☾ SO-DHV-810

KARL MARX

AN INTIMATE BIOGRAPHY

ABRIDGED EDITION

SAUL K. PADOVER

A MENTOR BOOK

NEW AMERICAN LIBRARY

TIMES MIRROR
NEW YORK AND SCARBOROUGH, ONTARIO

IMAGES OF MARX

"There is only one point, about which you have been clever enough to maintain a noble silence that all transcendentalism cannot do away with— I mean filthy money, the value of which . . . you still do not seem to understand. I do not deny that sometimes I reproach myself for having kept too loose a rein on you . . ."

—Heinrich Marx (Karl's father)

"Dr. Marx, this is the name of my idol, is still a very young man, who will give the coup de grâce to the medieval religion and politics; he combines the deepest philosophical seriousness with the most cutting wit; think of Rousseau, Voltaire, Holbach, Lessing, Heine and Hegel united in one person; I say *united,* not tossed together—and you have Dr. Marx."

—Moses Hess, socialist philosopher

"Marx is of medium height . . . his figure is powerful. . . . His large piercing eyes have something uncannily demonic about them. At first glance one sees in him a man of genius and energy; his intellectual superiority exerts irresistible power on his surroundings. . . . In private life he is a highly disorderly, cynical person, a poor host; he leads a real gypsy existence."

—from a spy's report in the Berlin secret archives

DR. SAUL K. PADOVER is a Distinguished Service Professor of Political Science, Graduate Faculty, New School for Social Research. He is the author of numerous biographies and books on European and American history, including *The Essential Marx, Jefferson: A Great American's Life and Ideas, Thomas Jefferson on Democracy, The Living U.S. Constitution* (all available in Mentor editions), and the seven-volume *Karl Marx Library.*

Recommended MENTOR Reading

CONTENTS

Acknowledgments

I wish to express my thanks to:

Dr. Hans Pelger of the Karl-Marx-Haus in Trier for his helpfulness, particularly in opening this Marx museum for my researches;

the Internationaal Instituut voor Sociale Geschiedenis (International Institute of Social History) in Amsterdam, which contains a wealth of material on the Marx family and on persons connected with them;

and, finally, the Inter-Nationes of the federal government in Bonn, Germany, for providing me with a photographer and with additional photographs related to Marx's life.

I also want to thank Dan Lacy, Senior Vice President of McGraw-Hill, for his patient encouragement of this biography, and Peggy Tsukahira, Associate Editor, for her fine editing of the book.

Author's Note

In this book, which has been twelve years in the making, I have aimed at something not available in other biographies of Marx: an objective account of him as a human being—lover, husbnd, friend, fighter, father, foe—rather than as the philosophic symbol and revolutionary idol that he has become. My approach is not that of the usual Marxologist or anti-Marxologist. I am, indeed, not a Marxist but a Jeffersonian democrat. Essentially, I am an historian-biographer, trained in taking the long view, as was Marx himself, with a respect for historic facts and data. To me, a writer uninvolved in political dogma and unimpressed by psychohistory, Marx is worth knowing as a towering, vastly learned and extraordinarily gifted man who had his share of suffering, as recorded in this book.

This biography is based primarily on Marx's own writings and personal documents, in many cases published and translated here for the first time. What emerges is a man who, with all his faults, was one of the great men of our epoch worth knowing and remembering.

S.K.P.

Introduction

*Materials for a Marx Biography**

Until recently, biographies of Karl Marx have lacked detailed information about his background and youth. The socialist Franz Mehring in his standard life, *Karl Marx*, which was published in German in 1918 and which set the pattern for subsequent writings on the subject, devoted about one dozen paragraphs to Marx's origins, family, religion, youth and pre-university education. The crucial years in the formation of any human being, especially one as touched with greatness and as immensely complex as Karl Marx, could hardly be covered adequately in the four pages that Mehring devotes to it out of a total of nearly 600 in his book.

This long-existing blank in the life of Marx, particularly with regard to the Trier background and personal relationships, was due largely to a paucity of source materials, which have been either scattered or lost. The Rhineland has long been a target of wars and occupations, and records have inevitably disappeared. Marx's native Trier, now rebuilt, was heavily bombed in World War II. What is worse, Marx's literary executors saw fit to destroy a mass of his personal papers after his death in London.

In recent years, however, scholarly patience has resulted in the unearthing of scattered and often unknown materials, among them those relating to Marx's parents. Current scholarship, primarily German and Russian, is rectifying many omissions—obviously because Karl Marx is no longer a mere radical theorist, but the central intellectual and inspirational figure in much of the world today, including its two biggest nations, China and the Soviet Union. As a man of world importance,

*See also the Bibliography

he has stimulated wide curiosity even outside communist circles, as an activist revolutionary and thinker.

In recent decades the lacunae in Marx's life have been filled —as much as it is possible to do so under the circumstances— by a number of meticulous and scrupulous researchers, notably Werner Blumenberg, Bernhard Brilling, August Comte, Adolf Kober, Heinz Monz, and Edmund Silberner. Under the leadership of Dr. Hans Pelger, the Karl-Marx-Haus in Trier, Marx's birthplace, which is now a museum, publishes invaluable monographs and an excellent series of *Schriften* relating to Marx and those connected with him. These sources, and other Western scholars, have filled in gaps, especially in regard to background and personality, in the *Marx-Engels Werke,* the basic collection of letters, articles and assorted writings by Marx and Engels in 39 volumes, plus two suplementary ones, issued in German and in Russian translation, by Moscow's Marx-Lenin Institute. As of 1975, the series is beginning to be published in English. The *Werke* is a monumental work of devoted scholarship, replete with voluminous historical and explanatory notes, indispensable to any Marx biography.

There are still blanks in Marx's life, especially for the early period, which can probably never be filled. But we know much more about him than ever before. Thanks to the new research and the publications of the Marx-Lenin Institute, it is now, for the first time, possible to attempt a comprehensive biography, with special emphasis on Marx as a human being. The recent sources (especially Heinz Monz[1]) provide us with details, in many instances of vast amplitude on his personal life: his intimate relations with parents, wife, children and relatives; his attitudes toward colleagues and enemies (who were legion); his chronic illnesses and shocking poverty; and above all, the forces that buffeted, twisted and shaped him.

[1]See, for example, Monz's impressively original and detailed research on Trier: *Karl Marx. Grundlagen der Entwicklung zu Leben und Werk* (Trier, 1973:458 pp.).

I
The Family

He was one of eight children and was considered exceptional by his parents. His mother called him a *Glückskind*—child of Fortune. His father thought he was possessed of a demon, and feared for his future. The mother, thinking of material success, turned out to be wrong: her son was to have anything but *Glück* throughout his life. The father showed deeper insight. Heinrich Marx's oldest surviving son, Karl, was possessed of a demonic genius that was to transform the modern world.

Rabbinical Ancestors

Karl Marx was born at two o'clock in the morning of May 5, 1818, in an upstairs room of a rented house on Brückengasse No. 664 (now Brückenstrasse No. 10), in Trier, Rhenish Prussia, the oldest city in Germany. Today, the Karl-Marx-Haus is administered as a museum by the Friedrich-Ebert-Stiftung, which is not inappropriate, since Ebert, the first President of the Weimar Republic, was a socialist.

The birth certificate, registered on May 7, records the name as "Carl" and those of his parents as Heinrich Marx and Henriette Presborck. The mother's name is a variant of Presborg or Presburg, derived from the Slovak city of Pressburg (Bratislava), whence the family was said to have come to Holland in the 16th century.

Marx was a descendant of rabbis on both sides of his family. Since the 17th century, virtually all the rabbis of Trier were his paternal ancestors. It was a magnificent intellectual heritage, which may perhaps explain Karl Marx's dialectical brilliance and moral passion, but he was not proud of it. He was to evince a lifelong antipathy for Jews privately and a contempt for Judaism publicly.

Joshua Heschel Lvov was the father of Moses Lvov, another Trier rabbi, who was the stepfather of Meyer (Mordechai) Halevi, known as Marx Levi,[1] also a rabbi in Trier. Karl Marx probably did not know this, but Rabbi Joshua Heschel Lvov was the author of a Hebrew book, *She'elot Uteshuvot P'nay Levana* [*Responsa: The Face of the Moon*], published in Altona in 1765, which in such secular questions as equitability of taxes and community participation expressed a position that can be described as strongly democratic. Rabbi Meyer was the father of Heschel, Karl Marx's father. Meyer was succeeded in the Trier rabbinate by his eldest son Samuel, who became Chief Rabbi of the Department of the Saar in the period of the French Revolution. Rabbi Samuel, Karl's uncle, was also a member of the Great Sanhedrin, a Council established by Napoleon I for the regulation of Jewish affairs.

It is not known what, if any, contact Karl had with Rabbi Samuel, who died in 1827, when Karl, already baptized as a Lutheran, was nine years old. In the light of Karl's ignorance of Judaism and his later distortion of its meaning, it may be assumed that his exposure to his rabbinical uncle was minimal.

Apart from the Trier rabbis, the Marx genealogy shows a long line of rabbis and scholars elsewhere in Europe, going back to the fifteenth century. Many were men of great eminence. Among the most famous Marx ancestors were Joseph ben Gerson Hacohen[2] (1511–1591), a distinguished scholar of Cracow, Poland, and Meyer ben Yitzchak (Isaac) Katzenellenbogen (1482–1565), chief rabbi of Venice-Padua, Italy. The renown of these erudite Marx ancestors was widespread, at least among the Jewish communities of Europe.[3]

No such details are available for Karl Marx's maternal family, the Presburgs of Nijmegen [French: Nimêgue], Holland, except that it, too, is known to have a rabbinical lineage. Marx's mother, Henriette (born in Nijmegen on September 20, 1788), was the daughter of Isaac Presburg

---

[1]Levi, Levy, Halevi, Halevy, phonetically derived from the Hebrew, are variants of the same name.

[2]Like Levi and its variants, so also Hacohen, Cohen, Cohn, Cahan, Cahane, Kohn, etc., are variants of the same Hebrew name, meaning priest, or more specifically, a descendant of the tribe of Aaron.

[3]See Appendix II.

and Nannette Cohen. Isaac Presburg's father—Karl Marx's maternal great-grandfather—was rabbi in Nijmegen. Referring to the Dutch side of her ancestry, Marx's daughter Eleanor wrote after her father's death, "the sons of the family have been rabbis for centuries."

Karl Marx's Father

Heinrich Marx, who died when Karl was twenty years old, was a key figure in his son's early life. The father not only molded his oldest surviving son (the first-born, Moritz David, had died in infancy), but nurtured him with exceptional care and loved him with fussy tenderness, at least until the last two years of his life. And Karl Marx, who, except for his love for his wife and children, was not affectionate, reciprocated his father's devotion and respect.

Like many a father of a famous son, Heinrich [Heschel or Hirschel] Marx is not well known to posterity. Indeed, until recently he was hardly kown at all, except as a name. Today, despite large gaps in information that still exist and may never be filled, enough is available about him to provide us with an understanding of his character and personality.

Heschel-Heinrich Marx was born in 1777 (not in 1782, as was formerly believed) in Sarrelouis [German: Saarlouis], a small town on the left bank of the Saar River, which Louis XIV's great engineer-architect, the Marquis de Vauban, had transformed into a fortress in 1680-85.

One can only surmise as to the origin of the name "Marx." It is not intrinsically a Jewish name, but is also borne by many Christian Germans. Marx is a German form of Mark, the New Testament apostle. In the Sarrelouis archives there are some documents from 1783 which are titled in French, *"les papiers du rabbin Marc Levy."* This Marc Levy (or Halevy) probably carried French personal documents with that name when he moved to Trier. There, Marc could easily have been Germanized into Marx. In any case, Karl's grandfather, when he was rabbi in Trier, began to refer to himself as Marx-Levy, and then simply as Marx. By the time Karl was born, the family name was documentarily established as Marx.

When Karl's father was a young boy, the family moved from Sarrelouis thirty miles northward to Trier, a German town which became French (Trèves) when Heschel-Heinrich

Marx was seventeen years old. He was deeply influenced by French culture, since he was born and for a long time lived under the French flag. Eleanor Marx wrote that her grandfather, of whom she knew only what her parents had told her, was a "real 'Frenchman' of the Eighteenth Century. He knew Voltaire and Rousseau by heart."

Karl Marx was to absorb a love for French culture and ideas from his father, and to have a lifelong interest in all things French. Many of his non-economic writings were to deal with French affairs; much of his preoccupation was to be with French politics. Two of his three daughters were to marry Frenchmen, and he himself learned to write and speak the language of Molière and Descartes flawlessly, although he was never to rid himself of his heavy Teutonic accent in speaking it.

Stimulated by the liberating currents of the French Revolution, Heschel Marx broke out of the confining rabbinical circle and moved into the larger world. He somehow acquired a classical education and training in law, which then meant French law. (The Code Napoléon [*Code Civil*] was introduced in the Rhineland in 1807 and the *Code Pénal* in 1810.) How he managed to get his education, or who his teachers were, is not known. But apparently it involved a bitter and prolonged struggle on his part, which left scars. It seems that only his widowed mother stood lovingly by him. In later years, Karl's father spoke of his own *dornige Jugend* [thorny youth] and of his painful path when he set out to prove, in an anti-Semitic environment, that a Jew had the talent and the probity to be a lawyer.

Like other educated men of his time, Heschel Marx was familiar with the great writers and thinkers of the modern age, both French and German. He knew the writings of philosophers like John Locke and Immanuel Kant, and also the ideas of scientists like Gottfried Wilhelm Leibniz and Isaac Newton. Imbued with the Enlightenment notions of tolerance, progress and human dignity, he detested tyranny and came to abhor what he called "Napoleonic arbitrariness," under which he lived, and presumably practiced law, for about fifteen years.

Despite what must have been almost insuperable obstacles, Heschel Marx, a man without money and without social position in the Christian world, succeeded not only in becoming a lawyer, the first Jew to do so in predominantly Catholic Trier, but also the leading member of the local bar. His first years of practice, before Karl was born, must still have been "thorny," for there is no record that he possessed anything taxable before his marriage, which took place at the rather late age of thirty-seven, probably because he could not afford a wife and children up to that time. He never became a wealthy man, but eventually he achieved a good practice and acquired a fairly substantial estate, including one or two small vineyards on the Mosel River, of which the wine-loving Karl Marx was to be proud in later years.

Karl Marx's Mother

It is not known how, or if, Heschel Marx and Henriette Presburg met before their engagement. The contact between the German lawyer and the Dutch girl, living at least 100 miles apart in different countries, although under the same French empire, may have been made through a traditional Jewish *shadkhen* [marriage broker] or, more likely, through relatives living in Holland.

There is a French saying that a marriage has a good chance of success if the wife is half the age of her husband, plus seven years. This was almost exactly the case with Karl Marx's parents. When Heschel Marx married Henriette Presburg, he was over thirty-seven years old and she had just passed her twenty-sixth birthday. Theirs, as it happened, turned out to be a singularly happy union.

They were married on November 22, 1814, in a civil ceremony by the Mayor in the Mairie of Nijmegen, the Dutch city that then formed part of the French Département de Bouches du Rhin. Four local businessmen served as witnesses to the marriage between the attorney from Trèves, "Hendrik Marx," as the name is given in the French marriage certificate, and Henriette Presburg, a local girl listed as being *"sans occupation."*

Almost nothing is known of Henriette's girlhood, but much can be surmised from her background as a Dutch Jew and the granddaughter of a rabbi. The Jews of Holland did not suffer from the religious discriminations or persecutions common in the rest of Europe. Long before the Batavian Republic granted Jews full civil rights *de jure* in September 1796, they had enjoyed religious and economic freedom *de facto*. They were accepted and respected as an integral part of the national community. Protestant Dutch, mostly members of the Calvinist Reformed Church, often referred to Jews as the "Sons of the Old [Biblical] people" and as "our Jewish fellow Christians." Jews pursued occupations and commerce in a normal, uninhibited way.

Henriette's father, Isaac Presburg, was a Nijmegen businessman and almost certainly well-to-do, judged by her considerable dowry and by the fact that her younger sister Nannette Sophie married a Jewish banker from nearby Zalt-Bommel.

Henriette brought with her a dowry of 8,100 Dutch Gulden, the equivalent of 4,536 German Taler, of which she retained considerable control. The marriage agreement also provided her with a legal claim to one-fourth of her husband's estate and one-fourth of his income.

Judged by purchasing power, Henriette's dowry was substantial. In those days, government salaries ranged from 900 to 1,400 Taler annually. In Trier, for example, the highest salary, that of Ludwig von Westphalen, Karl Marx's future father-in-law, was 1,800 Taler. Poorer people lived on about 200 Taler a year. In Trier, two furnished rooms could be rented for six to seven Taler monthly, and a month's board consisting of four meals a day cost about the same.

Over the years, either through inheritance or investment, or both, Henriette Marx was able greatly to increase her economic assets. In 1833, when Karl was fifteen, his mother's personal property was estimated at 11,136 Taler—about two and a half times her original dowry. This put her—and her husband—solidly in the middle class. After the death of her husband, whom she outlived by a quarter of a century, the widow Marx carefully nursed and increased her estate, to the open anger of her perpetually impecunious and debt-ridden son, who engaged in tireless and not always successful efforts to "squeeze" money out of *die Alte* [the Old Woman, or Old Lady], as he came to call her. Although as a youngster he had called her "*Mütterchen*" [little mother] and "*Engelsmutter*" [angel-mother], in his adult correspondence he rarely referred to her as "Mother."

His relations were more friendly with the family of his mother's sister Sophie. The banker whom she married, Lion Benjamin Philips (1794–1866), was later to play a role in Karl's life, particularly after the widow Marx appointed Philips executor of her will and made him her trusted business adviser. In his years in exile, in desperate need of money, Marx paid several visits to his uncle in Zalt-Bommel, ingratiating himself through flattery and his pose as an important writer who knew famous people such as Ferdinand Lassalle. Nephew Karl, despite his notoriety as a radical, was always received generously and hospitably by his rich Dutch uncle and warmly by his girl cousins, especially young Antoinette (Nannette) Philips, with whom he carried on a flirtation. Marx, who had no affection for his own mother and siblings, was always proud of his prosperous and successful Dutch relatives.

Unlike her husband, Henriette was not well educated, but she may have attended a secular school in Holland, for she could read and write the language of her native country, an unusual accomplishment for women, even Jewish women, in that period, unless they belonged to exceptional or prosperous families.

Henriette seems to have learned no German in her childhood or youth, but acquired the language painfully after she married Heinrich, with whom she first communicated in Dutch, which he understood, but spoke poorly. In the first years of her marriage, she lived in Trier "as in a foreign country." She never really mastered the German language. Her few surviving letters to Karl show tortured syntax, less than adequate grammar, and almost nonexistent punctuation. Her German pronunciation remained heavily Dutchified, as can be seen from some of her letters. She made the hard German "g" sound like the Dutch "gh," pronounced "ch." Such speech must have sounded illiterate to her oldest son, who became a man of immense literary culture and intellectual sophistication. According to Karl himself, his mother never even pronounced his name in the German way. She called him "Karell."

"Karell" himself obviously absorbed the Dutch language in his childhood. He could read and speak it, but perhaps out of antipathy for his mother he pretended not to know it well and seems not to have bothered to cultivate it, although he became a skilled linguist, at home in nearly all European languages, including Russian.

Marx's Dutch mother was not a woman of culture or intellect—to the end of her life, despite her special love for little Karl, she was never able to understand, let alone sympathize with the kind of son she had brought into the world and reared; and he, in turn, was to have no respect for her in later years. Her life was concentrated on her husband, who loved her, and her large family, on whom she lavished a fussy and energetic care. Henriette Marx had all the sterling virtues of an old-fashioned mother and housewife—a Dutch tidiness and orderliness, frugality, buoyancy and respect for material possessions, which she was not above flaunting. These were down-to-earth qualities which Karl came to loathe as "bourgeois" and "philistine," two words which became his favorite epithets for everything he detested, including the whole existing social order of Europe. In his personal life, Karl Marx was to evince qualities of attitude and behavior—untidiness, improvidence, slothfulness, contempt for material accumulation, among others—that were the exact antithesis of those that characterized his bourgeois Dutch mother.

Heinrich Marx's Conversion to Christianity

Sometime between April 23, 1816, and August 17, 1817—that is, one or two years before Karl was born—Heschel Marx had himself baptized as a Christian. Baptism among educated Prussian Jews in the first third of the 19th century was far from uncommon. The voluntary conversion of Jews to Christianity, an unusual phenomenon in Europe at any time, was the consequence, paradoxically, of both German anti-Semitism and the Enlightenment.

In Germany, anti-Semitism had long roots, dating back to the Crusades, when whole Jewish communities were exterminated by the Crusaders. There were pogroms in the Rhineland as late as the 1820's, when Karl Marx was a little boy.

Anti-Semitism, in Germany and elsewhere, had two primary causes, economic and religious. In Germany, where most people still lived in small towns and villages, a strong middle class had not yet emerged in the first half of the 19th century. Hence a handful of Jews played a dominant role in the economy—and indirectly in the politics—of the numerous small German states, whose princelings were financed by so-called *Hofjuden* [court Jews]. Other Jews, excluded from most decent occupations, had to resort to petty trading and money-lending. In consequence, Jews, both rich and poor, were hated as usurers by the oppressed and debt-ridden masses, particularly the still feudalized peasants.

Popular enmity was aggravated by religion. In the public mind, Jews were not only economic exploiters but also enemies of the true religion, accursed by God because they had rejected Christ. It was commonly believed that the Jews' own religion taught nothing but corruption and the worship of one exclusive and jealous god—Money. Ironically enough, Karl Marx absorbed this Christian belief in his youth (but not from his father) and was never to lose it.

On March 11, 1812, Friedrich Wilhelm III, "by the grace of God, King of Prussia," issued a sweeping edict granting Jews citizenship on condition that they adopt German surnames and keep their business books and contracts in German or "some other living language" written in Latin script, rather than in Hebrew or Yiddish. The decree abolished special taxes and other discriminatory provisions against the Jews, opened schools and universities (but not professorships) to them, and made them subject to military service. But a number of restrictions still remained in force; government positions and the practice of certain professions, including the law, continued to be closed to Jews. These and other disabilities could be removed only by baptism, which the Prussian government encouraged. Those who wished to be baptized, an order from Berlin stated, should have no difficulties put in their way by local officials, but "rather given all possible assistance." In other words, before Jews could become full citizens they had first to become Christians.

The great majority of Prussian Jews did not leave the synagogue for the church, but a small number did. Most of the conversions were to Protestantism, for two main reasons. The rulers of Prussia were pious Protestants, and the majority of the population, around 55%, was Evangelical. Protestantism was thus the religion of those in power. Secondly, it was considered more "modern," keeping up with the new philosophy and the secular scholarship of the time, and less dogmatic and intolerant than Catholicism. Hence Protestantism was palatable to educated Jews like Karl Marx's father, who had already lost faith in their own ancestral orthodoxy.

Among the converts of the period was Heinrich Heine, one of Germany's greatest poets. He was baptized (he called it ironically "sprinkled") as a matter of expediency at age twenty-eight, in 1825, the same year as Marx's mother. Baptism, Heine said, was "an entrance card into the community of European culture."

Heschel Marx's baptism was not a matter of conviction but of necessity. It was a step not lightly taken, particularly for one who did not believe in any creeds and was not anti-Jewish. His religion, as he told his son Karl, consisted only of "a pure belief in God" and was not concerned with organized dogmas. It is significant that in Heschel Marx's library—which consisted mostly of legal works in French and German, and had an estimated value of 208 Taler—there were no books on religion or theology, either Christian or Jewish.

Trier, perhaps because of the liberating influences of the French Revolution that affected the Rhineland, was an exceptional city in regard to religious tolerance. There was no religious friction at the time when Karl Marx was growing up. In 1828, when Karl was a boy of ten, Trier's Oberbürgermeister, Wilhelm Haw, reported: "Everybody, Catholics, Protestants and Israelites, moves about in the greatest harmony."

Heschel Marx had hoped that, in view of Trier's prevailing tolerance and the high esteem in which he was held by his Christian colleagues in the city, an exception might be made in his case and he would be permitted to continue practicing his legal profession. On April 23, 1816, Sethe, the President of the *Landesgericht* [Provincial Supreme Court] in Trier, interceded for him in Berlin. Less than two weeks later, on May 4, 1816, Kircheisen, the Prussian Minister of Justice, issued a ruling that excluded Jews from the practice of law. He refused to make an exception in Marx's case, just as he had systematically rejected the appeals of other Jewish lawyers.

Heschel was then confronted with the choice of either abandoning the law, which he loved, or giving up Judaism, in which he no longer believed. Leaving the synagogue was compartively easy, but was still an affront to his pride as a Jew and a denial of his ancestry. Conversion to Christianity—a religion in which, as a Rousseauist and Voltairean, he did not at heart believe—also involved hurting the feelings of his mother and a possible break with his family, including his rabbinical brother Samuel in Trier. For a man as affectionate as Heschel Marx, it must have been a painful dilemma. In the end, however, probably soon after his mother's death, he chose baptism and took the Christian name of Heinrich.

It is noteworthy that neither his young wife, Henriette, nor his infant daughter, Sophie, born in 1816, was baptized at that time. Nor was Karl at his birth in 1818. Henriette and her children remained Jewish for the time being. Karl Marx was thus born a Jew, and may even have been circumcised (although there is no record of it), since according to Jewish law, a child follows the religion of its mother.

After baptism, there were no obstacles to Heinrich Marx's

career under the Prussian regime. He had hitherto been merely an *Advokat* [lawyer or barrister], which, according to the Rhineland rules of those days, limited his practice to penal matters. For other cases, he had to employ an *Anwalt* [lawyer or solicitor] and pay him a fee. His income was small. By 1821, Heinrich had become an *Advokatanwalt*, a combination of the two, without limit to his practice. His income, therefore, began to rise accordingly. The *Advokatanwälte* were the elite among lawyers. In Heinrich's days, Trier had between twelve and fourteen of them.

He was accepted socially and professionally by the Trier community, where the great majority of Catholics and the tiny minority of Protestants lived in harmony. Heinrich Marx's integrity and ability won him the respect of his colleagues and fellow-citizens, and he became an esteemed member of the prestigious Casino Society—Trier's "country club," to which the town's leading burghers and professional men belonged. After becoming an *Advokat am Ober-Appellationsgericht* [Attorney at the Supreme Court of Appeals] in Trier, Heinrich Marx acquired the coveted title of *Justizrat* [Councilor of Justice: the equivalent of a King's Counsel in England] and the distinction of becoming the *batônnier* of the local bar.

II
Youth

Trier

When Karl was two years old, in 1820, the Marx family moved from the Brückengasse, where he was born, to Simeongasse No. 1070 (today: Simeonstrasse No. 8), on Trier's main street. Heinrich Marx bought the house on October 1, 1819, for the fairly substantial sum of 3,650 Taler (the equivalent of more than 13,000 French francs), with a down payment of 1,050 Taler, the rest to be paid within six years in three instalments, at 5% interest.

The house on Simeongasse was about fifty yards from the Porta Nigra, Trier's oldest and most magnificent monument, which dominated the landscape of Marx's childhood and boyhood. The Porta Nigra had three-story towers—the tallest of them 95 feet high—and two 23-foot gateways. It was constructed by the Romans of huge blocks of sandstone in the 3rd century A.D. To a boy with historic imagination, it was a constant reminder of the grandeur and power of the Roman Empire.

Both the Porta Nigra and the neighboring Marx family house still stand virtually as they were in Karl's youth; the former is increasingly blackened with age and the latter is occupied by an optical shop. The house, which is approximately twenty feet wide and flush with the sidewalk, had eight rooms and a kitchen on the two main floors and three more small chambers under the mansard roof. There was also an outbuilding with four rooms and a scullery in the rear. It was in this solid middle-class house—both its cost and the tax on it (26 francs per annum) represented the Trier bourgeois average—that Karl Marx lived until he left home for the University at the age of seventeen.

Trier provided a special historical stimulus. It is the oldest town in Germany, founded by Caesar Augustus in the terri-

tory of a tribe of Gauls called the Treveri. In the 4th century
A.D., the settlement, known as *Augusta Treverorum,* was often the residence of Roman Emperors. Christianity was introduced there by Constantine I and as early as 314 A.D. the
town had a Bishop. For almost 1,500 years, Trier was the
residence of Bishops, Archbishops and ecclesiastical princes
known as Electors. The Elector [in German: *Kurfürst*] was
for centuries the spiritual-temporal ruler of Trier and the surrounding area. In August 1794, the French captured the
town, instituted a civil administration, and introduced the
ideas and institutions of the French Revolution.

Trier, which remained in French hands for twenty-one
years, was thus a community rooted in four historic traditions
and cultures: the Imperial Roman, the medieval Catholic, the
indigenous German, and the Revolutionary French. In Karl's
youth all the traditions were still palpable; there was no escaping the Roman remains or the Catholic churches or the
German language or the new French ideas.

Located picturesquely on the right bank of the Mosel
River, Trier was surrounded by vine-clad slopes and wooded
hills, through which Karl used to roam as a boy. It was a
quiet town, with gardens and orchards and narrow, winding
streets, leading here and there to some fine public buildings
and impressive historic ruins. Among the former were the
Obergerichtoshof [Superior Court], where Heinrich Marx
practiced his profession, and the Friedrich Wilhelm Gymnasium, which Karl attended. Among the historic remains, in
addition to the Porta Nigra, were the ruins of a big Roman
palace, Roman baths, and a Roman amphitheatre with a
seating capacity of some 8,000, surrounded by vineyards.

The birthplace of the man who made famous the slogan,
"religion is the opium of the people," was preponderantly a
city of churches and ecclesiastical institutions. Within a few
minutes' walk from Karl's home were the Archepiscopal
Palace; the immense Cathedral, built in the 4th century and
rebuilt in the early Middle Ages; and the brick Basilica, the
construction of which dated back to the Emperor Constantine
I. In Trier, whose population was 93% Catholic, the impression of ecclesiasticism, at least in its physical manifesta-
tions, was overpowering.

Trier in Marx's day was characterized not only by
churches and ecclesiastical edifices but also by wine. Its culti-
vation on the slopes along the Mosel River was the region's
most important single economic enterprise, both for the grow-

ers and the townspeople, many of whom, like Heinrich Marx, owned vineyards. The Mosel wines, indeed, may have been what first attracted the Romans to settle in Trier. The town's reputation as a wine center has been embodied in medieval Latin verse:

> *Trevir metropolis, urbs amoenissima,*
> *Quae Bacchum recolis, Baccho gratissima,*
> *Da tuis incolis vina fortissima,*
> *Per dulcor!*[1]

In Karl Marx's youth, as for centuries before, the spirit of Bacchus lingered in Trier. He imbibed it, and developed a lifelong taste for wine. Even as a poor refugee in London, he and his wife drank it whenever he could afford it. When he was well, he drank it for pleasure; when he was sick, he drank it as medicine (physicians used to prescribe it in those days).

Thomas Jefferson once remarked that wine-growing regions were likely to be economically poor. For one thing, the cultivators of the vine tended to love their product too much; for another, wine is not as fruitful, either in economic yield or in nourishment, as rice, wheat or olives. Trier essentially confirmed Jefferson's observation. Without industrialization or capitalist enterprise, it was economically a poor town, remaining throughout Karl's youth what it had been for centuries—a market place. The Markt Platz, a few hundred yards from Marx's home at the other end of Simeongasse, was and is the heart of town and an administrative center. Trier's population consisted chiefly of *Beamten* [civil servants], ecclesiastics, small merchants, and craftsmen, who provided services and goods for the surrounding countryside. It had a small-town intellectual climate with a sprinkling of educated men, lawyers, teachers, government officials.

Economically, Trier was pre-industrial and traditional, far removed from the world of capitalism. The statistics for 1828, when Karl was ten years old, show that it was primarily a "service" town, as it continued to be for decades after-

[1]Freely translated, it reads:

Treves metropolis, most delightful city,
You, who cultivate the grape, are most
*   pleasing to Bacchus.*
Give your inhabitants the wines
*   strongest for sweetness!*

wards. It had an astonishing number of eating-and-drinking places and small shops. In a population of approximately 12,-000 there were 40 restaurants, 48 inns, and 83 saloons—or about one for every sixty persons. The town was also replete with old-fashioned trades and occupations. Trier had 21 tinsmiths, 39 housepainters, 40 blacksmiths, 55 tanners, 89 butchers, 118 masons, 160 carpenters, 166 bakers, 204 tailors and 256 shoemakers. There were also nearly 1,300 domestic servants, mostly female—more than 10% of the total population.

But one thing nonindustrial Trier shared with cities where capitalism was emerging—for example, the textile towns of Barmen and Elberfeld, and the metallurgical ones of Remscheid and Solingen—was the poverty and misery of the lower classes. In 1830, when Karl was a boy of twelve, Trier's Oberbürgermeister, Wilhelm Haw, reported that one out of every four persons in town was jobless, but the figure was probably much higher. In the winter of that year, soup kitchens, supported by charity, ladled out 57,315 portions of soup—made of potatoes, peas or oats—averaging 520 portions per day, to keep the hungry from outright starvation. The more hopeless cases of the indigent and the sick were confined to the overcrowded poorhouse, which, in Karl's boyhood, contained on an average nearly 500 inmates.

Young Karl always saw beggars and prostitutes on Trier's streets. The town had public bordellos, as well as many unregistered whores. The town's desperate poverty also fostered a great deal of petty crime, including stealing; the police listed 728 cases in 1828 alone. Part of Heinrich Marx's law practice consisted of defending those accused of thievery.

As the son of a well-to-do lawyer, Karl, of course, belonged to Trier's privileged class, small but influential, socially secure, well sheltered, well clad and well fed. But he would have had to be insensitive or blind—and Karl Marx was neither—not to be affected by the prevailing misery and the cruel economic inequalities of the environment in which he was born and grew up.

Karl's Siblings and Baptism

Karl spent his childhood and boyhood in a happy and increasingly crowded home. The house was crammed with heavy Germanic furniture and, within a few years after the family moved in, teemed with children. By the time Karl was eight years old, the house on the Simeongasse contained twelve people, including two maids.

Henriette and Heinrich Marx were exceedingly prolific. They produced children with the regularity of the seasons. The first, Moritz-David, conceived right after the wedding, was born in 1815 and died in infancy. The second, Sophie, was born in the following year, in 1816. Karl came two years later. Thereafter, Henriette gave birth to a child annually: Hermann was born in 1819, Henriette in 1820, Luise in 1821, and Emilie in 1822. Two more came within two-year intervals: Karoline in 1824, and Eduard in 1826.[2]

Karl thus grew up in a family with seven siblings, two brothers and five sisters, all but Sophie younger than he. Not much is known about his brothers and sisters, except that most of them were sickly and not outstanding in any way. Karl, always energetic, dominated them quite early; later, he probably also despised them for being slow intellectually. As a little boy, he played with his siblings, using them for horses, galloping down the nearby Markusberg. When they were angry with him, he would try to win them over by telling them wonderful stories, for he had a fertile imagination. His surviving sisters, according to his daughter, remembered Karl as a "terrible tyrant" in their youth.

Heinrich, the doting father, may consciously or unconsciously have encouraged Karl's imperiousness and the resulting arrogance which later marked his personality. Very early in Karl's life, his father detected "splendid natural gifts" in his oldest son and treated him accordingly. At the same time, Heinrich recognized the mediocrity of his other children.

Karl's two brothers and one sister died quite early of tuberculosis, which seems to have run in the family—Hermann and Karoline at the age of twenty-three, and Eduard at the age of eleven. While they were alive, Karl, when away from home, did not bother to write to them or to send greetings. Later, a second sister, Henriette (Jettchen), also died of tuberculosis in great pain. But Jettchen did survive for a dozen years after her marriage, finally dying at the age of thirty-six, in 1856.

Karl, too, was tubercular, and, according to him, the affliction kept him out of Prussian military service. When, in October 1845, he was threatened with expulsion from Brussels

[2]See Appendix IV: Marx's Siblings.

and was thinking of emigrating to the United States, he wrote to the Oberbürgermeister of Trier for an exit permit, explaining that he was free of his military obligation, since, in 1838, the doctor in Berlin had considered him "unfit for now, owing to a weak chest and periodic spitting of blood." He added that three years later, in May 1841, the military Super-Revisions Commission finally declared him "completely invalid because of the affected lungs."

Little information is available about Karl's pre-school days. It is not known, for example, whether there were any religious observances or influences in the house. Did Heinrich ever talk to his children, especially his eldest son Karl, about religion or prayer or God? Did Henriette observe the time-hallowed blessing of the candles on Friday night? Were there any prayers said in the Marx home? Was there any observance of the Sabbath? Did Henriette, a woman of strong character, suddenly give up the cherished Jewish rituals because of her husband's baptism? These questions cannot be answered.

Nor is there any record that Heinrich attended Protestant church services or took part in Evangelical community affairs, or that he was expected to do so. In the light of Heinrich's lack of admiration for Christianity, it is fair to assume that his participation in religious matters was minimal, and so probably was any discussion of the subject with his children. Karl may have picked up a few notions and expressions from his mother, but in all likelihood he had no religious education before he went to school.

In the Prussia of that day, however, the religious question was inescapable. When Karl reached school age in 1824, his father had to make the same kind of decision for him that he had made for himself some seven years earlier. On September 13, 1824, a Prussian government decree confirmed a long-standing practice that non-Christians could not attend public schools. For a Jewish child, this meant either an inferior private institution or a Hebrew school. For Heinrich Marx, ambitious for his gifted son, the first choice was unthinkable and the second impossible.

Three months after Karl's sixth birthday, on August 26, 1824, he and his siblings—eight-year-old Sophie, five-year-old Hermann, four-year-old Henriette, three-year-old Luise, two-year-old Emilie and the three-week-old infant Karoline—received baptism in the Trier Evangelical church, which then held its services in a Jesuit church assigned to it by the Prussian government. A decade later, on March 23, 1834, Karl, at the age of sixteen, was confirmed at the altar of the same Jesuit church. Five couples and a single woman served as the god-parents. Three of the godfathers were Heinrich Marx's fellow-lawyers and one was a government official. The baptismal register recorded that Henriette Marx, the mother, had not yet converted to Christianity because her parents were still alive, but that she granted permission for the baptism of her seven children.

What religion Karl knew, he learned at school. The *Volksschule* [elementary school] which he attended was Evangelical. Its director was Johann Abraham Küpper, the pastor who had prepared him for baptism. Later, in the Gymnasium [secondary school], Karl was exposed to compulsory religious instruction for two hours every week. The teacher for the Evangelical students was the same Pastor Küpper, who became proud of his pupil. The other Gymnasium teachers were reasonably well satisfied with Karl's knowledge of Christianity, in which they examined him before graduation. In his diploma, it was noted that his "knowledge of the Christian faith and morals" was "pretty clear and well-founded" and that he also knew "a little of the history of the Christian church." From these restrained comments it may be surmised that religion was not one of Karl's favorite subjects.

Gymnasium

Only with his Gymnasium days do we begin to get specific details about the life of young Marx. The record of his studies and grades, as well as his graduation essays and the opinion of his teachers, have been preserved. They cast the first direct light on Karl Marx's formative years. It was in the Gymnasium that the larger world of culture and of radical ideas was opened up to him.

Marx entered the Friedrich Wilhelm Gymnasium in October 1830, at the age of twelve. He remained there until his graduation in 1835.

The Gymnasium, founded as a Jesuit school in 1563, enjoyed an excellent scholastic reputation. The building, a fine example of late-Renaissance architecture constructed in 1611-1614—two small, pointed towers flanking a four-story facade, with a statue in the front courtyard—still stands as it was in Karl's student days, although it ceased to be a

Gymnasium in 1944. Contrary to previous assertions,[3] the Gymnasium was not Jesuit, or even Catholic, when Karl was a student there. From 1815, when the Prussians took over the territory, the Gymnasium was a government school, operating under the jurisdiction—and, one should add, the surveillance—of the Ministry of Education in Berlin, which looked upon the country's secondary schools with suspicion as hotbeds of anti-Prussianism and radicalism.

Scholastically, Karl, despite his brilliance, was not at the top of his class, probably because a number of courses in the largely compulsory curriculum—Religion and Physics, for example—did not interest him. Other courses that were voluntary, like Hebrew, Drawing and Singing, he did not take. In the crucial final examinations, which consisted of written and oral tests and lasted a grueling week (September 17 to 23, 1835), Karl's grades were no better than average. The examinations, in which the whole faculty participated under the official chairmanship of a government inspector, Education Councillor Theodor Brüggemann, were formidable and would probably stump most American college graduates today.

His overall average was 2.4, or slightly under the American equivalent of B plus. If the examinations were an accurate reflection of his knowledge and interests, Karl apparently excelled only in German and Latin composition. In other academic subjects, he ranged from adequate to mediocre.

Jenny von Westphalen

At the time he finished Gymnasium, Karl was secretly engaged to the lovely Jenny von Westphalen. He himself was far from handsome. Somebody who knew the swarthy, stocky, hirsute Karl as a youth in Trier recalled him as "nearly the most unattractive man on whom the sun ever shone."

Karl may have been unattractive to others but not to the romantic Jenny von Westphalen. Her early pictures show a bright-eyed young woman with a perfectly oval face, a fine short nose and soft mouth. She was considered Trier's most attractive and desirable girl. Twenty years after their mar-

---

[3]See, for example, Werner Blumenberg, *Karl Marx: In Selbstzeugnissen und Bilddokumenten* (1962), p. 17: "Karl Marx attended the Jesuit Gymnasium in Trier for five years."

riage, Marx, on his last visit to Trier soon after his mother's death, wrote to his wife (December 15, 1863):

> I have made daily pilgrimages to the old Westphalen house [on the Römerstrasse], which interested me more than all the Roman antiquities, because it reminded me of the happiest period of my youth and had sheltered my best treasure. Furthermore, I am asked daily, right and left, about the erstwhile "most beautiful girl in Trier," and the "Queen of the Ball." It is damned agreeable for a man when his wife lives in the imagination of a whole city as an "enchanted princess."

Jenny was well educated for a girl of her time, had serious intellectual interests, personal style and humor. When she and Karl lived in Paris in the 1840's, her charm and humor captivated Heinrich Heine, the wittiest of poets. In later years, during their often bitter London exile days, she and her husband frequently found a relief from their material misery in hearty laughter. In time, her wit became as sardonic as Karl's, and even more amusing. She was so scintillating, especially when describing fakes and windbags, for whom she had an unerring eye, that Karl came to call her the best letter-writer in the family. Unfortunately, most of her letters have been destroyed, but those that have survived show that her husband's high estimate of her talents was justified.

Jenny was the daughter of a German aristocrat, Johann Ludwig von Westphalen, who had come to Trier as a high government official in 1816, the year after the town was annexed by Prussia. Previous to that he had been president of the Provincial Court in Salzwedel, where Jenny was born on February 12, 1814. Von Westphalen had no wealth or property, but his high salary as a Prussian *Regierungsrat* [State Councillor] enabled him to live comfortably in a spacious house with a big garden, where Jenny and her young brother Edgar frequently played with her friends Sophie and Karl Marx.

Baron von Westphalen may or may not have been aware of the developing romance between his lovely daughter Jenny and young Karl, but he does not seem to have taken it seriously at first. Neither, for that matter, did Jenny herself, who was four years older than Karl. She was full of doubts about her relationship with the infatuated, homely boy, although their attraction to each other was growing irresistibly. Her

uncertainty was not due to the disparity of social status between herself and Karl, nor to his ancestry. She was an inde-
pendent-minded girl, not given to aristocratic pretensions.
Her own mother, Karoline, von Westphalen's second wife,
was the daughter of a petty Prussian government official
named Heubel. To Jenny, who loved her mother, rank was
unimportant; some members of her family, particularly her
older half-brother, Ferdinand Otto von Westphalen, who later
(1850-1858) became a reactionary Prussian Minister of the
Interior, felt differently.

What worried Jenny was not Karl's social status or Jewish
descent—like Karl, she was raised in the Protestant faith and
later became an atheist—but stark practicality. How could
Karl, who hoped to be a poet and litterateur, ever support
her? Poets, Heinrich Marx did not fail to point out to his son,
were notoriously impecunious; they always had to depend financially upon the whim of some patron. Jenny herself, although a baroness, had no property of her own and no
expectation of any inheritance. Karl could hope to inherit
someday from the estate of his prosperous mother, but she
was in her prime, and it might be a long wait; even then, he
would have to share the inheritance with his siblings, of
whom there were seven when Jenny and Karl fell in love. His
prospects for a career in law or government service remunerative enough to support a wife and children in the comfort to
which she and Karl were accustomed might be favorable, but
it would mean a wait of at least half a dozen years, probably
more. When Karl was ready for the University, he was a boy
of seventeen and a half and she was a young woman of
twenty-one. By the time he would be able to support her, she
would be nearing thirty. Could the sought-after "Queen of
the Ball" afford to wait that long?

Apparently they did become engaged before Karl left for
the University; or, at least, following the romantic tradition of
the time, they secretly plighted each other their eternal troth.
There is no exact information as to when that happened,
since after Karl Marx's death his daughter Laura Lafargue
saw fit to destroy all her parents' correspondence. To keep
the secret, at least temporarily, Jenny and Karl seem to have
decided not to write to each other. She would often visit the
Marx home to obtain news about him, and he, in Bonn,
would simply fret.

In the meantime, Karl went off to the University, leaving a
deeply troubled Jenny behind him in Trier. She was sure

about her love for Karl but not about their future. There is
no evidence that he shared Jenny's worries. For one thing, to
an exuberant *Glückskind*, bursting with ideas, the future was
not a pressing reality. Like Micawber, Marx was always an
optimist. Moreover, neither as a student nor as a grown man
did he ever show any practical financial sense. Nor did he
ever have a head for figures; in later years, his statistical
tables were the despair of Frederick Engels, when Engels undertook to bring out the second and third volumes of *Das
Kapital*, left unfinished at Marx's death. Marx, the great
economic theorist who could write deep metaphysical disser-
tations about money, could hardly keep accurate household
accounts, and his wife turned out to be no more practical
than he. What little money he ever had, including occasional
chunks of inheritance which would have kept an ordinary
family in reasonable comfort for years, he used up quickly
and often improvidently, and then resorted desperately either
to pawning everything movable—family silver, linens, his
wife's and children's clothing—or to borrowing at exorbitant
rates of interest. He came to live mostly on credit, and was
nearly always in debt, often to several people at the same
time.

In Trier, Jenny alternated between hope and depression.
Family pressures, unconsummated love, and worry about the
future brought about periods of illness, some of it grave. But
underneath Jenny's feminine fragility was a woman whose
determined will matched Karl's.

A woman in love, she learned how to wait. She waited
eight years to marry her *Schwarzwildchen*.

III
Bonn University
(1835-1836)

The Matriculant

Three weeks after his graduation from the Gymnasium, on Saturday, October 17, 1835, at early dawn, Karl Marx was at the pier in Trier. With him was the whole family—father, mother, brothers and sisters—for it was a great occasion. The *Glückskind*, the luminous hope of the family, was going off to the University, the first Marx ever to do so—and the last. Heinrich Marx had anxiously planned this event for years. "I want to see in you," the father told Karl, "what I could have become if I had come into the world under the same favorable auspices as you."

At four in the morning, Karl embarked on the roofed boat, the *Eiljacht* [express yacht] sailing on the Mosel to Coblentz. There he transferred to a steamer for a forty-mile journey on the picturesque Rhine to Bonn, where he was going "to study Jurisprudence," as it stated on his Gymnasium diploma.

Upon his arrival in Bonn, Karl took the most expensive rooms in a rooming house opposite the University at 764 Josephstrasse and then registered, together with six other Trier students, in the Faculty of Jurisprudence. This was one of five major faculties into which the University was divided (the others being Philosophy, Medicine, Protestant Theology and Catholic Theology). The Faculty of Jurisprudence had about seven professors, who lectured in their particular specialties—Roman law, German law, canon law (Protestant and Catholic), international law, criminal law, Prussian law, and legal philosophy and methodology. Instruction was in the form of lectures, some of them open to the public, some exclusively for students, but attendance was not compulsory. Students were on their own; all they needed at the end of each semester was the professor's signature in the appropriate column of their Student Book.

For Karl, Bonn was an exciting place. The town itself, with a population of about 40,000, was four times larger than Trier. It was dominated by the University, which had a number of distinguished professors (a total of about 57 in 1839) and some 700 colorful and carousing students, of whom the local wine-imbibing burghers were quite proud. It was a gay life.

Karl plunged into it with the ebullience of an energetic seventeen-year-old. His behavior indicates that he was glad to be away from parental supervision and fussing. For the first three weeks, he did not write home at all. It did not seem to have bothered him that his overprotective father would be concerned about his studies and that his doting mother would be worried about the health and welfare of her *Glückskind*. Six weeks after Karl's matriculation at Bonn, his father complained to him, "It is amazing that we do not even have your exact address yet." That letter was written on November 18, one month after Karl left home, and was not mailed until eleven days later—waiting for the Bonn address to arrive. In the first three months at Bonn, Karl wrote home only twice, hurried notes mostly asking for money, since, despite the generous paternal allowance, he soon got into debt. "Your letter," his father replied to one of them, ". . . was barely legible."

Karl's parents fretted about him because they knew that he was prone to excess and that his health was fragile, a combination that could be destructive.

"And so, dear Karl," his father wrote him in his first letter, "be well, and when you give your soul truly robust and healthy nourishment, do not forget that on this wretched earth the body is its constant companion and conditions the well-being of the whole machine. A sick scholar is the most unfortunate being on earth."

Karl did not answer his father's letter or the long postscript his mother attached to it. Henriette Marx's first known letter to her "most beloved and best" son, as she called him, expressed deep maternal devotion and practical concern. She wanted to know whether he kept his rooms in order, whether he kept himself clean and scrubbed at least once a week, whether he was frugal in his expenditures, and whether he did not drink too much coffee. Written on November 29, 1835, in faulty German, poorly spelled and almost without punctuation, Henriette's letter, which throws an indirect light on Karl's personal habits, also has a special flavor:[1]

Greatly belov'd dear Carl!
with much pleasure I seize the pen to write to you—long already the letter of your dear father is ready and always I am holding back, with this I could already have had a letter from you, which would attest to your well-being for you can believe me that I greatly yearn for you thank Heaven we are all quite healthy everybody is active and diligent also Eduard vexes himself so that we hope yet to make an efficient person out of him now you cannot ascribe it to the weakness of my sex if I am curious to know how you arranged your small household, if frugality plays the main role in big as well as in little household expenses which is an indispensable necessity, in addition I permit myself to remark dear Carl that you must never regard cleanliness and orderliness as unimportant because health and cheerfulness depend upon them see to it punctually that your rooms are scrubbed often set a regular time for it—and you scrub my beloved Carl weekly with sponge and soap—how goes it with the coffee Do you fabricate it yourself or what, I beg you to report to me everything about the housekeeping, your amiable Muse will not feel offended by the Prose of your Mother, tell Her that through the inferior the superior and the better are attained, and so keep well if you have a wish for Christmas that I can satisfy I am prepared for it with pleasure so keep well my beloved dear Carl be worthy and good and always keep God and your Parents before your eyes adieu your loving Mother Henriette Marx.
All the children greet you and kiss you and you are as always the most beloved and best.

The First-Year Student

Karl registered for nine courses in the winter semester. When his father finally heard about it, he warned him, "Nine courses seem to be somewhat excessive, and I don't want you

[1] I have tried to retain the tone and syntax of the original in my translation. S.K.P.

to do more than body and soul can bear." Karl then dropped three of his courses—on aesthetics and Greek literature. Of the six he retained, three were in law and three in poetry and art.

Karl apparently attended the lectures quite regularly. In his Student Book, under the column "Testimony of the Instructors on Lecture Attendance," all his professors pronounced him "diligent and attentive."[2] These remarks were in lieu of grades, which did not exist in German universities.

Karl plunged into his studies and student life with the kind of excess against which his father constantly warned him. Early in 1836, in one of the two letters he wrote to his parents that semester, he briefly informed them that his health had broken down. They reacted characteristically, Heinrich with a moral homily against immoderation, suspecting that Karl was smoking and drinking too much and working too hard, and Henriette with specific motherly advice on how to live moderately. If, the father wrote to his son, the report of his health was not poetically exaggerated, as, knowing Karl, he suspected it might be, then he must take greater care of himself.

Heinrich urged that Karl lead a moral and abstemious life and that he exercise regularly, taking walks and riding.

The mother showed her anxiety in her own fashion. She wanted him to give up stimulants and spicy foods and tobacco and go to bed early and thus spare his health:

Beloved dear Carl! Your indisposition has saddened us all, still I hope and wish that you are again restored— and even though I am very anxious in regard to the health of my dear children, I am nevertheless convinced that you beloved Carl can reach a high old age if you behave reasonably, you should not get heated up or drink much wine or coffee and eat nothing sharp much pepper or other spices, you should not smoke tobacco nor stay up late at night and rise early. Watch out also for colds and don't dance dear Carl until you are fully recovered, it may appear ridiculous to you dear Carl that I made like a Doctor you don't know how it hurts the hearts of parents when their children are unwell and how many sad hours this has already caused us—you

[2]Bonn University, "Departure Certificate," August 4, 1836; photocopy in Bonn Archives.

children should only see to it that you remain morally and physically healthy and for the rest don't worry, the dear father was well the whole Winter thank Heavens and there is no lack of work and we are all well. . . . write soon dear Carl better a little than letting it go by too long adieu your loving [Mother] I kiss you in my thoughts beloved Carl your mother Henriette Marx.

There is no evidence that Karl heeded his parents' advice—then or later. He did not inform them about what he was doing. A scrap of a letter from Heinrich to Karl, dated July 1, 1836, preserved in Amsterdam,[3] reads: "I plead with you, dear Carl, write about anything, but write. . . . Comfort your dear good mother. . . ." The only concession he seems to have made to his father was to reduce his courses in the spring semester from six to four, three in jurisprudence and one in literature.

By now, Karl had lost interest in the academic curriculum. He found the lectures, particularly in jurisprudence, arid and intellectually unsatisfying. He began to study on his own and became increasingly involved in the turbulent life of the students, of whom he soon became a leader.

Student Societies

Karl became a member of two student societies, one literary and one social. Still hoping to be a poet and litterateur, he joined the *Poetenbund*, a circle of young writers founded by revolutionary students, which was in competition with a similar group in the Hanoverian University of Göttingen.

The news of Karl's membership in the Poetry Circle added to his father's worries. For a gifted young man destined to become a lawyer to spend precious time on poetry and to take his effusions seriously was disturbing to the prosaic Heinrich. He feared that poetry was an escape from reality for his exuberant son and suspected that the boy had no genuine talent for it.

But neither then nor for the next half dozen years did Karl give up the Muse. During most of his student days, both in Bonn and Berlin, he poured his emotions and visions into

[3]Ms G352, in the *International Institute for Social History*, Amsterdam.

verse, filling notebooks with *Lieder*, lyrics, ballads and assorted versifications.

The other society Karl joined in Bonn was a *Landsmann-schaft*—a regional fraternity. For a student, membership in a *Landsmannschaft* was all but compulsory. It not only fulfilled a psychological need of belonging but was also a social-intellectual necessity, since outside of classroom lectures, the University provided nothing else for the students, who were left to their own devices.

The student situation was practically tailor-made for class conflict between the arrogant nobles and the defensively derisive bourgeois, of whom the pugnacious young Marx, with his sarcastic tongue and generous paternal allowance, soon became one of the leaders. But the potential enemies actually had much in common; they led the same kind of wild student life. Both the aristocrats and the bourgeois were a carousing lot, drinking heavily, singing boisterously at all hours of the night, engaging in fistfights and duels.

Duels and Debts

Pugnacious as always, Karl carried a dueling weapon (probably a stiletto), jeered sarcastically at the Borussians, roared student songs, and drank his quota of brimming steins. He was arrested in nearby Cologne for carrying a weapon, an offense which the police considered serious enough to report to the Bonn University authorities.[4] It is not known what, if any, action the University took against him, for the Bonn student Record Book for 1836-37 has been lost. In June 1836, the Bonn University authorities jailed Karl for twenty-four hours in the *Karzer* [student prison] for rowdiness, not a severe punishment, as he was permitted visits from fellow students, many of whom had shared the same jolly experience. In the year 1836, no fewer than fifty-two students were thus "incarcerated" in the University *Karzer*, some of them for as many as eight days (for dueling).[5]

[4]Report of von Salomon to von Rehfus, September 5, 1836: MS in Bonn Kuratorial Archive E 9, ID: "Die akademische Gerichtsbarkeit betreffend" [Concerning Academic Jurisdiction], June 1834 to May 1837.
[5]"Verzeichnis der verurtheilten studirenden" [List of sentenced students], MS in Bonn University Rektorsakten, G.6.

All this was made part of the student's record. Karl's Leaving-Certificate from Bonn contains the following comment:

It is to be remarked that because of nightly uproarious disturbances of the peace and drunkenness, he incurred the penalty of one day's imprisonment—otherwise nothing prejudicial against him from a moral and economic point of view has been made known. Subsequently he has been accused of carrying a forbidden weapon in Cologne. The investigation is still pending.[6]

Karl spent money riotously. Early in 1836, his father sent him a check for an extra 50 Taler. But the debts kept on mounting and he could not or would not explain them satisfactorily to his worried father. "Your accounts, dear Karl," Heinrich rebuked him, "are à la Carl,[7] without coherence, without purpose. . . . Even from a scholar one has a right to expect orderliness." In that year, Heinrich's property was estimated at 21,594 Taler; his income was declining with his health and he had so little cash—less than 500 Taler altogether—that the family had to count pennies, economizing even on postal rates. A letter by regular mail express cost one Taler. Heinrich advised his son to write by slower freight mail: "Let it swell to a package and send it with the goodsvan. I hope you don't take amiss these small remarks about economizing." By March, Karl was 160 Taler in debt. His father warned him, "Dear Karl, I repeat to you, I do everything that is necessary, but I am the father of many children—and you know very well that I am not rich."

The reports that reached Trier of Karl's drinking, disorderly conduct, and carrying dueling weapons dismayed Heinrich. He feared his intemperate son would get himself killed.

Sometime in the summer of 1836, Karl either challenged or was challenged to a duel, probably by a member of the *Corps Borussia*, but whoever his opponent was he turned out to be a better swordsman than the lawyer's son from Trier. Karl was wounded on the right eye.

This was too much for Heinrich Marx. For some months now he had felt that Bonn was not the proper University for his son, and Karl apparently agreed. On July 1, 1836, Heinrich Marx sent a brief, lawyerish note to "Herrn Carl, Studi-

---

[6]Bonn University Leaving-Certificate, August 22, 1836; MS in Bonn University Archives.
[7]Karl's father used "Karl" and "Carl" interchangeably.

osus Juris," stating: "I not only grant my son Carl Marx permission but also [express] my intention . . . that he transfer to the University of Berlin in the next Semester." The note was signed formally, "Marx, *Justizrat* and Attorney."[8]

On August 22, 1836, Karl left Bonn for Trier, where he spent his vacation. He and Jenny became secretly engaged, with the approval of his parents. Heinrich and Jenny—though apparently not Karl—were worried about the reaction of *her* parents when they found out.

IV
Berlin University
(1836-1841)

In the middle of October 1836, Karl left Trier for Berlin, a city which Prussia's Rhineland subjects, including Trierites, considered an alien capital. But it had a University of great renown, a center of learning not dominated by carousing students but by ambitious and hard-working Prussians.

Karl traveled by post coach, for there was as yet no railroad. The trip to Berlin took five days. It was not a happy trip, for Karl, eighteen and a half years old and passionately in love with Jenny, was tormented by the physical ache of parting from his beloved, as well as by uncertainty about the future, both personal and professional. Karl nursed his despair, which he communicated to his father more than a year later, in his famous letter of November 18, 1837—the confession of a soul in torment. About his journey to Berlin, he wrote:

> When I left home, a new world had opened up for me, one of love and, at first, a love drunk with longing and empty of hope. Even the trip to Berlin, which otherwise would have enchanted me to the highest degree, would have inspired me to contemplate nature and inflamed me to a joy of living, left me cold, indeed, depressed me considerably. For the rocks I saw before me were no steeper, no harsher than the sensations of my soul, the broad cities no livelier than the surging of my blood, the restaurant tables no more overloaded with indigestible food than the contents of my imagination, and, finally, art itself, which was not as beautiful as Jenny.

The University of Berlin was a far cry from Bonn, and at first its size and intellectual ferment may well have intimidated a young man from the provinces. It had over 2,000 students, three times as many as Bonn, and professors whose fame was nationwide and, indeed, in some cases almost legendary. The University was young in years, as European universities went, intellectually bold, challenging and vigorous. Despite the prevailing political autocracy of the Prussian government, its University enjoyed a surprising amount of freedom.

It had been established only a little over a quarter of a century before Karl Marx matriculated there. Its founder, Karl Wilhelm von Humboldt, a philologist, was himself a man of genius and older brother of an even greater genius, Alexander von Humboldt. Karl Wilhelm von Humboldt had told King Friedrich Wilhelm III after Napoleon I had destroyed Prussian power at Jena in 1806: "The State must replace by intellectual force what it has lost in physical force." With an initial royal grant of 150,000 Taler, von Humboldt proceeded to lay the foundations of the University, including Academies of Arts and Sciences, libraries, botanical gardens, an anatomical museum, and similar institutions. He raided the older German universities for the best scholars and scientists.

When the University opened in 1810, it had the most distinguished faculty in Germany and possibly in Europe. Among the renowned names were Christoph Wilhelm Hufeland in medicine; Johann Gottlieb Fichte in philosophy; Friedrich Schleiermacher in theology; Heinrich Klaproth in orientology; Barthold Georg Niebuhr in Roman history; and Friedrich Karl von Savigny in Roman law. These men were pioneers in their fields. The greatest and ultimately the most influential professor, Georg Wilhelm Hegel, came to Berlin in 1818, and remained there until his death in 1831. His philosophy revolutionized the University.

Classes and Professors

When Karl entered the University of Berlin, it had already shifted or was in the process of shifting much of its emphasis from philosophy to jurisprudence and the historical sciences. In history, philosophical speculation was being replaced increasingly by the documentary evidence method, of which the foremost practitioner was Leopold von Ranke, who came to Berlin in 1825. Ranke, who wrote, "In all history God dwells, lives, is to be seen," claimed that meticulous study of documents could demonstrate the past *"wie es eigentlich gewesen ist"* [as it really was]. Through his pioneering seminars, which were to extend over a period of sixty years (he died in 1886, at the age of ninety-one), Ranke created a new school of historians who transformed the writing of history not only in Germany but in the Western world.[1] His presence was strongly felt at the University, although much of his presumable "scientific" new history was burdened by an overdose of factualism and microscopism.

In his mature years, Marx, recalling the "little twerp" Ranke from his student days, referred to him contemptuously as a "flunkey" who spent his time in "silly rummaging in anecdotes and ascribing all great events to trifles and lousinesses."

Karl's interest in lecture courses soon waned. There were three semesters in which he attended none at all. Altogether, during his nine semesters in Berlin, from fall 1836 to spring 1841, he took a total of twelve courses, of which only a few were in law. His other courses included anthropology, geography, art history, and Euripides, as well as one on Isaiah by the theologian Bruno Bauer, with whom Marx was to maintain a stormy relationship for many years. Instead of formal classes, Karl pursued studies on his own.

Most of the original giants, who had lent glory to the University and had attracted students from all over Germany, were no longer alive when Karl matriculated, but their aura and influence were still palpable. At least two of the professors he respected, Friedrich Karl von Savigny and Eduard Gans, had been students of Hegel, whom they interpreted in different ways. They stimulated young Karl, in this formative period, as they themselves had been inspired by the great philosopher. During his first year at the University, Karl dipped into Hegel's *Phaenomenologie des Geistes* [*Phenomenology of the Mind*] but did not then become a Hegelian. As he wrote his father on November 10, 1837, "I had read fragments of Hegel's philosophy, the grotesque, rocklike melody of which did not appeal to me."

While attending von Savigny's lectures, Karl read the professor's first important book, *Das Recht des Besitzes* [*The*

[1] See "The Ranke School" by Saul K. Padover, in James Westfall Thompson, *A History of Historical Writing* (New York, 1942), II, Ch. XLII.

Law of Property], a pioneer work in jurisprudence which extended the concept of property to include other possessions, as well as his monumental six-volume *Geschichte des römischen Rechts im Mittelalter* [*History of Roman Law in the Middle Ages*]. In his lectures and writings, von Savigny stressed two main ideas, institutional integralism and historical continuity. To von Savigny, the law was an integral part of the total life of a nation. "I regard the law of each country," he wrote, "as a member of its body, not as a garment which has been made merely to please the fancy or that could be taken off at pleasure and exchanged for another." As for continuity, von Savigny rejected as superficial the notion that each generation was "free and independent" of its past. In the preface of the first number of the *Zeitschrift für geschichtliche Rechtswissenschaft* [*Journal of Historical Jurisprudence*] (1815), he stated; "Each age does not act arbitrarily or in an egoistic independence, but is entirely held to the past by common and indissoluble bonds." Strains of this formulation can be detected in the later "Marxist" doctrine of historical materialism.

The second outstanding personality whose lectures Karl attended was Eduard Gans, who, like von Savigny, was both a jurist and a Hegelian. Two years after becoming a professor in Berlin, in 1820, Hegel brought the brilliant twenty-three-year-old Gans, who had been a student of his at Heidelberg, to the University, to counteract the conservative influence of von Savigny, who by then had a massive reputation as the founder of the historical school of jurisprudence. After Hegel's death in 1831, his two former students heightened the intellectual ferment at the University by their opposing interpretations of the subtle philosophy of their teacher.

Each of the two Hegelians reflected a significant aspect of Hegel's thought. Von Savigny's historical approach to institutions implied support for the political status quo. This was, of course, in line with Hegel's "absolute Idea"—an immutable universalism not subject to human control. Hegel himself had given the autocratic Prussian government philosophic support when he declared it to be the "realization of the absolute Idea." But keen students of Hegel, like Gans—and later, Marx—stressed another great element in Hegelianism, that of dialectics. Just as the "absolute Idea" was static and retrospective, so the Hegelian concept of dialectics was evolutionary and forward-looking. For in essence, and by definition, the dialectical process meant movement and change, presumably for the better.

Although Marx had found his first taste of Hegel unpalatable, he soon fell under the great philosopher's spell. Within a year, he read Hegel's *Outlines of the Philosophy of Right* and *Lectures on the Philosophy of History*, both of which had been brought out by Eduard Gans, as well as the *Phenomenology of the Mind*, *The Science of Logic*, and the *Encyclopedia of the Philosophic Sciences in Outline*. As a student, Karl wrote a few "Hegel Epigrams." One of them reads:

> Because in mind I have discovered the Highest and · Deepest, I am coarse, like a God, and, like him, envelop myself in Darkness.
>
> Long have I searched and moved on the surging sea of thought, and there I found the Word, and clung to it fast.[2]

In 1837, in the second year at the University, Karl joined the circle of the Young Hegelians.

After having registered for his University courses, Karl plunged into a storm of work. He stayed up night after night, eating irregularly, smoking heavily, devouring books and filling notebooks. "I sought," he said later, "to immerse myself in scholarship and art." Setting himself a frenetic pace, he raced from law to philosophy to poetry to aesthetics, then to writing plays and stories, then back to philosophy and poetry.

For a student in his eighteenth year, Marx's self-guided reading during the first semester was remarkable. In law, he hurried to master the major works of Roman and German jurisprudence. In Roman law, he read the basic digests, known as the Pandects.

Not satisfied with mere reading, he made voluminous extracts and translated the first two books of the Pandects into German. Then he rushed on to organize the available fragments of Roman law into a coherent system that would yield some philosophic meaning.

At the end of the first semester, Karl had a mental crisis. The furious pace he set himself and the frustration involved

[2]*Weil ich das Höchste endeckt und die Tiefe sinnend gefunden, Bin ich grob, wei ein Gott, hüll' mich in Dunkel, wie er. Lange forscht' ich und trieb auf dem wogenden Meer der Gedanken, Und da fand ich das Wort, halt' am Gefundenen fest.*

in his "fruitless intellectual labors" churned up in him a "consuming anger." Rage and strain, aggravated by news of Jenny's illness in Trier and her continued silence, caused a physical and mental breakdown. The smoke-filled room and the sleepless nights were too much for his tubercular lungs. "My physical condition," Karl wrote to his father on November 1, 1837, "deteriorated, and a doctor recommended the countryside; and thus, for the first time, I traversed the whole spreading city to the gate of Stralow." Stralow [strelau] was a village on the outskirts of Berlin on the Spree River. It took two days for the raging young man to calm down. He stayed in a house near the Spree, and at first he ran around the garden "like a madman." Gradually, Karl settled down to enjoy fresh air and country life. "I even joined my landlord in a hunting party," he told his father. His health was soon restored. He returned to Berlin so well and elated that he "felt like embracing every loafer at street corners."

The euphoria did not last. Once again, he resumed his habit of excessive work and equally extravagant pursuit of universal meaning, with a greater emphasis on law and legal philosophy. He sought answers in the writings of scientists and juridical theorists, the canon law and the contemporary German legal system.

In science, he read Francis Bacon's *De dignitate et augmentis scientiarum* (1623), and Hermann Samuel Reimarus' work on animal instincts.[3] In theory, in addition to Hegel, whom he began to study seriously during his second semester, he read Fichte on natural law[4] and Schelling on natural philosophy.[5] In ecclesiastical law, he read and excerpted "virtually the whole corpus" of Gratian's *Concordia*[6] and Lancelotti's *Institutiones*,[7] both classics in canon law. In German jurisprudence, he read and extracted from the work of his professor, von Savigny, on property;[8] Klein's legislative

---

[3] Reimarus, *Allgemeine Betrachtungen über die Triebe der Thiere* [*General Observations on Instincts in Animals*] (1760).

[4] Johann Gottlieb Fichte, *Grundlage des Naturrechts nach Prinzipien der Wissenschaftslehre* [*Elements of Natural Law According to the Principles of Scientific Theory*] (1796).

[5] Friedrich Wilhelm Joseph Schelling, *Philosophische Schriften* [*Philosophical Writings*] (Vol. I, 1809).

[6] *Concordia discordantium canonum* [ca.1140], containing about 3,500 texts of church councils, decretals and other ecclesiastical acts.

[7] Giovanni Paolo Lancelotti, *Institutiones iuris canonici*.

[8] Friedrich Carl von Savigny, *Das Recht des Besitzes* [*The Law of Property*] (1803).

Annals;[9] Feuerbach's positive penal law;[10] and von Grol-mann's principles of the science of criminal law.[11]

As he made clear in his letter of November 10, 1837, to his father, he did not read those works on jurisprudence primarily to become a lawyer, but rather to find metaphysical answers. "I . . . tried to work out a philosophy of law while studying law." He devoured the tomes, he admitted, uncritically and "in schoolboy fashion," never ceasing in his search for the Absolute in terms of principles, definitions and concepts.

[9]Ernst Ferdinand Klein, *Annalen der Gesetzgebung . . . in den Preussischen Staaten* [*Annals of Legislation . . . in the Prussian States*] (26 vols., 1788-1809).

[10]Johann Paul Anselm Feuerbach, *Lehrbuch des gemeinen in Deutschland gültigen peinlichen Rechts* [*Manual of Common Penal Law Applicable in Germany*] (1808).

[11]Karl von Grolmann, *Grundsätze der Criminalrechts-Wissenschaft* [*Principles of the Science of Criminal Law*] (4th ed., 1825).

V
Sturm und Drang

Emotional Turmoil

In his eighteenth year, Karl underwent a devastating crisis of heart and mind. Undirected in his studies and unclear in his purposes, consumed by a gigantic intellectual hunger, he was buffeted by incessant external proddings and internal pressures. The external goads came from his father, whose normal tendency to fuss and fret was now aggravated by deteriorating health, declining income and worries about the future of his family, which included five unmarried daughters for whom dowries had to be provided. All his life's hopes were pinned on his eldest son, for whom his ambitions were exceeded only by his doubts about Karl's stability of character and purpose. Would he measure up to his father's soaring expectations?

Adding to Heinrich's anxieties was Jenny, whom he came to treat as if she were his own daughter. The father was not sure that his son was mature enough to measure the consequences of his betrothal to a gentle and trusting young woman. Or perhaps, Heinrich suspected the worst and dreaded the future—if so, his fears were prophetic. He poured his worries into letters to his son that were relentless in their exhortations, moralizing and meddling. Even their obvious good intentions, which Karl never doubted, did nothing for his peace of mind. Loving his father as he did and wrestling with his personal demon, he did not know how to cope with the implacable tyranny of paternal love. The main effect of Heinrich's admonishments—which continued for two more years, until his death in 1838, to batter Karl—was to unsettle his son's already troubled spirit still further.

For Karl, his love for Jenny was a torment. He suffered Werther-like sorrows, for the sentimental-romantic spirit of Goethe's 18th century novel was still alive in early 19th century Germany.[1] Karl, as well as Jenny, had a strong strain of romanticism, which was later reflected in their ardent and persistent revolutionism. But there were also practical reasons for Karl's *Angst*. His secret betrothal to Trier's most beautiful girl seemed to be a hopeless engagement. What did an impecunious young student, unsure about his career and uncertain about the future, have to offer her?

Karl's torment was aggravated by a lack of correspondence between the two lovers. For Jenny, either because she considered it disrespectful for a daughter to act behind the back of loving and beloved parents, or because of some contemporary romantic tradition, would not write to her betrothed or answer his letters until their engagement had parental approval—a reluctant approval that was not granted until 1837, after Karl and Jenny had both made themselves sick with waiting.

Plays and Poems

While frantically chasing after elusive metaphysical absolutes through volumes of law and philosophy, Karl did not neglect his chief passion, the arts, and particularly his own literary writings. At the end of the first semester, he wrote, "I again sought the dances of the Muses and the music of Satyrs." Spurred by the philosophy of Idealism, he turned out what he called a "few bad productions," such as *Der Besuch* [*The Visit*]; *Scorpion und Felix*, a "humorous romance"; and *Oulanem*, a tragedy in non-rhyming verse, which he referred to as a "drama of the fantastic." *Scorpion* was not really very humorous, at least not intentionally, and *Oulanem*, while perhaps fantastic, was not much of a drama, as Karl soon discovered for himself.

Karl's state of emotional upheaval did not submerge his innate critical sense for long. By the time he was nineteen, he realized that he was dabbling in pseudo-philosophy and that, apart from his poetry, his literary concoctions had little merit.

---

[1]Goethe's *The Sorrows of Werther* (1774) dealt with a sensitive young student who committed suicide because of unrequited love. Thomas Carlyle wrote of the book: "*Werther*, infusing itself into the core and whole spirit of literature, gave birth to a race of sentimentalists, who raged and wailed in every part of the world till better light dawned on them, or at any rate till exhausted nature laid itself to sleep, and it was discovered that lamenting was an unproductive labour."

He recognized that *Scorpion und Felix* contained "forced humor" and that *Oulanem* was "inept." These writings, he finally admitted to his father, to whom he had sent them, were "mostly without inspired objects or vibrant ideas."

All this time, he wrote, "the realm of true poetry shone at me like a distant fairy palace" and helped to dissolve his other creations "into nothingness." Poetry became "my heaven, my art" and a constant "companion." It centered around his love for Jenny, transporting him into a "remote other-world" without boundaries, where "everything real grew blurred."

By November 1836, Karl had filled three notebooks with poems, entitling the first two, *Buch der Liebe* [*Book of Love*], and the third, *Buch der Lieder* [*Book of Songs*]. The three notebooks, which had long been lost when they were published in 1929, consisted of 262 pages and contained a total of fifty-six poems; lyrics, ballads, and sonnets. Thirty-five of them carried the superscription "To Jenny"—and many of the poems had such sentimental titles as "Song to the Stars," "Yearning," "Son of a Sailor at Sea," "The Harp Songstresses," "The Melancholy Girl," "The Pale Maiden." At eighteen, and violently in love, Karl was, after all, entitled to be romantic.

Final Sonnet to Jenny

One thing more, my child, I must tell:
Joyously I end with this song of farewell;
For the last silvery waves so roll
As on Jenny's breath to find their soul,
Leaping boldly over rock and tower,
Running through rising flood and shower,
While the hours with life pulsate
Their fulfillment in you to consecrate.

Boldly envelop'd in ardor's mantle wide,
The luminous heart lifted with pride,
Triumphantly freed from force and strain
I tread firmly through the spacious terrain,
Pain shattering before your visage that gleams,
And from life's tree sprout the dreams.[2]

²Schluss-Sonnett an Jenny

Eines muss ich Dir, mein Kind, noch sagen,
  Fröhlich schiesst mein Abschiedssang der Rhein,
Denn die letzten Silberwellen schlagen,

Karl inscribed his collection of poems "To my dear, eternally beloved Jenny von Westphalen," and in December 1836 he sent it to Trier. At Christmastime, Jenny visited the Marx family, where she stayed as usual until 10 o'clock in the evening, and was given the lyrics. She read them, Karl's sister Sophie wrote him, with tears of "joy and sorrow."

Subsequently, Karl also gathered international folksongs—in Spanish, Greek, Lettish, Lapp, Estonian, Albanian, as well as in German dialects—and sent the collection to "my sweet beloved Jennychen." The cover carried a stanza from an "old folksong":

> Have never forgotten thee,
> Have ever thought of thee,
> Thou liest always in my heart,
> Heart, heart,
> Clinging like a rose on a branch.[8]

Jenny treasured Karl's lyrics to the end of her days. She never showed them to anybody, not even to members of her immediate family. The poems remained a symbol of their love, cherished long after she and Karl had found them jejune and ridiculous. "I must tell you," Laura Lafargue wrote Franz Mehring after Marx's death, "that my father treated those poems very disrespectfully; every time my parents came to talk about them, they laughed heartily over those youthful follies."

By early 1837, Karl's father seems to have reluctantly

> Sich in Jennys Hauche Klang zu leihn,
> So wird kühn durch Felsensprung und Ragen,
> Lauf durch Flutenfall und Hain,
> Fort derf Stundenlauf des Lebens schlagen,
> Zur Vollendung sich in Dir zu weihn.
>
> Kühn gehüllt in weiten Glutgewanden,
> Lichtverklärt das stolzbehob' ne Herz,
> Herrschend losgesagt von Zwang und Banden
> Tret' ich feston Schritt's durch weite Räume,
> Schmett' re vor Dein Antlitz hin den Schmerz
> Und zum Lebensbaum entsprühn die Träume!"

> [8]Hab' Deiner nievergessen,
> Hab' alzeit an Dih gedenkt,
> Du liegst mir stets am Herzen,
> Herzen, Herzen,
> Wie d' Ros' am Stiele hängt.

reconciled himself to the unhappy idea that his son might choose authorship as his career. But if Karl must be an author, he should, to begin with, consider writing about "philosophical or juridical subjects," or both together, and let verse "take second place." Poetry could do no harm in one's career, provided it was not "genuine poetry" but only "light verse." If original and written in a novel style, such verse could even help to enhance Karl's reputation and enable him, "reasonably and surely," to obtain a professorship or some other worthy post.

But, above all, Karl must stop flitting about from subject to subject, wasting his time in footling pursuits. He ought to make up his mind about a career and stick to it: "You must come to a firm decision—if not this second, then certainly this year, and once made, it should be kept firmly in mind and pursued unswervingly." Such a decision was a necessity, particularly for Jenny's peace of mind. Karl must not keep her in an agony of uncertainty about the future.

As one of the steps towards practicability, Heinrich advised, Karl should try to find a publisher. That, the father added, might well be the hardest thing for an unknown young writer to achieve. Still, for Karl it might not be impossible, for, his father reminded him, "you are altogether a *Glückskind.*"

The *Glückskind,* still thinking of himself primarily as a poet, was not far behind his father in his anxiety to see his name in print; and, like any fledgling author, he was cruelly disappointed by his first rejection slip. In 1837, Karl sent some of his poems to the *Deutsche Musenalmanach* and was turned down curtly by the co-editor, Adalbert von Chamisso, the French-born German poet to whom the world is indebted for *Schlemihl,*[4] the man who sold his shadow. "Herr von Chamisso," Karl wrote to his father, "sent me a measly note in which he says 'he regrets that his Almanac cannot use my contributions because it has long since gone to press.' I swallowed his note in anger." Karl then tried two Leipzig publishers, Otto Wiegand and Julius Wunder, without success.

For Heinrich's sixtieth birthday, in April 1837, Karl selected a number of his poems, put them in a separate notebook with the inscription "Dedication to the Father," and sent them to Trier as a "feeble token of eternal love." The poems

[4]Adalbert von Chamisso, *Peter Schlemihl's Wunderbare Geschichte* [*Peter Schlemihl's Wonderful History*].

included: "Creation" [*Schöpfung*], "Poetry" [*Dichtung*], "Song of a Sailor at Sea" [*Lied eines Schiffers auf der See*], "The Fiddler" [*Der Spielmann*], and "Night Love" [*Nachtliebe*].

It was not until four years later that some of Marx's poetry got into print. In Jaunary 1841, *Athenäum*, a Berlin weekly devoted to culture,[5] published two poems, "The Fiddler" and "Night Love," from Karl's manuscript collection of what he called *Wilde Lieder* [*Wild Songs*].

The Letter of November 10, 1837

On November 10, 1837, Karl finally replied in full to his father's persistent hectoring, advice and admonitions. This communication is rare on many counts. It is the first of Marx's letters that has been preserved and the only personal letter in existence from his early years. Otherwise, the first available correspondence does not begin until 1842, when he was twenty-four years old.

The letter of November 10, 1837, probably escaped destruction because it was tucked away among Henriette Marx's papers. Upon her death in 1863, it was found and kept by Karl's older sister, Sophie Schmalhausen, who left it to her family. Karl apparently did not know of its existence, or he might have destroyed it when he visited Trier in 1863; at least, so his daughter Eleanor remarked when she first made it public sixty years after it was written.[6]

The letter is, indeed, a remarkable document. About four thousand words long, it took all night to write. It came to an end only when the guttering candle died out and Karl's eyes became blurred and his mind overcome with weariness and emotion. As an unsparing account of a young man in an agony of self-searching, it is memorable in itself. As a self-portrait of Karl Marx in the throes of his first intellectual development, it is invaluable. The letter throws a flood of

[5] *Athenäum's* subtitle was: *Zeitschrift für das gebildete Deutschland* [*Journal for Educated Germany*].

[6] Eleanor Marx-Aveling, in *Die Neue Zeit*, 1897: "The letter submitted here was sent to me a few months ago by my cousin, Frau Karoline Smith, who found it among the papers of her Sophie. . . . Marx himself was in Trier at the time of his mother's death in 1863, but he surely did not know of the existence of the letter and that his sister had it— fortunately so, or he undoubtedly would have destroyed it."

light on the mind of young Marx, revealing the strengths and weakness associated with the later Marx: a tendency to generalization, a sense of sharp criticism, a relentless chase after ideas and systems. The extraordinary letter begins with a broad generalization:

Dear Father:

There are moments in life which stand as landmarks, terminating the past and at the same time pointing firmly in a new direction. At such a point of transition, we feel compelled to contemplate, with the eagle eye of thought, the past and the present, in order to arrive at a true awareness of our actual situation. Indeed, world history itself loves such a retrospect, seeming to move backwards and to stand still, whereas in reality it leans back in the armchair to understand itself and to penetrate intellectually its own action, the action of the mind.

From world history, Karl moved to the individual, and from there to himself and his relation to his parents:

The individual, however, becomes lyrical in such moments, because metamorphosis is partly swan song, partly overture to a great new poem that tries to gain shape amidst the still hazy, brilliant hues; and yet we should erect a monument to what we have already experienced, so that it should regain in sensibility what it has lost in action; and where could we find a more sacred abode than in the hearts of our parents, the most indulgent judges, the most intimate participants, the sun of love whose fire warms our innermost strivings! What better way is there to correct and to receive forgiveness for what is displeasing and blameworthy in our character than to look at it as an essentially necessary condition? In what other way, at least, could the frequently hostile turn of fortune and the aberration of spirit escape the reproach of being due to a twisted heart?

Karl proceeded to review the events of his year in Berlin and to examine his "view of life" as an "expression of reflection taking shape in all directions—in science, in art, in private endeavors." He described his experience with poetry and his need for it, his search for philosophical definitions and concepts, his attempt to build a structure and a theory of law, his habit of making excerpts from all the works on philosophy and jurisprudence that he read. He discussed his literary efforts and his frustrations over them and the breakdown in his health, and his resumption of his studies and writings upon his recovery.

Karl then took up the subject that preyed so much on his father's mind—his career. He was beginning to lean in the direction of government service. He had met, he wrote, a man named Schmidthänner, an *Assessor*, who advised him to enter the judiciary. "This," Karl added, "would appeal to me all the more since I really prefer jurisprudence to . . . public administration." According to Schmidthänner, in some parts of Germany, such as Westphalia, promotion was faster than in Berlin. It was possible to become an *Assessor* in three years, and if, thereafter, you acquired a doctorate, you had a prospect of becoming a professor of jurisprudence.

The concluding paragraphs of the letter were out of tune with the rest of it. They contained expressions of effusive filial affection and family sentimentality—something that Karl, according to Heinrich, had never before indulged in. Karl now referred to his mother as *Engelsmutter*—Angelic Mother—and implored his father not to show her the part of the letter which suggested the possibility of his coming home: "My unexpected arrival may perhaps cheer up that great, splendid woman." The letter ends on a note of extreme and rare personal emotion:

In the hope that the clouds which hang over our family will gradually pass; that I may be permitted to share your sufferings and mingle my tears with yours, and perhaps in your presence demonstrate the deep affection, the boundless love, which I have often expressed poorly; in the hope that you too, dear, eternally beloved father, mindful of the confused state of my storm-tossed soul, will forgive where the heart must often have seemed to err as my overburdened spirit stifled it; in the hope that you will soon be fully restored to health so that I shall be able to press you close to my heart and tell you all I feel,

I remain your ever-loving son,

KARL.

There were two postscripts:

Forgive, dear father, the illegible handwriting and the poor style; it is nearly 4 o'clock; the candle has burned out entirely, and my eyes are clouded; a deep restlessness has overwhelmed me; I shall not be able to lay the specters haunting me until I am in your dear presence.

The other postscript was for Jenny, who had recently been induced finally to write him a letter:

Please give my love to my sweet, splendid Jenny. I have already read her letter twelve times, and each time I discover new charms in it. In every respect, it is the most beautiful letter I can imagine a woman writing.

The Father's Last Letters[7]

Karl's long letter, making its slow way by post coach from Berlin to Trier, crossed one in the reverse direction. This was a letter from his father, dated November 17, in which Heinrich castigated his son for his negativism, particularly his complaints about Jenny's silence:

Your pessimism disgusts me, and I least expected it from you. What reason can you have for it? Has not everything been smiling for you since your cradle? Has not nature endowed you richly? . . . And had you not, in the most incomprehensible way, carried off the heart of a girl whom thousands envy you? And yet the first setback and the first unfulfilled desire bring forth only pessimism! Is this strength? Is this manly character?[7]

And now came Karl's long outpouring of November 10. It both angered and offended Heinrich, who was in the throes of pain from throat, liver and lung ailments. He was wracked by constant coughs, and probably suspected that he had not long to live. The least his eldest son could do, he felt, was to evince some sympathy for the family and hurry on with his practical career. But Karl's elaborate letter showed that his

[7]In the International Institute for Social History, Amsterdam, D3270/3288, there are eighteen photocopies of Heinrich Marx's manuscript letters to Karl, the last one dated February 10, 1838.

overriding concern was with his inner self and his personal passions. Of the approximately 3,000 words in the November 10 letter, fewer than 200 mentioned career and less than 100 referred to family. The rest was entirely *Karl*.

On December 9, 1837, Heinrich, obviously in a state of barely controlled agitation, wrote Karl a long letter. It consisted of a detailed list of complaints—to "have you swallow them like pills." The letter lashed at Karl for his selfishness, accused him of disorderliness, upbraided him for squandering time and money. This was the last letter of any length that Heinrich was to write to his son.

Heinrich castigated his son for his numerous failures in all areas of human relationship and responsibility. His letter was a substantial catalog of transgressions, a number of which are ironically reminiscent of the accusations made against Karl Marx by his enemies in later years. Heinrich charged Karl with being a slovenly barbarian, an antisocial person, a wretched son, an indifferent brother, a selfish lover, an irresponsible student, and a reckless spendthrift.

Heinrich wrote that he blamed himself for his indulgence of Karl and that he felt guilty in having encouraged the romance with Jenny. He and his wife had done so in the hope that the engagement would have a beneficent effect on Karl's character. But, Heinrich asked rhetorically, what harvest did they reap? "I want and must tell you that you have given your parents much displeasure and little or no joy." He then accused him of neglecting his parents by rarely bothering to keep in touch with them in any meaningful sense. His letter, a characteristic example of his selfishness, had been aggravated by his enclosure of his latest literary effort which so offended Heinrich that he condemned it as a piece of monstrous trash, a "crazy concoction" in the fashion of the current fiendish avant-garde, a "deluge of words" without sense or meaning.

Heinrich also took his son to task for his spendthrift ways. In one year, Karl spent more money than an average wealthy family. He had already exhausted his annual allowance and had again piled up a debt, as he had previously done when he was a student at Bonn. Heinrich told his son that he had paid a debt of 160 Taler, for which Karl had signed a check, but warned him that this could not go on: "As for the future, I don't want to expect many more such."

In January 1838, Heinrich Marx took to bed, wracked by coughs and liver pains. His thoughts continued to be with his son, to whom he could no longer write long letters, but on his sickbed he read Karl's letters, according to the mother, "over and over again." Heinrich's last communication to Karl consisted of an addendum to a letter that Henriette wrote on February 10, in which she reported on the course of her husband's illness: "Your father's cough is much better, but he suffers from a loss of appetite, and on account of his long sickness has become awfully irritable." She begged Karl to write him "very tenderly." Heinrich's last written words to Karl show how tormented he was by the thought of his son's continued disregard for what he ironically called "filthy money." The father's remarks had a pathetic prescience:

There is only one point, about which you have been clever enough to maintain a noble silence, that all transcendentalism cannot do away with—I mean filthy money, the value of which for a father of a family you still do not seem to understand and which I, therefore, do the more so. I do not deny that sometimes I reproach myself for having kept too loose a rein on you. Thus we are now in the fourth month of the judicial calendar, and already you have drawn 280 Taler. I have not earned that much this winter.

Karl received the 280 Taler from Henriette, who signed her letter "Your Mother who loves you."[8] There were to be few such letters thereafter.

On May 10, 1838, Heinrich Marx died in Trier at the age of sixty. Karl was not present and there is no record of his reaction to his father's death. Heinrich apparently died of tuberculosis, complicated by inflammation and swelling of the liver. Karl seems to have inherited from his father, as he always claimed, a susceptibility to lung and liver ailments, afflictions which were to torment him all his life. When, in March 1853, he came down with an "inflammation of the liver," he wrote to Engels: "It is hereditary in my family. My Old Man died of it."[9]

[8]MS, D3287, in the International Institute for Social History, Amsterdam.
[9]On March 10, 1853, Jenny wrote from London to Adolf Cluss, a friend in Washington, D.C., "My dear Karl has been suffering for weeks, and a few days ago his old liver trouble acted up, to the point of inflammation, a sickness which is to me the more worrisome as it is hereditary in his family and was the fatal cause of his father's death."

The Mother

Heinrich's death marked the end of a crucial period in Karl Marx's life. It was the termination of whatever dependence he ever had on a parent. With the father dead, the last restraint on Karl, frail as that may have been, was gone. So were any emotional ties with his family in Trier. He never seems to have had any particular attachment to his brothers and sisters, and no real affection for his mother. Words like *"Engelsmutter"* and "magnificent woman," which Karl had used occasionally, were more routine than heartfelt expressions, written in deference to his father. But now the mother, a bourgeoise who owned property in Trier, became to Karl hardly anything more than a possible source of money.

In October 1838, about half a year after Heinrich's death, Henriette sent Karl 160 Taler, which he apparently told his mother he needed "for graduation." But he was far from graduation. He gave up any pretense that he was studying to become a lawyer, and spent the next three years in Berlin in the company of the Young Hegelians, and preparing for his doctorate in philosophy. He kept on pressing his mother for money, which she supplied with increasing misgivings. Her last letter to Karl that has been preserved, written in May 1840, is full of grievances. She complained that Jenny's family, the von Westphalens, arrogantly ignored her—*"keine juste millieu findet da nicht Stat"* [no proper relationship takes place], as she wrote in her Dutch-German—and scolded her son for his behavior towards his own family. He, Karl, she told him, had entirely abandoned everything that was "once valuable and dear" to him, saying "you will never make the moral sacrifices for your family that your family made for you." She added: "I want to know if you have *pronovirt*."[10]

Altogether, up to the time he took his doctorate, in 1841, his mother sent him a total of 1,111 Taler. This sum was an advance on his inheritance, from his deceased father. When Heinrich Marx's estate was finally settled, in 1841, it amounted to a total of 22,110 Taler, 5 Groschen, and 11 Pfennigs.

---

[10]The German word *promoviert* [with an "m"] means taking a doctor's degree.

Half of this, 11,136 Taler, was Henriette's own property, which she had brought as a dowry, and was left to her. The other half, amounting to slightly more than 9,000 Taler after deductions for some debts, was divided among Karl and his six siblings. Karl's final share from his father's estate added up to little more than 800 Taler. This did not last him long.

The widow Marx was not a wealthy woman, although Karl always acted as if she were. An estate worth around 11,000 Taler did not provide an opulent income. Assuming Karl's mother had investments in real estate and stocks (through her brother-in-law, the Dutch banker Lion Philips, who was her testamentary executor), her income may have come to 8% per annum, which was double the interest that Trier banks paid on savings in those days. But an annual income of between 900 and 1,000 Taler was not overabundant for a widow with six children, five of whom were marriageable daughters. In any case, she did not live like a rich woman or the widow of the town's leading lawyer. The upper-class von Westphalens, who had been friends of Heinrich's, ignored her, although Jenny, who liked her no more than did Karl, continued to visit her. Henriette's environment was lower-middle-class. The first testament that she drew up, in 1849, was witnessed by an innkeeper, a shoemaker, and a carpenter; the second one, of November 1859, by a shoemaker and an upholsterer. By that time, Karl had long ceased to have any filial contact with his mother.

VI

Doctor of Philosophy

The Young Hegelians

In Berlin, Marx's intellectual contacts were with the Young Hegelians, among whom he made strong friends. The so-called Doctors' Club of Hegelians consisted of both students and Ph.D.'s. They met regularly in coffee houses, which also had reading rooms, and debated philosophical and theological ideas, which had far-reaching political implications. The Doctors' Club attracted both literary and philosophical members, but it tended increasingly to pivot around Hegelianism, with its conservative and revolutionary aspects.

Marx was a frequent visitor to the Club, where he participated in the voluble conversations and disputations. Much of the talk was cleverly garrulous and some of it witty, fueled by steins of beer and bottles of wine. There was a special wise-guy Berlin atmosphere in the Club of aspiring philosophers and would-be political leaders. The leading members of the Club were at least a decade older than Marx, but he matched them in volubility and brilliance. Among those who became his close friends, at least for the time being, were Bruno Bauer, Adolf Rutenberg, and Karl Friedrich Köppen.

Bauer, born in 1809, was then already a *Dozent* on the Faculty of Theology. Of medium size, with a ready smile, pointed nose, high forehead, and finely shaped mouth, Bauer was "practically a Napoleonic figure." Erudite, bold, ironic, windy, and skeptical—especially about the Christian state and dogma—a born disputant, he was the intellectual leader of the Young Hegelians. Marx was to break with Bauer within half a dozen years and to pour ridicule upon him in his polemic *The Holy Family*.

Dr. Adolf Rutenberg, whom Marx called his best friend as early as 1837, in his second year at the University, was an old *Burschenschafter* [radical fraternity man], had been a teacher of geography and history in a military school, and had been frequently jailed by the Prussian government for his liberalism. Ten years older than Marx, Rutenberg was then a leading newspaperman in Berlin, a correspondent for provincial papers, and a facile writer who knew how to be adroit in his journalistic generalities to escape the ubiquitous Prussian censorship. In 1842, Rutenberg became editor of the *Rheinische Zeitung*, a position from which he was dismissed and in which he was succeeded by Marx, who considered his erstwhile friend "incompetent."

Marx's third Young Hegelian friend, Karl Friedrich Köppen, was also his senior by ten years. Frederick Engels, who was a gifted cartoonist, met Köppen in Berlin some time after Marx had left the city, and drew him as he saw him. Engels' caricature shows a bespectacled Köppen with his beaked nose almost meeting his pointed chin, wearing an epauletted overcoat and rapier, sitting round-shouldered over a table covered with half-empty wine bottles and glasses. A boon companion, Köppen, by profession a teacher of history, was an erudite scholar and a courageous socialist. He was so impressed by the youthful Marx that he dedicated his book on Frederick the Great to "my friend Karl Heinrich Marx from Trier."[1] In 1841, after Marx had left Berlin, Köppen wrote him: "You are a storehouse of thoughts, a workhouse, or, to speak Berlinish, a bullhead of ideas." Marx retained a lifelong affection for him. In 1861, two years before Köppen's death, Marx visited him in Berlin and took delight in his drinking company.

The Doctoral Dissertation

At the end of 1839, Marx began to work on his doctoral dissertation. He chose the field of late Greek philosophy, about which little scholarly work had been done. The title of his dissertation was *Differenz der demokritischen und epikureischen Naturphilosophie* [Difference Between the Democritean and Epicurean Philosophy of Nature]—a subject which he hoped some day to enlarge upon, in order to cover this whole field of thought. The time had come, he felt,

---

[1] Karl Friedrich Köppen, *Friedrich der Grosse und seine Widersacher* [*Frederick the Great and His Opponents*] (Leipzig, 1840).

for an understanding of the Epicureans, Stoics and Skeptics as "philosophers of self-consciousness."

Marx plunged into the study of Greek philosophy with his customary enthusiasm and thoroughness. The drafts, outlines and notes, which have been preserved, show astonishing penetration and erudition for a young man of twenty-one and twenty-two. Sweeping through all the original materials, he read and annotated—in Greek and Latin—the following classical philosophers, historians, dramatists, poets, and essayists: Aeschylus, Aristotle, Athenaeus, Aurelius, Augustinus, Cicero, Clemens Alexandrinus, Diogenes Laertius, Epicurus, Eusebius Pamphilus, Hesiod, Lucretius, Ovid, Plato, Plutarch, Pseudo-Plutarch, Seneca, Sextus Empiricus, Stobaeus, and Tacitus.

Marx structured his dissertation into two parts, a general and a particular. Each was divided into five sections. Part I dealt with the subject of the treatise; the relationship between the Democritean and Epicurean physics; the difficulties in identifying the philosophy of the two thinkers; the general differences in principles between them; and the result. Part II had five chapters: the decline of the atom from the straight line; the qualities of the atom; $\mathring{a}\tau o\mu o\acute{\iota}$ $\mathring{a}\rho\chi a\iota$ and $\mathring{a}\tau o\mu a$ $\sigma\tau o\iota\chi\epsilon\tilde{\iota}a$; time; and the meteors.

Marx viewed Epicurus as the more subtle and influential of the two philosophers. He considered Democritus the "foremost encyclopedic intellect among the Greeks." But he paid a greater tribute to Epicurus, calling him the "true radical enlightener of Antiquity, who openly attacked the ancient religion, and from whom also Roman atheism, insofar as it existed, emanated."

The Epicurean philosophy was regarded as a fully developed materialist system in the classic age, after it was eternalized in Lucretius' *De rerum natura*. Of Democritus, however, little was known, and only fragments of his writings have been preserved. In his dissertation, Marx set himself the task of reconstructing and reevaluating their respective philosophies out of whatever original materials were available.

Democritus was the philosopher closest to materialism—a philosophy which young Marx, still a Hegelian Idealist, had not yet embraced at that point. In Democritean thought, nothing that exists can be destroyed. Nothing happens accidentally, but with reason and necessity. Nothing exists but infinite numbers and varieties of atoms—and the void. Change is merely a separation and a uniting of parts. The collisions and rotations of the atoms result in continuing world-formations.

Epicurus, taking over this conception of nature from Democritus, made certain changes, the most important of which was the idea of the "swerving of the atoms," that is, their falling away from a straight line, instead of vertically. This idea has been ridiculed; Immanuel Kant, for example, who otherwise admired Epicurus, called it "an insolent invention." Marx, too, was critical of Epicurus' "reckless irresponsibility" in the explanation of material phenomena, but argued that there was a philosophic reason in what seemed to be physical unreason. For unlike Democritus, Epicurus was not concerned primarily with nature as an end in itself, but only as a support for his philosophic system, which was, for him, rooted in individual man's consciousness of the self.

As for the core of the dissertation, the difference between the natural philosophy of Democritus and Epicurus, Marx developed the idea that while Democritus was interested entirely in the material existence of the atom, Epicurus viewed it also as a symbol. To Epicurus, the atom, in addition to being the physical foundation of phenomena, represented individual man and his self-consciousness.

To Democritus, the vertical fall of the atom showed the necessity, or the fixed unavoidability, of all occurrences, whereas to Epicurus, the swerving of the atoms meant irregularity, that is, a departure from eternal or inexorable fate. This, as Lucretius pointed out, was the origin of man's individuality and his free will. Thus the Epicurean principle of individualism and indeterminism, among other things, freed man from bondage to the gods, which was the implication of the inflexible Democritean cosmology.

"Hence," Marx wrote, "Epicurus is the greatest enlightener, and he deserves the eulogy bestowed upon him by Lucretius":

When, before the eyes of men, disgraceful life on earth
Was bowed down by the burden of oppressive religion,
Which extended its head from the high regions of heaven,
And with gruesome grotesqueness frightfully threatened
    mankind,
A Greek first ventured to raise his mortal eye
Against the monster and boldly resisted it.
Neither the fable of god, nor lightning or thunder of heaven,
Scared him with their threat. . . .

Thus, as in reprisal, religion lies at our feet,
Completely defeated,
But, as for us, triumph raises us up to heaven.[2]

An appendix to the dissertation, consisting of two sections,
treated Plutarch's polemic against Epicurus. The appendix
was essentially a philosophical exploration of religion, with
particular emphasis on the existence of God, a subject that
was to occupy Marx for the next two or three years, after
which he dropped it forever as a topic for serious thought. A
decade after he completed his dissertation, he referred to religion as "this boring theme."

Marx hoped to publish his dissertation, and in March
1841, he wrote a brief preface for it. Although the hope did
not materialize, because, as he wrote later, "political and philosophical affairs of quite another kind" intervened, the preface is illuminating for its tone of challenge and its assertion
of the sovereignty of philosophy.

Marx stated that his dissertation was only a forerunner of
a large work on the cycle of Epicurean, Stoical and Skeptical ideas in their connection with the whole Greek speculative
philosophy. He praised Hegel's approach to Greek thought,
but pointed out that the "giant thinker," in his admirable *History of Philosophy*, had failed to recognize the great significance of the Greek speculative systems, which were the "keys
to the real history of Greek philosophy." Marx also explained
that the reason he included in his appendix a critique of Plutarch's polemic against Epicurus' theology was that the
former was a typical representative of those who "theol-
ogized" philosophy, that is, dragged philosophy into the
"forum of religion," instead of letting it reign independently
on its own. After quoting from David Hume's *A Treatise of
Human Nature* (1739) that philosophy was "outraged" when

[2]Lucretius, *De rerum natura:*

Humana ante oculos foede quum vita jaceret,
In terreis oppressa gravi sub relligione,
Quae caput a coeli regionibus ostendebat,
Horribili super aspectu mortalibus instans:
Primum Grajus homo mortaleis tollere contra
Est oculos ausus, primusque obsistere contra;
Quem nec fama Deum nec fulmina nec minitanti
Murmure compressit coelum. . . .
Quare relligio pedibus subjecta vicissim
Obteritur, nos exaequat victoria coelo.
                              —Translated by S.K.P.

it was forced to defend its own "sovereign character," Marx
continued:

> Philosophy, so long as a drop of blood still pulsates in
> its world-conquering, absolutely free heart, will always
> call out to its opponents, with Epicurus:
> "Impious is not he who rejects the God of the multi-
> tude, but he who attributes the conceptions of the multi-
> tude to the Gods."[3]

Early in 1841, Marx completed his *Differenz der demokritischen und epikuräischen Naturphilosophie*. The dissertation
no longer exists in its entirety. Chapters IV and V of Part I
have been lost, and only fragments and notes from the appendix survive.

For political reasons, however, Marx did not submit his
dissertation to Berlin University. In 1840, the Prussian government appointed Johann Albrecht Friedrich Eichhorn as
Minister of Culture. Eichhorn, in turn, named Professor
Schelling as Rector of the University. Both the Minister and
the Rector were then clericalists, determined to put an end to
the influence of the Young Hegelians. As a protégé and
friend of Bruno Bauer, a known critic of religion, Marx
could expect to be harassed, perhaps even rejected, by the
Berlin University's pro-clerical examiners. Bauer, who had
left Berlin for Bonn University in 1839, and had been urging
Marx to get his doctorate in order to be able to join him
there on the faculty, advised him to submit his dissertation to
Jena and take his degree there. Jena, in the Grand Duchy of
Saxe-Weimar, was outside the jurisdiction of Prussia. A small
University, it had, since the 18th century, a tradition of intellectual eminence—Fichte, Hegel, and Schiller had taught
there—of *Freiheit* [freedom] and liberalism.

Marx accepted Bauer's advice. On March 30, 1841, he received his *Abgangszeugnis* [departure certificate] from the
University of Berlin, officially terminating his studies there.
He had a professional copyist make a clean copy of his dissertation (Marx's own handwriting was always crabbed and
almost illegible) and, on April 6, 1841, he sent it to Karl
Friedrich Bachmann, Professor of Philosophy at Jena. Included with the dissertation were the usual requirements: the
litterae petitoriae [candidate's presentation], the curriculum

[3]From Epicurus' letter to Menoikeus.

vitae, the *Abgangszeugnis* from Berlin, and the legal fees of twelve *Friedrichsdor*. Marx's covering letter to the "*Hochwohlgeborener*" [Right Honorable] Professor Bachmann supplicated him, if the dissertation was satisfactory to the faculty, "to expedite the granting of the Doctoral Honor as soon as possible," because he could remain in Berlin only a few weeks more and it would be highly desirable for him to have the doctorate before his departure.

The Jena Faculty acted expeditiously. Within about a week, on April 15, 1841, Jena University awarded "Carolo Henrico Marx" the degree of "Doctoris Philosophiae Honores," in absentia.

VII
Return to the Rhineland

Trier and Bonn

In mid-April, the new *Herr Doktor*, twenty-three years old and full of exuberance, left Berlin, a city where he had spent nearly five years but which he had never come to like. A Rhinelander imbued with French culture, Marx was disdainful of the Prussians, who to him were no better than Russians, and had an antipathy for the Hohenzollern capital, located as it was on the border of the Slavic world.

On his way to Trier, Marx stopped in Cologne, the liveliest and wealthiest city in the Rhineland. Here he met a group of Young Hegelians, among them Moses Hess, a socialist philosopher six years older than he, on whom he made an overwhelming impression with his prodigal learning and exuberance. Hess thought that Marx, despite his youth, was the greatest, perhaps the only, living real philosopher in Germany. Compared to this young man—"my idol"—he felt himself like a "clumsy bungler" in philosophy, although, he wrote, that was his own field. In a letter written a few months after their meeting, to the novelist Berthold Auerbach, Hess expressed his opinion of Marx in extravagant terms:

> You will be glad to get to know a man here who now belongs among our friends. . . . Dr. Marx, this is the name of my idol, is still a very young man (at most some twenty-four years old[1]), who will give the coup de grâce to the medieval religion and politics; he combines the deepest philosophical seriousness with the most cutting wit; think of Rousseau, Voltaire, Holbach, Lessing,

---

[1]When Hess wrote that letter, September 2, 1841, Marx was only twenty-three years old.

Heine and Hegel united in one person; I say *united*, not tossed together—and you have Dr. Marx.

In Trier, Marx took some practical steps. He had himself finally released from Prussian military duty (Frederick Engels, whom Marx did not yet know, was then doing his one-year stint as an artillery lieutenant in Berlin) because of his affected lungs. He also concluded an official *Erbvertrag* [settlement of inheritance] with his worried and wary mother, signing it "Dr. K.H. Marx." She did not pay him in full.

Early in July, he went to Bonn, where Bruno Bauer was a *Privatdozent* [lecturer, or reader] of philosophy in the department of theology. Marx hoped, through Bauer's influence, also to teach philosophy there. But Bauer was already in deep trouble himself. At the University, both Protestant and Catholic theologians, although usually in doctrinal rivalry, combined against Bauer, whom they considered "godless." His lectures caused student disturbances.

The controversy over Bauer led Friedrich Wilhelm IV, Prussia's pietistic King, personally to order that the iconoclastic professor must under no circumstances be permitted to continue to teach in Bonn, which meant that every Prussian university would be closed to him, Early in March 1842, Bauer informed Marx that he had been removed from his position in Bonn *"par lit de justice"* [by order of the king], for his presumably atheistic views. To all intents and purposes, this also ended Marx's hopes for an academic career.

Journalism and Censorship

Even before Bauer's official dismissal from the University, Marx realized that there was no academic future for him in Prussia, or, for that matter, anywhere else in Germany. He would have to find some other occupation, if he was ever to marry Jenny and support her properly.

In the Germany of the mid-19th century, careers in established institutions were being increasingly closed to the most gifted individuals if they had the audacity to question the mystical-traditional foundations of Christianity, as did Bruno Bauer and Ludwig Feuerbach, or the social system, as did Marx and Engels and other Young Hegelians. Germany, like the rest of monarchical Europe, provided no institutionalized outlet for the energies and imaginations and aspirations

of young idealists, which, incidentally, helps to explain why
such a large number of Germans emigrated to the United
States in the 1840's and 1850's (Marx, too, at one time had
vague plans to emigrate). If they gave up their rebelliousness,
they could hope to find a haven in some safe educational,
governmental, or ecclesiastical bureaucracy. If they did not,
and if they continued to feel alienated in religion and in politics, they turned to revolutionary expression or activity.

Marx, like many other such *déraciné* intellectuals of his
time, entered one of the few fields open to him—journalism.
Given the conditions of the period, with Germany, as well as
the rest of continental Europe, in nationalist ferment and social unrest, and with governments, almost without exception,
monarchic and oppressive, journalism could not be a neutral
occupation. The journalist had the choice of either defending
the status quo, in which case he was likely to be rewarded
with money and other favors, or attacking it, which was certain to expose him to harassment, legal prosecution, and in
the end, exile. Marx, by inclination a nonconformist and by
philosophical conviction a rebel determined to rearrange the
universe around him, chose the latter alternative. Although
Jenny appealed to him not to meddle in politics, he did not
really know how to write except critically, polemically, dispu-
tatiously. From the very first, Marx's type of writing, regardless of subject matter, had political implications. Its
object was to expose existing institutions and ideas, to clear
the way for new ones. As he put it in his succinct *Theses on
Feuerbach* (1845): "The philosophers have only *interpreted*
the world in various ways; the point, however, is to change
it." Philosophy and jurisprudence, in both of which he was
steeped, were to serve as instruments of that change. Marx
thus became a journalist *engagé*, committed to battle. Journalism was the only profession he ever had and the only
career he was ever to pursue.

Everywhere, however, the journalist and the free intellectual in general had to contend with the bane of the writing
profession: censorship. There was no First Amendment in
Germany. Press and publication were not free; they were not
protected by government, but threatened by it. At about the
time that Marx was making his debut as a professional journalist, freedom of expression came under increasingly severe
restrictions. On December 24, 1841, three leading Prussian
Cabinet members—Minister of Culture Eichhorn, Minister of
Foreign Affairs von Maltzan, and Minister of Interior [Po-

lice] von Rochow—issued a combined censorship decree, which elaborated on the comparatively mild censorship edict which had been in force since October 18, 1819. The new decree aimed to suppress anything that was critical of the "fundamental principles of religion" and "offensive to morality and good will."[2] It gave sweeping powers to the censors to decide not merely the actual content of any piece of writing but, what was more devastating, its *tendency*, that is, the presumed intent of the author.

Within two or three weeks of its promulgation, Marx, bravely or rashly, undertook a critique of the new censorship edict. It was his first important political article. Entitled "Remarks on the Latest Prussian Censorship Instruction," the article was lengthy, somewhat too polemical to be intellectually focused, but contained fine verbal flashes and sharp logical thrusts, and altogether it constituted, in the words of Arnold Ruge, "without doubt the best work on freedom of the press written until now."

His method of treating the subject was to take up the leading arguments against a fully free press, as enunciated by the various speakers in the Rhenish Diet, and attempt to demolish them with a mixture of sarcasm, logic and historical example.

To the "paradoxical" argument, as he called it, that censorship actually helped to improve the press, Marx replied, "The greatest orator of the French Revolution, Mirabeau, . . . had trained himself in prison. Are, therefore, prisons the colleges of oratory?"

One of the speakers in the Rhenish Diet had argued that freedom was an ideal of perfection that could not be granted to society, in the form of a free press, because man was immature and imperfect. Marx's devastating riposte:

What follows from this? That the reasoning of our speaker is imperfect, governments are imperfect, the Diets are imperfect, freedom of the press is imperfect, every sphere of human activity is imperfect. If, therefore, one of those spheres ought not to exist because of its imperfection, then nobody has the right to exist, and man altogether has no right to exist.

[2]Text in Joseph Hansen, ed., *Rheinische Briefe und Akten zur Geschichte der politischen Bewegung* 1830–1850 [*Rhenish Letters and Documents for the History of the Political Movement* 1830–1850] (Essen, 1919).

Another speaker had attacked freedom of the press because it was productive of evil. Marx asked, if freedom was evil, why it was that government publications enjoyed absolute freedom, inquiring, "Does not the censor daily exercise an absolute freedom of the press, if not directly, then indirectly?"

Marx went on to point out that freedom had always existed, but that the only question was whether it should be "the privilege of a few or of the human spirit in general."

If, he argued, a free press is repudiated as the embodiment of "general freedom," then the censored press should be rejected even more, because it represents a "particular freedom." For how, he asked, can the species be good if the genus is bad? If the speaker were consistent, Marx wrote, he would have to repudiate, not the free press, but the press altogether: "According to [the speaker], the press would be good only if it were not the product of freedom, that is, not a human product. Thus, only *animals* and *Gods* would be entitled to a press at all."

Censorship of the press, Marx continued, was, among other things, also a bad police measure because it achieves the opposite of what it intends. It aims to prevent free expression as "something displeasing," but by allowing only selected pieces of writing, it actually creates a mystery around the forbidden ones and consequently arouses a widespread interest in them.

Freedom of the press, on the other hand, would remove all mystery from writing and provide a normal outlet for the ordinary, as well as the extraordinary, activities of societies. Marx then proceeded to eulogize the role of a free press in idealistic, almost rhapsodic terms:

The free press is the omnipresent open eye of the spirit of the people, the embodied confidence of a people in itself, the articulate bond that ties the individual with the State and the world, the incorporated culture which transfigures material struggles into intellectual ones, and idealizes its raw, material shape. It is the ruthless confession of a people to itself, and it is well-known that the power of confession is redeeming. The free press is the intellectual mirror in which a people sees itself, and self-viewing is the first condition of wisdom. It is the mind of the State that can be peddled in every cottage, cheaper than material gas. It is universal, omnipresent, omniscient. It is the ideal world, which constantly gushes from the real one, and streams back to it, ever richer and animated anew.

Marx attacked the new censorship from what might be called a libertarian—that is, a non-Marxist—point of view. The censorship, he pointed out, was both absurd and nihilistic. It made, in effect, mere bureaucrats, untrained in philosophy, literature or science, the supreme judges of their intellectual superiors, the writers. It was fundamentally nihilistic in that, in applying the vague and indefinable notion of *tendency* as a criterion, it abolished all objective standards of truth and science. In the concluding paragraph of his article, Marx stated bluntly: "The real, *radical cure of the censorship* is its *abolition.* For it as a bad institution."

Feuerbach and Religion

In Trier and Bonn, Marx was doing serious reading, particularly in religious philosophy, a subject then much in the air in Germany. A critical tone towards Christianity and institutions connected with it was then spreading in intellectual circles. An attack on the basic principles of the dominant religion was, at the same time, an assault on the foundations of the "Christian state" that Prussia and other European monarchies then claimed to be. As the effect of Voltaire's writings showed in the 18th century, criticism (in his case, also ridicule) of the church was a first step towards dissolving its affiliated secular institutions.

The most important book that Marx read, and one that was clearly a turning point in his own intellectual development from idealism to materialism, was Ludwig Feuerbach's recently published *Das Wesen des Christentums* [*The Essence of Christianity*] (Leipzig, 1841).[8] In it, Feuerbach undertook to humanize theology and to develop what he called a "true or anthropological essence of religion." Rejecting Hegelian idealism in favor of materialism, Feuerbach denied the existence of God as an "absolute Idea" and asserted that nothing exists outside of nature and of man. Religion existed only in man's mind; it was man's "consciousness of the

---

[8] It was translated into English by the novelist George Eliot under the title *The Essence of Religion* (London, 1853). An earlier English translation, under Frederick Engels' supervision, was being prepared in Manchester in 1844, but was never published.

infinite." God did not create man, but man created God, who is only the outward expression of man's inner nature. God having no separate existence outside of man, various aspects of existing religion merely correspond to some "feature or need of human nature." Religious beliefs were thus not divine, or even noble, and some of them, such as the sacraments, actually led to superstition and immorality. Feuerbach was not only critical of Christianity but also, like Bruno Bauer, of Judaism, which he condemned as egoistic and interested only in personal gain—a position that Marx adopted. Feuerbach's book had a stunning effect on Marx, as it did on Engels, who read it at about the same time.

In Marx's earliest piece on religion, "Luther as Arbiter between Strauss and Feuerbach," which he wrote in January 1842 and published in Ruge's *Anekdota*, he suggested, with a touch of irony, that if Christian theologians and speculative philosophers wanted to liberate themselves from their preconceptions about such subjects as *providence, omnipotence, creation, miracles*, and *faith*, they would have to turn to Feuerbach. Marx concluded with a pun. For the theologians and the idealistic philosophers, he wrote, "there is no other road to *truth* and *freedom* except the one that leads through the *Feuerbach* [firestream]." Feuerbach, Marx concluded, was "the purgatory of the present day."

VIII
The Rheinische Zeitung

Founding

In May 1842, Marx, while still living in Bonn, became a regular contributor to the *Rheinische Zeitung* in Cologne. The newspaper, the full title of which was *Rheinische Zeitung für Politik, Handel und Gewärbe* [*Rhenish Gazette for Politics, Commerce and Trade*], was then only about four months old and had not yet found its direction.

It was established, on December 15, 1841, as a stock company with a capitalization of 30,000 Taler, a substantial sum that was to be doubled by the sale of an additional 1,200 shares at 25 Taler each. There were 400 subscribers. On the first day of the year 1842, the *Rheinische Zeitung* was launched with champagne.

The new journal was the product of special conditions prevailing in Cologne, then the most progressive city in the Prussian kingdom (acquired by the Hohenzollerns after the defeat of Napoleon at Waterloo in 1815). With a population of about 80,000, Cologne was the center of emerging industry and of energetic businessmen of enlightened, modern views. The city's Catholic population in general and the business entrepreneurs in particular were in strong opposition to the Prussian government in Berlin, the former for religious reasons and the latter on economic-social grounds.

Rhineland Catholics were ultramontanes with a historic antipathy for the Prussian Protestants who now ruled them from afar. The Cologne bankers and industrialists, some of whom were Jews and a number of whom associated with progressive intellectuals such as Moses Hess, viewed the government in Berlin with no less distaste than did the population at large. To Rhinelanders, the Prussian monarchy was a feudal, if not boorish, anachronism. The cultured and Western-minded Rhineland leaders were at variance with the parochialism and autocracy of Old Prussia. They favored a unification of the splintered German states that would make a wider market possible; a reform of the existing political institutions along democratic lines to enable them to participate in political power; and, finally, a constitution that would guarantee personal rights, including trial by jury, freedom of the press and freedom of religion, the last of particular importance to Cologne's cultured Jewish bourgeoisie.

These were the aims for which the *Rheinische Zeitung* was established by Cologne's liberal elements. Among the new journal's founders, directors and shareholders were professional men, doctors and lawyers, as well as outstanding business leaders.

Politics and Religion

In the summer of 1842, while Marx was still in Trier, where he lived with the von Westphalens, the *Kölnische Zeitung's* political editor, who bore the Olympian name Karl Heinrich Hermes, published articles in which he criticized Marx's views on censorship and argued against granting "civil equality to Jews," which the *Rheinische Zeitung* was then advocating. Hermes held the traditionally Catholic position on the "Christian state": that non-Christians may not claim equality in a Christian political system. Marx, despite his professed aversion for Judaism, which he was to castigate in the following year in his essay *On the Jewish Question*, picked up the gauntlet, and came out bluntly in defense of secularism and against clericalism.

In a three-installment polemic, entitled "The Leading Article in No. 179 of the *Kölnische Zeitung*,"[1] Marx took on Hermes and his newspaper's policies.

The lengthy polemic was discursive, philosophical, and exhibitionistically erudite. Marx referred to a galaxy of great names, including classical writers and thinkers, such as Aristotle, Epicurus, Lucian, Socrates and Tertullian, and later ones like Campanella, Condorcet, Grotius, Hegel, Hobbes, Leibniz, Montesquieu, Newton, Rousseau, Shakespeare, Spinoza and Voltaire. He was, after all, a recent Ph.D. in philosophy, and the urge to show off his knowledge was not easily resisted. But the article also showed gleams of insight, inspired by a fundamental humanism.

[1] *Rheinische Zeitung*, July 10, 12, 14, 1842.

In the course of his arguments against the *Kölnische Zeitung,* Marx also discoursed on the function of the press, the meaning of philosophy, the nature of religion, the role of Christianity in politics. It was, in short, an essay in traditional liberalism, written a few short years before Marx adopted his rigorous doctrine of materialist determinism and class conflict.

The Fighting Editor

Until Marx's arrival on the scene as contributor and then as editor, the *Rheinische Zeitung,* while slowly growing in circulation, was without firm leadership or focused editorial policy. Adolf Rutenberg, the editor, was a Young Hegelian Ph.D. journalist, whom Marx called "my most intimate Berlin friend."

The Prussian authorities helped to get Rutenberg out of the paper. Somehow they considered him dangerous and demanded that he be removed from his post. In Marx's sardonic opinion, Rutenberg was "dangerous to nobody except the *Rheinische Zeitung* and himself," but the owners of the paper had to yield to government pressure. On October 15, 1842, Marx, having replaced the ousted Rutenberg as editor, moved to Cologne to direct the newspaper. A new era began for the *Rheinische Zeitung.*

Marx set about to move the *Rheinische Zeitung* in a leftward, although not communist, direction. At that point he was not a communist, nor even much of a social radical. He was, rather, a humanist, interested in justice and enlightenment, in the tradition of the French Revolution of 1789, a tradition he had absorbed from his father and his teachers in the Trier Gymnasium.

Marx at that time knew little about economics and not much about communism. In his first article on the subject, published in the *Rheinische Zeitung* on the day after he took over as editor, he wrote, "The *Rheinische Zeitung,* which cannot concede the theoretical reality of communist ideas even in their present form, and can even less wish or consider possible their practical realization, will submit these ideas to a thorough scrutiny."[2]

[2]"Communism and the Augsburg *Allgemeine Zeitung,*" October 16, 1842.

In the fall of 1842, Marx began to familiarize himself with contemporary French utopian and socialist theorists. He read Étienne Cabet's *Voyage en Icarie* (1842), Victor Considérant's *Destineé Sociale* (1834–38), Théodore Dézamy's *Calomnies et Politique de M. Cabet* (1842), Charles Fourier's *Théorie des Quatre Mouvements et des Destinées Générales* (2nd ed., 1841), Pierre Leroux's *De l'Humanité* (1840), and Pierre-Joseph Proudhon's *Qu' est-ce que la Propriété?* (1841). These writers did not convert Marx to communism but they aroused his interest. He arrived at communism one or two years later, not so much through the utopians, as through economics, the serious study of which he did not begin until after he had left the *Rheinische Zeitung* and settled in Paris at the end of 1843.

If Marx did not turn the *Rheinische Zeitung* into a revolutionary newspaper, he nevertheless changed it into a fighting organ. Other German journals, either from timidity or opportunism, were then mostly satisfied with being carriers of official handouts and repeaters of sanctimonious platitudes. Marx said that he did not want the *Rheinische Zeitung* to be "merely a mindless amalgam of dry reporting and base flattery." He turned it into an escharotic organ, taking pleasure in contention for its own sake, attacking other newspapers—even outside Cologne—in polemics, criticizing bureaucrats and questioning government policies. There was method in his seeming rashness, as he wrote to a friend a decade later: "Polemic is a necessity for every journal, so long as it has to struggle."[3]

The Fatal Censorship

The paper was censored as a daily routine by a dull bureaucrat named Laurenz Dolleschall, whose policy, he said, was not to permit "making fun of divine things." He struck out much of what he did not understand and everything that appeared to him to be suspicious—for example, the section on marriage in Marx's article "The Philosophical Manifesto of the Historical School of Law."[4] Marx enjoyed quoting Dolleschall: "Now it's a matter of my bread and butter. Now I strike out everything."

---

[3]Marx to Adolf Cluss, September 15, 1853.
[4]*Rheinische Zeitung*, August 9, 1842.

The censorship system required that proof sheets be brought to the home of the censor every evening, and since the *Rheinische Zeitung* was a morning paper, it meant that editor and writers had to stay up late at night to redo their copy after the red-penciling.

On January 4, 1843, the *Rheinische Zeitung* published an attack on Czarist military despotism. The news of it enraged the Russian despot himself. Czar Nicholas I blustered, berated the Prussian Ambassador von Lieberman about the liberal German press, and wrote a protest to the King in Berlin. Since Russia was Prussia's chief ally in Europe, King Friedrich Wilhelm was shaken by the Czar's outburst. On January 21, 1843, the cowed Prussian monarch assembled a Ministerial Council, which decided to kill the *Rheinische Zeitung*, as of March 31.

IX
Love and Marriage

Jenny

In the seven years of her engagement to Karl, Jenny had had to endure a variety of torments: personal anxieties, unfulfilled desire, and family opposition. In addition to the ever-unresolved doubt as to Karl's ability to earn a steady living, the discrepancy in their ages was increasingly troublesome as time went on. She was four years older than Karl, and the interminable wait for him, requiring her to pass up opportunities to make a "practical" marriage, stirred in her the fear of becoming an old maid, not a happy lot in a gossipy small town.

Despite inner doubts and outer pressures, she remained steadfastly in love with her "Karlchen," her *"Liebchen,"* her "lord and master." Hers was what she herself called a *"schwärmerische Jugendliebe"* [ecstatic young love], unrestrained in its virginal passion. Brought up in a respectable Evangelical family, in which some of her close relatives were rigid, stiff pietists, Jenny also had a prim and puritanical streak (which became pronounced in later years), and it is more than likely that, despite her ardent temperament, she remained a virgin throughout her engagment to Karl. The continuing sexual repression heightened her tensions.

The few of her letters to Karl that have survived from this period are extravagant, sometimes near-hysterical, outpourings of her unfulfilled passion.

Darling *Schwarzwildchen:*
How glad I am that you are gay and that my letter has cheered you and that you yearn for me and that you live in tapestried rooms and that you drank champagne in Cologne and that there are Hegel Clubs and that you

dreamt [of me] and that, in short, you, my beloved, are mine, my own *Schwarzwildchen.* . . .

She went on to say that her heart so overflowed with love and longing and "ardent desire for you, the endlessly beloved," that it caused her sleepless nights thinking of him and praying for him and blessing him. And when she slept, she dreamt sweet dreams of "all the bliss that was and will be." She pined for him so that, as a symbol of her yearning, she kept her valises all ready and packed: "dresses and collars and bonnets in the neatest order." She apostrophized the letter, which she wrote with a kiss on every finger:

Fly, fly to my Karl and press yourself on his lips and then stop being the mute messenger of love and whisper to him all the small sweet secret sweetnesses . . . tell him all—but no, *leave* a little bit for your lady.

She concluded:

Adieu, beloved little man of the railroad. Adieu, thou dear little man. Is it not true that I can marry you after all? Farewell, farewell, my *Liebchen.*

In another letter, she wrote that on a visit to friends in Neuss, the Rhine town some ninety miles north of Trier, she walked in the evening along the banks of the great river and her thoughts were filled with Karl. The "love stars shone bright and clear," radiantly lighting her path and celebrating the love in her heart:

Karl, Karl, how I love you! . . . Everything I bear in my heart, all my senses and thoughts, everything past, present, future, is only an utterance, a sign, a tone, and when it rings, it means this only: I love you inexpressibly, limitlessly, timelessly, immeasurably. . . .

Karl had constant and harsh quarrels with his mother about Jenny whenever he visited Trier. "For years," he wrote to Arnold Ruge, on March 13, 1843, "I and my bride have had to fight more unnecessary and exhausting battles than many others who are three times older and who constantly speak of their 'life experience.' "

After her gentle husband's death, it had become increasingly difficult to reconcile Henriette Marx to her son's involvement with Jenny and to his impractical ways. A widow with a fixed income, she had to concern herself with her five unmarried daughters and one sick younger son. It was a household plagued by illnesses. In 1842, at the height of Karl's quarrel with his family, his twenty-three-year-old brother Hermann died of tuberculosis. Widow Marx, bearing the whole family burden, could not understand why her gifted *Glückskind* was not only no help but actually an impediment to her. Karl seemed to be not merely impractical, but callously indifferent to his own flesh and blood. Instead of supporting his mother and siblings, Karl, with all his superior education, would not or could not make a decent living and constantly asked his mother for money.

Karl, who rarely permitted himself to understand other people, did not have the slightest comprehension of his mother's point of view. Ever prone to be suspicious, a trait that was aggravated in later years to the point where it embittered many of his personal relationships, Marx was convinced that the struggle with his mother was fomented by outsiders.

His mother also heaped reproaches on Jenny, because she thought that it was the duty of a fiancée to lead her man in the "right path." But Jenny had no more practical sense than Karl, and neither of them shared Henriette Marx's down-to-earth utilitarianism. Jenny considered her somewhat crude, with a tendency to flaunt her finery. Frau Marx, who may have felt uncomfortable with the beautiful young baroness, returned Jenny's coolness. She addressed Jenny, whom, after all, she had known since childhood, not by the familiar German *Du*, but by the formal *Sie*. Except for Karl's oldest sister Sophie, with whom she had gone to school, the whole Marx family, Jenny once confided to a friend, "stood alien and remote to me."

While Jenny's father, Ludwig von Westphalen, was alive, both Jenny and Karl had a friend in him. A tolerant and cultured gentleman, he had no social or religious objections to his daughter's engagement to Karl, who, early in 1842, finding his mother's home intolerable, moved in with the von Westphalens. But on March 3, 1842, von Westphalen died at the age of seventy-two after a long illness. Jenny now lost the strongest support within her own family. Her difficulties mounted.

One of them was financial. Ludwig von Westphalen possessed the title of baron but had no property. After forty years of public service, he had retired on a relatively modest pension of 1,125 Taler per annum, a considerable portion of which was consumed by medical expenses in the last year of his life. For Jenny there was no inheritance and no dowry. Her mother, Karoline, von Westphalen's second wife, was a commoner who had no means of her own. Her widow's pension was so meager that, to Jenny's constant distress, she was to live the rest of her life in respectable poverty.

The practical thing for the twenty-eight-year-old, dowerless Jenny was to marry some man who could support her in comfort, and there was no lack of suitors for the hand of "the most beautiful girl in Trier." There were "endless" and intense conflicts and quarrels within the von Westphalen family. The opposition to Marx was led by Jenny's "crazy, egoistical" uncle, Heinrich Georg von Westphalen, and her half-brother, Ferdinand Otto Wilhelm von Westphalen, her father's son by a previous marriage, whom her mother, Karoline, had raised as if he were one of her own children.

Jenny, as Marx told Ruge, had to fight the "hardest battles" with these conservative and narrow-minded relatives. To them, as Marx put it, "the 'Lord in Heaven' and the 'Lord in Berlin' are equal objects of worship."[1] Karl, like Jenny, came to despise his brother-in-law, the "*Herr Staatsminster.*" In an article he once wrote for the *New-York Daily Tribune,*[2] he referred to him as a "weak-minded and fanatical reactionist (Herr von Westphalen being my brother-in-law I had ample opportunity of becoming acquainted with the mental powers of the man)."

Marx always vehemently denied the existence of religious or racial prejudice against him in the Westphalen family, but that he harbored resentment is revealed by his violent reaction to an obituary for Jenny written by Marx's son-in-law, Charles Longuet, five days after her death. "One surmises," Longuet wrote somewhat delicately in *La Justice* (December 7, 1881), a Paris daily of which he was an editor, "that her marriage to Karl Marx, son of a Trier lawyer, did not take place without trouble. There were *many prejudices to overcome, the strongest of which was race prejudice.* It is known that the illustrious socialist is of Jewish origin."

When Marx read this, he flew into a rage and accused his son-in-law of being a liar; he wrote his daughter that her hus-

[1] Marx to Ruge, March 13, 1843.
[2] "The Berlin Conspiracy," April 18, 1853.

band's account was *"simple invention"* and that "there was no prejudice to overcome." He concluded harshly: "Longuet would greatly oblige me by never mentioning my name in *his* writings."

From Marx's violent reaction it would seem that the statement that his marriage was impeded by religious and racial prejudice hit a sensitive nerve. Longuet, a French journalist from Normandy, could not have made up such a story. He must have heard it from his wife or mother-in-law.

Honeymoon

In March 1843, Marx's last month on the *Rheinische Zeitung*, he was occupied with two important projects. One was to publish, with Arnold Ruge, a literary-cultural magazine, *Deutsch-Französische Jahrbücher*, abroad, preferably in Paris. The other was what he called his *"private plan"*—to marry Jenny. "Without any romanticism," he wrote to Ruge on March 13, 1843, "I can assure you that I am head over heels in love."

As the time of marriage drew near, Jenny could not contain her happiness. She and Karl excitedly discussed their wedding plans, including the exhilarating prospect of shopping in Paris. In one of her last letters to Karl while he was still in Cologne, Jenny addressed him already as "my rightful, altar-dignified, darling husband," and told him to leave shopping to her:

This morning I saw many new laces in Wolf's shop. If you cannot buy them cheaply or have anybody else find them, I beg you, dear *Herzchen*, to leave the article to me. In general, *Herzchen*, I would *truly prefer now* that you buy nothing, and save your money for the trip [to Paris]. You see, *Herzchen*, I will then be with you, and we will buy together, and if we are cheated, it will be in company—please, *Herzchen*, no buying now. The same with the garland of flowers. I fear you would pay too much, and it would be nice to buy it together. Should you insist on flowers, then get roses. They would best suit my green dress. But I would be happier if you left the whole business to me.

Then she veered away from this topic and gave vent to a burst of jealousy.

Did you behave well on the steamer [i.e., on his return to Cologne from Trier, where he had recently visited her], or was there another Madame Hermann aboard? You wicked rascal. I am going to drive away this sort of thing once and for all. Always on the steamers. Such-like straying I am going to put in the interdict in our *contrat social*, in our marriage contract, and will punish such irregularities verbally. I will make a specific list of all such cases and put them under penance, and I will create a second penal law comparable to the marriage law. I want to catch you.

The archness of her tone did not conceal her real pangs. She was, indeed, always fiercely jealous of her Karlchen, and he, a naturally flirtatious male, had to watch his step with the circumspection of any tame bourgeois husband.

Her letter concluded:

Farewell, solely beloved, dark, sweet, divine, darling man, "what," how! Ay, you rogue-face. Talatta, talatta, farewell, write soon, talatta, talatta.

Even after he had left the *Rheinische Zeitung*, Marx continued to live in Cologne, where he was working on some serious articles, including a critique of Hegel's "philosophy of right," to explore the relations between the "political state" and "civil society." At the same time he was planning and negotiating with Arnold Ruge the publication of the *Deutsch-Französiche Jahrbücher*, a venture which, he hoped, would enable him financially to marry Jenny.

At the end of May, Marx moved into the home of Jenny's mother in Bad Kreuznach, about fifty miles east of Trier. Bad Kreuznach, on the Nahe River, was a picturesque watering-place, whose salt baths, taken in the *Kurhaus*, were supposed to cure skin diseases.

Karl Marx, who was soon to write that "religion is the opium of the people," and Jenny, who spent her mature life as an atheist, had a church wedding. The banns were published on June 13. Six days later, on June 19, according to the Marriage Certificate, "Carl Marx, Doctor of Science, . . . Evangelical Faith," and "Julie Bertha Jänni von Westphalen,

. . . Evangelical Faith," were married in the Protestant church in Bad Kreuznach. Few people attended the wedding. On Jenny's side, only her mother and younger brother Edgar were present. The other von Westphalen relatives stayed away. Of Marx's family, there was nobody—neither his mother nor any of his five sisters attended.

Following the custom of honeymooners of the time, the newlyweds went to the Rheinpfalz, in Switzerland, to see the falls of the Rhine. They traveled there by carriage via Schaffhausen. The honeymoon was paid for by Frau von Westphalen, who had come into a small legacy. Karl and Jenny carried the money in a small, two-handled strongbox, which they were in the habit of leaving open in hotel rooms; they shared the cash with anyone in need. Upon their return to Bad Kreuznach, by slow stages through Baden-Baden, there was nothing left in the strongbox. But the happy couple did not worry. Neither then nor in all the subsequent years of their penury did Karl and Jenny evince any more "money sense" than they did on their honeymoon.

These were his and Jenny's "golden days." They were blissfully happy and deeply in love, a love that was to survive the heartaches of personal tragedies and the ravages of poverty in exile. In one of his later newspaper articles,[3] Marx once quoted his and his father's favorite German poet:[4]

> *O zarte Sehnsucht, süsses Hoffen,*
> *Der ersten Liebe gold'ne Zeit!*
> *Das Auge sieht den Himmel offen,*
> *Es Schwelgt das Herz in Seligkeit.*
> *O dass sie ewig grünen bliebe,*
> *Die schöne Zeit der jungen Liebe!*

Marx himself translated this as:

> Oh, tender longings, sweet hopes,
> Golden time of first love!
> The eye sees heavens open,
> The heart luxuriates in bliss.
> Oh, that it could bloom forever,
> That golden time of young love!

[3]"Prussia. The New Ministry," in *New-York Daily Tribune*, November 24, 1858.
[4]Friedrich von Schiller, *Das Lied von der Glocke.*

X
Philosophy and Religion

Hegelianism

After returning to Kreuznach from his honeymoon, Marx devoted the summer and fall to writing on political philosophy, notably Hegel, and on political problems, such as civil emancipation in a Christian state. While waiting for Ruge, who visited him in Kreuznach at the end of July, to consummate the final plans for the *Deutsch-Französische Jahrbücher*, Marx read or reread a number of philosophical and political classics, among them Hegel's *Grundlinien der Philosophie des Rechts oder Naturrecht im Umrisse*,[1] in the 1833 edition of his Berlin University professor Eduard Gans; Machiavelli's *Il Principe;* Montesquieu's *L'Esprit des Lois;* and Rousseau's Le *Contrat Social*, as well as works on the French Revolution, a subject of lifelong interest to Marx, and on German history, particularly the work of Leopold von Ranke, whom he despised. Still under the influence of Feuerbach, Marx investigated religious problems from the political point of view. His concern was not with theology as such, but with religion and ecclesiasticism as it shaped men and affected institutions. Thus he read—and soon attacked—two recent publications by his friend, the religious philosopher Bruno Bauer: a book entitled *Die Judenfrage*,[2] and an article, *"Die Fähigkeit der heutigen Juden und Christen, frei zu werden."*[3]

The fruit of his studies was three critical articles, two on Hegel, with whom he had been preoccupied for more than a year, and one on the Jewish question. These two subjects,

---

[1]*Base-Lines of the Philosophy of Right or Natural Right in Outline.*
[2]Bauer, *The Jewish Question* (Brunswick, 1843).
[3]Bauer, "The Ability of Today's Jews and Christians to Become Free," in *Einundzwanzig Bogen aus der Schweiz* [Twenty-one Sheets from Switzerland], edited by Georg Herwegh (Zurich and Winterthur, 1843).

Hegelianism and Judaism, had a special significance in the evolution of Marx's position, for they represented both intellectual emancipation and psychological self-clarification. The Hegel essay constituted, in effect, the beginnings of his repudiation of his great philosophical model; the article on Judaism was a final repudiation, couched in philosophic but harsh language, of the faith of his ancestors.[4]

Marx's capacity for intellectual concentration and work, which he was to evince all his life until sickness mastered him, is seen in his critique of Hegel. The first part of it was written while he was still basking in his honeymoon period and living in an attractive and leisurely resort town. When posthumously published under the title *"Zur Kritik der Hegelschen Rechtsphilosophie,"*[5] it amounted to a book of 130 printed pages. In it, he took up Paragraphs 261 to 313 of Hegel's *Grundlinien*, which dealt with *Staatsrecht*,[6] including the state and its relation to civil society, government, bureaucracy and democracy, and dissected them point by point.

So awesome was Hegel's stature that Marx approached him with what was for him extraordinary restraint. Unlike Marx's other critical writings, past and future, which were abrasively polemical, his analysis of Hegel was calm and objective, even where he strongly disagreed with him. A philosopher, after all, such as Marx considered himself to be, did not treat a man like Hegel lightly or sarcastically.

The critique of the *Kritik* was opaque and convoluted, for Marx was following the Hegelian pattern and using Hegelian language (which he learned to discard in his mature writings in later years) but his basic criticism was that Hegel treated institutions and ideas as if they were outside human effort, and not as they were encountered in reality. For to Hegel, everything flowed from and was shaped by a pre-existing Universal Idea.

Marx discerned contradictions in Hegel. Hegel viewed monarchy as the embodiment of the Universal, but within Hegel's own framework, monarchy, being necessarily limited to a few, could logically be only a fraction of the Universal,

---

[4]For a psychological analysis of Marx's hatred of Judaism and Jews, see Arnold Künzli, *Karl Marx. Eine Psychographie* (Vienna, 1966), Part II: "Psyche."

[5]"Toward the Critique of Hegel's Philosophy of Law," in Marx-Engels, *Werke* (Berlin, 1964), Vol. I, pp. 201–333.

[6]*Staatsrecht* means constitutional law; in the Hegelian context, it might also be translated as the philosophy of the state.

subsumed under the general species, "and a bad one at that."
To be consistent, Hegel's conception of the state would have
to be a democracy, which is universalized in all its citizens,
rather than in a few. Marx wrote, in viscous Hegelianese:

> Democracy is the Truth of monarchy, monarchy is not
> the Truth of democracy. . . . Monarchy cannot, while
> democracy can, be comprehended from within itself. In
> democracy, no factor attains any significance other than
> what belongs to it. It is in reality the only factor of the
> whole demos. In monarchy, a part determines the char-
> acter of the whole. . . . Democracy is content and
> form. Monarchy is *supposed* to be only form, but it fal-
> sifies content. . . .

Marx attempted to reverse Hegel's idea that institutions are
the product of the Universal. The contrary was likely to be
the truth. It is the actual human being, and only he, who
creates his own social and religious systems; he does so, not
at the behest of or in obedience to an abstract notion, but in
response to his own existence: "Just as religion does not
create man, but man creates religion, so the constitution [of
a state] does not create the people, but the people create the
constitution. . . . Man does not exist for the law, but the law
exists for man."

Marx wrote the second part of his Hegel *Critique*, which
he subtitled "Introduction," probably because it was merely
fourteen printed pages long, soon after he moved to Paris at
the end of 1843. It was published in the short-lived *Deutsch-
Französische Jahrbücher.*[7]

The article is memorable for having introduced two
concepts with which Marx's name has always been connected: religion as "opium," and the "proletariat." Marx opened
his piece with sweeping discussion of the meaning of religion
for men living in this world. Religion, he asserted, is man's
escape from unpleasant reality. It is man's search for a "su-
pernatural being in the fantastic reality of heaven." It
expresses real misery and at the same time protests against it.
"Religion is the sigh of the distressed creature, the soul of a

[7]"Toward the Critique of Hegel's Philosophy of Law: Introduction,"
in *Deutsch-Französische Jahrbücher*, February 1844; part of the text
appears in Saul K. Padover, ed., *Karl Marx on Revolution* (New York,
1971), pp. 422–426.

heartless world, as it is also the spirit of spiritless conditions. It is the *opium* of the people."

Since man is a living creature, a member of the state and society, and "not an abstract being crouching outside the world," his pursuit of religion is an illusion. It cannot solve his real problems. To achieve the real happiness of the people, it is necessary to abolish the *illusory* religious one. This involves the elimination of conditions that require such illusions. The first step in this direction must be an attack on religion. "Criticism of religion is the prelude of all criticism."

Marx then proceeded to more specific revolutionary affirmation, bringing forth the proletariat and assigning to it its historic role. He came to the proletariat, by way of the Hegelian dialectic with its negations and syntheses, in the following manner. Philosophy, which is universal truth, leads to the proletariat, which is the universal class, since it does not belong to any of the existing classes of society. In the dialectical process, the two universals exchange roles. "As philosophy finds its material weapons in the proletariat, so the proletariat finds in philosophy its intellectual weapons." Since the proletariat is universal in character, it cannot emancipate itself without emancipating everybody else. It can redeem itself only by redeeming the whole society. And it can redeem the whole society only by the latter's dissolution, to be followed by the synthesis, a new society.

Marx applied this dialectical process particularly to Germany, which he viewed as partly feudal and completely enslaved. Hence Germany was ripe for a thorough revolution which, in turn, would revolutionize the rest of the world. Marx summed up his article:

In Germany *no* sort of bondage can be broken without *every* sort of bondage being broken. Thorough-minded Germans cannot make a revolution without making a fundamental revolution. *The emancipation of Germany is the emancipation of mankind.* The *head* of this emancipation is philosophy, its *heart* is the *proletariat.*

He concluded:

When all the inner conditions are fulfilled, the day of German resurrection will be heralded by the crowing of the Gallic rooster.

Marx's brilliantly dogmatic assertions were to have consequences for the future, but, ironically, not in his native country. Neither in Marx's lifetime nor thereafter did the proletariat revolutionize or "emancipate" Germany. The "Gallic rooster" also remained silent.

"On the Jewish Question"

Marx's second subject of self-clarification, or possibly self-purging, was Judaism. On a conscious level, he seems to have had no interest in Judaism or Jewish subjects. Nevertheless, in this early period of his life he could not escape the "Jewish problem," particularly as religion was then a major preoccupation of such writers and thinkers as Ludwig Feuerbach and Bruno Bauer, who were interested in the general question of intellectual-political emancipation.

In the last month of his editorship of the *Rheinische Zeitung*, Marx made a revealing statement in a letter to Arnold Ruge:

> Just now the chief of the local Israelites came to see me and asked me to forward a petition for the Jews to the Landtag [Diet], and I want to do it. Revolting [*widerlich*][8] though the Israelite religion is to me, nevertheless Bauer's opinion in *Die Judenfrage* seems to me to be too abstract.[9]

The petition, signed in the name of Cologne's Jewish community, which then consisted of about forty-six families and whose leader was coincidentally also named Marx (Raphael), appealed for the political equality of Jews with other citizens. Despite his revulsion for Judaism, Marx undertook to forward it. The reason for his gesture was political. "The point is," he went on, "to puncture in the Christian state as many holes as possible and to smuggle in, insofar as it is up to us, what is rational." He expected—and probably hoped—that the petition would be thrown out, but he said, "At least one should try it—and the embitterment grows with each petition that is rejected." To everyone's surprise, the petition, support-

---

[8]The German word *widerlich* can also be translated as "repulsive," "loathsome," "nauseating."
[9]Marx to Ruge, March 13, 1843.

ed by a number of Christian liberals, was approved by the Rhenish Diet. It was the first time that a German parliament had granted the "complete equality of Jews in civil and political matters."

Marx's anti-Jewishness reflected the deeply ingrained anti-Semitism of Germany's leading writers and thinkers (with probably the sole exception of Lessing), who assumed as a matter of course that Judaism, against which Christendom had warred for a millennium, was a degraded religion of materialism and arrogance, and its practitioners, the Jews, were thus necessarily a debased people. This was a dogma that prevailed almost universally in Marx's time. Johann Gottlieb Fichte, a distinguished philosopher and patriotic writer, referred to Jews as a "hate-filled nation." Even Goethe was opposed to Jewish "liberation." So long as Jews professed their religion, they would continue to be something less than human. To become really human, and thus fit to be citizens in a Christian society, Jews would have to give up their religion. Such was the argument even of not particularly anti-Semitic writers like Bauer. In his book *Die Judenfrage* [*The Jewish Question*], published in 1843, Bauer put it thus:

> The question is whether the Jew as such is capable of accepting human rights and conceding them to others. His religion and way of life force him to eternal separation, for it is their essence. Their essence make him, not a human being, but a Jew.

Bauer's basic argument was that religion as it prevailed at the time was a bar to social emancipation. So long as men clung to the existing faith they could not be free. This was true also for Christians, for whom, however, emancipation was easier, since essentially their religion was a superior one. A Christian had to take but one step to universalize his religion, but a Jew, trapped in his primitive and egoistic faith, had first of all to get rid of Judaism altogether before he could move towards universality.

Marx vented his own views in a review of *Die Judenfrage*, along with another book of Bauer's, for the *Deutsch-Französische Jahrbücher* which appeared the following February.[10] In the article, written in September and October 1843

---

[10]English text in Saul K. Padover, ed., *Karl Marx on Religion* (New York, 1974), p. 169-192.

and titled *"Zur Judenfrange"* [On the Jewish Question], Marx agreed with his friend Bauer's fundamental premises about Judaism and Jews, but differed from Bauer in that he rejected all religion, both Christian and Jewish, as a condition of political emancipation or of civil rights. In Marx's view, the situation should be reversed. It was the state rather than the citizen that ought to give up claims to any religion, which, as a proper political state, it had no business asserting or dictating: "The *political* emancipation of the Jew, the Christian, or the religious man in general is the *emancipation of the state* from Judaism, from Christianity, from religion generally."

The real problem, according to Marx, lay in religion as connected with *Schacher*—haggling or bargaining—and it is here that the Jews come in for castigation. For their religion had not only corrupted Christian society with its materialistic spirit, but they themselves personified such corruption in practice. Here Marx reechoed the ancient anti-Semitic charges that Judaism was a Mammon-oriented religion and the Jews its money-worshipping votaries. As if to curry favor with Christian anti-Semites, Marx went far beyond Bauer in his brutal accusations against Jews and Judaism. He made his charges in apodictic sentences, as if they were self-evident truths:

> Let us consider the actual, secular Jew, not the *Sabbath* Jew, as Bauer does, but the *everyday* Jew.
>
> Let us not look for the secret of the Jew in his religion, but let us look for the secret of religion in the actual Jew.
>
> What is the secular basis of Judaism? Practical *need, self-interest*.
>
> What is the worldly cult of the Jew? *Schacher*. What is his worldly god? Money!

Marx repeated his accusations like hammer blows:

> What actually was the foundation, in and of itself, of the Jewish religion? Practical need, egoism. Hence the Jew's monotheism is in reality a polytheism of many needs, a polytheism that makes even the toilet an object of divine law . . . The god of *practical need and self-interest* is *Money*.
>
> Money is the jealous god of Israel before whom no other god may exist. Money degrades all the gods of

mankind—and converts them into commodities. . . .

The god of the Jews has been secularized and has become the god of the world. His god is only an illusory bill of exchange. . . .

What is contained abstractly in the Jewish religion—contempt for theory, for art, for history, for man as an end in himself—is the *actual conscious* standpoint and virtue of the money-man. . . .

Marx concluded that so long as this Jewish spirit of money pervades society, it cannot be free. Nor can Jews be free while they worship a Mammon religion. Both society and Jews must get rid of Judaism and the profit motive which lies at its core. "*Zur Judenfrage*" concluded with these words: "The social *emancipation* of the Jew is the *emancipation of society from Jewishness.*"

Marx's slander of Jews as hagglers and money-men by nature was factually as well as theologically inaccurate, and reflected nearly total ignorance, possibly willful, of the lives and faith of the people from whom he descended. In his time, the vast majority of Europe's Jews were neither capitalists nor merchants, but were poor, often pitifully exploited working people. Of the 10,000 Jews in Bavaria when "*Zur Judenfrage*" was published, well over half made their living as craftsmen, on the land, or in some pursuit other than retail trade or the professions. In that same year, according to the historian Simon Dubnow, of some 5,000 Jews in two typical German cities, Breslau and Oppeln, only 20 percent lived by trade. Among the rest were 1,160 innkeepers; 669 mechanics, craftsmen, or artists; 625 domestic servants; 344 horse dealers; 270 doctors and teachers; 152 farmers; and 81 wage laborers. There were also 233 beggars and 484 inmates of poorhouses and infirmaries.[11] In Russia, where the great majority of Europe's Jews lived, they were without civil rights, huddled in miserable ghettos, and, next to the serfs, the most oppressed people in Czardom. (Neither then nor later did Marx, whose heart bled for the world's other poor, show Jews the slightest sympathy.)

After writing "*Zur Judenfrage*," Marx never returned to the subject as such. Having solved the problems to his own satisfaction and having settled with his family background, he

[11]Dubnow, *Weltgeschichte des jüdischen Volkes* [*World History of the Jewish People*] (Jerusalem, 1938), Vol. 3, p. 73.

dropped the whole matter. Neither did he write extensively on religion in general in later years. He found it, he told Engels in 1851, a "boring theme."

Marx never retracted his defamation of the Jews, and this was to have its influence on socialist thinking.[12] On the contrary, he harbored a lifelong hostility towards them. In his *Theses on Feuerbach* (1845), a brief compilation of pithy sayings, he thought it necessary to drag in his bias, referring to the "dirty Jewish" aspect of Christianity. His private letters are replete with anti-Semitic remarks, caricatures, and crude epithets: "Levy's Jewish nose," "usurers," "Jew-boy," "nigger-Jew," etc. For reasons perhaps explainable by the German concept *Selbsthass* [self-hate],[13] Marx's hatred of Jews was a canker which neither time nor experience ever eradicated from his soul.

[12]See Edmund Silberner, "The Anti-Semitic Tradition in Modern Socialism," Inaugural Address delivered at Hebrew University of Jerusalem, January 4, 1953.

[13]See Theodor Lessing, *Der Jüdische Selbsthass* [*Jewish Self-Hate*] (Berlin, Der Jüdischer Verlag, 1900).

XI
Paris

The Deutsch-Französische Jahrbücher

By September 1843, Arnold Ruge had definitely decided that the *Deutsch-Französische Jahrbücher,* which he and Marx had been discussing for so many months, should be published in Paris. Marx was pleased for two reasons. One was an eagerly sought opportunity to leave his native country. The other reason was living in exciting Paris itself.

Despite the word *Yearbooks* in the title, the journal was originally planned to appear in twelve monthly instalments. It was to be published bilingually and was to serve as a "French-German scientific alliance," as Marx explained in a letter to Feuerbach, on October 3, 1843, inviting him to contribute an article on the German philosopher Friedrich Wilhelm Joseph von Schelling. Feuerbach declined the invitation on the grounds that he was busy with other work.

In his September 1843 letter to Ruge, Marx formulated his ideas for the new journal. It was, he stated, to have a universal, philosophical approach, and avoid a partial or one-sided viewpoint. At the same time, the *Deutsch-Französische Jahrbücher* should combine ruthless criticism with deep humanism. Hence it should not support or identify with any of the existing radical dogmas, particularly those of communism, which were incomplete because they expressed "only one aspect of [human] reality."

At the end of October, Marx and his wife moved to Paris, where Ruge had already preceded them.

In Paris, they moved into a house inhabited by other Germans, including the Ruges: 38 rue Vanneau, in the Faubourg St. Germain. The publishing address of their *Bureau des Annales* [Office of the Yearbooks] was nearby, at 22 rue Vanneau. Ruge fell ill, and Marx brought out the journal by himself.

The first and last issue of the *Deutsch-Französische Jahrbücher* came out as a double number in February 1844, in an edition of 1,000 copies. It was a book-length magazine, with some lively content, giving an impression of youthful revolutionary lustiness. It included Marx's articles on Hegelianism and Judaism, and his correspondence with Ruge, satiric poems on King Ludwig I of Bavaria by Heinrich Heine, as well as pieces by the poet Georg Friedrich Herwegh and the Russian revolutionist Bakunin (the only non-German contributor) and two essays by Frederick Engels, mailed in from Manchester. Of Engels' two articles, "Outlines for a Critique of National Economy," and "The Condition of England" (a review of Thomas Carlyle's *Past and Present*), the former was of special importance, for it not only stimulated Marx's interest in economic studies but also initiated what was to become a lifelong contact between them.

Of more immediate consequence was Marx's increasing conflict with Ruge. Ruge was not happy with what he called "Marx's epigrams," considering some too artificial and others too raw. "If I had not been sick," he said, "I would have corrected some of the crude things" in the journal. Moreover, as a liberal democrat, and not a communist, he objected to Marx's discovery, in his Hegel article, of the proletariat as the dissolver of the existing order and as the "emancipator" of humanity.

Early in March, Ruge suspended further plans for the publication of the *Deutsch-Französische Jahrbücher*, and latent hostility between him and Marx led to a final break at the end of that month.

In financial straits as always, and with a wife seven months pregnant, Marx had previously pressed Ruge for his salary, to which he may or may not have been legally entitled. Ruge would not pay him in money, but in copies of the *Deutsch-Französische Jahrbücher*. Friends in Cologne came to Marx's rescue. At the instigation of his admirer, the wealthy Georg Jung, 1,000 Taler were collected among his friends. The money was raised, according to a letter written to Marx on March 14, 1844, by Heinrich Joseph Claessen, a physician and stockholder of the *Rheinische Zeitung*, as a "tribute" which "we bring with a glad heart to your talents and effectiveness," in order to "compensate you for the sacrifices which you have made for the common cause." A few months later, on July 31, Jung sent Marx 800 francs, in compensation for 100 copies of the *Deutsch-Französische Jahrbücher* which had been smuggled into Germany. Jung's handout relieved Marx of his financial distress, at least temporarily, and enabled him to devote himself to serious study and writing in Paris.

Marx never forgave Ruge. He pursued him with relentless hatred for the rest of his life, rarely passing up an opportunity to sneer at his former friend and heap calumny on him in both private letters and public polemics, often in the crudest terms.

Contacts

Despite the failure of the *Deutsch-Französische Jahrbücher*, Marx's residence in Paris, from October 1843 to February 1845, was one of the happiest and most productive periods of his life. It also marked a turning point, for it was in Paris that he definitely became a communist.

The dazzling French capital was endlessly stimulating to the exuberant young Marx. The city was then the home of a galaxy of literary and artistic talents perhaps unexcelled in any other modern epoch. Among the most renowned were the astonishingly fecund Honoré de Balzac, whom Marx read with admiration and later quoted in *Das Kapital*;[1] the adroit Victor Hugo, whom he considered "brilliant"; and George Sand, the pseudonymous woman novelist, whom he cited with approval in his polemical work against Proudhon, *The Poverty of Philosophy* (1847).[2] It is also likely that Marx met a number of Paris luminaries in the Countess d'Agoult's salon. Among those who attended her musical soirées were the composers Frédéric Chopin and Giacomo Meyerbeer (neither of whom was a Frenchman), the critic Charles Augustin Sainte-Beuve, the painter Jean Auguste Dominique Ingres, the poets Alfred de Musset and Alfred de Vigny, and Heinrich Heine. Whether the two men knew it or not, Heine was a cousin of Marx's mother, both of them being descendants of Simon Pressburg.

Marx had met Heine, either through Moses Hess or Ruge, sometime in December 1843, not long after his arrival in

---

[1] In *Das Kapital*, Vol. III, Ch. 1, sec. 1, Marx praised Balzac as "generally remarkable for his profound grasp of actual conditions"; he also cited him in Vol. I, Ch. 22, sec. 7, footnote.

[2] The quotation, from Sand's novel *Jean Ziska*, reads: "Combat or death; sanguinary struggle or nothingness. It is thus that the question is invincibly posed."

Paris. The famous poet and the quondam poet struck up a warm friendship, despite the twenty-one years that separated them in age. They were men of similar background: both found Germany spiritually uncongenial and moved abroad, where each spent the rest of his life as an exile, Heine in Paris since 1831 and Marx in London after 1849. Both were deeply influenced by Hegel, Heine as a direct student of the great philosopher at the University of Berlin. Both were baptized German Jews, which put them in a special category, men who were neither Christian nor Jewish. Both were men of acute critical faculties and flashing wit.

Heine often visited the Marx *ménage*. He was probaby attracted as much by Jenny's beauty and wit as by Marx's intellect. She had the ability to cheer him when he was in one of his fits of depression. Heine often brought along his latest verses for reading and discussion. One day, soon after the first Marx child, Jenny, was born on May 1, 1844, Heine came to visit and found the young parents standing by helpless and desperate, while the baby was in convulsions. "The child," said the poet, "needs a bath," and forthwith proceeded to give her one. Marx was henceforth sure that Heine had saved little Jenny's life.

In his later years, Heine finally became disillusioned with the arrogance and dogmatism of the German radicals, including Marx. They reminded him, he wrote, of the Babylonian king Nebuchadnezzar, who fell from God's grace and was condemned to eat grass like an animal in the field, as told in the "splendid" Book of Daniel:[3] "I recommend it for the edification of my good friend Ruge, and also to my much more stubborn friend Marx . . . and the rest of the crowd of godless, self-appointed gods."

Marx, while sardonically amused at Heine's return to religion in his last years, did not cease to appreciate the poet's writings. A would-be poet himself, and a lifelong reader of poetry in the major European languages, Marx had a special fondness for Heine's brand of irony and humor. Heine was to be one of the few friends whom Marx did not attack in the end; instead, he quoted him with relish on numerous occasions.

---

[3]Daniel: 4, 29: "And thou shalt be driven from men, and thy dwelling shall be with the beasts of the field; thou shalt be made to eat grass as oxen. . . . The same hour was the thing fulfilled upon Nebuchadnezzar; and he was driven from men, and did eat grass as oxen, and his body was wet with the dew of heaven, till his hair was grown like eagles' feathers, and his nails like birds' claws."

Among other individuals of great importance in the history of 19th-century European radicalism whom Marx met in Paris in 1844 were Michael Bakunin and Pierre Joseph Proudhon. Marx was later to be at war with both of them.

He and Bakunin, a Russian aristocrat four years his senior and a man of giant stature and reckless courage in the cause of the oppressed, had an uneasy relationship from the first. The two men both admired and feared each other. The Russian revolutionist, who was to spend years in exile in Siberia and to make a legendary escape from there, was impressed by Marx's erudition and brilliance. He often sought Marx's conversation, which he said was "always instructive and witty." But at the same time he found Marx to be vain, arrogant and spiteful.

Marx, in turn, basically distrusted the intellectually undisciplined Russian, a product of a country that he always considered, and dreaded as, barbaric. In his later polemics against Bakunin,[4] he referred to him contemptuously as a "Cossack." The mutual antipathy of these two radical chiefs, despite their occasional protestations of friendship, was to shatter the Marx-led First International in 1872.

Marx had no such personal feelings about Proudhon, whose first book, *What Is Property?* (Paris, 1840), he admired and called "epoch-making," but whose later work he criticized mercilessly. The two men met during July 1844, and they spent, as Marx tells it, long hours, "often lasting all night," discussing social and philosophical problems. "I infected him to his great injury with Hegelianism, which, owing to his ignorance of the German language, he could not study properly." Proudhon, a self-educated man, never did master the intricacies of Hegel, or, for that matter, of technical economics, as Marx was to point out later.

But a greater influence on Marx's development came not from contact with famous individuals, but from meeting with workers. Paris, in addition to being the heart of Continental culture, was the home of European revolution and radical ferment. The great Revolution of 1789 continued to be a living tradition, both for the triumphant middle class, now seemingly in solid control of all levers of power under Louis Philippe, and the discontented and intelligent workers, seething with radical idealism. In Paris, class divisions were

[4]See Saul K. Padover, ed., *Karl Marx on the First International* (New York, 1973).

palpable, sharp and uncompromising. Marx did not have to imagine or invent the class struggle; he only had to look around him.

Paris provided Marx with the opportunity of getting to know real proletarians, not just theorists like Proudhon. He was introduced to working class radicals by a few men from the circle of German refugee intellectuals centered around Moses Hess, his friend and admirer from Cologne. Now in Paris, Hess devoted himself, as he wrote to his friend, the novelist Auerbach, "to philosophic projects of communism." His "communism," being both philosophic and democratic, was of a different brand from that associated with the name of Marx, with whom he was soon to break. But for the time being, Hess exerted some influence on the development of Marx's ideas.

Paris had a colony of about 10,000 German artisans and journeymen—"shoemaker" was then virtually synonymous with "German"—with strong communist leanings. In the Faubourg St. Antoine, there were often violent street clashes between the German workers, who spoke no French, and the Parisian proletarians, who resented the foreigners for under-cutting their wages. It was, of course, a classic confrontation. Marx was introduced to the German artisans by a refugee physician, August Hermann Ewerbeck, who was both a member of the *Bund der Kommunisten* [Communist League] and chief of the secret society *Bund der Gerechten* [League of the Just].

The League of the Just, prototype of the subsequent communist leagues and organizations, left its imprint on Marx's development as a communist. It was founded in Paris in 1836, by German artisans under the inspiration of Christian Wilhelm Weitling, a natty tailor and a fuzzy utopian communist, whose naive self-confidence and ideas of "Christian love"[5] Marx was soon to shatter.

Marx attended some of the meetings of both the German communists and the French. A police spy (Paris was then teeming with them) reported that in the summer of 1844 he often saw Marx visiting the meetings of the French communist groups in the Barrière du Trône, on the rue de Vincennes. But Marx did not become a member of either group.

[5] Wilhelm Weitling, *Die Menschheit, Wie Sie Ist und Wie Sie Sein Sollte* [*Mankind, As It Is and As It Should Be*] (1838): "The law of nature and of Christian love is the basis of all laws to be made for society."

The French workers impressed Marx enormously with their intelligence, energy and idealism. "In the meetings of the communist artisans," he wrote, "brotherhood is not a phrase but the truth, and nobility shines from the labor-hardened faces."

Paris was always to remain a focal point in Marx's political thinking. His interest in French affairs continued to be as strong as his romantic illusions about the French proletariat. His major noneconomic writings—*The Class Struggles in France,* 1848–1850 (1850); *The Eighteenth Brumaire of Louis Napoleon*[6] (1852); *The Civil War in France* (1871)—were passionate polemics about French politics.

Engels

It was young Frederick Engels, then twenty-four years old, who was influential in Marx's conversion to communism in 1844. Engels provided Marx with a strong stimulus for the study of economics and inspired him with enthusiasm for the communist cause. For Marx, economic studies were to become a lifelong interest and to serve as the underpinning of his communist theories.

Marx had been deeply impressed by the two articles that Engels had contributed to the *Deutsch-Französische Jahrbücher,* especially the essay "Outlines of a Critique of Political Economy," which dealt with the development of modern capitalism, from mercantilism to the contemporary English factory system. England, Engels wrote, was then of "immeasurable importance for history and for all other countries," because it was a pioneer in the development of the institutions and methods of modern capitalism. The article, touching upon commerce, competition, value, ground rents, capital and labor, was a sweeping review of the whole subject, about which Engels already knew a great deal and Marx as yet very little.

Marx's decision to adopt communism, towards which he had been shifting for a number of months, was finally made when Engels stopped off in Paris, on the way from Manchester to his native Barmen, Germany. He visited Marx, whom he had met briefly in the *Rheinische Zeitung* days in Cologne,

---

[6] In the second German edition, this was retitled *The Eighteenth Brumaire of Louis Bonaparte* (Hamburg, 1869).

and the two enthusiastic young Germans spent ten days together, from August 28 to September 6, 1844, discovering each other's minds, attitudes, reactions and opinions. They discussed the whole range of philosophic and social problems, particularly as they related to German and European radicalism. An inextinguishable spark was struck between them. They found themselves, in the words of Engels, "in accord in all theoretical fields," and they decided then and there to collaborate in their future work as slashing critics of existing society. Their intellectual assault on the status quo in all its aspects—literary, philosophic, religious, economic and political—was to be rooted in the materialist viewpoint that has come to be known as "Marxism."

The first product of the Marx-Engels collaboration, which also marked a definite break with traditional idealism, was *Critique of Critical Critique*, over which the title *The Holy Family* was superimposed while it was being printed. Engels wrote the first four chapters while he was still in Paris; Marx finished the last four chapters and postscript in November.

The Holy Family, subtitled *Against Bruno Bauer & Associates*, was a satire against the Young Hegelians who were led by Bauer and grouped around the *Allgemeine Literatur-Zeitung*, a Berlin monthly. In that publication, Bauer "& Associates" were making the lofty claim of elevating theoretical criticism into a transcendental essence, beyond and above all human experience.

Marx wanted to publish this "brochure against Bauer," as he called it, in Paris, so as to have it printed under his eyes, but he found no publisher. At the end of November, he sent the manuscript to a Frankfurt publisher named Löwenthal, who brought out *The Holy Family* in February 1845, under the imprint "Literarische Anstalt (J. Rütten)." Marx received an honorarium of 1,000 francs. It was his first book royalty.

Marx and Engels had roughly similar backgrounds. Both were products of the German middle class, sons of well-to-do bourgeois parents, imbued with the prevailing virtues of material ambition, hard work and discipline. Where Marx's father was a conservative provincial lawyer, Engels' parent was a reactionary small-town manufacturer. Neither in the Marx nor in the Engels household was there any tradition or atmosphere of radicalism. Marx and Engels, however, had different reactions to their parents. Marx loved and admired his father, a skeptic and a liberal in religion, and had neither affection nor esteem for his mother. Engels, on the other

hand, disliked his "*Schweinhund*" of a father, a dour Lutheran religious fanatic, but loved and respected his mother.

Engels was born on November 28, 1820, in Barmen, a
small manufacturing town that now forms part of Elberfeld,
in the Wupper Valley, Rhenish Prussia. He was the oldest of
the six children of Friedrich and Elisabeth Franziska Mauri-
tia Engels, a Protestant couple in a predominantly Protestant
town. After attending elementary school in Barmen, young
Frederick entered the Gymnasium at Elberfeld at the age of
fourteen, but left it after three years. He had no further
schooling and, unlike Marx, he never became a "*Herr
Doktor.*" Under pressure from his tyrannical father, he became a business apprentice in Barmen and then in Bremen,
but he soon called it a "dog's life" and left business at the
age of twenty. He was then in full rebellion not only against
his dreary family home, which he called a "Zion of obscuran-
tism," but also against the "penny-pinching" world of commerce, which he labeled "*Schacher*" [haggling].

Engels was to remain a lifelong enemy of organized religion and an implacable foe of capitalism, although necessity
forced him to return to business, which he did in November
1850, when he found himself unable to earn a living as a
journalist in London. Unlike Marx, he had such a well-or-
ganized and practical mind that, despite his contempt for
commerce, he joined his father's textile firm in Manchester
and became a successful businessman. By the time he was
fifty he had accumulated enough capital to retire and support
himself, as well as the Marx family, in comfort. Through Engels, Manchester capitalism was thus to contribute to the
propagation and crystallization of communist ideas, including
Marx's writings.

Engels, blond, elegant, slender and Teutonic-looking, had a
brilliant but not profound mind and was quick, sharp and unerring in his judgments. His versatility was astonishing. In his
maturity he showed a grasp of virtually every branch of the
natural sciences, biology, chemistry, botany and physics. His
reading was as wide-ranging as that of Marx, his writings on
military affairs and tactics, a minor specialty of his, commanded respect. By the time he had reached middle age, he
had mastered, to the point of reading and writing, nearly two
dozen languages, including the Slavic ones, on which he
planned to write a comparative grammar; this was a specialty
of some piquancy, since he had a Teutonic contempt for
Slavs, including Poles, whom Marx romantically admired.

Engels also taught himself Gothic, Old Nordic, and Old Saxon, studied Arabic, and once learned Persian in three weeks: "a mere child's play," he said. His English was impeccable. Since he had a tendency to stammer when excited, he was said to "stutter in twenty languages."

In Manchester, after his business success was assured, Engels came to live the comfortable life of a capitalist gentleman. He maintained two homes—one for appearance, as befitted a member of the local Stock Exchange, and another for his Irish mistress, Mary, and then, after her death, her sister, Lydia ("Lizzy") Burns, whom in later years he called "my wife." He was a lover of good food, a connoisseur of vintage wines, and a robust singer of *Lieder*. In Manchester, like a good capitalist, he had his own horse and rode to hounds with the local gentry, whom as a communist he despised, but by whose antic behavior he was sardonically amused.

Marx and Engels shared not merely a common philosophy but also certain common traits of behavior. Both were brash and witty, voluble with ideas, intolerant of opposition. Each was blunt and capable of bawdiness. Both had tendencies toward vulgarity, particularly in characterizing their opponents. They both loved to polemicize, for which they had a special gift. Their polemics were not infrequently steeped in malice. There was also a streak of harshness in both men, particularly vis-à-vis the "philistines" (one of Marx's favorite pejoratives) and any capitalists with whom they happened to be in conflict at the moment.

First Efforts at Economics

In Paris, Marx continued to pursue one of his unquenchable passions, a love of books, among them the novels of the extremely popular Eugène Sue, who produced them in multiples of ten—*Les Mystères de Paris* (10 vols., 1842-43); *Le Juif Errant* (10 vols., 1844-45)—and whom he and Engels were soon to lampoon in *The Holy Family*. Ruge said of Marx: "he reads much, works with uncommon intensity, does not go to bed for three, four nights in succession, and constantly plunges anew into an endless ocean of books."

Among the "ocean of books" were works on economics, which Marx not only read but annotated. He had begun to keep notes of his economic studies the year before and now continued the practice, in the hope of making a mark in the field of political economy. He made extensive extracts from the works that deeply impressed him. He read, in French translation, James Mill's *Elements of Political Economy* (London, 1821), a "great work," as he called it, from which he made excerpts that, when posthumously published, ran into nineteen printed pages. He also studied the other classic English economists, John Ramsay MacCulloch, or McCulloch, *The Principles of Political Economy* (London, 1830); David Ricardo, *On the Principles of Political Economy and Taxation* (London, 1817); and Adam Smith, *An Inquiry into the Nature and Causes of the Wealth of Nations* (London, 1776). These works were then available in French translation. The English economists made a lasting impression on Marx, as can be seen from his numerous references to them in his own later economic writings and from the voluminous extracts and critical comments on them in the so-called volume IV of *Kapital*.[7]

He also read the leading French economic theorists, including Michel Chevalier's *Des Intérêts matérials en France* (Paris-Brussels, 1838); Jean Baptiste Say's *Traité d'économie politique* (3d ed., Paris, 1817); and the Polish-born Frédéric Skarbek's *Théories des richesses sociales* (Paris, 1829). Attempting to supplement theory with some practical knowledge of the workings of the French financial system, which then and later played such a pervasive role in the politics of France, he bought a book on the Stock Exchange by a French lawyer, Antoine Simon Gabriel Coffinières, entitled *De la bourse et des spéculations sur les effets publics* (Paris, 1824), but found it shallow and worthless. But there was then little reliable material on this crucial subject.

Intellectually restless, with concepts taken from Hegel and Feuerbach still struggling in his mind, ambitious to establish himself quickly as a writer, Marx again indulged one of his compulsions, that of generalizing the results of his serious readings and formulating them in absolute categories. Just as he had rushed to restructure ancient Roman law after studying the Pandects and other juridical works as a student at the University of Berlin, only to throw out his hasty "system" as

---

[7]Progress Publishers, Moscow, brought out *Theories of Surplus Value*, which it subtitled Vol. IV of *Kapital*, in 1963 (Part I), 1968 (Part II), 1971 (Part III). The material in these posthumous volumes consists primarily of comments and excerpts, which Marx had not integrated into a book before his death.

inadequate, so now he was in a hurry to do the same with his readings in political economy, and with approximately similar results.

In the spring of 1844, before he had actually mastered any of the major elements of economics, he wrote a long essay on "Wages, Profit of Capital, Ground Rents, Alienation of Labor," which he did not complete, or publish. At the same time, between April and August, he wrote down his thoughts on these economic subjects and their interrelation with "the state, law, ethics, civil life, etc." This further attempt at universalizing also went unpublished, and a number of the manuscript pages have been lost since. What survived did not see print until almost a century later, when the Moscow Institute of Marxism-Leninism published it in 1932, under the title *Economic and Philosophic Manuscripts of 1844*.

These writings contain more philosophy (or philosophic psychology) than concrete economics, but the thrust is definitely in the direction of political economy. Many of their fundamental concepts—words like *aufheben* [to abolish, or to raise], *entäussern* [to give up, or part with], *Gattungswesen*[8] [species-being]—come from the German philosophy of Hegel and Feuerbach.

One concept, *Entfremdung* [alienation or estrangement], was used by Marx in a novel way. In both Hegel and Feuerbach, *Entfremdung* was a philosophic abstraction. Marx gave it a new meaning by relating it to the material world, particularly the world of human feelings and actions.

Marx distinguished four forms of alienation. He saw man as alienated from nature when living in a state of civilization. Man is also alienated from his *Gattungswesen*, or species-being. By the same token, man is alienated from his fellow-men. And he is likewise alienated from his own self and his activities. Applied to the economic world, this means that the worker, producing goods for others, is alienated from what he makes. Thus we have "alienated labor" in capitalist society.

This Marxian concept of alienation was to open up new vistas, not only in economics, but also in the realms of psychology and human behavior, and has resulted in frequent references to *Economic and Philosophic Manuscripts of*

---

[8]The German word *Wesen*, which Marx used often, has no precise English equivalent. Its many meanings include "being," "existence," "substance," "essence," "reality," "nature," "matter," etc. *Gattungswesen* is usually translated by the hybrid term given here.

1884, otherwise a sketchy and derivative work, by social scientists in our own day.

Marx managed to find a German publisher. On February 1, 1845, he signed a contract with Karl Wilhelm Leske of Darmstadt, for a two-volume work, to be entitled *Kritik der Politik und Nationalökonomie* [*Critique of Policy and National Economy*]. Leske gave him an advance of 1,500 francs. But Marx never completed the work. Two days after he signed the contract, he was expelled from Paris and moved to Brussels, where conditions for sustained study were not favorable. After the lapse of a year and a half, Leske, under police investigation and harassment, worriedly asked Marx whether his book would be really "scientific." Marx replied sharply on August 1, 1846: "The book is scientific, but not scientific in the Prussian government's sense." He offered to return the advance as soon as he had found another publisher. He never did.

German publishers were either cowed by the prevailing censorship or too conservative. None dared risk police displeasure by bringing out a radical book. Marx even dreamed of founding an independent radical press for the publication of a journal and books. The press was to be financed by subscription, at 25 Taler per share, but there were no buyers. The scheme had to be dropped. Marx said that he would have to resort to writing in French, or not at all.

Another dozen years were to pass before Marx published his first book on economics.

Jenny and Jennychen

The first of Marx's seven children, one of the three daughters to survive and grow into adulthood, was born on February 1, 1844, in the small apartment on the rue Vanneau. She was named Jenny, after her mother, and was naturally called "Jennychen," or little Jenny. She was to grow into a beautiful and spirited woman and to be her father's favorite daughter. Her death, which was to occur thirty-nine years later, two months before Marx's own, was for him the final shattering blow.

Jennychen was the joy and despair of her parents, for she was a weak and sickly child who seemed unlikely to survive infancy. After six weeks of struggle, finding themselves unable to cope, they decided that Jenny should take the baby to her mother, who had in the meantime moved from Bad Kreuznach back to Trier. In the middle of June, as Jenny tells it in her brief *Reminiscences,* "I took the mail coach to Trier with my mortally sick child."

Jenny spent the summer in Trier, where, she wrote to her husband, "my mother waits on me hand and foot in the most tender way," and "my little one is being cherished and tended." Her letters to Karl contain vivid vignettes of his native city, mixed with outpourings of passion for him, and touching personal drama. She wrote him how she put on her best Parisian finery and acted the happy wife of a successful journalist in Paris, to impress the gossipy small town, which clearly had doubts about her marriage and her husband.

Then there was the story of her visit to old Mrs. Marx and her daughters. With her customary dramatic flair, Jenny, maintaining her role as the wife of a successful author, chose her wedding anniversary to call on her husband's mother and sisters, who had stayed away from her wedding. Wearing her chic Parisian dress, her face flushed with anxiety and her heart beating with excitement, she took, as she told Karl, the "difficult road" to the Marx family home to seek reconciliation.

When I rang, my heart thudded almost audibly. Everything passed through my soul. The door opened, and Jettchen [Marx's sister Henriette] came out, fell on my neck, kissed me and led me into the room where your mother and Sophie sat. Both embraced me, your mother immediately called me *Du,* and Sophie pulled me over to the couch. She is frightfully ravaged [by tuberculosis]. . . . And yet Jettchen [also tubercular] is even more miserable. Only your mother is blooming and well and cheerfulness itself, virtually merry and wanton. *Ach,* this jollity is so sinister. All the girls are equally cordial, especially Carolinchen [Marx's youngest sister Caroline].

The next morning, at 9 o'clock, Henriette returned the visit, to see her first grandchild, "our dear little angel." Later the Marx sisters dropped in. Jenny was pleased, and so was her mother, but she could not help being skeptical about all this friendliness. It was obvious to her that the new-found cordiality on the part of the Marx women, particularly Karl's mother, was due to their belief, which Jenny carefully fostered, that Karl was at long last doing really well. As she put it to her husband, "It shows what success can do, or rather, in our case, the *semblance* of success, which I know how to maintain with the finest tactics."

But Jenny did not really deceive Henriette Marx, who remained basically unfriendly. The mutual visits soon ceased. "I have not seen your family for a long time," Jenny wrote to Karl seven weeks after the first visit. She could not hide her distaste for her mother-in-law, whose insensitivity and crassness offended her. She was horrified to notice how Henriette was gaily making preparations for the marriage of Karl's sister Jettchen to Theodor Simons, a village architect, at a time when the twenty-four-year-old girl (she died at the age of thirty-six) was coughing desperately and "looks like a ghost." Everybody, Jenny reported to her husband, "thinks it shocking and conscienceless." She did not understand the "character of your family, to be so gay and contented" under such circumstances. How could the Marx women gad about to their "glossy parties" and brag about their brooches and earrings and scarves, she asked indignantly. "Your mother herself had told us that she believes Jettchen has tuberculosis, and she lets her marry nevertheless."

Jenny spent the summer in Trier, oscillating between intense happiness and fear for the future. She was daily more and more enchanted by her first child, naturally the most beautiful baby in the world. "You cannot even imagine," she wrote her husband, "the beauty of its forehead, the transparency of its skin, the wonderful daintiness of its little hands." Her passion for her husband, procreator of this miraculous infant, was at as high a pitch as ever. "You can hardly believe, my heart's beloved," she wrote him in one of her letters, "how deeply happy your letters make me, and your last pastoral one, Thou High Priest and Bishop of the Heart, has again lulled your poor sheep into calm and peace."

"Write me real soon," she concluded, "I am much too happy even at the mere sight of your handwriting. You good, dear, sweet *Schwarzwildchen*, you darling father of my *Püppchen* [little doll]." Jenny dreaded and hoped that with the passion she and her husband had for each other, they would make another baby as soon as she returned to Paris. "Karlchen," she wrote, "how long do you think the little doll will remain a solo party? I fear, I fear that when Papa and

Mama are again together and live as husband and wife, there will soon be a duo."

As Jenny had foreseen, after she returned to Paris she became pregnant with her second child. This continued almost annually until her menopause. Marx, preoccupied with the economic consequences of capitalism, was oblivious to the economic consequences of sex.

Expulsion from Paris

In July, 1844, while Jenny was still in Trier, Marx made contact with *Vorwärts! Pariser Deutsche Zeitschrift*. This was a semiweekly German-language publication, founded by Heinrich Boernstein, edited by Karl Ludwig Bernays and financially supported by the Berlin-born composer Giacomo Meyerbeer. Within a few weeks Marx joined the staff and helped to radicalize the journal—and thereby ultimately to kill it.

In the August 7 and 10 issues of *Vorwärts!* Marx published a two-part article entitled "Critical Marginal Notes on the [*Vorwärts!*] Article 'The King of Prussia and Social Reform. By a Prussian.'" [9] Since the Prussian in question was Arnold Ruge, it gave Marx an opportunity to lambaste his enemy and at the same time to analyze the need and meaning of revolution in Prussia.

Ruge's piece had dealt with the Silesian weavers whose revolt of June 4–6 had been easily crushed with a minimal show of force. He asserted that in suppressing the uprising with only a few troops, the Prussian King had not acted out of "fear," as was charged in the Paris daily, *La Réforme*, but with a "Christian heart" and "Christian feeling."

In his lengthy and contentious reply, which he admitted was marked by "long-windedness," Marx accused Ruge of "literary charlatanism" and ridiculed him for his rhetoric in making the "absurd" distinction between political and social revolution. Any revolution, Marx argued, was both: insofar as it dissolved the old order, it was social; insofar as it abolished the old power, it was political. He concluded that such revolution—the overthrow of both the social and political order—was necessary for the attainment of socialism in Prussia.

[9] For text, see Saul K. Padover, ed., *Karl Marx on Revolution* (New York, 1971), pp. 7-22.

The Berlin authorities, whose Paris agents were still reporting about Marx, interpreted his article as an unmistakable
call to revolution. Just as the Russian Czar in 1842 had
brought pressure to bear on the Prussian King to act against
the *Rheinische Zeitung,* so now the Prussian King exerted his
influence with King Louis Philippe of France to take steps
against *Vorwärts!* The Prussian ambassador, Karl Eduard Arnim, protested to the French Premier, the historian-politician
François Guizot. Then the Prussian King sent Alexander von
Humboldt, the distinguished German scientist, to the French
King, with a lengthy letter and a "splendid porcelain vase" as
a royal gift. Louis Philippe assured von Humboldt that he
would rid Paris of the German radicals and atheists connected with *Vorwärts!*

The next move, made by the French Ministry of the Interior on January 11, 1845, was an order of expulsion. It was
handed to Marx in the morning of January 25, which was a
Saturday. As Jenny tells it in her *Reminiscences,* "Suddenly,
. . . the police commissioner came to our house and showed
us an order of expulsion . . . 'Karl Marx must leave Paris
within 24 hours,' it read."

Actually he was given a week's grace.

XII
Brussels

The Beginning of Exile

Marx left Paris on Saturday, February 1, exactly one week after receiving the expulsion notice. He took the *messagerie* [stagecoach] to Belgium, in the company of two friends, the publisher Karl Wilhelm Leske and the communist journalist Heinrich Buergers. The three of them had the coach to themselves up to the Belgian frontier, and they spent their time talking and singing. They stayed one night in Liège and on February 3 arrived in Brussels, where they put up in the Hôtel de Saxe, rue de Neuve.

Marx then moved to a tavern, Au Bois Sauvage, 19–21 Plaine Sainte-Gudule, owned by Jean Baptiste Lannoy, a middle-aged man who was kind to German refugees. In mid-February, Jenny and her eight-month-old baby, after a journey in "bitter cold weather," joined Marx in the tavern, where they stayed for about a month. She was ill, and pregnant again, and there was no money at all.

Engels, then still in Barmen and on the verge of breaking with his father, came to their financial rescue with 50 Taler, borrowed, he wrote, "from my Old Man." He also opened a collection campaign for the Marx family among Rhineland communists; by early April, it had netted 750 francs, enough to provide temporarily for groceries and rent.

In the three years that Marx lived in Brussels, he moved several times, either into friends' houses or from one slummy quarter to another. From the Bois Sauvage, he settled temporarily in the Rue Pacheco, where the poet Ferdinand Freiligrath lived briefly. Later, he found a shabby apartment at 5 Rue d'Alliance, outside the Porte de Louvain, a district which Jenny called a "pauper colony." It was here that the second Marx baby, Laura, was born on September 26, 1845. But in the following year Marx had to give up the little apartment and return temporarily to the Bois Sauvage tavern with his wife and two babies. In 1848, the Marxes, who by that time had three children, moved back to the Bois Sauvage for the third and last time. Every change of address was reported by the *Fremdenpolizei* [police in charge of aliens] to the *Sûreté Publique*.[1]

To pay for rent, food and other necessities in an expensive country, Marx resorted to borrowing from friends and acquaintances, a habit he continued throughout most of his life. Where attempts at direct borrowing failed, friends took up collections. Early in 1846, Marx needed to pay an urgent debt of 1,200 francs, and appealed to everybody he knew, including his mother (through Jenny, who was then visiting her own sick mother in Trier) and her business friends. By that time, they were aware of Marx's chronic improvidence and turned a deaf ear to his pleas.

Marx continued to live on borrowed money and occasional donations, but he paid a heavy price for this form of financing. Constant borrowing from all and sundry hurt his pride. This resulted in rages, and in attempting to suppress them he injured his health. Virtually every financial crisis in the Marx household drove him or his wife, and often both of them together, to bed with some form of illness. In the summer of 1846, Marx had an attack of asthma so severe that it frightened Jenny, who also became ill, as well as their friends. This was the first of an endless chain of varied afflictions from which Marx and Jenny were to suffer chronically throughout their lifelong exile.

When, early in the year 1848, Marx finally received the remainder of his inheritance, which amounted to around 6,000 francs, instead of husbanding the money for the support of his family, he spent about 5,000 francs helping to buy arms for radical workers in Brussels during the February uprising. He was convinced that the European revolution had at last arrived. His immediate reward was to be promptly kicked out of Belgium.

"Lenchen"

In April 1845, about two months after Jenny arrived in Brussels, her mother, aware that her daughter had no skill or

---

[1] Copies of police reports in the International Institute for Social History, Amsterdam, MSS E17 and E20.

experience in coping with a household, especially one with children, sent her her own maid, "the faithful, dear Lenchen." This was Helene (or Helena) Demuth, who was then twenty-one years old and had been with the von Westphalens since she was a girl of eleven or twelve. She was ten years younger than Jenny, whom she loved with total devotion. Lenchen immediately took over the Marx household, such as it was, and when Marx was too poor to pay her and suggested that she return to Trier, Lenchen refused. She cast her lot with the Marx family forever.

Helene Demuth was, by all accounts, a remarkable servant and a rare woman. She even became the subject of a novel after her death.[2] A daughter of peasants from the Saar, she had no formal education, but as a Sarroise she spoke French, which was, of course, helpful in Brussels. Strong, energetic, and cheerful, Lenchen had been trained in all the household arts by Frau von Westphalen. This "treasure," as Jenny called her, did the cooking, housecleaning, laundering, dressmaking, nursing, wet-nursing, household planning and every other practical task, including taking articles to the pawn shop when hunger or eviction threatened. She became a second mother to the Marx children, who repaid her with filial love and respect. Marx's youngest daughter Eleanor, in her *Reminiscences*, called Lenchen "as noble a woman as ever lived."

As long as Jenny and Karl Marx were alive, Lenchen ran their household like a benevolent dictator, and after the latter's death, Engels was happy to have her move in with him. Her dictatorship was lightened by her sturdy cheerfulness and sense of humor, traits she shared with both Marxes. In the words of Wilhelm Liebknecht, an intimate friend of Marx, whom he visited often when he lived in London, "Marx submitted [to Lenchen] like a lamb."

Worshiped by his wife and adored by his children, Marx was, nevertheless, not a hero to Lenchen. Nobody knew his faults and weaknesses of the flesh and of the spirit better than this shrewd and intimate servant. She had no difficulty in "twisting him around her little finger," or squelching him when the occasion called for it. His customary rages might terrify others, but not Lenchen. Liebknecht recalls that Marx "might storm and thunder ever so much, keeping everybody at a distance. Lenchen went into the lion's den, and if he

[2] Stefan Grossmann, *Lenchen Demuth und andere Novellen* (Berlin, 1925).

growled she gave him such a severe lecture that the lion became meek as a lamb."

If Lenchen was not particularly impressed by the master of the house, the master was impressed by Lenchen. His affectionate pun on her name—"*Demuth* [Humility], *Wehmuth* [Melancholy], *Hochmuth* [Pride]"—reflects his honest appreciation of the intelligence and native ability of this untutored peasant woman. She was not only able to beat him in chess but also to give him hard-headed advice in party politics—advice which Engels later also sought and accepted.

Helene Demuth, who died on November 4, 1890, of cancer of the bowels, at the age of sixty-six[8], now lies buried in the same grave as Marx and Jenny in London's Highgate Cemetery. Her final resting place was chosen by Marx's surviving daughters, who knew better than anyone else that in the years of exile and destitution, the family might have perished without Lenchen.

Man Without a Country

When Marx arrived in Brussels, he had registered as an alien with the *Sûreté Publique* and formally petitioned for the right to live in Belgium. His petition, written in French, and addressed to King Leopold I on February 7, 1845, read:

The undersigned Karl Marx, Doctor of Philosophy, twenty-six years old, from Trier, Kingdom of Prussia, with the intention of settling with his wife and child in the states of Your Majesty, most respectfully and humbly takes the liberty of requesting Your Majesty to grant him permission to take up his residence in Belgium.

With deepest respect, I have the honor to be Your Majesty's very humble and very obedient servant.

Dr. Karl Marx.

His Majesty, not a Belgian but a native German from Coburg (uncle of England's Queen Victoria), who had been elected King of the Belgians at the creation of the country in 1831, did not reply directly. The new kingdom, flanked as it

[8]The death certificate in Somerset House, London, gives her age erroneously as "67 years," and the cause of death as "cancer of Bowell [*sic*] perforative peritonitis."

was by a covetous France and an unfriendly Holland, did not feel secure with refugees. Marx, like other foreigners, was permitted to remain in Belgium on condition that he refrain from writing about current politics.

With this exception, he felt himself free to propagate communism, as he and Engels now began to develop it; build a local communist organization, such as it was; maintain active contact with communists and other leftists abroad; and make plans for a European revolution. But his proceedings did not go unobserved. Prussian police spies reported on him to Berlin, which in turn began to apply pressure on the government in Brussels to expel him. Faced with a repetition of the Paris experience, and furious at being harassed by his native country, which he contemptuously called a "hither-Russian colony," Marx took the rash step of cutting his legal ties with Prussia.

On October 17, 1845, he applied to Oberbürgermeister Goertz of Trier for an *Auswanderungsschein* [Emigration Certificate or Exit Permit] to enable him to emigrate to the "United North American States." He reminded the Mayor that he was no longer subject to military service (on account of his infected lungs), and hence there should be no legal obstacle to granting him the desired permission. Getting no answer from Goertz, Marx again wrote him, on November 10, asking both for the *Auswanderungsschein* and for a "release" from the "association of Royal Prussian subjects"; in other words, he renounced his Prussian citizenship. This step was neither prudent nor practical, and Marx lived to regret it.

On November 23, at the suggestion of the Rhine Province's *Regierungspräsident* [Governor] Rudolf von Auerswald that it would be wise to get rid of the traitor, Berlin granted Marx's request for denaturalization.

Henceforth Marx spent his life as a stateless person, a man without a country.

Engels

After Marx settled in Brussels, he was joined by a number of other refugees, among them Michael Bakunin and Moses Hess and his wife Sybille, whom gossips spoke of as a former prostitute. The small colony met evenings in a pleasant cafe. They were joined occasionally by a Belgian communist, Philippe Gigot, and by a few non-radical Poles and Russians, including the distinguished Polish historian Joachim Lelewel, usually wearing a blue blouse, and Pavel Vasilyevich Annenkov, a liberal Russian landowner who became a friend of Marx.

But for Marx the most important arrival in Brussels was that of Engels, who had been in a state of rebellion and disgust in Barmen, where, he wrote, he led a "life such as the most splendid philistine would dream of." To please his parents, he had made an effort to work in his father's factory, but the "low trade" of business *"Schacher* [haggling]" revolted him. He was determined to be a writer and propagandist for communism, and not a "trading animal." He wrote to Marx on January 2, 1845:

> I was sorry even before I began to work. The haggling business is too abominable, Barmen is too abominable, the waste of time is too abominable, and in particular it is too abominable not only to be a bourgeois but a manufacturer, to remain a bourgeois active against the proletariat. A few days in my Old Man's factory again brought before my eyes this abomination.

Engels found the father-dominated household stifling. His behavior was under the constant scrutiny of his sanctimonious Old Man and his siblings. It infuriated him. "I cannot eat, drink, sleep or fart without seeing those accursed children-of-God faces." The family suspected him of debauchery and of conspiracy against the existing social order, a fairly well justified suspicion, since he not only had affairs with girls but also associated with communists in Barmen and lectured on communism in Elberfeld. Pursuing both girls and communism was a cardinal sin in the eyes of his father, who, Engels wrote, was tormented by "trite visions of hell" and was impervious to the most elementary principles of logic. "In addition," Engels went on, "the Old Man is so dumb that he throws communism and liberalism into the same box, and, despite all my counter-arguments, he constantly holds me responsible for the infamies of the English bourgeoisie in Parliament!"

Engels endured the pietistic family atmosphere with its "Christian malice," which was enough "to drive one nuts," only because of his suffering mother. She loved young Frederick but was scared of her tyrannical husband, and under the intensity of the conflict between father and son, she sought refuge in illness.

Early in April 1845, Engels finally broke with his father and left Barmen. He came to Brussels, where he was warmly welcomed by Marx—and by Jenny, who had never met him before—and settled next door to them, in the rue d'Alliance.

By that time, Engels, at twenty-five, had already developed the main outlines of his ideas, including the materialist philosophy of history.

The German Ideology

In September 1845, half a year after the publication of *The Holy Family*, Marx and Engels began their second book, *The German Ideology*. They worked on it until the summer of 1846, when Engels left to do propaganda work in Paris, but never really completed it. *The German Ideology* was, in effect, a continuation of *The Holy Family*, attacking German writers and radicals of the Hegel-Feuerbach school. In *The Holy Family*, their main targets had been Bauer ("Saint Bruno") and his associates. In *The German Ideology*, the polemic artillery was aimed mainly at Max Stirner, Karl Grün and the so-called "true socialists."

Stirner, a pseudonym for Johann Caspar Schmidt, was a relatively obscure teacher in a girls' school who had recently published a book, *Der Einzige und sein Eigentum* [*The Individual and His Property*] (Leipzig, 1845), which became briefly popular in Germany. In the same year, Karl Grün, a well-known German socialist living in exile in Paris, published a book, *Die soziale Bewegung in Frankreich und Belgien* [*The Social Movement in France and Belgium*] (Darmstadt, 1845), as well as a few articles on socialism.

The philosophy of Stirner, who is ridiculed in *The German Ideology* as "Saint Max," is summed up in the title of his book. *Der Einzige* means "the unique," "the individual" or "the only one"; this and the individual, not society, is at the core of Stirner's philosophy. All political and moral ties are superstitions; generalities like rights and obligations are not related to psychological reality. There is only one reality—*Der Einzige* himself, who consciously determines the needs of his own individual ego, such as family relations, human contacts, mundane activities, all of which become his personal *Eigentum*. *Der Einzige* is neither aristocrat nor superman nor

anarchist. He is simply Everyman, a kind of universal proletarian. Stirner was essentially a democrat, voicing a view
calculated to appeal to ordinary people. His philosophy was
the antithesis of communism or socialism, which both presuppose social-political organization and action, and was clearly
inimical to that of Marx and Engels, who decided to demolish him by mockery. In the printed edition of *The German
Ideology*,[4] out of 596 pages of text by Marx and Engels,
nearly 499 are devoted to "Saint Max."

Karl Grün rated less space in *The German Ideology*, but
he was pursued with more hate by Marx in public and in private.[5] Grün's "true socialism" was attacked for its disregard
of historical and class distinctions. But Marx's virulence
against a man who had ostensibly been his friend, since their
University days,[6] was probably also rooted in fierce personal
jealousy, fed by hate and malice, traits which, according to
such men as Michael Bakunin and Karl Heinzen who first
admired and later detested him, he always showed towards
actual or potential rivals.

The German Ideology, discursive, incomplete, and often
trivial, is not exclusively polemical and sarcastic. It has valuable pages. The first section, "Feuerbach," is a fairly comprehensive critique of idealism and the formulation of historical
materialism. It also contains an opaque statement of what
Marx and Engels meant by communism:

> Communism differs from all previous movements in that
> it overturns the basis of all earlier relations of produc
> tion and *Verkehr* [intercourse], and for the first time
> consciously treats all natural presuppositions as the crea
> tures of hitherto existing men, strips them of their
> natural character and subjugates them to the power of
> the united individuals. Its organization is, therefore, es
> sentially economic, the material production of the condi
> tions of this unity. The reality which communism is
> creating is precisely the true basis for rendering it impos
> sible that anything should exist independently of individ-

[4] English edition: Progress Publishers, Moscow, 1964.
[5] For an account of a controversy between Marx and Grün. see
Deutsche-Brüsseler-Zeitung, April 8, 1847. Marx's attack on Grün's
book and the "true socialists," which forms Ch. IV of *The German
Ideology*, was first published in the Bielefeld monthly, *Das Westphälische Dampfboot*, in August and September 1847.
[6] Cf. Grün to Hess, September 1, 1845.

uals, insofar as reality is only a product of the preceding intercourse of individuals themselves. Thus the communists in practice treat the conditions created up to now by production and intercourse as inorganic conditions. . . .

This philosophic section on communism concludes with an explication on the role assigned to the proletariat in the communist philosophy:

For the proletarians, on the other hand, the condition of their own existence, labor, and with it all the conditions of existence governing modern society, has become something accidental, something over which they, as separate individuals, have no control, and over which no *social* organization can give them control. . . . The proletarians, if they are to assert themselves as individuals, will have to abolish the very condition of their existence (which has, moreover, been that of all society up to the present), namely, labor. Thus they find themselves directly opposed to the form in which, hitherto, the individuals, of which society consists, have given themselves collective expression, that is, the State, and must overthrow the State in order to assert their own personality.

This was, of course, extensively echoed in the *Communist Manifesto,* which Marx and Engels were soon to write.

They had a good time writing *The German Ideology,* often working until three or four o'clock in the morning and roaring with laughter at their own irreverence, oblivious to the fact that their hilarity kept Jenny, Lenchen and the two babies awake.

The book was never published in its entirety during the authors' lifetime. Marx and Engels could not find a publisher in Germany. A communist polemic that derided other socialists was not a popular subject. In 1846, a Bielefeld socialist businessman, Julius Meyer, who had promised to finance the publication of *The German Ideology,* withdrew his offer after reading its ridicule of the "true socialists." Some twenty years later, Marx heard with malicious pleasure that Meyer, while on a business trip in Warsaw, "threw himself out of the window and obligingly broke his neck."[7]

The writing of *The German Ideology,* however, did achieve

[7]Marx to Engels, May 7, 1867.

one main purpose, according to Engels, namely, "self-under-standing." The unpublished manuscript, he wrote, was left to the "gnawing criticism of the mice." This may have been literally true. After Marx's death, Engels wrote to a Berlin school teacher that he still had the manuscript, "insofar as the mice haven't gnawed it up yet."[8]

The German Ideology was not published until nearly half a century after Marx's death. In 1932, the Moscow Marx-Engels-Lenin Institute brought out the book, of which some pages had been damaged, in its entirety for the first time. A full English translation appeared in Moscow thirty years later.

[8]Engels to Max Hildebrand, October 22, 1889.

XIII

Communists and the Manifesto

Communist Organizations

In the summer of 1845, while Jenny, who was pregnant, and Lenchen went to stay with Frau von Westphalen in Trier, Marx and Engels traveled to England. It was Marx's first visit to the country that was then the center of world capitalism. The two spent a couple of weeks in Manchester, with which Engels was of course familiar, where they took advantage of the Chetham Library there to study leading English economists. Marx made excerpts from the works of such writers as William Cobbett, William Petty, William Thompson and Thomas Tooke, and later used his notes both in the *Grundrisse* and in *Kapital*.

In London, Marx and Engels made contact with foreign communists and English radicals. The British capital was the home of left-wing Chartism, whose weekly, *The Northern Star*, under the editorship of George Julian Harney, was so sympathetic to European radicalism that Engels began to write for it in September 1845. London also harbored many political refugees, including German communists who belonged to the League of the Just and whose organization was the *Deutsche Bildungs-Gesellschaft für Arbeiter* [German Workers Educational Society], or *Arbeiterbildungsverein* for short, founded in 1840. Among its founders were the utopian communist Wilhelm Weitling and the revolutionary activist Karl Schapper, with both of whom Marx was soon to be in conflict.

The London police left the radicals, both homegrown and Continental, unmolested, a situation that was undoubtedly appealing to Marx after his experiences in Cologne and Paris. Police nonintervention was, of course, due basically to securely established British freedom, which did not feel threatened by a handful of aliens. The foreigners, moreover, were peaceful and clearly did not advocate the overthrow of the British Government.

The London communists were, in fact, generally opposed to violence and to secret conspiracies. They were gradualists, using the heady rhetoric of revolution, but postponing it until a more propitious time. Their aim, basically shared by Marx, was to prepare the ground for revolution slowly, through education and propaganda.

Revolutionary generalities were obfuscated by the imprecise terminology then used to express them. The words "socialism" and "communism," popularized by the utopian writings of Fourier and Saint-Simon, had no sharply defined meaning. The same was true of the term "democracy," which, though not a popular subject among Continental theorists, had a friendly sound to radicals. All these terms were often used interchangeably. Communists not infrequently called themselves socialists, and considered themselves democrats, in the general sense that they believed that government should be by and for the people, instead of being for privileged groups, by aristocrats or monarchs.

Marx and Engels returned to Brussels around August 24, after having spent about six weeks in England. Before they left London, they attended a conference which adopted a proposal made by Engels that an organization be set up in London for the mutual exchange of information about revolutionary activities in other countries. This was the Communist Correspondence Committee.

In Brussels, Marx and Engels, assisted by the Belgian librarian Philippe Gigot, formed the Communist Correspondence Committee. They made it, in essence, a nuclear communist party, aimed to bring about clarification and conformity of ideas among German, French and English communists and socialists.

The Correspondence Committee came to an end as an organization in the summer of 1847, following a decision by the communists in London to reorganize the League of the Just and call the new group *Bund der Kommunisten*, the Communist League. Marx joined the League, and in August 1847, he became president of its Brussels branch, as well as a member of its district committee.

Communist Friends

The number of communists and socialists with whom Marx worked closely, in person or through correspondence, was not large, amounting to perhaps eighteen individuals altogether. With some of them his contact was transient or short-lived, with others it was reasonably friendly and durable, with a few it developed into hostility and prolonged conflict.

Communist friends on visits to Brussels would sometimes stay with the hospitable Marxes, as did the German poets Georg Weerth and Ferdinand Freiligrath. With congenial friends, Marx, ordinarily a harsh intellectual critic, was a boon companion, ready for merriment and conviviality. He played as hard as he worked, when the occasion offered, or when he had money to spend.

The core of Marx's communist circle was made up of Germans. Marx dominated it intellectually and by sheer force of personality. Even the wives were impressed by him. Frau Freiligrath, after she met him in Brussels, called him "a very important and original man." With the possible exception of a couple of typesetters, none of the German communists with whom Marx had a close relationship was a proletarian in the Marxist sense. They were primarily either professional persons or intellectuals of one kind or another. Among them were three physicians and about nine journalists and writers, including two poets. In 1845, their average age was twenty-eight. This was the nucleus of what Marx and Engels hoped would constitute an international proletarian party.

Some of the communists of the Brussels period remained loyal to Marx, and were useful to him later in exile. Freiligrath, a poet with an established reputation who subsequently had a well-paying job in a bank in London, was to help Marx financially, particularly by cashing promissory notes. But their friendship became increasingly strained after 1859–60, at a time when Marx came to be obsessed by a feeling of persecution. Weydemeyer, the Westphalian artillery lieutenant turned communist, continued after his emigration to the United States in 1851 to be a staunch friend and an American "Marxist" until his death fifteen years later.

Next to Engels, perhaps the most loyal and steadfast of Marx's communist friends was Wilhelm Wolff, nicknamed "Lupus," a self-taught agitator and journalist, son of East

German peasants who were practically serfs. A miserable childhood, scarred by hunger and two broken legs, had left bitter memories that turned Wolff into a courageous and determined revolutionist. After escaping from a Prussian prison, where he was incarcerated for violating the press laws, he came to Brussels in the spring of 1846, a seasoned revolutionist of thirty-seven, and thenceforth became a close colleague of Marx and Engels, finally settling, as they did, in England.

"Lupus," who never married, came to look upon the Marx family as if it were his own. When he died in Manchester on May 9, 1864, at the age of fifty-five, he left most of his small estate, including his books and effects, to Marx and his family. It consisted mainly of money that "Lupus" had saved up as a much beloved private tutor. Marx's inheritance from "Lupus" came to £824.14.9,[1] not an insignificant sum for a poor man. However, in Marx's hands it did not last long.

Wilhelm Weitling

Marx's relations with Wilhelm Weitling, the earliest German proletarian theorist, were not happy. Weitling was a special type of communist, with a different background from that of middle-class intellectuals like Marx, Engels or Hess. Born in 1808 in Magdeburg, he was the illegitimate son of a German working woman and a French officer stationed there. He grew up never knowing his father's name, suffering the misery and humiliation of a lower-class, fatherless child. As a boy he was apprenticed to a tailor and as a young man did military service, from which he deserted to become an international revolutionist.

In 1837, he helped found the utopian communist League of the Just and remained its leading spirit for the next seven years. He wrote its theoretical program in a book entitled *Die Menschheit, wie sie ist und wie sie sein sollte* [*Humanity, As It Is and As It Should Be*] (1838). After participating in Auguste Blanqui's abortive uprising in Paris in 1839, Weitling escaped to Switzerland, where he continued his activities. In 1842, he published *Garantien der Harmonie und Freiheit* [*Guarantees of Harmony and Freedom*], in which he combined communism with democracy. He visualized a future

[1] A final account of Wolff's estate, probated at £1,384.17, can be found in Engels' letter to Marx, March 11, 1865.

communist society in which the individual, after performing the minimum obligatory labor necessary for his existence, would be free to pursue his personal inclinations. Individual freedom would thus guarantee social harmony.

On September 22, 1845, in a letter to Marx, Engels and Hess, whom he addressed quaintly as *"Lieben Jungens!"* [Dear Boys], Weitling invited himself to Brussels. He wrote fatuously: "I would like for once to see your women, drink your beer, taste your *Frass* [grub], and smoke your cigars; the rest: it goes without saying." He was treated by Karl and Jenny Marx with generous hospitality.

It was soon clear that Weitling had his own communist theory and was too intractable to fit it into Marx's—or anybody else's. In Marx's view, he had to be demolished. It was a task that Marx carried out with characteristic ruthlessness.

The memorable confrontation between Marx and Weitling occurred on March 30, 1846, in Marx's home at an evening session of the Correspondence Committee. In addition to Marx, Engels and Weitling, half a dozen others were present, five of them communists: Philippe Gigot, Louis Heilberg, Sebastian Seiler, Edgar von Westphalen and Joseph Weydemeyer. The sixth was an outsider, the Russian non-communist Pavel Annenkov, whom Marx had invited as a guest. It is to Annenkov that we owe the detailed report of what took place.[2]

He began with a vivid portrait, the first of its kind, of Marx in action and appearance:

Marx himself was the type of man who is made up of energy, will power and unshakable conviction, a type highly remarkable also in outward appearance. A mane of thick black hair, hairy hands, his coat buttoned crookedly, he nevertheless looked like a man who had the right and the power to command respect, even though his appearance and behavior might seem peculiar enough. His movements were clumsy, but bold and self-assured; his manners defied all the usual social conventions. But they were proud, with a tinge of contempt, and his sharp, metallic voice was remarkably suited to the radical judgments he delivered on men and things.

[2]Annenkov, in *Vyestnik Yevropy*, April 1880, pp. 497-99; German translation "Eine russische Stimme über Karl Marx," in *Die Neue Zeit* (Stuttgart), 1883, pp. 236-41.

He spoke in nothing but imperatives, the words tolerating
no opposition, penetrating everything he said with a
harsh tone that jarred me almost painfully. The tone
expressed his firm conviction of his mission to dominate
men's minds and to prescribe laws for them.

Annenkov concluded:

Before my eyes stood the personification of a democratic
dictator, such as might float before one's mind in a moment of fantasy.

Annenkov, who himself remained silent during the whole
evening's meeting, was surprised at Weitling's outward appearance. He expected a disheveled proletarian fanatic, but
what he saw was a carefully groomed man who looked like a
traveling salesman: "The tailor-agitator Weitling was a handsome, fair-haired young man[3] in a coat of elegant cut, with a
coquettishly trimmed small beard, more like a commercial
traveler than the stern, embittered worker that I had expected
to meet."

Marx dominated the meeting, as he always did. The men
seated themselves around a small green table, Marx at the
narrow end of it, "pencil in hand, his leonine head bent over
a piece of paper." According to Weitling's own account,[4] Sebastian Seiler suggested that the topic of the evening's session
should be: How best to carry on propaganda in Germany.
Marx asked him to elaborate, and when Seiler refused, he angrily did so himself. Marx summarized the problem as follows:

1. A testing of the communist party must be undertaken.
2. This can be achieved by criticizing the incompetent
and separating them from the sources of money.
3. This testing is now the most important thing that can
be done in the interest of communism.
4. Whoever has the power to get the money from the
money-men also has the means to oust the others and
it would be well to do so.

[3] Weitling was then actually thirty-seven years old, Annenkov thirty-
three.
[4] Weitling to Hess, March 31, 1846.

5. "Artisan communism," "philosophical communism,"[5] must be fought, and the feeling that it is all merely a daydream must be ridiculed; word-of-mouth propaganda, secret propaganda, the word propaganda in general, must not be used in the future.
6. The early realization of communism is out of the question; the bourgeoisie must first come to the helm.

Engels, of course, supported Marx. In Annenkov's version, Engels, "tall, straight, elegant in an English way and serious," opened the discussion on the necessity for a firm theoretical program to be carried out by men devoted to the communist cause. Such a program, said Marx's "constant companion and comrade," should enable those who had time or the possibility for theorizing to unite under its banner. Hardly had Engels finished when Marx raised his head and turned directly to Weitling with a harsh question:

"Tell us, Weitling, you who have made so much noise in Germany with your communist preachings, you who have won over so many workers that they thereby lost their work and their bread, on what grounds do you justify your social-revolutionary activities, and on what do you expect to base them in the future?"

A vehement debate ensued, and Weitling began to explain that it was not his aim to create new economic theories, but only to adopt those which, as the experience in France had shown, were most suitable to open the eyes of the workers to their dreadful condition; that the workers had learned not to trust others for the solution of the injustices committed against them; that their hope rested only on themselves and their own democratic and communist organizations. Weitling repeated himself, lost himself in generalities, stumbled in his rhetoric. He was obviously out of his depth and looked worried when he realized, as Annenkov observed, that this was a very different audience from the one that "usually surrounded his work-bench" or read his pamphlets.

Weitling would have gone stumbling on, had not Marx, "his brows in an angry frown," interrupted him with a harsh and sarcastic rejoinder. Marx's speech, according to Annenkov, boiled down to this:

[5]Weitling explained that it was Marx who used these phrases, "not I."

It is simply a fraud to arouse the people without providing them with firm, carefully thought out principles for their actions. The arousing of fantastic hopes, of the kind just heard here, would only end in the downfall of the suffering people, and not in their salvation. In Germany, to appeal to the workers without a strict scientific idea and without a positive doctrine, is like an empty and conscienceless game of propaganda, which on the one hand presupposes an inspired prophet and on the other, only donkeys listening to him with open mouth.

With a violent gesture, Marx then suddenly pointed to Annenkov and said, "Here is a Russian among us. In Russia, Weitling, your kind of role would find a place. Only there could a successful union between a confused prophet and addled followers be actually established and maintained." But in a civilized country like Germany, Marx went on rudely, people without a positive doctrine can achieve nothing, and in fact have hitherto achieved nothing except noise, harmful revolts and the destruction of the very cause to which they were dedicated.

Weitling, his cheeks flushed with anger, took up the offensive. In a voice trembling with excitement, he plunged into vehement speech, the substance of which was summarized by Annenkov:

A person [like Weitling] who has brought together hundreds of men in the name of Justice, Solidarity and Brotherly Love cannot be called empty and pointless. In the face of this attack tonight, he consoled himself with the memory of the hundreds of letters and declarations of gratitude he received from all parts of the Fatherland, and that his modest preparatory labors were perhaps more important for the common cause than the theories and the analytical ivory tower doctrines that are remote from the suffering world and the oppressions of the people.

These last remarks were aimed directly at Marx, who was well aware that, unlike Weitling, he had never been a suffering worker and had never lived as a proletarian. Stung, Marx flew into a great rage. He pounded his fist on the table so violently that it shook and the lamp on it rattled. Then he jumped to his feet and shouted, "Ignorance has never yet helped anybody!" He strode up and down the room in uncontrolled fury, while everybody, including Annenkov, hastily took his leave in embarrassment.

Weitling had no money and no job and did not know where to turn. In his despair, he appealed to Hess for travel money to be able to leave Brussels. The gentle Hess, outraged at Marx's treatment of a fellow-communist writer and revolted by his cruelty, wrote him bluntly on May 20, 1846, "His [Weitling's] mistrust of you two has reached a peak. You two have driven him crazy and now you wonder that he is mad. I do not wish to have anything more to do with this whole affair; it makes me want to vomit. Shit in all dimensions."

Weitling finally raised enough *Reisegeld* [travel money] to go to America that year—"to try out the prophet business there," as Engels put it. He came back to Germany in the revolutionary year 1848, and in 1849 returned to America. In New York, he published a journal, *Die Republik der Arbeiter* [*The Republic of Workers*], and in Iowa some of his followers established a utopian community, *Communia*. Neither had a long life. *Communia* dissolved in 1853 and *Die Republik der Arbeiter* ceased publication in 1855. The influence of Weitling, who died in 1871 at the age of sixty-three, gradually faded away.

The Poverty of Philosophy

After Weitling, Marx turned his fire on Proudhon, whom he had formerly tried to teach Hegelian dialectics in Paris. His assault was a characteristic blend of intellectual brilliance and personal disparagement. Marx seemed incapable of handling the ideas of an adversary solely on their merits; he had to annihilate his opponent altogether.

His criticism of Proudhon was basically justified on the grounds of logic and socialist-communist objectives. Despite his fame, Proudhon was ignorant of economics and, as Marx said, "petty bourgeois" in his outlook and prejudices. But there was a personal animus, too. It had it seeds in the spring of 1846, when Marx invited Proudhon to become a member of the Communist Correspondence Committee.

Proudhon's reply was polite but devastating. He advised Marx not to fall into the same trap as Martin Luther, who, after overthrowing the Catholic system, set up his own "apparatus of excommunication and anathemas." He urged, in the name of humanity, that all opinions be welcomed and freely discussed, and all dogmatism be rejected: "Let us not make ourselves the leaders of a new intolerance." This was a viewpoint that Marx was psychologically incapable of accepting.

Proudhon went on to expound his own idea of social change. He did not believe in revolution: a proper economic and political theory, propagated openly among workers, would lead to a peaceful transformation of property through liberty and equality. Thus, violent revolution, with its bloodshed and extermination, would be avoided. Proudhon, who was proud of his descent from a working-class father and a peasant mother, reminded Marx that, in any case, French workers would not tolerate his kind of revolution. "Our proletarians," he concluded, "have such a great thirst for knowledge that you would receive short shrift from them if you offered them only blood to drink."

It was a stinging rebuke, which Marx was not likely to forgive. Proudhon soon supplied Marx with an opportunity to retaliate when, later that year, he published in Paris a two-volume work, *Système des Contradictions Économiques, ou Philosophie de la Misère* [*System of Economic Contradictions, or Philosophy of Poverty*]. Before its publication, he had informed Marx about it in a long letter, adding, somewhat rashly, *"J'attends votre férule critique"* [I await the lash of your criticism].

Marx received a copy of Proudhon's *Philosophy of Poverty*, as the work came to be known, sometime in December 1846. At the same time, Engels wrote him from Paris that he had made critical extracts from the work, and would be glad to send his manuscript to Marx in Brussels, except that "it is not worth the 15 francs it would cost to mail it." Marx read Proudhon's book in two days, and came to the same conclusion as Engels. He then set about to demolish Proudhon. Between the end of December 1846 and the beginning of April 1847, Marx wrote, in French, his *Misère de la Philosophie* [*The Poverty of Philosophy*]. It was subtitled *Réponse à la Philosophie de la Misère de M. Proudhon* [*Reply to M. Proudhon's Philosophy of Poverty*]. This was the first book that Marx wrote entirely by himself, and not in collaboration with Engels.[6]

The essential content of Marx's formidable polemic against Proudhon was brilliantly summarized by him in a lengthy letter which he wrote, again in French, to his friend Annenkov in Paris.[7] The letter, like *Misère de la Philosophie* itself, shows Marx's sweeping critical sense and his great gift for social-economic generalization. It also contains seeds of Marxist philosophy that he was to develop more fully in later writings.

Marx began his epistolary demolition of the *Philosophy of Poverty* as follows: "I admit to you frankly that I find the book as a whole bad, very bad. You yourself in your letter make fun of the 'bit of German philosophy' which M. Proudhon parades in this shapeless and presumptuous work, but you assume that the economic presentation has been infected by the philosophic poison. . . . M. Proudhon does not give you a false criticism of political economy because he is the possessor of a ridiculous philosophy, but he gives you a ridiculous philosophy because he has not understood the present social conditions in their *engrènement* [concatenation]—to use a word which, like much else, M. Proudhon has borrowed from Fourier."

Why, Marx went on, does Proudhon speak about God, a manifest universal reason, and impersonal forces in history, all of which he cannot explain? Why does he "play with feeble Hegelianism"? Because, Marx explained, in the absence of understanding of man's historical development, it is easy to "invent mystical causes" and to fall back on high-sounding words. He then formulated his own materialist interpretation of history:

What is society, whatever its form may be? The product of men's reciprocal activities. Are men free to choose

[6]*Misère de la Philosophie* came out, in 1847, under the imprint of two different firms: C. G. Vogler (a member of the Communist League) in Brussels, and A. Frank in Paris, in an edition of 1,500 copies. Marx paid for the printing cost, Vogler and Frank serving as his *"agents de vente"* [salesmen]. In 1865, Frank sold his business to the publisher F. Vieweg. By that time, most of the edition had been sold out. In 1868, Marx inquired how many copies were left in Paris and was informed that there were only ninety-two. He then moved to have his son-in-law, Paul Lafargue, acquire them and "sell them among his friends" in Paris. "It would be nice, after all," Marx wrote to Engels on October 15, 1868, "if I could realize a few *Batzen* [pretty pennies]."

[7]December 28, 1846. The letter, when printed, ran into twelve pages.

this or that social form? Not at all. Presuppose a particular state of development of men's faculties, and you will have a corresponding form of commerce and consumption. Presuppose a certain stage of development of production, commerce and consumption, and you will have a corresponding form of social constitution, a corresponding organization of the family, orders or classes, in a word, a civil society.

This, Marx added, "is what M. Proudhon will never understand," because he "confuses ideas with things." Nor does he perceive that social and economic developments are not permanently fixed, but transitory and historical: "M. Proudhon, incapable of following the real movement of history, gives you a phantasmagoria which has the presumption of being a dialectical phantasmagoria. He feels no need to speak of the 17th, 18th, and 19th centuries, for his history takes place in the nebulous milieu of the imagination and rises high above time and place. In a word, it is Hegelian *vieillerie* [rubbish]."

Marx's *The Poverty of Philosophy* was an elaboration of the arguments against Proudhon presented in the letter to Annenkov. Marx could not resist the temptation of introducing his book with a sneer. In his brief Foreword, written on June 15, 1847, he remarks:

M. Proudhon has the misfortune of being singularly misunderstood in Europe. In France, he has the right to be a bad economist, because he passes for a good German philosopher. In Germany, he has the right to be a bad philosopher, because he passes for one of the strongest French economists. We, in our capacity as a German and an economist at the same time, wish to protest against this double error.

The book against Proudhon, Marx wrote some two decades later, "ended our friendship for ever."[8]

The Communist Manifesto

It was at the urging of Engels, then living in Paris, that Marx agreed to attend the second congress of the Communist

[8]Marx to Johann Baptist von Schweitzer, January 24, 1865.

League in London. On November 23/24, 1847, Engels arranged a rendezvous with Marx in Ostend, to discuss plans for the congress before going to London. Engels went on to say that the forthcoming Communist League congress "must be decisive," adding in English the words, which he underlined: *as this time we shall have it all our own way.*

He also urged Marx to give some thought to a statement of the communist creed. "Do reflect on the *Glaubensbekenntnis* [confession of faith]. I believe we would do best to leave out the catechistic form and entitle the thing: Communist *Manifesto*."

Engels himself prepared a catechism consisting of twenty-five questions and answers. As a primer of basic communism, the document is of historic interest. Some of the questions:

1. Q. What is communism?
   A. Communism is the doctrine of the conditions for the liberation of the proletariat.
2. Q. What is the proletariat?
   A. The proletariat is the only social class which derives its livelihood solely from the sale of its labor and not from the profit of capital. . . .
4. Q. How did the proletariat arise?
   A. It arose through the Industrial Revolution. . . .
5. Q. Under what conditions does the proletariat's sale of its labor to the bourgeoisie take place?
   A. Labor is a commodity like any other, and its price is determined by precisely the same laws as any other commodity. . . .

The answer to question 10, "What course of development will this revolution take?"constituted, in effect, a blueprint for a proletarian dictatorship of the kind that was to be established by Lenin, a lifelong student of Marxism, seventy years later. As Engels put it, "democracy would be thoroughly useless" if the proletariat did not use it to attack private property and take immediate measures to secure its own existence. The catechism proposed a twelve-point communist program:

1. Limitation of private property through progressive taxation and heavy inheritance taxes.
2. Gradual expropriation of landed property, manufacturers, railroad magnates, and shipowners . .

3. Confiscation of the property of all emigrants and rebels against the majority of the people.
4. Organization of labor through the employment of the proletarians in the national properties, factories and shops.
5. Equal compulsory labor of all members of society until the completion of the abolition of private property; formation of industrial armies, particularly for agriculture.
6. Centralization of the credit system and banking in the hands of the state through a national bank, and elimination of all private banks and bankers.
7. Augmentation of the national factories, shops, railroads and ships, and improvement of agricultural lands.
8. Raising all children in national institutions, at public expense.
9. Construction of great palaces on national properties for public housing.
10. Demolition of all unhealthy and badly built housing and city slums.
11. Equal right of inheritance for legitimate and illegitimate children.
12. Concentration of all means of transportation in the hands of the nation.

On November 27, Marx, traveling in the company of the Belgian communist Victor Tedesco, took the train to Ostend to meet Engels. He went as the delegate of the Belgian *Association Démocratique,* a communist organization which he had helped found and of which he had become vice president two weeks earlier.

Marx left his family in a wretched condition. The children were sick. Jenny, eight months pregnant, was also ailing. The household was, as usual, hounded by creditors. The 150 francs which, on November 15, Marx received as a loan from his Maastricht brother-in-law, Wilhelm Robert Schmalhausen, did not stretch far. He had exhausted his other credit resources. In London, his concern about his distressed family was so great that on December 9 he beseeched his Russian friend Annenkov, then living in Paris, to send 100 or 200 francs to Jenny in Brussels.

Financial worries and family illness did not dampen Marx's enthusiasm for the revolutionary cause. In London, among his fellow-radicals, he pursued the goal of revolution with his customary vigor, participating in the meetings, which were held at night, and giving talks. He lectured before the German Educational Association, which met in a hall on Great Windmill Street; and when the Chartists, on November 29, organized a meeting in commemoration of the Polish insurrection of 1830, Marx, along with Engels and the Chartist leaders George Julian Harney and Ernest Jones, was one of the speakers. In his brief speech, echoes of which were soon to be found in the *Communist Manifesto*, Marx spoke of the conflict between bourgeois and proletarian, and assigned the leading role of liberators of mankind to the English proletariat:

> Of all countries, England is the one where the conflict between proletariat and bourgeoisie is most developed. Hence the victory of the English proletarians over the English bourgeoisie is decisive for the victory of all the oppressed over their oppressors. Hence Poland is not to be freed in Poland, but in England. You Chartists therefore do not have to express pious wishes for the liberation of nations. Defeat your own internal enemies and you will have the proud awareness of having defeated the entire old social system.[9]

It was advice that the English proletariat, which had never heard of Marxist theory, did not heed, then or later.

At the Communist League congress, Marx and Engels, in contrast to so many of their logomachic, windy fellow communists, knew precisely what they wanted. They were energetic and single-minded in the pursuit of their objectives in a congress which, for ten days, argued vehemently about principles and ideas. In the end, the congress, of which Karl Schapper was president and Engels secretary, adopted new statutes, providing for an organization consisting of Communities, Circles, Guiding Circles, a Central Committee, and a Congress. In Article 1, the objective of the Communist League was stated to be ". . . the overthrow of the bourgeoisie, the rule of the proletariat, the annihilation of the old bourgeois society based on class contradictions, and the es-

---

[9]Text in *Deutsche-Brüsseler-Zeitung*, December 9, 1847; English translation in Saul K. Padover, ed., *Karl Marx on Revolution* (New York, 1971), pp. 35-36. A slightly different and abbreviated version appeared in the Chartist weekly *The Northern Star*, December 4, 1847.

tablishment of a new society without classes and without private property."

The old motto, "All Men Are Brethren," was replaced by a new one:

"Proletarians of All Countries, Unite!"

On the same day that the new statutes were adopted, December 8, 1847, the League authorized Marx to draft a "detailed theoretical and practical party program," to serve as a manifesto of the communist party.

On December 17, 1847, about four days after Marx returned from London, Jenny gave birth to their third child. It was a boy they named Edgar, after her younger brother, Edgar von Westphalen. The baby looked like his father and was not pretty like his little sisters. As Jenny said with loving irony: "An Adonis the boy will never be." Marx adored his little son.

After her delivery, Jenny served as Marx's copyist and secretary, a task that she was to perform lovingly and happily for many years to come. The writing of the *Manifesto* did not progress rapidly, probably because Marx kept on consulting Engels, who had gone back to Paris from London. There is no evidence to indicate that the Communist League had included Engels in its authorization to draft a manifesto. Marx, nevertheless, brought him in as his literary partner, and history has since regarded both men as its authors. Judged by style and historic sweep, the primary writing was probably by Marx, but the ideas were shared by both. Marx, for example, incorporated in its entirety the twelve-point communist program (reduced in the *Manifesto* to ten points) which Engels had listed in his catechism. But the key concept of class struggle and the role of the proletariat was Marx's own, according to Engels.

Four main strains are interwoven in the *Manifesto*—prophetic, historic, moral and revolutionary. It opened with the prophetic assertion: "A specter is haunting Europe—the specter of communism." Next came a sweeping historic declaration: "The history of all hitherto existing society is the history of class struggles." This was a statement of such dubious validity that Engels himself, in his brief preface to the German edition of 1883, suggested that it really meant all history "since the dissolution of the primeval communal land ownership." Throughout the *Manifesto* there are expressions of indignation at injustices committed against the exploited. Finally, it concluded with the ringing revolutionary proclamation:

> The proletarians have nothing to lose but their chains. They have a world to win.
> Proletarians[10] of all countries, unite!

The *Manifesto* introduced a new and baneful note into the revolutionary movement—the idea of conflict and hate. Up to that time, socialists had tended to be humanists and utopians, emphasizing the brotherhood of man, rather than the solidarity of class. But in the *Manifesto,* Marx stressed struggle, violence and class. He viewed men not as brothers, but as constant enemies who fight for power, and not for humane ideals. He also declared war on Europe's assorted forms of socialism. The concept of class conflict was designed to separate socialists, who believed in humanitarianism and democracy, from communists, who were now armed with a new historic revelation of their presumably inevitable victory through class war. In the *Manifesto,* Marx supplied communists with a battle rationale against the civilized world.

Marx completed the *Manifesto* at the end of January 1848, and sent it to London. There the text, in German, was printed in the office of the *Bildungs-Gesellschaft für Arbeiter* (46 Liverpool Street), as a twenty-one-page brochure, in a first edition of 500 copies. There were no authors' names. The title page read: *Manifest der Kommunistischen Partei. Veröffentlicht im Februar* 1848. *Proletarier aller Länder vereinigt Euch![11]* It was not until 1850, when George Julian Harney published the first English translation of the *Manifesto* (by Helen MacFarlane) in his weekly *The Red Republican* (Nos. 21–24), that Marx and Engels were mentioned as its authors. In printing the *Manifesto,* in abbreviated form, Harney stated in a marginal note that it was "the most revolutionary document ever given to the world."

Although the *Manifesto* appeared in the same month that the 1848 European revolutions broke out, it had no influence on the revolts which were then spreading on the Continent. There were Danish, Flemish, French, Italian, Polish and

---

[10]Contrary to English translations, which use the word "Workingmen," Marx himself wrote *"Proletarier"* [Proletarians].

[11]Manifesto of the Communist Party. Published in February 1848. Proletarians of all countries, unite!

Swedish translations in 1848, but their impact was not noticeable. The *Manifesto* made its way inexorably during the following decades. A Russian and a new French translation came out in 1869. An abbreviated edition, "Manifesto of the German Communist Party," was published in *Woodhull & Claflin's Weekly* (December 30, 1871) in New York City. Since then, there have been countless translations and editions.

The worldwide influence of Marx's masterpiece of revolutionary propaganda has been incalculable. In 1888, five years after Marx's death, Engels wrote in the preface to the "Authorized English Translation" of the *Manifesto* that it was "presently beyond doubt the most widespread, most international work in the entire socialist literature, a common program which is acknowledged by millions from Siberia to California."

—————— XIV ——————
The Year of Revolution

Expulsion from Brussels

The "mad and holy year" of revolution opened in Paris, the capital of European revolutions, on February 22, 1848, when demonstrating students and workers set up barricades against the bourgeois government of Louis Philippe and his conservative Minister, François Guizot. Two days later, on February 24, Louis Philippe abdicated, and that evening a provisional republic was proclaimed—the second in French history. The new republican government was dominated by the poet Alphonse de Lamartine, on the right, and supported by the socialist Louis Blanc, on the left. The uneasy Republic was not destined to live long. In June it was swept away in a bloody insurrection, which was suppressed by General Louis Cavaignac, who became a temporary military dictator, and was replaced in December by Louis Napoleon, nephew of Napoleon I, as president. Two years later, in 1852, through a coup d'état, Louis Napoleon made himself emperor-dictator under the title of Napoleon III.

"The February revolution," wrote Marx,[1] "was the *beautiful* revolution, the revolution of general sympathies. . . . The June revolution is the *ugly* revolution, the repulsive revolution." The beautiful revolution of February 1848 triggered uprisings in other European capitals. In Brussels, the news from Paris was hailed with tremendous excitement by the radicals. Marx, who avidly read all the newspapers he could lay his hands on, shared in the excitement, convinced that the events in France knelled the doom of the bourgeoisie and heralded a new order of society. He, together with Engels, who had been expelled from Paris in January, moved the *Association Démocratique* to petition the Brussels City Council

—————————————————————
[1]"The June Revolution," in *Neue Rheinische Zeitung*, June 29, 1848.

to arm the workers. The cry now rang: *"Aux armes, citoy-ens!"*

The German workers in Brussels began to arm. With the 6,000 francs Marx had received from his father's estate, they acquired "daggers, revolvers, etc.," according to his wife. This subversive action by a foreigner, who had, moreover, pledged himself not to meddle in Belgian politics, naturally interested the Brussels police. They asked the Procurator in Trier about the origin of the money, and were informed that Marx's mother was rich enough to afford such a sum.

The Belgian authorities moved promptly against both the indigenous and foreign revolutionists. King Leopold, a son-in-law of Louis Philippe, brought in troops, declared martial law, broke up workers' meetings, and jailed the leaders. Thirty-four Belgian and five German radicals were imprisoned in the Brussels jail, Petits Carmes. According to Marx, his friend and colleague Wilhelm Wolff (Lupus) was savagely beaten. On March 1, Wolff and the other foreign radicals were handed passes of expulsion from Belgium.

Marx's turn came next. On the afternoon of March 3, the central committee of the Communist League met in Marx's home and authorized him to set up headquarters in Paris. Early that evening, he received a police order to leave Belgium within twenty-four hours. Later in the night, while he was making preparations to leave, a police commissioner and ten gendarmes broke into his residence, ransacked it, and arrested him on the pretext that he had no proper papers.

In her "terrible anxiety," Jenny Marx rushed to see Lucien Leopold Jottrand, a radical Belgian lawyer who was president of the *Association Démocratique,* asking for help. When she returned home, she found, at the front door, a police agent who told her that if she wanted to see her husband she should follow him to the Police Préfecture. There, instead of her husband, she found a commissioner, who treated her rudely. When Philippe Charles Gigot, the Belgian communist who had come with her, protested on her behalf, he was arrested. Then, under pretext of vagrancy, she was led off to jail in the Hôtel de Ville and locked up in a cell with derelicts and prostitutes.

At 11 o'clock in the morning, she was escorted by gendarmes to the office of an examining magistrate for interrogation. She was questioned for two hours. After spending eighteen hours in jail, Jenny was released in the evening, and went back "to my three poor little children." Marx came home from prison a little later. Their twenty-four-hour time limit was up, and they had to leave Brussels without delay.

The Marxes were not unhappy to depart from Brussels, after three years of exile there. In the heady winter and spring days of 1848, the place for a revolutionist to be was not a provincial capital like Brussels, but Paris, the great city that was once more seething with political intoxication.

Even before his arrest, Marx had taken steps to return to Paris, appealing to the new French government to annul Louis Philippe's expulsion order of 1845. On or about March 1, Ferdinand Flocon, a member of the provisional government who was also the editor of *La Réforme*, sent Marx an invitation to return, couched in the grandiloquent French rhetoric of contemporary romantics:

Brave and loyal Marx.
The soil of the French Republic is a field of asylum for all the friends of liberty.
Tyranny had exiled you. Free France opens its gates to you and to all those who fight for the sacred cause, the fraternal cause of all the peoples.
Every agent of the government ought to interpret his mission in this sense.
Salutation and fraternity.

Marx and his wife packed in a hurry. They sold a few things, but left their chests, which contained Jenny's silver and the better linen, with a friendly bookdealer named Vogler. On March 4, they took the train, which was crowded with soldiers, to France. Belgian police accompanied them to the French border. "It was a very cold, gloomy day . . ." Jenny recalled. "We had great trouble keeping the little children, of whom the youngest was one year old, warm."

Paris Again

The trip to Paris through northern France was not smooth. Not only was the train crowded, but there were delays as a result of the recent violence. At Valenciennes, the tracks were torn up, necessitating a half hour's detour by omnibus. Nearer Paris, at Pontoise, locomotives and cars lay smashed on twisted tracks. At St. Denis, the station was burned out. Despite these obstacles, the Marx family arrived on March 5 and put up in a hotel. Their mailing address, however, was care of Madame Gsell, 75 Boulevard Beaumarchais.

The Marxes visited old friends, including the Georg Herweghs, whom they found changed—or perhaps they themselves had changed in the three years of their absence from Paris.

Marx went to see his old friend Heinrich Heine, but no meaningful communication with the sick poet was now possible. Heine, however, retained his wit. As Marx entered, two nurses were taking him to bed, and Heine greeted the visitor in a feeble voice: "You see, dear Marx, the ladies are still carrying me in their arms."

In Paris, the signs of recent revolution were everywhere: chopped-down trees, piled-up flagstones for barricades, smashed windows, and demolished omnibuses. At the Palais Royal, all the windows were broken and the guardhouse burned. The tricolor waved over the Tuileries, where Marx's friend, the journalist Jacques Imbert, was now governor. In the Louvre, there was a Workers' Parliament under the presidency of Louis Blanc, the socialist author of *Organisation du Travail* (1839), who, on February 26, had set up National Workshops to provide work for the unemployed. On the streets, which showed red flags of revolution, one could hear not only the stirring *Marseillaise* but also the old Girondist song:

> *Mourir pour la patrie*
> *C'est le sort le plus beau*
> *Le plus digne d'envie.*[2]

For the Germans living in Paris, the news from the *Vaterland* was particularly thrilling. The hitherto passive Germanic lands were in the throes of protest and rebellion. Formerly stolid and obedient Germans were suddenly acting like effervescent Frenchmen, as Marx had predicted that they would. The delighted Engels reported to Marx on March 18, just before he left Brussels for Paris: "In Germany things go truly well, uprisings everywhere."

There were uprisings and demonstrations in the various German states, from Baden to East Prussia. In the cities,

[2]To die for the fatherland—
This is the finest fate,
The most worthy of envy.

workers struck for higher wages, and in the countryside—in Prussia, Mecklenburg, Saxony, Thuringia—aroused peasant organizations demanded land and a reduction in taxes.

For Marx and the German refugees in Paris, the most important news came from Berlin, for it was the capital of the most powerful German state. If a revolution could succeed it would mean that the German feudal autocracies were really crumbling. Throughout the month of March 1848, Berlin was the scene of demonstrations, revolts and barricades, hitherto unheard of in tightly ruled, orderly Prussia. For the moment, both the hungry workers and the well-to-do bourgeois liberals seemed united in their protests against the Hohenzollern autocracy. King Friedrich Wilhelm IV was so shaken by the revolutionary events in his capital that he granted the demands for the withdrawal of the Prussian army from Berlin, the establishment of an armed citizens' National Guard, freedom of the press, and the convocation cf a *Landtag* [Diet]. Marx, in Paris, was reminded of Louis XVI and France in 1789.

The Prussian King was also frightened into appointing a middle-class Ministry. In place of the Junkers who had traditionally ruled Prussia, he named two bourgeois from Cologne—the banker Ludolf Camphausen and the industrialist David Justus Hansemann—as Prime Minister and Finance Minister respectively.

Their regime, like the democratic upsurge in general, was not destined to last. The workers had no real power, the middle class no governmental experience, and the German people no political maturity. They were no match for a tenacious and resourceful Prussian monarchy, backed by tough and disciplined military Junkers. Within a few months, to Marx's rage, the King recovered his nerve, put down revolutionary activities, and drove the Diet out of Berlin at bayonet point. The same thing happened to Germany's first united Parliament, which opened in Frankfurt in May 1848, and which, after a year of futility and ineptness described by Marx as "parliamentary cretinism," was ignominiously chased out of existence by Prussian and other royalist troops.

In Paris, where the immigrants, Belgians, Italians, Poles, were forming military legions to fight for freedom in their homelands, the Germans, too, caught the fever. Before Marx's arrival in Paris, at a large meeting of the German Democratic Club, consisting of artisans, workers and middle-class socialists and presided over by Georg Herwegh, it had

been enthusiastically decided to organize a German Legion
for battle in the *Vaterland*.

The Legion and their leaders were interested in German
freedom, not in communism. Therefore, as soon as Marx arrived in Paris, he plunged into battle against them. He invited
Engels to return from Brussels and help in the fight against
the nationalists. "The bourgeoisie here," he wrote him on
March 16, "is again horrible, insolent and reactionary, *mais
elle verra* [but it will see]." Other communists arrived from
London: Karl Schapper, a giant of a man, pursuing his lifetime career as a revolutionist, the shoemaker Heinrich Bauer
and the watchmaker Joseph Moll. They broke with the German Democratic Club, organized their own Workers' Club,
and reconstituted the Communist League, with Marx as
president and Schapper as secretary. Communists in Germany were alerted.

Between March 21 and 29, Marx and Engels drafted a
short program for the Communist League to be distributed as
a handbill in Germany. Entitled "Demands of the Communist
Party in Germany,"[3] it contained seventeen points:

1. All of Germany to be a "united, indivisible republic."
2. All Germans over twenty-one to be entitled to vote
   and hold office.
3. The representatives of the people to be paid, so that
   workers too could sit in Parliament.
4. General arming of the people; the armies to work
   and to produce more than the cost of their main-
   tenance.
5. A free administration of justice.
6. All feudal dues on the peasants to be abolished
   "without compensation."
7. Feudal estates, mines, etc., to be transformed into
   national property.
8. Peasant mortgages to be declared state property.
9. Ground rents or tenant dues on leaseholds to be
   paid to the state as taxes.
10. Private banks to be replaced by a state bank, whose
    paper currency is to be legal tender.

[3]Printed in Paris on March 30 and in Cologne on September 10,
1848, it was also published in a few radical German newspapers:
*Berliner Zeitungs-Halle, Mannheimer Abendzeitung, Triev'sche Zeitung,
Deutsche Allgemeine Zeitung*.

11. All means of transportation—railroads, canals, steamers, roads—to be taken over by the state.
12. Civil servants' salaries to be determined by the size and needs of their families.
13. Complete separation of church and state.
14. Limitation of the right of inheritance.
15. Steep progressive taxation, and elimination of consumer taxes.
16. National workshops, with the state guaranteeing all workers their livelihood.
17. Free universal education.

The communist program was not aimed at German nationalists or the middle class, whose interests and outlook it ignored. It was designed to appeal to the "German proletariat, the small bourgeoisie, and the peasantry." If these millions of "exploited and oppressed" would combine, the program stated, they would attain power, which "properly belongs to them as the producers of all wealth." Such a victory could only be achieved through propaganda among the proletariat, and not by a few armed adventurers invading Germany from France.

In the face of the enthusiastic support given to the German Legion by the workers in Paris, Marx took the unpopular position of opposing both its existence and its aims. He attacked such bourgeois leaders as Georg Herwegh and Adalbert von Bornstedt as irresponsible *Lumpen*. He believed that armed intervention by ill-trained and poorly armed German enthusiasts could only lead to their destruction—an opinion which turned out to be correct. When the Legionaires crossed the German frontier, they were routed by disciplined royalist troops.

In Marx's opinion, the time was not ripe for German workers to take action. For the time being, he argued, the place for German revolutionists was not Germany, but Paris, where the outcome of the revolutions in Europe would be decided.

This advise, offensive to German nationalist feelings, was received with a resounding lack of enthusiasm. In an outburst of heated rhetoric, Marx was accused of being a traitor and a coward. Morally and intellectually Marx was a brave man, but, unlike Engels, who was soon to participate in military engagements in Baden, he was averse to physical combat, and was never known to hurl a bomb, tote a musket or fire from behind a barricade.

Marx's position on the German revolution was demonstrably self-defeating. It was clear that he could not remain in Paris while others were active in Germany. His friend Georg Weerth wrote him on March 25, from Cologne, which was then an armed city in rebellion against the monarchy in Berlin, that he had better come home, where he was needed to fight for communism, which had become a "scare word." Weerth informed him that his communist friends—Heinrich Buergers, Dr. Roland Daniels, Dr. Karl Ludwig d'Ester—were thinking of establishing a newspaper, if they could raise the money. The time was ripe: freedom of the press prevailed and the Prussian authorities were intimidated.

Cologne

Despite his theory that the European revolution would be decided in Paris, Marx decided to return to the *Vaterland*. He would go to Cologne, Germany's wealthiest city, to prepare for the publication of a revolutionary newspaper, while his family stayed with Jenny's mother in Trier.

On March 30, the Prefect of Police gave Marx, "*Docteur en Philosophie*," a French passport, valid for one year. A week later, on April 6, Marx, accompanied by Engels and a few other communists, left Paris. They stopped off in Mainz, on the left bank of the Rhine, where they saw evidence of widespread enthusiasm for the apparently successful revolution in France and the spreading one in Germany. The streets of Mainz, which like Trier had once been under French control, resounded with orators, the sidewalks were colorful with the uniforms of the feather-hatted civil guards, the walls were plastered with posters: *Vive la République!* In Trier, Jenny found the same kind of republican enthusiasm—black-red-gold flags, cockades on men's hats, ribbons in schoolgirls' hair and a civil guard in defiance of Prussian troops.

Marx and Engels arrived in Cologne, which was brimful with anti-Prussian and anti-monarchical ferment, on April 11, 1848, and forthwith began to lay plans for their newspaper. On April 13, Marx, having renounced his Prussian citizenship in 1845, made an application to the Cologne Director of Police for citizenship and permission to settle there.

Cologne granted his application to remain, but his citizenship was unresolved. Later that summer, when he was in bitter opposition to the Berlin government, the Rhenish provincial administration declared him a foreigner. Marx protested in vain: "I consider myself, as hitherto, a German citizen."[4] On September 12, Friedrich Christian Hubert von Kühlwetter, Prussian Minister of Interior, rejected his appeal for a restoration of his citizenship. Thus Marx found himself fighting for revolution in Germany not as a citizen, but as a stateless individual, vulnerable to expulsion.

In April, the Central Committee of the Communist League in Cologne sent emissaries to German cities to determine the possibility of establishing a nationwide proletarian party, to be made up of workers and peasants, and to sell shares for the projected *Neue Rheinische Zeitung*. Engels went north to Barmen and Elberfeld; Schapper to Mainz and Wiesbaden; Ernst Dronke, a twenty-six-year-old author and journalist, to Coblenz, Cassel and Frankfurt; Wilhelm Wolff to Berlin and Breslau. Their reports were uniformly discouraging. They found that the communists, meager in numbers, were in disarray, and the workers in general were without the experience, organization or will to play the revolutionary role that Marxian theory assigned to them. And everywhere the middle class, while battling for a free parliamentary system, hated and feared communists and communism.

The obvious impotence of the Communist League caused Marx and Engels to drop it as a political instrument and to concentrate, instead, on influencing the bourgeois revolution through a radical newspaper. They urged communists to join democratic societies and carry on their propaganda among them, from the inside. This tactical change led to a bitter conflict with the Cologne Workers' Association under the leadership of Andreas Gottschalk, a communist physician, and August von Willich, an aristocrat who had been a lieutenant of artillery in the Prussian army. Gottschalk, soon to be jailed for subversion, died in 1849. Willich, after fighting in the Baden revolution, emigrated to the United States in 1852 and during the Civil War became a Union brigadier general.[5]

---

[4] Marx to Police Director Wilhelm Arnold Geiger, August 5, 1848.
[5] On other Germans fighting in the Civil War, see Saul K. Padover, ed., *Karl Marx on America and the Civil War* (New York, 1972).

Neue Rheinische Zeitung

The plans for the *Neue Rheinische Zeitung* called for a funding of 30,000 Taler, to be obtained by selling shares at 50 Taler each. But there were not many takers. Those who had confidence in a radical newspaper had no money, and those who had money had no such confidence. For a workingman, 50 Taler was a considerable sum. Marx and Engels had to fall back on the bourgeoisie, but their sales pitch met with more suspicion than success.

Engels explained to Marx that he had "put the bite" on his crusty father. But, he added sardonically, "my Old Man" would rather "hang on our heads 1,000 cartridge-bullets than 1,000 Taler." Despite his rich contacts and persuasiveness, he was able to dispose of a mere fourteen shares.

By the end of May only 13,000 Taler were raised, about half of that sum coming from unsuspecting bourgeois. Marx added some of his own inheritance money. There seemed to be no possibility of selling any more shares, despite advertisements and wall posters, and Marx and Engels decided to advance the publication of their paper by one month, to issue it on June 1 instead of July 1, as originally planned. The enterprise began in serious financial difficulties, and was to end in near-bankruptcy.

The first issue of the *Neue Rheinische Zeitung,* dated June 1, 1848, appeared on the evening of May 31. It was subtitled *Organ of Democracy,* which it was not, at least not in the accepted Western sense.

It was a newspaper entirely run by communists. The front page of the first issue listed the editorial board: Editor in Chief, Karl Marx; Editors, Heinrich Buergers, Ernst Dronke, Friedrich Engels, Georg Weerth, Ferdinand Wolff and Wilhelm Wolff.

Every one of them had been a member of the Communist League. Each of the editors had his own specialty. Wilhelm Wolff, for example, wrote on agriculture. Georg Weerth, a poet, composed feuilletons and satires. His most notorious piece was the anonymously published "Life and Exploits of the Famous Knight Schnapphahnski [Snatch-Rooster-ski]," a satire on a powerful Prussian Junker General, Prince Felix

Maria von Lichnowski. The Prussian government considered it virtually *lèse majesté*.

Next to Marx himself, Engels was the most important staff member, and the bluntest and roughest political writer on the paper. He wrote the bulk of the editorials, and much else besides. Altogether, he and Marx between them contributed some 227 articles, a number of them in several installments. The *Neue Rheinische Zeitung* also published reports from cities in rebellion: Berlin, Paris, Prague and Vienna.

Marx, the editor in chief, was in charge of everything, including finances. He was the absolute, unquestioned boss of the paper, controlling its policies and dictating its politics. His "dictatorship," according to Engels, was "gladly accepted by us all." With the control of a radical newspaper fully in his hands, Marx showed himself to be arrogant in public, boorish towards opponents and contemptuous of all opinions not his own. He made enemies with practiced ease. Carl Schurz, a nineteen-year-old German revolutionary who later became a Union General and Republican statesman in the United States, met Marx in Cologne at a conference in the summer of 1848, and remembered him in these words: "I have never seen a man whose bearing was so provoking and intolerable. To no opinion, which differed from his, he accorded the honor of even a condescending consideration. Everyone who contradicted him he treated with abject contempt: every argument that he did not like he answered either with biting scorn at the unfathomable ignorance that had prompted it, or with opprobrious aspersions upon the motives of him who had advanced it. I remember most distinctly the cutting disdain with which he pronounced the word bourgeois—that is, as a detestable example of the deepest mental and moral degeneracy—he denounced everyone that dared to oppose his opinion."[6]

Marxian arrogance and intolerance also marked the *Neue Rheinische Zeitung,* which added to its financial woes. Middleclass supporters were soon alienated, particularly after the paper showed its contempt for the Frankfurt National Assembly, on which German democrats pinned their hopes for a parliamentary system and for national unity.

Middle-class subscribers were further antagonized when, in a series of articles, the *Neue Rheinische Zeitung* excoriated the brutality with which General Cavaignac suppressed the

[6]Schurz, *Reminiscences* (New York, 1907-1908).

June 23 uprising in Paris.[7] All this dried up the sources of desperately needed cash and necessitated fund-raising expeditions. One such excursion, undertaken by Marx in August–September 1848, to Vienna and Berlin, raised 1,950 Taler from Polish democrats, most of which went to pay immediate debts, including a 500-Taler installment on the printing machine. The *Neue Rheinische Zeitung,* with its circulation of about 5,000, selling at one silver Groschen and five Pfennigs, continued to be chronically short of money.

Marx conceived the *Neue Rheinische Zeitung* as an instrument for kindling what he hoped would be a real revolution. For this purpose, he used the tactic, which was to be adopted by generations of communists after him, of fomenting suspicions, exposing evil and inciting hatred against the authorities, always in indignant rhetoric. In truth, he often had objective justification for his anger and indignation at the Prussian government and those who, like the Frankfurt Assembly, failed to take effective steps to curb its tyranny.

Until its very end, the paper directed a steady drumfire of criticisms, exposés and sarcasm not only at government policies but also at the assorted democrats and liberals who, both in the Prussian Diet in Berlin and the National Assembly in Frankfurt, were fumbling to transform the prevailing German autocracies into a parliamentary democracy. Their incompetence and an absence of national unity, were indeed monumental, causing the impatient and scornful Marx to heap contempt upon them. It must be said, however, that Marx never really appreciated any parliamentary system.

One of the *Neue Rheinische Zeitung* articles dealt with the arrest of Friedrich Anneke, a Cologne communist, and infuriated the local *Oberprokurator* [Chief Prosecutor] Zweiffel[8] by hinting that one of the arresting gendarmes was drunk: "between six and seven in the morning, six or seven gendarmes entered Anneke's home, immediately manhandled the maid in the entrance hall and sneaked silently up the stairs. Three of them remained in the vestibule, four broke into the bedroom, where Anneke and his pregnant wife were sleeping. Of these four pillars of justice, one was reeling, at this early

[7] *Neue Rheinische Zeitung,* June 26, 28, and 29, 1848; the articles were written by Engels.

[8] Later, in the course of his battles with the Chief Prosecutor, Marx could not resist the temptation of punning on the name *Zweiffel*—the word (with one "f") meaning "doubt" in German.

morning hour already more or less filled with 'spirit,' the
water of true life, the burnt water."[9]

Chief Prosecutor Zweiffel and the gendarmes were duly insulted, and hauled Marx and his publisher, Hermann Korff,
into court for "slander." After two hours of interrogation, the
examining magistrate, the Chief Prosecutor and the Police
Commissioner raided the offices of the *Neue Rheinische Zeitung* and found a manuscript which they mistakenly thought
to be that of the offending article, the authorship of which
Marx refused to divulge. The affair, including police harassment and interrogation, dragged on for weeks.

On July 20, two weeks after the Anneke article, Marx took
up the question of a new censorship law, reported to be pending in Berlin. He attacked it as a repetition of the old "Napoleonic press despotism." His comments on censorship now
differed from those he had written for the old *Rheinische Zeitung* six years earlier, when he had fought for freedom of the
press within the established order and in a liberal bourgeois
framework. Now, in 1848, Marx was a communist, no longer
interested in the potential for freedom within a middle-class
democratic system, but in the overthrow of the whole social
order. This time, his approach was not philosophical or theoretical but bluntly combative:

From the day that the law goes into force, the [Prus-
sian] officials can commit any despotism, any tyranny,
any illegality with impunity; they can coolly flog or order to be flogged, arrest, and hold without a hearing; the
effective control, the press, has been made ineffective.
On the day that the law goes into force, the bureaucracy
can celebrate a feast of joy . . . In fact, what remains
of freedom of the press, when that which *deserves* public
contempt can no longer be exposed to public contempt?[10]

As the revolutionary situation in Berlin and other German
cities was still fluid, the government was not sufficiently sure
of itself to take immediate steps against Marx and his newspaper. That summer Marx helped to organize so-called Democratic Associations in Cologne and in the rest of the

[9]"Arrests," in *Neue Rheinische Zeitung*, July 5, 1848. The words,
"water of . . . life" and "burnt water," are, of course, literal translations of *eau de vie* and *brandy*.
[10]"The Prussian Press Bill," in *Neue Rheinische Zeitung*, July 20,
1848.

Rhineland, for the purpose of carrying on revolutionary agitation among workers and peasants. On September 25, a revolt broke out in Cologne and martial law was declared. The military commandant closed the *Neue Rheinische Zeitung*, as well as the smaller radical journals,[11] for about two weeks. They were permitted to resume publication on October 12.

As the government was steadily gaining the upper hand in the revolutionary struggles, it felt free to start suppressing the channels of hostile opinion. Early in October, the Cologne Prosecutor's office began to move against the editors of the *Neue Rheinische Zeitung*. Warrants were issued for the arrest of Buergers, Dronke, and Engels, who fled the city. In the beginning of November, Marx, accompanied by a friendly crowd, was summoned to court for a renewed interrogation. Later that month, news came from Berlin that the government had suspended all but the conservative newspapers there, had disarmed the people's militia, and had driven out the Prussian Assembly at bayonet point. The humiliated Assembly moved to a hotel and voted unanimously to suspend the payment of taxes. Whereupon Marx issued an Extra: "NO MORE TAXES!!!" It concluded, "Thus from today on, taxes are suspended!!! The payment of taxes is high treason, the denial of taxes the first duty of the citizen!"[12]

Towards the end of November, Marx underwent two more court hearings and was indicted on three counts. They included the "crimes," as he called them sarcastically, of having insulted *Herr Oberprokurator* Zweiffel and the gendarmerie in the Anneke affair; of having satirized the Junkers in the Schnapphahnski piece; and of "incitement to rebellion" in the anti-tax campaign. The indictments were combined into two separate cases, one dealing with "insult" and the other with "rebellion." The trial, set for December 20, was postponed to February 7, 1849.

Marx made a propaganda show out of the jury trial before

[11]*Neue Kölnische Zeitung für Bürger, Bauern und Soldaten* [*New Cologne Gazette for Townsmen, Peasants and Soldiers*], a communist daily published by Friedrich Anneke and Friedrich von Beust; *Zeitung des Arbeiter-Vereins zu Köln* [*Gazette of the Workers Association in Cologne*], a communist daily published by Gottschalk, Moll and Schapper; *Der Wächter am Rhein* [*The Watchman on the Rhine*], a radical daily.
[12]*Neue Rheinische Zeitung*, Extra, November 17, 1848.

the Court of Assizes. He had the courtroom filled with communist supporters. His tactic was not to defend himself, but to attack the prosecution. This he did with open contempt.

The "insult" case came first. After the Prosecutor and the defense attorney had presented their sides, Marx rose and spoke for about an hour. Chief Prosecutor Zweiffel, he pointed out, had built his case on Article 222 of the old Napoleonic *Code Pénal*, which dealt with resistance to authority. The Article referred to *"outrages par paroles"*—offenses by words. Marx argued that *"paroles"* meant spoken words, and did not apply to written or printed ones. As for injury done to the honor and sensibilities of offended officials, he claimed that a man's feelings were a subjective and unmeasurable quantity, and hence not judicable:

> What is honor, what is sensitivity? What is injury in regard to them? This depends entirely on the individual with whom I have to deal, on the level of his education, on his prejudices, on his conceit. There is no other yardstick to measure the *noli me tangere* [touch me not] of the pompous vanity of an official who deems himself to be incomparable.

The Prussian Minister of the Interior asked Franz August Eichmann, Governor of the Rhine Province, to have Marx expelled from Cologne. Fearing trouble from radicals, Eichmann counseled delay, but advised that at the first opportune moment the *Neue Rheinische Zeitung*'s communist editor should be driven out of Prussia altogether. Marx soon presented Berlin with its opportunity. On May 10, 1849, he published a brutal indictment not merely of Prussia's reigning monarch, but of the whole Hohenzollern dynasty. To show his contempt, he did not even deign to refer to the King by name or title, but called him "Herr Hohenzollern." He enumerated the historic examples of the "breaches of faith, the perfidies, the legacy huntings by which this family of corporals" had made itself great.[13] In the course of his almost hysterical denunciation, Marx quoted from Heinrich Heine's poem *Der Wechselbalg* [*The Changeling* or *Monster*]:

[13]"The Deeds of the House of Hohenzollern," in *Neue Rheinische Zeitung*, May 10, 1849; text in Saul K. Padover, ed., *Karl Marx on Revolution* (New York, 1971), pp. 477–81.

A child with a big pumpkin head,
With long mustache and gray pigtail,
With spidery-long but strong little arms,
With a gigantic gizzard, but short entrails,
A monster. . . .[14]

The *Neue Rheinische Zeitung* was nearing the end of its existence. It was practically bankrupt, and the government was moving against it. In the middle of April, Marx undertook a three-week money-raising tour, going as far north as Hamburg and Bremen; the total result was *"nichts"* [nothing]. While he was away, a Cologne official named Moeller drew up an order for Marx's expulsion, on the ground that he was an alien who had abused Prussian hospitality.

The expulsion order, dated May 11, was delivered by the Cologne Police Director, Wilhelm Arnold Geiger, at Marx's home, while he was still absent, five days later. Upon his return, he had just enough time to liquidate the newspaper. He sold the printing press and his own furniture, and borrowed an additional 300 Taler to pay the typesetters, office employees, editorial personnel and paper suppliers. Altogether, the *Neue Rheinische Zeitung* cost him personally about 7,000 Taler. It was the kind of loss a man in his financial position could not afford. He was never to be free of debt until years later when Engels settled an annuity on him.

He prepared the last issue of the now "meager" *Neue Rheinische Zeitung* while he was in hiding. It appeared on May 19, 1849, and was printed in red ink. In the words of Jenny Marx, the "red number" was a "real firebrand in form and content." The front page, directly below the title, carried a poem, "Word of Farewell of the *Neue Rheinische Zeitung*," by Ferdinand Freiligrath, which contained five romantic-revolutionary verses, the last of which read:

When the last Crown shatters like glass
In battle's lightnings and flames,
When the people utter their final "Guilty!,"
We will again stand together in line,

[14]*Ein Kind mit grossen Kürbiskopf,*
  Mit Langem [sic] Schnurrbart, greisem Zopf,
  Mit spinnig langen, doch starken Ärmchen,
  Mit Riesenmagen, doch kurzen Gedärmchen,
  Ein Wechselbalg. . . .

With word, with sword, on the Danube, on the Rhine. . . .[15]

Marx's own last editorial flung furious defiance at his enemies and hurled a promise of future revenge:

We are ruthless, we ask no consideration from you. When our turn comes, we will not conceal our terrorism. But the *royal terrorists,* the terrorists by the Grace-and-Law of God, are brutal, contemptible and vulgar in practice, cowardly, covert and deceitful in theory, and *dishonorable* in both.

Marx and his family departed from Cologne around May 19 or 20. Once more they were penniless refugees. Jenny redeemed her last pieces of family silver from the pawnshop in Brussels and sold the furniture before it could be distrained. Marx's personal library, consisting of some 400 titles, including Greek and Roman classics, German poetry and French novels, was left with his communist friend, Dr. Roland Daniels. He did not get his collection back until about a dozen years later,[16] and then a number of valuable books were missing.[17]

The Marxes went to Frankfurt, where they stayed with the Weydemeyers. Jenny pawned the silver, which went in and out of pawnshops for many years to come. "Weydemeyer and his wife," she wrote later, "again gave us hospitality and were very helpful to me in my dealings with the pawnbroker." She needed the money to pay the fare to Trier, whither she, Lenchen and the three children went, via Bingen, "to see my old home town and my dear mother." She was now, indeed, as she had wryly called herself in the previous year, a *"Vagabundin."*

Marx, joined by Engels, tried to persuade the Leftists in the Frankfurt Assembly to head an armed revolt in southwest

[15]*Wenn die letzte Krone wie Glas zerbricht,*
In des Kampfes Wettern und Flammen,
Wenn das Volk sein letztes "Schuldig!" spricht,
Dann stehen wir wider zusammen!
Mit dem Wort, mit dem Schwert, an der Donau, am Rhein. . . .
[16]Marx to Engels, December 12, 1860: "My library has arrived. Still in the Custom House, since the Commissioners have not yet decided whether I should receive the books duty free."
[17]Marx to Engels, February 27, 1861.

Germany. They encountered total indifference. They went on a tour, urging the same course of revolutionary action on a few radicals in Mannheim, Ludwigshafen, Karlsruhe and other southwestern German cities, but met with the same response as in Frankfurt. By the end of May, the two young Germans in search of a revolution—Marx was thirty-one, Engels twenty-nine—were arrested by Hessian soldiers in Bingen, brought to Darmstadt, and then to Frankfurt, where they were released. It was the end of the line for Marx's career as an active revolutionist.

Early in June, he and Engels separated. Engels, the more athletic and military of the two, went to Kaiserslautern, the temporary capital of Baden, to join the forces of its threatened provisional government, commanded by August von Willich. He participated in a few skirmishes. After the Badeners were routed by the disciplined Prussian and other royalist forces in July, Engels managed to escape to Switzerland and then make his way to London. His military experience was to win him among his friends, including the Marx family, the affectionate sobriquet of *"Der General"* [The General]. He was German enough to love it.

Paris Interlude and Exile

Marx went to Paris, city of chronic revolutions, home of irrepressible radicals. Hiding from the French police, he found lodgings on the Left Bank, 45 rue de Lille, where he lived under the pseudonym "Ramboz." He made contact with German communists, among them Dronke, Ewerbeck and Seiler. Conversation and observation convinced him that the French capital was a "revolutionary crater" and on the verge of a new outbreak. Always the optimist, he wrote to Engels in Baden that in a few days he expected to have *"several* revolutionary journals at my disposal." It was a pipe dream. A brief uprising did take place in the middle of June, but it was easily suppressed.

Paris was then experiencing not a revolution, but a different kind of agony—a cholera epidemic. The horror was underlined by the long lines of hearses rushing to the cemeteries to dispose of the infected bodies as quickly as possible. Marx seemed to be unaffected; he remained, in the words of his wife, "confident and cheerful."

It was Jenny who suffered. She was staying with her

mother in Trier, but found her unpleasantly changed. Lone-
liness and poverty had brought out qualities of unexpected
hardness and selfishness in old Frau von Westphalen. Trier itself became unbearable. Jenny thought the town to be the
"pettiest, most wretched nest, full of ridiculous local deifica-
tion." Her heart was filled with "sorrow and melancholy," aggravated by longing and concern for her "dear husband" in
plague-stricken Paris.

On July 7, Jenny with her three children and Lenchen
came to Paris, all of them crowding into the lodgings on 45
rue de Lille. Jenny was again with child.

The Marx family was penniless and, as always, prone to
illness. Sometimes all of them were sick at the same time. As
usual, Marx had recourse to the pawnshop, but that was not
an inexhaustible resource. Once again, he made an appeal to
his friends in Germany, Freiligrath, Daniels and Lassalle, to
help out. On July 13 he wrote desperately to Weydemeyer in
Frankfurt, "I tell you that if I do not get help from some-
where, I am *perdu* since my family is here with me and my
wife's last piece of jewelry has already wandered off to the
pawnshop."

Friends in Germany came to the rescue. Lassalle in-
discreetly instituted a public collection among his Rhineland
friends. He raised some 200 Taler, amounting to 430 francs,
which Marx received at the end of July. But the news of the
public collection infuriated him "inexpressibly." He protested
to Lassalle and wrote to Freiligrath on July 31: "To me the
greatest financial embarrassment is preferable to public beg-
gary."

In the meantime, the Paris police had caught up with
Marx. On July 19, a police agent came to the house, asked
for *"Marx et sa dame,"* and handed him an order of banishment to Morbihan in Brittany. It was reputed to be an
unhealthful region, and Marx was convinced that the order
was a deliberate attempt by the French government to kill
him. When the news reached Freiligrath in Cologne, he advised Marx on July 29 to seek refuge in England.

The execution of the order of banishment was delayed,
pending an appeal by Marx. The postponement lasted about
five days, during which time, he wrote, "the sword of Damo-
cles still hangs over my head."[18] The appeal was hopeless, and
Marx decided that if he was to avoid being exiled to Mor-

[18]Marx to Weydemeyer, August 1, 1849.

bihan, he would have to leave Paris. On August 23, he wrote
to Engels, who was then in Lausanne, "I am exiled to the
Morbihan Department, in the Pontine Marshes of Brittany.
You understand that I am not enthusiastic about this cloaked
attempt at murder. Hence I leave France."

There was no country open to Marx on the Continent.
Even Switzerland was impossible, since he had no passport
for it. Moreover, he was convinced that Switzerland would
soon be hermetically sealed and the refugees there would be
caught like mice in a trap. The only possibility was London,
where, he informed Engels, he had "*positive* prospects" of
founding a German journal, with a portion of the necessary
funds already "assured." On August 23 he urged Engels to
join him there: "I absolutely count on it that you will not
leave me in the lurch."

On August 24, Marx left Paris for London. Engels, after a
five-week ocean voyage from Genoa, joined him there on
November 10.

They thought that their stay in the British capital would be
short. In their view, the defeats of the uprisings in Europe
were merely temporary interruptions in the inexorable tide of
revolution. They were soon to be disillusioned. The economic
prosperity that followed the violence of 1848–1849 produced
not revolution, but stability. There was to be no revolution in
Europe (except for the short-lived Paris Commune in 1871)
for the rest of the 19th century.

Marx was to spend the remaining thirty-four years of his
life in London, a totally uprooted man, profoundly alienated
from the institutions of the country that provided him with a
secure refuge. Except for one brief instance when he wanted
a passport, he never even bothered to apply for British citizenship.

XV

London

Lodgings in Misery

Marx came to London without money, without prospects and without a knowledge of the language of the country. Having no lodgings of his own, he stayed with Karl Blind, a twenty-three-year-old German refugee journalist, at Peterson's Coffeehouse, Grosvenor Square. He was "frightfully tired" and within a week of his arrival, he caught a "kind of cholera." Aggravating his distress was worry about Jenny and the children, whom he had left behind in Paris, where she was under police orders to leave the country: "I am now truly in a difficult position," Marx wrote on September 5, 1849, to Freiligrath, who had sent Jenny 100 francs to pay pressing debts. "My wife is highly pregnant, she must leave Paris on the 15th, and I don't know where to turn to raise the necessary money for fare and for lodgings here."

Jenny, more than seven months pregnant, arrived in London on September 17. The day was foggy and bleak. She came, as she wrote later, "sick and exhausted with my three poor persecuted little children." At the steamer on the Thames, she was received not by her husband, who was sick, but by Georg Weerth, the young poet who had been one of the editors of the *Neue Rheinische Zeitung*. Weerth took the frightened and miserable Marx family to a boardinghouse on Leicester Square, where they obtained a single furnished room. For several days the Marxes huddled in this wretched chamber. Then they moved to 4 Anderson Street, Chelsea, to quarters a little larger but no less dingy. "The next two years," Jenny recalled later, "were for us a time of the greatest hardship, of continual acute anxiety, great privations of all kinds, and actual need."

On November 5, seven weeks after her arrival in London, Jenny gave birth to her fourth child, a boy. It was Guy

Fawkes Day, when Londoners were celebrating the suppression of the Gunpowder Plot of 1605 with fireworks and assorted merriments. The boy was named Edmund Heinrich Guy, Heinrich after Marx's father, and Guy after Fawkes, the "great conspirator," as Jenny called him. The baby, the first of several English-born Marx children, was registered in Somerset House as Henry Edward Guy Marx. But the family, with its penchant for nicknames, called the child Guido or Föxchen, "Little Fox."

In their first winter in London the Marx family—two adults and four children—lived in a single sleazy room. As foreigners, they were exploited and constantly threatened with eviction. The rent they paid was exorbitant, amounting to 250 Taler for the winter. Marx soon exhausted what small funds he had, and the family was thrown out of the room. This first eviction was a particularly brutal experience. Jenny tells how she was sitting one day feeding Föxchen from her bleeding breast, when the landlady suddenly burst in and demanded the £5 that was due. As Marx did not have the money, she took steps to evict the family. In her letter to Weydemeyer Jenny related:

> Two bailiffs came into the house, requisitioned all my little possessions, beds, linens, clothing, everything, including the cradle of my poor child, the better toys of the girls, who watched with hot tears in their eyes. In two hours, they threatened to take away everything—I lay down on the naked floor with the freezing children, with my sore breast.

The neighborhood apothecary, baker, butcher and milkman appeared with their bills and demanded payment. Jenny sold the beds to pay them. The beds were brought out to the sidewalk to be carted away. Despite the cold and the rain, two or three hundred people, "the whole Chelsea mob," as Jenny put it, assembled near the door to gape. By that time, however, it was after sunset, when, according to English law, evictions were forbidden. Two constables were on the scene. Despite the protesting landlord, the beds were taken back to the room until after sunrise, when the buyer picked them up.

Marx scoured the polyglot Chelsea area for new lodgings. A seedy and untidy foreigner, speaking broken English, did not look like a desirable tenant, even in that neighborhood. In addition, as Jenny wrote, "nobody wanted to take us, when he mentioned four children." They finally moved into a hotel for German refugees on Leicester Street, near Leicester Square. Here, too, the rent was inordinate. For one room with a small toilet they paid £5 10s. a week, more, as Jenny remarked bitterly, than the rent for "the biggest house in Germany." They had to pay by the week, and heaven help them if they were a day late. They were soon forced out. "One morning," Jenny wrote, "our worthy host refused to serve us breakfast." They moved to No. 64 Dean Street, Soho, where they occupied two tiny rooms in the home of a Jewish lace dealer.

In this squalid apartment the Marx family lived for six years. Their living conditions were not quite as bad as those of London's indigenous poor, which were among the worst in the Western world and which Marx was to castigate in *Capital*, but they were horrifying enough.

In Soho, the Marx family struck its first English roots. Here the children learned to speak English, which they preferred to German. Here Karl and Jenny became familiar with the mores of the country, which, but for the lack of money, had their agreeable side. London was then, as now, Europe's biggest city. As the center of capitalism and world empire, it was a lusty metropolis, bursting with vitality and enterprise. While it did not have the beauty and grace of Paris, it had great compensations, among them political freedom and stability. The police went unarmed: this was *unglaublich* to a German refugee. There was no censorship, and though the always suspicious Marx occasionally thought that his letters were being tampered with, this was not true as a rule. The police left him and the other foreigners unmolested, so long as they minded their own business and did not violate the law. Marx was not spied upon, except by foreign agents, mainly Prussian. In London, he was free to write what he pleased and to carry on communist agitation, intrigues and squabbles, which, however, were confined primarily to Germans and other foreigners.

The free air of London attracted numerous European refugees, particularly since the defeats of the 1848–49 revolutions had made the Continent inhospitable to radicals. For many of them, London was a stopover on the way to the United States or a temporary residence, while they waited for the opportunity to return to their homeland, as was the case with the French. For others, like Marx, it became a permanent residence. In the 1850s and 1860s, there were many visitors who supplied the refugee circles with zest and gossip. Among the foreigners whom Marx knew, or who visited him, were young German radicals like Ferdinand Lassalle and Wilhelm Liebknecht, the Russian Michael Bakunin, the Frenchman Louis Blanc and the Italian Giuseppe Mazzini.

London had other amenities. There were little coffee houses, where foreigners could meet their compatriots, exchange gossip, and hate each other, a not unpleasant occupation for uprooted people. There were also sporadic and generally short-lived foreign-language publications, including a humorous German weekly, in which editors and writers could snipe at their opponents.

On a higher level, London had fine parks, cultural events, concerts and theaters. Despite their indigence and frequent illnesses, the Marx family came to love the city and made it a habit to take long walks with friends—often singing while marching—in Hyde Park and Green Park when the weather was good. They also attended free public lectures and went to the theater, which Jenny in particular loved, whenever they had a few pence to buy the cheapest seats in the balcony.

In the end, despite their years of desolation and bereavements, the Marx family did not want to live anywhere but in England. The three surviving Marx daughters, brought up in English schools, also loved the country and its great literature. Eleanor, the youngest, became a part-time Shakespearean actress.

Soho had certain advantages for Marx. It was close to the center of London, near Oxford Street, Piccadilly, the Strand, Trafalgar Square and Westminster. It was also only a few minutes' walk from the British Museum, of special importance to Marx, who got into the habit of spending there whatever time he could spare from his household obligations and activities among the refugee communists, doing research in economics and, as of 1852, in politics for the numerous articles which he contributed to the *New-York Daily Tribune* and a few German-language newspapers on the Continent. Marx did his writing at night, when the children were asleep.

Another advantage of living in Soho was its familiar and friendly cosmopolitanism. The neighborhood teemed with foreigners, Frenchmen, Germans, Italians, Poles, Russians and Jews who were refugees from Russian pogroms. Here it was no shame to be poor. Everybody was poor. Above all, the tradesmen were in the habit of extending credit to impecunious foreigners.

A graphic description of Marx and his family in their Dean Street home is found in a report, which remained in the Berlin secret archives until 1921, by a Prussian police spy who visited there sometime in 1853. The spy, clearly a man of intelligence, went to Dean Street to acquaint himself with the leader of the German communists in London. Except for his reference to Heine, the spy's information was surprisingly accurate. He wrote:

> The chief of the party is Karl Marx; the deputy chiefs are Friedrich Engels in Manchester, Freiligrath and Wolff (called Lupus) in London, Heine in Paris, Weydemeyer and Cluss in America,[1] Buergers and Daniels in Cologne, Weerth in Hamburg. Except for these, all the rest are simple members. The creative and active spirit, the real soul of the party, however, is Marx; therefore I want to acquaint you with his personality.

The spy was as impressed by Marx's dynamic personality as Moses Hess had been in Cologne a dozen years earlier:

> Marx is of medium height, 34 years old; despite his relative youth, his hair is already turning gray; his figure is powerful; his features remind one of Szemere,[2] but his complexion is darker, his hair and beard, which he does not shave at all, very black. His large, piercing fiery eyes have something uncannily demonic about them. At first glance one sees in him a man of genius and energy; his intellectual superiority exerts irresistible power on his surroundings.

But in his personal habits, the spy reported, Marx was an unwashed bohemian revolutionist, a stranger to soap and to regular hours:

> In private life he is a highly disorderly, cynical person, a poor host; he leads a gypsy existence. Washing, grooming, and changing underwear are rarities with him; he gets drunk readily. Often he loafs all day long, but if he

[1] Weydemeyer was then a journalist in New York and Cluss worked for the Navy Department in Washington.
[2] Bertalan (Bartholomaeus) Szemere (1812–1869), a friend of Marx, was briefly the head of the Hungarian revolutionary government in 1849.

has work to do, he works day and night tirelessly. He does not have a fixed time for sleeping and staying up; very often he stays up all night, and at noon he lies down on the sofa fully dressed and sleeps until evening, unconcerned about the comings and goings around him.

The spy added that Jenny, "an educated, pleasant lady," had become accustomed to their gypsy life and "feels quite at home in this misery." He obviously did not see Jenny in one of her despairing moods. As for the three Marx children, they "are very good looking and have the intelligent eyes of their father." As husband and father, Marx, despite his wild character, "is the most tender and docile of men." The spy then went on to give a vivid description of the Marx domicile:

Marx lives in one of the worst, and thus cheapest, quarters in London. He lives in two rooms, the one with a view on the street is the living room, the one in the back is the bedroom. In the whole lodging not a single piece of good furniture is to be found; everything is broken, ragged and tattered; everything is covered with finger-thick dust; everywhere the greatest disorder. In the middle of the living room there is a big old table covered with oilcloth. On it lie manuscripts, books, newspapers, the childrens' toys, the scraps of his wife's sewing, tea cups with broken rims, dirty spoons, knives, forks, candlesticks, inkwell, drinking glasses, Dutch clay pipes, tobacco ashes—in a word, everything piled up helter-skelter on the same table.

Marx was an inveterate smoker, accustomed, since his student days, to staying up all night consuming tobacco while working, so that the room was simply fogged in. In later years he was to say that his income from *Capital* did not pay for the cigars he smoked while writing it. The smoke from coal, mixed with the fumes from tobacco, produced an opacity that made things almost invisible. The spy wrote:

When one enters Marx's room, the eyes get so dimmed by coal smoke and tobacco fumes that for the first moments one gropes as if in a cave until one gets gradually accustomed to the fumes and begins to distinguish objects as if in a fog. Everything is dirty, everything full of dust, sitting down becomes a truly dangerous business.

Here stands a chair with only three legs, there the children play and prepare food on another chair which happens to be still whole. The visitor is invited to sit down, but the children's chair has not been cleaned up, and one risks a pair of pants. But all this causes no embarrassment to Marx and his wife. One is received in the friendliest manner, is offered pipes, tobacco and whatever, with cordiality. Eventually a pleasant intellectual conversation makes amends for the household deficiencies, making the discomfort tolerable.

The spy concluded that once accustomed to the milieu, a person finds Marx's conversation so interesting and original that he longs for more. "This," he concluded, "is a faithful picture of the family life of the communist chief Marx."

Neue Rheinische Zeitung
Politisch-1 Ökonomische Revue

Marx's two early efforts at propagating communist ideas in London turned out to be failures. Upon his arrival, he tried to reorganize the Communist League, but intrigues and squabbles among communist refugees led him to dissolve the organization, as he announced to Engels on November 19, 1852.

Another enterprise was in the field of journalism. While still in Paris, Marx had begun negotiations for a new publication, a "political-economic monthly," as he wrote on August 1, 1849, to Engels, who had taken refuge in Switzerland.

Marx had grandiose plans. The new publication was to be called the *Neue Rheinische Zeitung*, with the addition of *Politisch-Ökonomische Revue* in the title. The *Revue* was to come out first as a monthly, then as a fortnightly, subsequently as a weekly and finally as a daily. Marx envisaged a publishing enterprise that would serve the "*propaganda* interests" of the German refugee communists, of whom there were many in London as well as in New York. For this he needed seed money which, he thought, could be raised only in America. He expected to raise 150 Taler to send Konrad Schramm, the business manager of the new *Revue*, to New York, where half-baked German refugee revolutionists were already biting "into the golden apple."[3]

[3]Marx to Ferdinand Freiligrath, January 10, 1850.

Little came of Marx's publishing dream. Engels joined him in London on November 10, 1849. By the middle of December, plans for the *Revue* were far enough advanced to make possible an agreement with Schubert & Co., a Hamburg music and book publisher, to print the journal. Another German publisher, F.E. Eisen'sche Buch-und-Kunsthandlung, of Cologne, offered to distribute the *Revue,* which sold for 10 Groschen, at a 50% discount.

But Marx could not raise the necessary funds and the journal did not appeal to many readers. There were no regular dates of publication. The first issue of the *Revue,* in an edition of 2,500 copies was dated January 1850, but came out on March 6. The other issues were also unsynchronized. The second one, dated February, appeared at the end of March. The third, dated May, was published on April 17. The fourth, dated March–April, was printed on May 19. The last issue was a double one; dated May–October, it was published on November 29.

The *Revue* was exclusively the product of Marx and Engels. A few of the articles were by Marx, many, perhaps most, by Engels. Some were collaborative. All were unsigned.

One of the consequences of the *Revue* fiasco was to convince Engels that he could not make a living as a journalist in London. Nor could he help the destitute Marx family. In mid-November 1850, a year after he had arrived in the British capital and in the same month that the *Revue* expired, Engels finally swallowed his pride and his hatred of "huckstering" and went to Manchester, where he entered his father's textile firm, Ermen and Engels, in a junior capacity. In 1852, his father made him business manager of the office, paying him £100 annually, together with 5% of the profits in the first four years, 7½% in the next four, and 10% thereafter. Fortunately for the Marx family, Engels was as talented in business as he was in everything else. In 1864, after he had inherited his father's share of the Manchester business, worth £10,000, he became a partner of the firm.

But during the first years in England, Engels earned too little in his father's business to be of substantial help. In the 1850s Engels could send Marx only driblets of money, which he occasionally had to take out of the till as an advance on his own salary. Sometimes he could do nothing more than guarantee Marx's loans or sign promissory notes, at usurious interest rates. But no matter how small the sum was, Engels never failed to respond to Marx's cry for help. During the day Engels was, in effect, a gentleman-merchant and at night a dedicated communist. He also had expensive tastes in imported wines and fine cigars and other amenities of a gentleman in the Victorian age. The upkeep of Engels' horse in a private stable cost more per month than Marx generally earned in any four-week period. Even so, over a period of two decades the total amount of cash that Engels sent Marx from Manchester may have amounted to about £4,000, averaging around £200 a year.

The Bitter Fruits of Poverty

Indigence, undernourishment, perpetual worry and constant harassment by creditors took their toll in the Marx household. Marx himself erupted in frequent rages—against individuals, creditors, money lenders, the bourgeois world and, on a less conscious level, against himself. He fell prey to a succession of illnesses, a number of which—liver ailments, lung congestion, and skin eruptions in the form of excruciatingly painful carbuncles—became chronic. His physical afflictions, curiously reminiscent of Job, often made it impossible for him to do any kind of work for weeks and months at a time.

Jenny was particularly affected by their poverty. As her pride was ground down, her health and nerves were affected. Indigence also took its toll on the children and resulted, Jenny was convinced, in the death of at least three of them.

The first bereavement occurred within a year of Jenny's arrival in London. On November 19, 1850, little Guido-Föxchen, suffering from pneumonia, suddenly ceased to breathe. It was a horrifying experience for the family.

Jenny, then in the sixth month of a new pregnancy, collapsed from shock and grief. Marx described it to Engels on November 23 as "a really dangerous state of agitation and exhaustion." It was the first child Jenny had lost, and the experience was devastating emotionally and psychologically. She moaned that the child was a "victim of bourgeois misery." Her bitterness over the loss of Guido persisted for years. She later wrote to a friend, when referring to Marx's enemies and detractors among the London refugees: "Who among them cared when I was deadly ill, when my child, who drank from my breast the torment and sorrow and cares, died therefrom . . . ?"[4]

The doctor did not help in her prostration. To take her away from the wretched lodgings which reminded her cruelly of her dead baby, Marx rented another little sleazy apartment, at number 28 on the same street, where they moved in December 1850. It consisted of two small rooms, including a tiny washroom and sink with running water.

Despite Jenny's sufferings, Marx apparently continued to believe in the traditional masculine prerogatives, regardless of the health of the woman involved. In a letter to Engels written on February 3, 1851, he referred to himself as a "strong-loined paterfamilias," adding ironically in French, *"mon mariage est plus productif que mon industrie* [my marriage is more productive than my work]."

On March 28, 1851, three months after the Marx family moved to 28 Dean Street, Jenny, then past her thirty–seventh birthday, gave birth to her fifth child, Franziska. Marx wrote to Engels on April 2, that he was disappointed that his wife "alas, was delivered of a girl, and not a *garçon*." But he had already sired a *garçon* when he lived at 64 Dean Street. When Franziska was born, Lenchen Demuth was six months pregnant by Marx. Her illegitimate son, officially registered as Henry Frederick Demuth ("Freddy"), was born on June 23.

Jenny, physically prostrated and in a state of near-hysteria, did not know that her husband was the father of Lenchen's baby. As the result of an understanding reached between Marx and Engels, Jenny and the rest of the family assumed that Engels, a gay bachelor, was the father, and the secret was preserved, apparently intact, to the end of Jenny's life.

The Marx household was in chaos. There was "literally not a farthing" in the house. Jenny suffered from "hysterical outbreaks," wailing and complaining. Marx did not blame her. He realized that she had good reason for her lamentations and rages, but it made life hellish, and he could not still his own furies.

At home [he wrote to Engels on July 31] where everything is always in a state of siege, the outbreaks of tears annoy and make me furious night after night, I cannot of course do much work. I am sorry for my wife. The

---

[4]Jenny Marx to Adolf Cluss, October 15, 1852.

main burden falls on her, and *au fond* she is right. *Il faut que l'industrie soit plus productive que le mariage* [work should be more productive than marriage]. Despite all this, you will recall that I am by nature *très peu endurant* [very impatient] and even *quelque peu dur* [a little hard], so that from time to time I lose my equanimity.

Marx feared that if the "gloomy" situation, with its "unending worries" and paltry struggles for existence, continued, "it will be the end of my wife."

On Easter 1852, Franziska died after three days of severe bronchitis. Like Guido, she was just a little over one year old at the time of her death. "When she died," Jenny wrote later, "we left her lifeless body in the back room, went into the front room and made our beds on the floor. Our three living children lay down by us and we all wept for the little angel whose livid lifeless body was in the next room."

A special horror connected with Franziska's death was that undertakers did not extend credit, and Marx did not have a penny for the burial. Interment was delayed, in the vain hope that financial help would arrive. Finally, on the day when the burial had to take place, Jenny hurried over to the home of a friendly French refugee and desperately begged for help. The kindly Frenchman gave her £2 for a coffin, or, as Marx put it, "to pay the English death-dogs." He was shaken by the whole experience. "Even though I have a tough skin," he wrote to Engels on April 28, "this time the whole shit has affected me deeply." Jenny's comment on the fate of Franziska had greater poignancy: "She had no cradle when she came into the world, and for a long time was denied a last resting place."

But a greater shock was still to come. In the winter of 1855, when Marx was suffering a persistent eye inflammation and enduring a "disgusting cough," his surviving son, seven-year-old Edgar, began to ail seriously. Edgar, whose nickname was "Colonel Musch," or simply, "Musch," was the darling of the household, pampered by the women and adored by his father. He was a chubby boy, full of mischief and jollity. The doting family treasured anecdotes about him.

By the middle of March 1855, Musch's illness seemed to be hopeless. He was suffering from tuberculosis of the bowels, a disease which Marx said was hereditary in his family. Jenny could not attend to her son, for she had recently given birth to another daughter—Eleanor, who came to be known as Tussy—and was sick herself. Marx, despite his own illness, stayed up with Musch night after night, nursing him tenderly. He came close to a breakdown. "My heart bleeds," he wrote to Engels on March 30, "and my head burns, although I must of course remain calm." On April 6, 1855, Musch died. Marx informed Engels in a brief note, written the same day: "Poor Musch is no more. He fell asleep (literally) in my arms between 5 and 6 o'clock."

Musch was the third Marx child to die. Jenny was prostrate. Marx was shattered. He developed a violent headache which deprived him of all power of thought, sight and hearing. Benumbed, he rode to the cemetery in silence, holding his head in his hands in mute desolation.

The death of Musch plunged the Marx household into prolonged despair and hopelessness. "The house," Marx wrote Engels a week later, "is desolated and deserted since the death of the dear child, whose animated soul he was. It is indescribable how we miss the child. I have experienced all kinds of bad luck, but only now do I understand what real misfortune is. I feel myself *broken down*."[5]

Marx's hair turned white from grief. Even philosophy failed to console him. Almost four months after the death of Musch, on July 28, he wrote to Lassalle:

Bacon says that really important people have so many relationships to nature and the world, so many objects of interest, that they easily get over any loss. I do not belong to these important people. The death of my child has deeply shattered my heart and brain, and I feel the loss as freshly as on the first day.

Jenny, too, continued to be, as Marx put it in English, completely "downbroken." To get away from the grieving, tragic atmosphere of the house, the Marx family moved to Camberwell, near London, to a cottage lent to them by Peter Imandt, a German communist refugee. In the middle of September, they went to stay with Engels in Manchester, where they remained until December.

Marx never got over the loss of his son. The shock was so

---

[5]Marx wrote the words "broken down" in English.

great that even the Soho neighborhood itself continued to upset him. Eight years after Musch's death, on February 13, 1863, he wrote to Engels, "the vicinity of Soho Square still frightens me whenever I accidentally come near it."

XVI
New-York Daily Tribune

The First Years

Marx's connection with the *New-York Daily Tribune* was one of the crucial events in his life. For one thing, it provided him with a platform from which he could express himself freely within the limitations of the factual requirements of journalism. American newspapers, unlike those he was accustomed to in Germany, were not subject to government harassment and censorship. For another, the *Tribune* correspondenceship kept him going financially in the decade 1851–61 during which he was the London correspondent. It was also a period when Engels could provide Marx with only limited financial assistance. When the correspondenceship ceased, so did Marx's sole means of more or less steady income.

The *New-York Daily Tribune* was then, in Marx's words, "the foremost English-language American newspaper." With a circulation of about 200,000, and selling for two pennies, it was also the largest and probably the most influential newspaper not only in New York City but also in the United States. The *Tribune*'s appeal was to educated people, and it provided its readers with substantial and serious reporting, both domestic and foreign. Its founder-publisher, Horace Greeley, was, in the time of Marx's correspondenceship, a powerful moral force for enlightened social ideas in the United States.[1] He was assisted by an able, liberal staff, notably the Transcen-

---

[1] "Greeley's own radical views were expressed fearlessly in his paper. He was an egalitarian, despising and fearing monopoly of any kind and class dominance; he espoused Fourierism and the agrarian movement; he supported cooperative shops and labor unions, opposed capital punishment, urged restrictions on liquor-selling." "Horace Greeley," in *Concise Dictionary of American Biography* (New York, 1964), p. 366.

dentalists George Ripley and Charles Anderson Dana, both of whom had spent years at Brook Farm. Dana was Greeley's second in command until 1862, when he resigned, founding the *New York Sun* six years later. Marx was proud to be associated with so eminent a newspaper, particularly one that generally advocated radical ideas.

Marx and Dana had met in Cologne in November 1848, when Marx, as editor of the *Neue Rheinische Zeitung*, was an important newspaperman. Dana, only one year younger than Marx, was then reporting to the *Tribune* on the various revolutions taking place in Europe, mainly in Austria, France and Germany. Dana's writing at the time shows that he shared Marx's pro-revolutionary sympathies.

In August 1851, Marx received a letter from Dana inviting him to write for the *Tribune*. The invitation came, miraculously, at a time when Marx was in such financial straits that he felt nearly suicidal.

Dana's invitation to Marx was both smart journalism and good business. For the failure of the 1848–49 European revolutions resulted in a flood of immigrants to the United States. Large numbers of them came from Germany. Between 1852 and 1854, for example, about half a million Germans landed in New York City. Obviously the immigrants retained an interest in the Old World, and the circulation of the *Tribune*, catering to this new readership, began to soar.

Marx eagerly welcomed the opportunity to be a *Tribune* correspondent, but the trouble was that he could not write in English. As usual when in difficulties, he turned to Engels for help. "If it were possible for you," he wrote him on August 8, 1851, "to supply an article in English on German conditions . . ., it would be a splendid beginning." Engels, a gifted linguist whose knowledge of the English language was impeccable, replied that he was ready to help his friend in need, but that he required further details. "Write me soon in what form it is to be—whether you want one suitable article or a series of them, and secondly, how the material is to be handled, for I know nothing whatever about the politics of the *New-York Tribune* except that it is American Whig." Marx replied on August 14, "Write a series of articles on Germany, from 1848 on. Clever and unceremonious. The gentlemen [of the *Tribune*] are *impudent* in the foreign [affairs] department."

Engels complied. For a whole year he wrote articles on Germany—there were nineteen altogether—and sent them to Marx, who in turn dispatched them, twice weekly (Tuesdays and Fridays), under his own name. They appeared in the *Tribune* between October 25, 1851, and October 23, 1852. The articles were later published in book form by Marx's daughter Eleanor in 1896,[2] under the title *Revolution and Counter-Revolution in Germany in 1848*. Eleanor mistakenly believed that her father was the author. It was not until 1913 that Engels' authorship became known.

Marx's own contribution to the *Tribune* did not begin until August 1852, one year after he received Dana's invitation. Even then he wrote his articles in German, sent them to Engels for translation, and then forwarded them to New York. Marx's own first article, which Engels divided for him into two parts—"The Elections in England: Tories and Whigs," and "The Chartists"—came out in the *Tribune* on August 21 and 25, 1852, respectively.

Marx made his first effort at English writing six months later. "Yesterday," he informed Engels on January 29, 1853, "for the first time, I risked writing an article for Dana in English. . . . If I could now obtain a decent grammar and stoutly plunge into the writing, it would go passably well." The *Tribune* featured the article, under the mixed title "Capital Punishment—Mr. Cobden's Pamphlets—Regulations of the Bank of England," on February 18, 1853.

Soon Marx's written English improved to such an extent that on June 1, 1853, Engels was moved to compliment him. "Your English," he wrote him, "is not only good, it is brilliant. Here and there a few catchwords are not woven in fluently enough, but this is the worst that can be said."

Flattered, Marx replied the next day: "The praise you bestow on my 'young' English has had a heartening effect on me. What I mainly lack is, first, grammatical sureness, and, secondly, a knack for certain secondary turnings of phrase, without which any *schlagfertige* [quick-witted] writing is impossible."

For the next decade Marx's style continued to improve. His early articles still showed evidence of ponderous Germanism, but the later ones were terse and muscular. The words

---

[2]A German translation also appeared in 1896, and a French one, by another Marx daughter, Laura Lafargue, in 1900.

were chosen with precision, and the style was frequently eloquent.

As a correspondent Marx had his own established routine. An interpretive journalist rather than an original investigator, he rarely reported from personal observation or interviews. On a few occasions he attended sessions of Parliament, as he did in July 1854, and reported his impressions in at least two articles.[3] It is a pity that he did not do much direct reporting, for he had a sharp eye.

In general, Marx's sources were almost entirely newspapers, of which he was an avid, lifelong reader. He perused both Continental and British newspapers, especially the influential and authoritative *Times* of London, from which he would quote extensively. Buying neswpapers daily was his main financial outlay as a correspondent, and often he could not afford even that. "I did not write the articles for Dana," he informed Engels on September 8, 1852, "because I did not have a penny to read the newpapers."

For economic and social materials Marx depended on the British Museum, where he often worked from ten in the morning to seven in the evening. There he read official reports and publications, making extensive notes of facts and figures which he wove into his articles for the *Tribune*. Many of them were so full of statistical data that they read like official reports themselves.

After assembling his notes and clippings, Marx often worked on his articles—two a week for a long time—until four in the morning, writing them in his cramped Germanic script that no English-language typesetter could possibly read. Jenny generally transcribed them, although Marx also had the occasional help of Wilhelm Pieper, a young German communist refugee who acted as his secretary. On Tuesdays and Fridays the articles were dispatched to New York. If an article missed the departing steamer, Marx would lose half a week's income. The pieces appeared in the *Tribune* on an average about two weeks after they were mailed in London, which was more or less the time it took a steamer to cross the Atlantic.

But the *Tribune* did not always treat Marx's correspon-

---

[3] "The War Debates in Parliament" and "The Austrian Policy—War Debates in the House of Commons," in *New-York Daily Tribune*, August 7 and 9, 1854.

dence scrupulously or considerately. Dana himself was unpredictable and either careless with Marx's contributions or cynical in his use of them. The *Tribune* editors took liberties with the articles, altering the text to suit their purposes, and often not printing them at all. Many of the dispatches were printed anonymously, often under a London dateline, headed: "From Our Own Correspondent." Others were published under trivial headlines, which Marx found offensive to his dignity as a writer. What particularly irked him was the way the *Tribune* exploited his work and made it its own. "Recently," he told Engels on April 22, 1854, "the *Tribune* has again appropriated all my articles as leaders and published only trash under *my* name." In fact, at least eighty-four of Marx's articles—nearly one-fourth of his total contributions—were published as "leaders," that is, as unsigned *Tribune* editorials, for which the author received no credit and little pay. Equally vexatious was the *Tribune*'s habit of accepting many of Marx's articles but failing to print them. On the other hand, in September 1856, the *Tribune* returned to him fifteen articles on Panslavism which did not suit its policies.

The money question was a source of frequent irritation. The *Tribune* paid per piece. If it chose not to print an article, Marx received no pay and thus lost endless hours of work. At first the compensation was £1, or $5, per article. This was not enough to live on, and Marx was desperate. Referring to the "chronic financial pressure" under which he labored at home, and the "loathsome" prospects of its indefinite continuance, he wrote to Engels on March 9, 1854, "From time to time I become wild at the thought that there is no end to the *Dreck* [filth]."

In all, the *Tribune* published at least 321 articles by Marx, about one-fourth of them as unsigned editorials. Another fourteen articles were written in cooperation with Engels, who contributed around 109 articles by himself.

In the eight years between 1853 and 1860, Marx's most creative period, he averaged around thirty-seven articles a year. The figure might conceivably be higher. Louis Lazarus, in the Appendix to H.M. Christman's *The American Journalism of Marx & Engels* (1966), lists twenty additional articles by Marx.

Well over half of Marx's *Tribune* articles dealt with foreign affairs: European countries, Russia, Turkey, the Middle East, the Crimean War, India and China. At least one-third of them centered on Britain, her domestic politics, foreign policy and economy. Some fifty pieces stressed economic subjects, including international trade and monetary affairs. In brief, as a *Tribune* correspondent, Marx was primarily a political, rather than an economic, reporter.

Gradual Loss of Income

Dana agreed to pay £2 per atricle and to buy two a week. Under this arrangement, which lasted about four years, Marx earned £4, or $20, weekly. But this did not mean a regular flow of income. Money orders were not infrequently delayed, and Marx often had to scramble to find somebody in the City with enough cash to take his promissory note on money from the *Tribune* that might or might not arrive in time. Furthermore, there was always the difficulty of cashing foreign money orders or checks. The *New-York Daily Tribune* was not that well known to London moneyed people.

In March 1857, Marx was informed that the *Tribune* would henceforth take only one article a week. This cut his already meager earnings in half. "While I wrote you from the upper floor," Marx informed Engels on December 8, 1857, "downstairs was besieged by hungry wolves." The pregnant Jenny was worried sick; everything that could be pawned was already in hock.

In February 1861, the month during which the seceded Southern American states organized their Confederate Government in Montgomery, Alabama, the *Tribune* suspended all foreign correspondents except Marx. But his retention was all but meaningless. For the next eight months, the *Tribune* printed none of his work, and hence paid nothing. In April, when the American Civil War opened with the bombardment of Fort Sumter and President Lincoln declared a state of "insurrection," Dana quit the *Tribune* in disagreement over its policy of compromise with the South.

In the latter part of 1861, the *Tribune* temporarily resumed printing some of Marx's articles, but only because they were connected with the American struggle. Between

October 11 and December 25, 1861, it published eight of his pieces, dealing with the effect of the Civil War on British commerce and public opinion.

The year 1861, when Marx earned practically nothing from the *Tribune* for eight months, was a particularly desperate one for him and his family. The eight articles the *Tribune* did print in 1861 brought him a total of £16, or $80, for the year. This did not even pay the most pressing debts. In November 1861, with a gift from Engels, Marx paid £18 to the butcher, baker, tea grocer, green grocer, oil man, and milkman; he spent 10 shillings for coal. But he had no money to pay the landlord, to whom he owed a year's rent and who constantly threatened him with eviction, or for school fees for his children, or for the cobbler, or the family's approaching winter needs, including food. He was at least £100 in debt. The situation, he said, was enough to drive a man crazy.

In an attempt to supplement his income, Marx reluctantly accepted an offer from Lassalle's cousin, Max Friedländer, who was publisher of *Die Presse*, Vienna's largest newspaper, to become its London correspondent. *Die Presse* only paid half the rates that the *Tribune* did: £1 per article and 10 shillings per newsletter. Furthermore, it printed only one out of every four articles Marx sent in, so that in one three-month period the *Presse* paid him a total of £6. After about a year as its correspondent, early in December 1862, Marx, disgusted with the "lousy fellows" in Vienna, stopped writing for them.

In 1862, the *Tribune* published only two articles by Marx, "English Public Opinion" on February 1, and "The Mexican Imbroglio" on March 10. The last piece was a sharp criticism of Britain's cynical diplomacy, a subject he had treated in a previous dispatch, in which he warned against the planned intervention of the European powers in Mexico while the United States was in the throes of the Civil War. "The contemplated intervention in Mexico by England, France, and Spain, is, in my opinion, one of the most monstrous enterprises ever chronicled in the annals of international history."[4]

The loss of regular income from the *Tribune* was all but irreplaceable. Debt-ridden and tormented by illnesses—he signed one of his letters to Engels, "Your Hemorrhoidarius"—

---

[4]"The Intervention in Mexico," in *New-York Daily Tribune,* November 23, 1861.

Marx hardly knew where to turn. On August 20, 1862, he wrote to Engels with bitter humor, "*Dear boy* [written in English], no matter what you may say, it is in reality painful to make so much *bother* for you with my miseries. If only I knew how to start some *business!* Gray, dear friend, is all theory, and only *business* is green."[5]

---

[5]Paraphrasing Goethe's *Faust*, Part I, Scene 4.

XVII
Political Economy

Research

In the summer of 1850, Marx began what was to become a systematic research in the field of political economy. He started with a study of the latest economic literature—dealing mainly with banking, prices and crises—utilizing the *Economist,* an invaluable London weekly devoted to economics and politics.[1] He attacked the subject with impatience, hoping to master it within a short time. During his first year of research, the "economic shit," as he called it, was beginning to bore him. He wrote to Engels on April 2, 1851, that "this science has made no further progress since A. Smith and D. Ricardo."

His plan was to gather materials for a German book on economics. In 1851, a Frankfurt publisher, Löwenthal, to whom the book was offered, rejected it. So did other publishers in Germany. Marx then asked his friend Joseph Weydemeyer, who had recently arrived in New York City, to set up a German publishing house there. Weydemeyer replied that the idea was not yet feasible, although a few months later, in the spring of 1852, he started a German-language monthly, *Die Revolution,* which published Marx's brilliant polemic *The Eighteenth Brumaire of Louis Napoleon.* The book on economics had to be postponed for several years.

It was the city of London and its British Museum that provided Marx with the great opportunity to master the field of political economy, a subject that was to occupy him intermittently for the rest of his working life.

The British Museum, with its priceless store of books and government reports, was not only a treasure house for an

---

[1] Its subtitle read: "Weekly Commercial Times, Bankers' Gazette, and Railway Monitor: A Political, Literary, and General Newspaper."

avid reader like Marx but it also served as an escape from
the wretchedness of his apartment. In the Museum's vast and
cathedral-like reading room, he could forget what he called
the "nagging" at home and the petty miseries of his daily existence. The reading room was also comfortable in all seasons.
"It is," Marx wrote to Engels on a hot summer day in 1854,
"the only cool place in London."

He went there as often as his chronic ill health permitted.
Frequently he could not work because hemorrhoids made it
too painful to sit. "The hemorrhoids," he wrote to Engels on
January 24, 1852, "have affected me this time more than the
French Revolution. . . . To go to the Library, the rear conditions do not permit this yet." There were occasions when he
could not go because his suit and overcoat were in hock. But
once in the Museum, he generally put in a ten-hour working
day.

Marx was a superlative researcher. He read everything
available in virtually all European languages and took copi-
ous notes. These were not mere research jottings, but often
short critical essays and acute comments on his readings, as
can be seen in the voluminous *Grundrisse* and in Volume IV
of *Capital (Theories of Surplus Value)*, both published posthumously. Marx's readings ranged through the spectrum of
political economy, including demography, mining, agriculture,
agronomy, credit, banking and finance, rent theory and
economic history. He studied, and excerpted from, not only
major works in English from Babbage[2] to Wakefield[3] and in
French, from Augier[4] to Sismondi,[5] but also in German,[6]

[2]Charles Babbage, *On the Economy of Machinery and Manufactures*
(London, 1832); Marx apparently read it in a French translation, by
E. Biot (Paris, 1833).

[3]Edward Gibbon Wakefield, *An Inquiry into the Nature and Causes
of the Wealth of Nations, by Adam Smith, With Notes from Ricardo,
McCulloch, Chalmers and other Eminent Political Economists* (new
ed. London, 1843).

[4]Marie Augier, *Du Crédit Public et de son histoire depuis les temps
anciens jusqu'à nos jours* (Paris, 1842).

[5]Jean Charles Leonard Simonde de Sismondi, *Études sur l'Économie
Politique* (2 vols., Brussels, 1837–1838); *Nouveaux Principes d'Économie
Politique, ou de la Richesse dans ses Rapports avec la Population* (2
vols., Paris, 1819).

[6]There were not many German economists in that period. In the
Grundrisse, there are frequent mentions of Hegel, who can hardly be
classified as an economist. Among German writers, Marx made extracts
from the following: Gustav von Gülich, *Die gesamten gewerblichen
Zustände in den bedeutendsten Ländern der Erde während der letzten*

Italian,[7] and Greek and Latin.[8] His immense researches also
included American authors, notably Benjamin Franklin on
paper money[9] and Henry Charles Carey on wages, class harmony and slavery.[10] Franklin impressed Marx as an original
thinker, "who formulated the basic law of modern political
economy." Marx considered Carey, with whose ideas he disagreed, "the only important American economist."[11]

In addition to works on political economy, Marx also
deepened his knowledge by reading important historians.
Among them were François Guizot's history of England, Nic-
colò Machiavelli's history of Florence, Barthold Georg Niebuhr's history of ancient Rome, and Augustin Thierry's
history of France. All this "bourgeois literature," as he called
it, reenforced his economic studies and provided him with essential data and insights, particularly in regard to the idea of
class and class struggle, which, he claimed, he did not invent.
"Insofar as I am concerned," he wrote to Weydemeyer on
March 5, 1852, "the merit of having discovered either the existence of classes in modern society or the class struggle does
not belong to me. Bourgeois historians have presented the historic development of this struggle of classes, and bourgeois
economists the economic anatomy of the same, long before
me."

Perhaps Marx's most innovative research was in the official

---

zwölf Jahre (3d vol., Jena, 1835); Karl Dietrich Hüllmann, Stadtwesen
des Mittelalters (Bonn, 1826); Justus von Liebig, Die organische
Chemie in ihrer Anwendung auf Agrikultur und Physiologie (4th ed.,
Brunswick, 1842); Adam Heinrich Müller, Die Elemente der Staatskunst
(2d part, Berlin, 1809); Johann Heinrich Moritz Poppe, Geschichte der
Technologie (Vol. I, Göttingen, 1807); Johann Friedrich Reitemeier,
Geschichte des Bergbaues und Hüttenwesens bey den alten Völkern
(Göttingen, 1785).

[7]Ferdinando Galiani, Della Moneta (Milan, 1803); Geminiano
Montanari, Della Moneta (Milan, 1804).

[8]Among the important classical authors from whom Marx made
excerpts were: Aristotle, Opera; Athenaeus, Deipnosophistae; Lucretius,
De Rerum Natura; Pliny, Histoire Naturelle (French and Latin texts);
Strabo, Rerum Geographicarum; Xenophon, Opuscula Politica.

[9]Franklin, "A modest inquiry into the nature and necessity of a
paper currency," in J. Sparks, ed., The Works of Benjamin Franklin
(Vol. II, Boston, 1836); "Remarks and facts relative to the American
paper money," in ibid.

[10]Carey, Essay on the Rate of Wages (Philadelphia and London,
1835); The Harmony of Interests (Philadelphia, 1851); The Slave Trade,
Domestic and Foreign (London, 1853).

[11]Marx to Joseph Weydemeyer, March 5, 1852.

literature of the British industrial system, namely, the remarkable Reports of the Factory Inspectors. Marx was deeply impressed by the honesty of these officials and their stark, factual accounts of what the factory machines did to their helpless operators, among them women and children. He used the materials from the Factory Reports with devastating effect both in his journalistic articles and, later, in *Capital*.[12] "We read of a young woman," Marx wrote in a newspaper article, "who lost her right arm," of a child that had "the bone in its nose crushed by the machine and lost the sight of both eyes," of a man who had "his left leg sawed off, the right arm broken in three or four places, the head frightfully mutilated," of a youth "whose left arm was torn from its socket, in addition to other injuries," and of another youth "who had both arms torn from their sockets, the abdomen ripped open so that the intestines broke out, both thighs and the head crushed," etc.

The Factory Inspectors' industrial bulletins, Marx commented, are "more horrible than any war bulletins from Crimea."[13]

Trouble with a Publisher

For more than half a dozen years Marx did intermittent research on his book on economics, even though he had no publisher for it. Despite his anxiety to produce a work that, he hoped, would advance the cause of revolution, he could not give it his full time. "The constant newspaper scribbling," he wrote on September 15, 1853, to Adolf Cluss, a communist friend who worked for the Navy Department in Washington, D.C., ". . . takes too much time, scatters my energies, and in the end it is for nothing."

Marx did not begin organizing the materials for his book *Zur Kritik der Politischen Oekonomie* [*Critique of Political Economy*] until the summer of 1857. The writing itself took about half a year, from August 1858, to January 1859. He worked mostly until about 4 o'clock in the morning.

Marx's friend the influential lawyer and political leader Ferdinand Lassalle (whom he generally reviled and ridiculed in private) found him a publisher, Franz Duncker, in Berlin.

[12]See, for example, Chapter VIII (Chapter X in the English edition): "The Working-Day."

[13]"Palmerston—Physiology of Great Britain's Ruling Classes," in *Neue Oder-Zeitung*, July 26, 1855.

Lassalle persuaded Duncker not only to publish Marx's book but also to pay him at a higher rate than was customary. Duncker agreed to pay Marx 3, instead of the usual 2, *Friedrichsdor,* a Prussian gold coin worth about 5½ Taler, per printer's sheet (16 printed pages). The total honorarium was to come to 33 *Friedrichsdor,* of which Marx received more than half—97 Taler and 15 silver groschen—in January 1859. Duncker was soon to regret bitterly ever having anything to do with Marx.

Zur Kritik der Politischen Oekonomie, Marx's first work on economics and his first book in more than a dozen years, was relatively short. A lengthy "Introduction" (about twenty-five pages), written in August–September 1857, was not included in the book but was published posthumously in 1903, in the Marxist monthly *Die Neue Zeit. Zur Kritik,* a hasty and incomplete work, dealt with commodities, theory of value and money. There was, in the latter subject, a bitter irony that did not escape Marx:

> The hapless manuscript [Marx wrote to Engels on January 21, 1859] is ready, but cannot be sent out as I do not have a farthing to mail or insure it. The latter is necessary, since I do not have a copy. . . . I do not believe that any one has ever written about "money" and suffered such a lack of it. Most authors on the subject have been in profound peace with the subject of their researches.

Marx delivered the manuscript to the London Packet Company on January 25; he now began to count the days. The Packet Company informed him that the package got to Berlin on January 30 and reached Duncker two days later, on February 1. The publisher acknowledged receipt almost a week later.

Two months passed and nothing happened. Marx was on tenterhooks, slowly boiling with anger at what he considered Duncker's procrastination. To add fuel to his impatience, Marx received a letter from the United States informing him that "party friends" there expected to order 100 copies of the book and wanted to know the price. Marx, suspecting Duncker of the worst intentions, including outright sabotage, peremptorily demanded that the publisher let him know the price of the book *"by return mail."* Duncker did not reply immediately, perhaps because he was not accustomed to arrogance from authors. The enraged Marx then decided to write the *Lauskerl* [lousy guy] in Berlin a *saugrob* [rude as hell] letter, as he told Engels. On May 28, one week after he had inquired about the price of the book, Marx did, indeed, write his publisher such a letter. It was vintage Marx:

Dear Sir:

You saw fit not to answer the letter I wrote you, asking for the price of my publication. This has made it impossible for me to answer my friends in America, since mail goes there only twice a week.

It took you fourteen days [actually, twelve] to acknowledge the receipt of my manuscript. You informed me then that printing would begin within a week. That one week became more than three weeks. About eight weeks ago, Lassalle wrote me that the thing would be finished in the middle of May. More than three weeks ago I received the last three printer's sheets. The corrections that needed to be made could have been done comfortably in *one* day.

Instead, despite the fact that the printing was *finished*, a complete cessation of activity seems to have taken place during this whole period.

Marx concluded his letter in a peremptory tone:

I hereby declare to you that I am tired of this *systematic and deliberate obstructiveness,* and I hereby demand, and indeed I do so categorically, that you put an end to these maneuvers, which appear to me to be highly suspicious. All my acquaintances in England share this opinion and have urged me to take this last step.

Yours truly,
Dr. Karl Marx.

Duncker replied three days later on May 31 that the "injurious charges of systematic obstructiveness, maneuvers, etc.," did not even remotely enter into the question. The delay, he explained, was due partly to the difficult conditions under which a German publisher had to operate and partly to his being taken up with the Leipzig Book Fair, "with all its sad conditions." He promised to publish the book within a week and to send Marx the rest of the honorarium. As for the retail price of the book, Duncker wrote, "in view of the risk involved in such a heavy scientific work," he could not sell it for less than one Prussian Taler.

Temporarily mollified, Marx apologized. "I am really sorry," he wrote to Duncker, "to have written you a wounding letter." For one thing, he explained, he had been away from Germany too long and had become too accustomed to "London conditions to appreciate properly German business methods." For another, he had been negotiating with a London publisher for an English translation, and the constantly misleading publication-date reports he was receiving from Berlin "sufficed to create in the mind of this John Bull the impression that I was a regular humbug." Duncker promptly replied that the book would appear within a few days, and Marx informed Engels on June 7. "The shit will be published in Berlin this week, I mean *Heft* One."

Three weeks passed, and still no book and no money from Berlin. The London publisher who had been negotiating for the translation lost interest and dropped the project.[14] On June 22, the furious Marx wrote Duncker another peremptory letter, demanding that the final honorarium be sent *"immediately,"* upbraiding him for his "principle that a 'strictly scientific work' cannot appear late enough," and warning him that his kind of delaying tactics could postpone publication "into the year 1860." Unless Duncker acted promptly, Marx threatened, he would make a *"public"* attack on him.

By now, Duncker was fed up. He replied by return mail on June 25 that *Zur Kritik der Politischen Oekonomie* had already come out—on June 11—that three free copies had been sent to London and that another nine copies were held for him in Berlin. Copies had also been sent to America. Duncker enclosed checks for the rest of the honorarium, 90 Taler, and told Marx that he wanted nothing more to do with him in the future.

Thus Marx, who had planned to bring out a second volume of his book, lost the only publisher who had been willing to take a chance on him. For the next several years he was to continue his economic work, which resulted in *Capital*, without a publisher in sight.

---

[14]An English translation, *Critique of Political Economy*, did not come out until 1909, more than a quarter of a century after Marx's death.

Critique of Political Economy

Zur Kritik der Politischen Oekonomie was an incomplete book which Marx viewed as a first installment of a larger work. Its importance lay mostly in the Preface, in which Marx presented the basic Marxist idea of "economic determinism." In essence, he wrote, economic foundations and what he called "relationships of production," rather than the human mind or will, shape social institutions and determine behavior. The real foundation of society was the economic structure, on which "a legal and political superstructure" is erected. The totality of economic relationships, Marx stated, conditions the "general process of social, political and intellectual life."

When economic conditions change, as they are bound to do, so do the relationships and the whole superstructure—legal, political, religious, artistic and philosophic. Then begins the era of social revolution, transforming everything; and men, becoming aware of those changes, fight them out. Thereafter, a new stage of development begins. This process of continuing transformation, Marx wrote, can be studied "with the precision of natural science." Since the anatomy of civil society, including the processes of revolutionary change, were to be found in political economy, said Marx, it was logical for him to seek—and, of course, to find—the truth of his ideas in that all-encompassing science.

Marx claimed that his approach to economics was that of a scientist, and not of an agitator like Weitling or a utopian like Proudhon. Such men, basically ignorant of economics, had made little effort to study, like Marx, either the profound economic theorists or the great political historians. According to Marx, economic conditions and the inevitable changes flowing from them were not constructs invented by him any more than the class struggle. As he visualized his role, he was only a scientist, scrupulously reporting the stark historic forces and realities as they manifested themselves—that is, as nature created them—regardless of the "interested prejudices, of the ruling classes." He, of course, had no prejudices, since he only recorded the findings of "science." At the entrance to science, as at the entrance to hell, Marx wrote at the end of his Preface, the motto must be, in the words of Dante's *Divine Comedy* "*Qui si convien lasciare ogni sos-*

petto/Ogni viltà convien che qui sia morta. [Here all distrust must be abandoned/Here all cowardice must be dead.]"

Marx's "science" was to be used to achieve communism. The first step, he believed, was to demolish the foundations of the prevailing European socialist theories of men like Proudhon and other "false brothers," as he called them; the second, to lay the scientific foundations of communism, that is, "Marxism."

The book was a failure. Duncker printed 1,000 copies, but there was practically no market for them in Germany, and hence no conduit for Marx's ideas in his homeland. Even socialists were disappointed, for they had expected a book propagating socialism and, instead, got a learned dissertation on economic categories. *Zur Kritik der Politischen Oekonomie* did not even enjoy a *succès d' estime*, since Germany's political economists, assuming they knew of the book's existence, did not bother to review it. As Marx put it, "not a single rooster has crowed over the thing." This further rejection by his native country strengthened his tendency to paranoia.

Marx was convinced that there was a plot against him and his book in Germany. His enemies, the "German literary rabble," he wrote, "honored" him with a "conspiracy of silence." His previous books, *The Poverty of Philosophy,* published in French in Brussels, and *The Eighteenth Brumaire of Louis Bonaparte,* published in German in New York City, had also been all but ignored in Germany. The failure of *Zur Kritik der Politischen Oekonomie* caused suffering for the whole Marx family.

Duncker might have been persuaded to bring out the second volume of the book, but Marx was too disheartened to go on with it. Penniless, in debt, threatened by the landlord with imminent eviction, he could not concentrate on his work. Until he had *"gecleart,"* as he wrote to Engels on October 5, 1859, the "worst bourgeois *Dreck,*" he was "absolutely incapable of continuing to write further." He did not, in fact, resume his work for another year and a half, during which time he developed the first of the liver afflictions that were to become acutely chronic and were ultimately one of the causes of his death.

XVIII
Herr Vogt

In the period of intense frustration following the publication of *Zur Kritik der Politischen Oekonomie,* which lasted to the end of the year 1860 and during which he and his wife came down with bouts of serious illnesses, Marx needed a specific target for his rage. This he found in Karl Vogt, a provincial German pedant-politician teaching geography in Geneva, who had published as a supplement to the June 2, 1859, issue of the Biel, Switzerland, daily *Schweizer Handels-Courier* a brochure, "Zur Warnung," containing some passages which Marx considered libelous. Instead of ignoring the obscure Vogt pamphlet, Marx plunged into an all-out attack against it. A pro-Marx German refugee weekly in London, *Das Volk,* opened with a polemic against Vogt on June 11. Then Marx set into operation a frantic and overwrought anti-Vogt campaign, in the course of which he attacked both enemies and friends. He also dragged in prominent acquaintances with requests that they supply him with character testimonials. Among those he asked for such references were Charles A. Dana, his employer on the *New-York Daily Tribune;* Ernest Jones, the Chartist publisher in London; and Joachim Lelewel, the eminent Polish historian whom he had known when they both lived in Brussels.

Marx's friends urged that he restrain himself. Even Engels, usually indulgent, thought it was a waste of time and energy to battle a "Herr Vogt." But Marx was unheeding in his rage. He plunged into the unpredictable and expensive course of legal action, determined to punish those who had the "insolence to print extracts from Vogt's slanderous work," as he wrote to a Hungarian acquaintance, Bartalan Szemere, on March 13, 1860.

Marx threatened to sue *The Daily Telegraph,* a London newspaper owned, as he said, by "polack Jews," which had the temerity to publish the Vogt "shit" against him.[1] After some backing and filling, which included anti-Semitic allusions by Marx, *The Daily Telegraph* offered to make an *amende honorable* and Marx finally dropped the libel suit.

But he did go through with a lawsuit against the *National-Zeitung,* a Berlin daily that had published extracts from the Vogt pamphlet. Lassalle, a brilliant lawyer, advised moderation, but this only infuriated Marx, who, in a letter to Engels written on February 9, 1860, referred to his well-wishing and always helpful friend in Berlin as "shameless," a "beast," a "pompous ape," a "Water-polack Jew." To Engels, who was not enthusiastic about this course of action, but who nevertheless subsidized it financially, Marx defended it, in a letter written on February 3, on grounds that since Vogt sought to present him as "an insignificant, rascally bourgeois scoundrel," the only way to counter it was by a "grand coup" of law in the Prussian capital that was bound, he was convinced, to become a "scandal throughout Germany."

The "grand coup" fizzled. Marx engaged a Berlin lawyer named Weber. To induce Weber to take the case, he wrote him that he himself was the son of a highly respected lawyer, the late Heinrich Marx, who had been the leader of the Trier bar. Marx sent Weber documents, which were inexpensive, and fees, which he could not afford. The retainer was 15 Taler, mailed to Weber on April 24. At the end of July, he sent Weber another 32 Taler and promised more. It was in vain. In October 1860, the *Obertribunal* in Berlin threw out the case, declaring in its final decision that it did not find in the Vogt article "either an objective injury to the honor of the plaintiff" or any intention to injure him.

Marx called the decision of the Berlin tribunal a "Prussian joke."

The libel suit cost him at least £100. The money had come mostly from Engels, who, upon the death of his father in the spring of 1860, became a partner in the Manchester business and could thus afford to help Marx with larger sums.

Marx also pursued Vogt in a book-sized polemic of about 300 pages, entitled *Herr Vogt.* Since no respectable publisher in Germany would touch it, he had it printed by a German

---

[1] Marx to Engels, February 9, 1860.

Left: The house where Marx was born, number 664 Bruckengasse (now number 10 Bruckenstrasse), Trier. Marx was born on May 5, 1818.

Right: 1070 Simeonsgasse (now 8 Simeonstrasse) in Trier, where Karl Marx lived throughout his boyhood from 1820 to 1835. The house was built in 1760. COURTESY INTER-NATIONES, BONN.

Right: Karl Marx in 1861 at the age of forty-three.

Below: The old Jewish cemetery of Trier, closed since 1922 and overlooked by the Nazis. Virtually all of Trier's rabbis since the middle of the 17th century were ancestors of Marx.

Top: Marx's daughters
Jennychen (1844-1883) and
Laura (1845-1911).

Middle: Marx's youngest
daughter, Eleanor (1855-
1898).

Bottom: Marx's son
Edgar or "Musch" (1847-
1855).

Karl Marx: Erster Entwurf z. ...

Opposite: The only surviving page of
Marx's draft of *The Communist Manifesto,*
written in December, 1847.

Above: Marx to his daughter, May 6, 1882:
"I am enclosing a photo for you and
for Fred [Engels]; no art could make a man
look worse." Taken in Algiers the year
before he died.

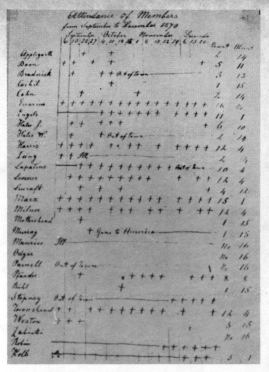

Opposite, top, left: Ferdinand Lassalle (1825-1864), founder of the German Labor Association in 1863, and a friend and enemy of Marx. COURTESY GERMAN INFORMATION CENTER.

Top right: Wilhelm Liegknecht (1826-1900), founder, with August Bebel, of the German Social Democratic party.

Bottom, left: Otto Meissner (1819-1902), publisher of *Das Kapital*.

Bottom, right: Frederick Engels (1820-1895). Portrait taken in London in the 1870s.

Above: Weekly attendance record of the General Council of the First International, September through December, 1870.

Charles-Jean Longuet (right), a Paris sculptor,
great-grandson of Karl Marx, with his wife, Simone,
and their two daughters, Frédérique and Anne,
at Trier in 1968.

book dealer in London,[2] at an initial cost of £25, which he could not, of course, afford.

Herr Vogt, a mixture of documents, quotations and accusations against a whole range of pet enemies, contained paragraphs of exceptional crudeness. A case in point is Marx's attack on Joseph Moses Levy, the publisher of the London *Daily Telegraph,* a more or less innocent bystander in the whole embranglement. The assault on Levy reached depths of vulgarity and anti-Semitism unprecedented even for Marx. Even Levy's "Jewish nose" was not spared:

> All London toilets discharge their physical ordure into the Thames through an ingenious system of underground sewer pipes. In the same way, through a system of goose quills, the world metropolis daily spits all its social ordure into a big paper-made central-sewer—*The Daily Telegraph.* . . . After he [Levy] has transformed the social ordure into newspaper articles, he transforms the newspaper articles into copper, and finally copper into gold. On the gate leading into the paper-made central-sewer are inscribed the words . . .: *"hic.* . . . *quisquam faxit oletum* [here a stink is made]," or, as Byron has translated into fine poetry: "Wanderer, stop and—piss!" . . .
>
> Levy wants to be an Anglo-Saxon. Hence at least once a month he attacks the un-British policies of Disraeli. . . . But of what use is it for Levy to attack Mr. Disraeli, . . . so long as Mother Nature has inscribed, with the wildest black letters, his family tree in the middle of his face. . . . Levy's nose constitutes a year's talk in the City of London. . . . The great art of Levy's nose in reality consists of cozying up to foul odor, to smell it out hundreds of miles away and to bring it forth. Thus Levy's nose serves *The Daily Telegraph* as an elephant snout, insect palp, lighthouse and telegraph. One can therefore say without exaggeration that Levy writes his newspaper with his nose.[3]

Herr Vogt was ignored by the press in Germany, and a French translation "disappeared on the *ukase* of the Imperial All-Highest" in France.[4] Jenny wrote bitterly to a friend in

[2] A. Petsch & Co., 78 Fenchurch St., London, E. C. (December, 1860).
[3] *Herr Vogt,* Ch. X.
[4] Marx to Johann Philipp Becker, February 26, 1862.

the United States that *Herr Vogt* was "being passed over in deathly silence by the cowardly and venal press" in Germany.[5] Marx, panting for attention in his native country, saw there the usual conspiracy against him.

The Vogt affair was not Marx's finest hour. An exercise in futile rage, it sapped his health, wasted his talents and consumed his pitifully meager resources. A year after the publication of *Herr Vogt*, he was sued in the Sheriff's Court in London for an additional £20 to pay the cost of publication.

Throughout the entire Vogt period, Marx did little serious work in economics, although he did publish about two dozen articles in the *New-York Daily Tribune* in 1860. It was only after he had purged himself of some of his bile by writing *Herr Vogt* that he could return to some intermittent economic research. In 1861, he began to work on *Das Kapital*.

[5] Jenny Marx to Louise Weydemeyer, March 11, 1861.

XIX
In Search of Geld

Zalt-Bommel

At the beginning of 1861, Marx's creditors were besieging him, he and his wife were constantly ailing, there was not a farthing in the house, and he did not know where to borrow money in London. As a last resort, he decided to take a trip to the Continent to seek financial support from rich relatives in Holland and political friends in Germany. Otherwise, he felt, he could not survive the winter.

Marx obtained a false passport under the name of Karl Johann Buehring, a German communist carpenter in London, and at the end of February he sailed for Holland on what Jenny called a "marauding expedition." In Zalt-Bommel, Holland, Marx hoped to "lure some dough" out of his rich uncle, the businessman-banker Lion Philips, who was the executor of his mother's estate.

A week after he arrived in Zalt-Bommel, Marx was able to send 60 guilders to his hard-pressed wife in London. Altogether, Marx wrote to Engels on May 7, 1861, he had "squeezed" the not inconsiderable sum of £160 out of his uncle, enough to pay his most pressing debts in London and reestablish his credit for new borrowing.

Following the maxim of La Rochefoucauld that gratitude is the expectation of future favors, Marx expressed his appreciation of his rich uncle even after he left Holland. On May 6, when he had returned to London, he wrote him a letter in which he cast a warm glow not only on the uncle but also on the offspring:[1]

---

[1]Antoinette Philips (*ca.* 1837–1885); August Philips (d. 1895), an Amsterdam lawyer; Friedrich Philips, a Zalt-Bommel banker; Jacques Philips, a Rotterdam lawyer; Jean Philips, an Aachen businessman; and Karl Philips, an Aachen businessman.

You will recall, dear Uncle, how often we used to jest about the fact that nowadays human breeding is inferior to cattle breeding. Now that I have seen your whole family I must declare you to be a *virtuoso in human breeding*. All your children are independent characters, each is individualistic, each possesses special intellectual superiority, and all are marked by a humane culture.

Marx was especially taken with his cousin Antoinette (Nannette) Philips, who was then about twenty-four years old. She was charming and witty and was equipped, as the forty-three-year-old Marx noted, with "dangerous black eyes." He paid unrestrained court to her,[2] and she frankly reciprocated by falling in love with him. Two days after he left Zalt-Bommel, Nannette wrote him, in English, asking him to write her a letter, "for our tranquillity," as soon as possible: ". . . As I am speaking so often of you, the family laughs at my attachment to you, which is not quite of so philosophical a character as yours."

Some of the relatives teased her. "But never mind! Now my dear Pacha! I fear that I have already too much abused of your time and patience, but I can't help for being so fond of speaking to you. Adieu my dear friend, take care to yourself and don't forget your affectionate Nannette."[3]

Marx's own letters to Nannette, were also flirtatious, but, coming from an uxorious husband, more coy. He was apparently as much in love with her as he dared to be. In his letters to Nannette, he addressed her as "My sweet little cousin" and concluded by calling her "My little enchantress." Marx returned to the obscure little Dutch town[4] often in the next four years, staying with the Philipses, who pampered him as a beloved and famous relative, for as long as two months at a time.

---

[2]Marx to Ferdinand Lassalle, May 8, 1861.
[3]Nannette Philips to Marx, May 18, 1861; MS, in the International Institute for Social History, Amsterdam (D 3665).
[4]Marx to Ferdinand Lassalle, March 7, 1861. "Zalt-Bommel is near Nymwegen. I don't belive you know the place. But it made itself noticeable during the recent floods."

Berlin

After enjoying the hospitality of the Philips family for about four weeks, Marx set out for Berlin. He was able to return to the Fatherland, after an absence of a dozen years, because of an amnesty that the Prussian King Wilhelm I had granted political exiles on January 12 of that year, upon the death of his insane brother, Friedrich Wilhelm IV.

In the Prussian capital, where Marx arrived on March 17, he was the guest of Ferdinand Lassalle, from whom he hoped to get financial assistance. Lassalle had a beautiful house on 13 Bellevuestrasse, which Marx called "one of the finest streets in Berlin." A famous lawyer and a powerful political figure in the Prussian capital, Lassalle gave Marx "an extraordinarily friendly welcome."[5] A major reason for this cordiality was the ambitious Lassalle's plan to finance a radical newspaper in Berlin, for which he was ready to raise the relatively large sum of 20,000 Taler.[6] Remembering Marx's fighting editorship of the *Rheinische Zeitung* and *Neue Rheinische Zeitung,* Lassalle wanted him to be the editor of his newspaper.

If Marx was to become an editor in Berlin he required a restoration of his Prussian citizenship, for which he applied on April 10. The Prussian government gave him a passport valid for one year, but it finally turned down his application on the ground that those who had been out of Prussia for ten years had forfeited their right to citizenship. This rejection led Marx to describe the royal amnesty as "pure deceit, fraud and snare."[7]

Marx's negotiations with Lassalle about the editorship, which had begun by correspondence while he was still in London and continued upon his return there, were half-hearted and probably not sincere, although the job was financially tempting. He hated the thought of moving from London, which, he confessed to Lassalle on May 8, had "an extraordinary fascination" for him, even though, he wrote, he lived there "like a hermit in a gigantic nest."

Jenny Marx, above all, was adamantly opposed to the

[5]Marx to Nannette Philips, March 24, 1861.
[6]Jenny Marx to Frederick Engels, early April 1861.
[7]Marx to Nannette Philips, July 17, 1861.

whole idea. She even resented Marx's visit to Lassalle in Berlin and his prolonged stay there. She could not understand, as she complained in a letter to Engels on April 3, why her husband was in "such a hurry to become a royal-Prussian 'subject.'" She would rather, she wrote, remain a *"lose jroschen"* [threepence] in London than be the wife of an editor in Berlin.

Marx tarried with Lassalle in Berlin mainly because he was having a good, relaxed time. Life in the Prussian capital, which Marx called "a metropolis of shakos without heads,"[8] was in itself boring, but Lassalle's high society friends, including generals, made up for it. They lionized Marx. He went to fine dinners, attended gala parties, met the local literati and once even dropped in on a session of the Prussian *Landtag,* which he observed from the press gallery.

Marx was particularly courted by Countess Sophie von Hatzfeldt, Lassalle's client and mistress, a bold and, some thought, a brazen lady. She was thirteen years older than Marx and twenty years older than her lover, but was still a striking woman, as Marx described her with some relish in a letter to Nannette Philips written on March 24. He observed that her eyes were blue and her hair "blond," but that she showed the traces of her age. The Countess wore artificial eyebrows; there were wrinkles in her face which she filled out with rouge.

Lassalle's "Egeria," as Marx called the Countess, tried hard to make him prolong his stay in Berlin. She entertained him in her house, took him to the theater, and once to a three-hour-long ballet, where, in order to insult the pietistic royal family, she took seats next to King Wilhelm I and his queen. Countess von Hatzfeldt's notoriety was such that when Jenny Marx learned that her husband had sat next to the "Babylonian woman" at dinner,[9] she was more determined than ever that he should not accept Lassalle's newspaper offer. "My wife," Marx wrote to his uncle on May 6 after he had returned to London, "is particularly opposed to moving to Berlin, because she does not want our daughters to be introduced to the Hatzfeldt circle."

On April 12 Marx reluctantly left Berlin and made his way back home by slow stages. After the fine gay times he had had in Zalt-Bommel and Berlin, he was obviously in no great

[8]Marx to Nannette Philips, April 13, 1861.
[9]Jenny Marx to Engels, end of March 1861.

hurry to return to London. He went by way of Elberfeld and Cologne, and then visited his seventy-year-old mother in Trier, where he spent two days. It was, as he wrote Lassalle on May 8, a "useful" trip, since the "old woman," who showed "imperturbable equanimity," canceled his long-outstanding promissory notes. Marx was agreeably surprised by this, particularly since the old woman, who he noted was now "rapidly approaching her end," did this without his asking.

From Trier, Marx went back briefly to Zalt-Bommel, via Aachen, where he had relatives, and to Rotterdam and Amsterdam to visit his Philips cousins. Seventeen days after he left Berlin, on April 29, he arrived in London, feeling triumphant. What with the money he had "squeezed" out of his Dutch uncle and his mother's forgiveness of his debt to her, his trip was a financial success. The family celebrated his homecoming through most of the night.

Engels to the Rescue

The euphoria and the money did not last long. The money was soon exhausted and Marx found himself again in a financial morass. He struggled to borrow where he could, but always returned to Engels with cries for help.

Engels was then in a financially difficult position, too. England was going through an economic crisis, aggravated by the American Civil War, which, among other things, had produced a cotton shortage.[10] In Engels' textile factory, the work was cut by half and his own income was so reduced that he could hardly pay for his lodgings. He stayed with Mary Burns, his Irish mistress for several years, "so as to spend little on rent."[11] Obviously he could be of little help to Marx in his destitution.

There was a moment in 1863 when the Marx-Engels friendship was nearly shattered. Mary Burns died suddenly of a heart attack and the grief-stricken Engels wrote to Marx on January 7, "I cannot convey to you how I feel. The poor girl had loved me with all her heart." Marx replied on January 8 with a letter full of his own financial woes, commenting on

---

[10]Saul K. Padover, ed., *Karl Marx on America and the Civil War* (New York, 1972); see especially pp. 62–65, 164–66, 276–77, on the cotton industry.

[11]Engels to Marx, February 28, 1862.

Mary in less than two dozen curt words: "The news of Mary's death has much surprised and upset me. She was very good-natured, witty and was devoted to you." Engels was understandably furious at what he thought was Marx's casualness and self-centeredness. His anger was so great that it was not until several days later, on January 13, that he felt cool enough to make a reply:

Dear Marx: You will find it proper that my own misfortune and your icy conception of it had made it impossible to answer you sooner. All my friends, including philistine acquaintances, have on this occasion, which had hit me so deeply, shown me more empathy and friendship than I had a right to expect. You found this moment fit to display the superiority of your own intellect. *Soit!* [So be it].

Engels coolly proceeded to give Marx advice on how to borrow money: from a loan society or an insurance company.

The shaken Marx did not answer Engels for eleven days—something of a record, since most of the time the two men corresponded almost daily—and then, on January 24, he wrote an apology:

It was very wrong of me to write you the letter I did, and I regretted it the moment it was mailed. But it was in no way due to heartlessness. My wife and children will testify that your letter [of January 7] (which came in the morning) shocked me as would the death of anyone closest to me.

He went on to explain that his seeming coldness was due to utter financial misery:

When I wrote you that night, I did so under the pressure of very desperate circumstances. In the house, there was the broker from the landlord, a protest from the butcher for unpaid bills, a lack of coal and groceries, and Jennychen sick in bed. Under such circumstances, I generally know only cyncism to help me. What drove me especially mad was that my wife thought that *I* did not report to you adequately our true situation.

Marx had exhausted all his financial possibilities. Attempts to borrow from moneylenders in London failed and appeals to friends and relatives in Germany went unheeded. He and Jenny were not only in want but felt a cruel sense of humiliation. The children could not go to school that quarter because there was no money for tuition and their clothes were not in presentable condition. In the depths of his disconsolateness, Marx thought of giving up the apartment (the landlord would keep the furniture to pay for the arrears in rent) and moving with eight-year-old Eleanor (Tussy), to a municipal charity lodging house. The older daughters, Jennychen and Laura, would become governesses in a family they knew named Cunningham and Lenchen would take up service in some other household. This despairing plan would, Marx felt, bring him some surcease and restore his and Jenny's self-confidence, which their cruel indigence had all but eroded.

It did not come to that. Engels, despite his own economic needs, was nevertheless a businessman with resources to fall back upon, and came to the rescue as usual. He also gladly accepted Marx's apology:

You understand yourself what an impression your penultimate letter had made upon me. One cannot live with a woman for so many years without feeling her death dreadfully. I feel as if with her I have buried the last piece of my youth. When I received your letter, she was not yet interred. I tell you, your letter was on my mind for a week, I could not forget it. Never mind, your last letter makes it quits, and I am glad that I did not lose, together with Mary, my oldest and best friend.

Then, with his usual generosity, Engels took some risky steps to help Marx financially. He arranged, with the help of friends, for a promissory note of £100, to fall due in about four months. This, he informed Marx on January 26, would at least for the time being, serve as "a reprieve from the gallows." Marx was deeply moved by this "big and unexpected help" from his friend. "I cannot be grateful enough, although *I*, deep inside of me, needed no *new* proof of your friendship to be convinced that it is self-sacrificing. Moreover, if you had seen the joy of my children, it would have been for you a beautiful reward."[12]

[12]Marx to Engels, January 28, 1863.

Inheritances

The end of the year 1863 and the middle of 1864 brought
Marx a windfall in the form of two inheritances. They involved fairly substantial sums of money, but gave no lasting
security to a family as improvident as the Marxes.

On November 30, 1863, Marx received a telegram from
Trier that his mother had just died. He was then so sick that,
as he put it, he "stood with one foot in the grave" himself,
but he was relieved that his mother had preceded him there.
"Under the circumstances," he wrote, "I am at any rate more
necessary than the old one." On the same day he asked Engels to send him "forthwith enough money so that I can start
for Trier immediately." Engels sent it by return mail.

Marx's mother left an estate worth 49,130.52 florins, invested by her brother-in-law Lion Philips, in solid Dutch mortgages and bonds. There was a debt of 7,808.90 florins. The
remaining 41,321.62 were divided equally between Marx and
his surviving three sisters, Emilie Conradi, Louise Juta, and
Sophie Schmalhausen. Lion Philips had already advanced 5,-
520 florins to Marx over the years. This meant that Marx
had a claim of 4,480 florins. In addition, his mother had provided another £270 for her only surviving son. All in all, the
inheritance—about £850 in sterling—was a great deal of
money in those days. When Marx was a full-time correspondent of the *New-York Daily Tribune,* his earnings had rarely
amounted to more than £100 a year.

In May 1864, Marx came into another inheritance.
William Wolff ("Lupus") died at the age of fifty-five and left
most of his estate, including his books, to the Marx family.
Wolff, a bachelor who supported himself by giving private
language lessons in Manchester, had lived so frugally that he
left an estate worth £1,000. Of this sum, £700 was be-
queathed to Marx. Altogether, in the course of about half a
year Marx inherited £1,550, which was more money than he
had ever possessed in his life.

One important consequence of Marx's sudden access to
wealth was a change of residence. As a result of the inheritance from his mother, he was able to move, in the spring of
1864, to a spacious house, 1 Modena Villas, Maitland Park,
Haverstock Hill, N.W. It was a three-story structure, with a
small garden in the back and a park in front. There was a

fireplace in every room. Marx's workroom was on the main floor; it was full of light, with bookshelves on every wall. Marx lived in this comfortable house for eleven years, until the spring of 1875, when he moved to 41 Maitland Park Road (or Crescent), where he spent the rest of his life. It was at 1 Modena Villas that he wrote *Capital* and directed the affairs of the First International.

Despite almost unrelieved illnesses, this was a happy home for the Marx family. Lenchen ran the kitchen downstairs, providing hearty culinary specialties, often enhanced by hampers of wine from Engels. Jenny built a small hothouse in the garden, and cultivated exotic plants. Here the older Marx daughters were courted. The youngest, Eleanor, filled the house and garden with her pets, which her father loved, too.

Annunity

In 1864, after having received an inheritance of £10,000 from his father, Engels became a partner in the paternal Manchester business of Engels and Ermen. Henceforth his main objective was to accumulate enough wealth to support himself and the Marx family in comfort. He invested his profits in basic English companies—waterworks, gasworks, railroads—that paid 7½% interest.[13]

Five years later, after protracted negotiations with his partner, Gottfried Ermen, Engels sold him his share for enough money to make him a relatively wealthy man. When the papers were signed, on the last day of June 1869, Engels was exultant. Marx's daughter Eleanor, who was then visiting him in Manchester, later wrote:

I shall never forget the triumphant "for the last time," which he shouted as he drew on his top boots in the morning to make his last journey to business. Some hours later, when we were standing at the door waiting for him, we saw him coming across the little field opposite his home. He was flourishing his walking stick in the air and singing, and laughing all over his face.

To Marx he wrote happily on July 1, "Dear Mohr, Hurrah! Today it is finished with the *doux commerce* [sweet

[13]Engels to his brother, Hermann Engels, July 15, 1869.

commerce], and I am a free man."[14] Marx replied on July 3, "Dear Fred, Congratulations on your flight from the Egyptian captivity," and drank a toast to his friend's freedom before sundown, "unlike the Prussian gendarmes."

Before liquidating his business, Engels made an extraordinarily generous arrangement for Marx. Carefully calculating his resources, he asked Marx to consult with his wife what his debts were and how much they would need to live on. On November 29, 1868, he offered to pay the debts and, what was more important, to provide Marx with a permanent annuity of £350. Marx was stunned by the offer. "I am," he replied to Engels on November 30 in his customary Germanlish, "entirely knocked down by your much too great generosity." It was indeed a generous annuity. When his former friend Ferdinand Freiligrath had been the manager of the London branch of Banque Générale Suisse, his annual salary had been no more than £200.

Marx received the first quarterly installment of the annuity on February 27, 1869. He could not, of course, manage to live within these generous means and frequently asked for additional handouts. After the second installment, Marx found that his wife had concealed or forgotten a debt of £75, telling Engels in annoyance on July 22 that "women need guardians." Engels paid the debt, but warned Marx on July 25, "See to it that it does not happen in the future since you know our arrangement is tight and leaves no *margin* for extravagances."

The Engels annuity liberated Marx from three nightmarish decades of insecurity and misery.

In September 1870, Engels moved to 122 Regent's Park Road in London, to be near Marx. Thereafter, until the end of Marx's life, the two men saw each other every day while they were in London.

----

[14] On the same day, Engels also wrote exultingly to his mother, "Today is the first day of my freedom, . . . and I feel ten years younger."

XX

Das Kapital

Interrupted Work

After the failure of *Zur Kritik der Politischen Oekonomie*, and after having purged himself of some of his rage through the Vogt affair, Marx went about seriously recasting the plan of his work on political economy. Instead of bringing it out piecemeal, in separate volumes, as he had originally intended, he would organize it along different lines. The new work, to which he and his family referred for years as *"das Buch,"* would be unified and comprehensive. It would also be published by a different German publisher, Karl Otto Meissner of Hamburg.[1] Marx's final plan resulted in *Das Kapital,* with a reminiscence of the old title in its subtitle: *Kritik der Politischen Oekonomie.* The work was to cover the whole range of political economy and was to be published in three volumes. This ambitious project was Marx's bid for immortality. But he succeeded in completing and publishing only the first volume in his lifetime. The other two, prepared by the faithful Engels, were brought out posthumously. Some three-quarters of a century after Marx's death, the Marx-Engels Institute in Moscow published Volumes IV and V of *Das Kapital (Theories of Surplus Value),* which are essentially a collection of Marx's voluminous notes.

The work on *Das Kapital* extended over a period of about half a dozen years, but there were long lacunae during which Marx did little writing. This was partly a matter of his own choosing and partly a result of wretched personal circumstances and debilitating illnesses. At times Marx worked on his opus "like a horse," as he wrote to Engels, whom he kept on consulting on technical points of business, practical com-

---

[1]Meissner also had an American outlet: L. W. Schmidt, 24 Barclay Street, New York City.

mercial problems and technology. But these periods of extreme exertion were infrequent.

A major reason for the delay in the completion of *Das Kapital* was psychological, as some scholars have suggested.[2] Marx may have wished to escape from public judgment on his work, fearing to expose himself to critics who, he was sure, were bound to be hostile or indifferent. As it turned out, this expectation was justified. Hence he postponed his work by engaging in activities extraneous to his theoretical and scientific endeavors.

In September 1864, before *Das Kapital* was anywhere near completion, Marx involved himself in the organization of the International Working Men's Association—the so-called First International[3]—and for the next eight years he was its active *de facto* leader, draftsman, champion and mentor. The First International, many of whose sessions were held in Marx's own home, consumed his time and energy, particularly since he was so prone to squabble with those he considered his opponents. The last four years of the First International, which Marx angrily liquidated in 1872, were so stormy that they drained his emotions, and helped to prevent him from completing the last two volumes of *Das Kapital*.

There were times, particularly in the first months of 1867, when Marx thought he was dying, when perhaps he wished he was dead, but was sustained by his fierce desire to finish his book. To a communist friend, the mining engineer Sigfrid Meyer, who had emigrated to the United States in 1866, Marx wrote on April 30, 1867:

Why did I not write you for such a long time? Because I have been continuously suspended over the edge of the grave. I had to utilize EVERY possible moment when I was capable of working, in order to complete my work for which I have sacrificed health, happiness and family. I hope this explanation needs no further elaboration. I laugh at the so-called "practical" men and their wisdom. If one wants to be an ox, then one can, of course, turn one's back on man's torments and tend to one's own

[2]See the comprehensive psychological study by Arnold Küenzli, *Karl Marx: Eine Psychographie* (Vienna, 1966).

[3]See Saul K. Padover, ed., *Karl Marx and the First International* (New York, 1973).

skin. But I would really have considered myself *impractical* if I had croaked without having finished my book, at least in manuscript.

A Visit to Germany

At the end of March 1867, Marx put the finishing touches on *Das Kapital*. Some four years had passed since he wrote Engels that he was preparing a final copy for publication. Now the manuscript was really finished, and, to prevent a repetition of the German publishing conspiracy he had suspected in the case of *Zur Kritik*, Marx decided to take the work personally to Otto Meissner in Hamburg. For the trip, he needed financial help from Engels. "Now," he wrote on April 2, "I must first redeem my clothes and watch from the pawnshop. And, also, I can hardly leave my family in the present condition, where it is without a sou and the creditors become daily more insolent."

Engels replied on April 4:

> Hurrah! The exclamation was irrepressible when I finally saw in black and white that Volume One *is* ready and that you want to go with it to Hamburg. So that you do not lack *Nervus Rerum* [the sinews of life], I am enclosing seven half-pound notes, a total of £35, the second half to be sent immediately upon receipt of the usual telegram.

After receiving the money, Marx, carrying with him the manuscript of *Das Kapital,* set out for Germany. He sailed from London on April 10, 1867, at 8 o'clock in the morning, on a vessel that carried passengers as well as pigs. The weather, in Marx's words, was "crazy" and stormy. Most passengers became sick, but not Marx. The voyage and the storm combined to give him a sense of liberation from the woes at home. He felt exhilarated, as "tremendously jolly as the 500 hogs." Only a few passengers remained on their feet, forming what Marx called a "small nucleus" of hardy males braving the elements. Marx, cooped up for so many years in London, loved every minute he spent in the company of these passengers.

After a voyage of two days, the boat arrived in Hamburg

at noon. Immediately upon landing, Marx went to the publisher's, but, finding that Meissner was not in, he left his calling card with an invitation for Meissner to join him for dinner. At 7 o'clock that evening the publisher came to see Marx. The two men—the author magnificently barbigerous and the publisher elegantly bearded but bald—then had a brief "pourparler" [palaver]. Marx decided that Meissner, "although somewhat Saxonish," was "all right." On the next day Marx brought his manuscript to Meissner, who put it in a safe. The publisher suggested that the work be published in three separate volumes, all of them within a year. Marx agreed. As he visualized it, Volume I, the *Production Process of Capital*, would contain a detailed description of the English proletariat during the last two decades, Volume II would be a continuation, and Volume III would constitute a history of political economy from the middle of the 17th century to the present.

Author and publisher celebrated their agreement in the spirit of Bacchus. "We began to tipple," Marx reported to Engels on April 13, "and he told me of his great 'delight' in making my worthy acquaintance. At any rate, *we* now have in Meissner a man entirely at our disposal; he has great contempt for the whole *Lumpenliteratenpack* [gang of literary rascals]."

In fact, Meissner's relations with Marx did not deteriorate into hostility, as had been the case with Franz Duncker in Berlin. In his correspondence, Meissner continued to address Marx as *"Lieber Herr Doktor* [Dear Herr Doctor]" and to sign his letters *"mit herzlichen Gruss* [with cordial greetings]."[4] The fact that Meissner published only Volume I of *Das Kapital* in Marx's lifetime was not the publisher's fault but the author's.

Meissner promised that the printing of Volume I would begin within a few days and then proceed quickly. He expected it to be completed in four or five weeks. There were, however, delays. Since Hamburg had neither enough printers nor skilled proofreaders, Meissner had his printing done by the house of Wigand and Co. in Leipzig. Easter week intervened, and Wigand did not begin printing until April 29, some two weeks after the manuscript was sent to him from Hamburg. Meissner asked Marx to stand by, so that he could be on

---

[4]Meissner's letters can be seen in the Karl-Marx Haus in Trier.

hand for the revision of the first proof sheets and decide if, for the purpose of quick publication, it would be possible to do with only one correction by the author. Marx, anxious to see his work in print as soon as possible, agreed with his publisher not to return to London as yet. In the meantime, he would take the opportunity of visiting his friend Dr. Ludwig Kugelmann in Hanover, the medium-sized capital of the province of the same name that had been incorporated by Prussia the year before.

The Kugelmann Interlude

On Tuesday, April 16, at 9 o'clock in the evening, Marx was met at the Hanover railroad station by Dr. Ludwig Kugelmann, whom he had informed of his arrival by telegram. Kugelmann took Marx to his home. It was Easter Week, and the Kugelmanns asked Marx whether he would join them on Good Friday to hear Bach's *Passion of Saint Matthew*. Marx regretfully declined, saying that despite his love of music, particularly of Bach, he had to leave Hanover on Maundy Thursday. But, in fact, Marx remained with the Kugelmanns for four weeks. It was one of the happiest months of his life.

The Kugelmanns made such a fuss over their distinguished visitor and pampered him so lovingly that his ailments suddenly vanished. There were no more carbuncles or furuncles. Even the liver trouble went away. Marx felt rejuvenated and gay.

Ludwig Kugelmann, then thirty-nine years old, was Hanover's leading gynecologist, brought in for consultation by doctors who had difficult cases. He corresponded with the great authorities in his field, such as Rudolf Virchow, the Prussian pathologist who was a founder of cellular pathology, and Ignaz Philipp Semmelweis, the Hungarian gynecologist whose pioneering in obstetrical antisepsis had saved numerous women's lives. Kugelmann himself was an inventor of many new surgical instruments. He told Marx that when he first began to practice he had encountered the professional jealousy and "stupidity" of the local doctors, who barred him from the medical association because they considered gynecology a *"Schweinerei"* [obscenity].

Kugelmann, a participant in the 1848 revolutions, was also a communist zealot. He was an active member of the First International, and he possessed a better collection of the writings of Marx and Engels than they themselves did. His unabashed and fanatical admiration for Marx was almost embarrassing. "He sometimes bores me with his enthusiasm," Marx wrote to Engels on April 24, "which is in contradiction to his cool objectivity as a medical man."

The distaff side of the Kugelmann household lavished special admiration and affection on Marx. The family consisted of Gertrud, *née* Oppenheim, the twenty-nine-year-old wife, and Franziska, the nine-year-old daughter. Gertrud, a gay Rhinelander, was charmed by Marx, a *Landsmann* from the Rhineland. Little Franziska, to whom Marx, the doting papa of three adoring daughters, paid special attention and with whom he knew how to talk and play, was particularly enchanted by the bushy-bearded guest. Indeed, most of what we know of Marx's visit to the Kugelmanns comes from Franziska's *Reminiscences*, which she wrote two years before her death, at the age of seventy-two, in 1930.[5]

Before Marx's arrival, Gertrud Kugelmann had worried about how she should treat the eminent visitor. She had expected a seedy revolutionist, absorbed in his radicalism and hating the world. Instead, she found "an elegant cavalier," smartly attired, exuding charm and courtliness. "Young dark eyes," Franziska recalled, "smiled at her from under a mane of grey hair." His gestures and conversation were "full of youthful freshness," and his warm Rhenish accent reminded Frau Kugelmann of her home.

Marx was a charming and entertaining guest. He would get up early for breakfast, join the Kugelmanns at the coffee table and chat for hours. Dr. Kugelmann, not wanting to miss a word that came from the lips of his hero, could hardly tear himself away to attend to his medical chores.

Marx became a part of the family to such an extent that he gave the Kugelmanns nicknames, an addiction he could never resist. Franziska became *"Madämchen"* [Dear Madam]. Frau Kugelmann was dubbed *"Gräfin"* [Countess] because

[5]Franziska Kugelmann, *Kleine Züge zu dem Grossen Charakterbild von Karl Marx* [*Small Outlines for the Large Character Portrait of Karl Marx*], written for the Moscow Institute of Marxism-Leninism, in 1928.

of her sure social graces, which Marx, himself the husband of a baroness, appreciated and respected. Dr. Kugelmann himself was given the name "Wenzel," after the good 10th-century Bohemian Prince Wenzel and the bad 14th-century King Wenzel, who murdered the national saint, John of Nepomuk (or Pomuk), by having him thrown into the Moldau River. Since Kugelmann was a man given to vehement utterances, Marx referred to him as the good or bad Wenzel, depending upon what he thought of the doctor's opinions at the moment. Later, when he sent him his photograph, he inscribed it to "my Wenzel."

Marx, in turn, reminded Kugelmann of Zeus Otricolus, of whom he had a bust in his music room. Everybody agreed that Marx, with his powerful head, splendid brow and thick hair, resembled the Olympian god. Once Kugelmann remarked that the gods of the classics, busts of whom were scattered throughout his house, were at "eternal rest without any passions." Marx, who had written his doctoral dissertation on the subject, replied that, on the contrary, they were at eternal passion without any unrest. Kugelmann told Marx that, like a modern Zeus, he too should finish his lightning and hurl his thunder at the world, and not waste his precious time in ordinary agitation (such as the First International). Kugelmann's conviction that Marx was wasting his time, particularly after the publication of Volume I of *Das Kapital*, was to be one of the causes that, some half a dozen years later, let to a permanent break in their friendship at the time when they were both on a cure in Karlsbad. Kugelmann's accusation infuriated Marx, probably because he sensed that it came cruelly close to the truth.

Marx felt almost smothered by his hosts' attentiveness. He wrote to Engels that they were really "splendid people" but that they left him no time to explore "the gloomy path of one's own self." The Kugelmanns made him part of their circle of friends, and he went out of his way to be charming to these provincial Germans. At dinners, he would put on his monocle and look approvingly at anyone who made a sensible remark. He did not suffer fools gladly, but he lost his temper only once, when a man asked him whether in a future egalitarian state he would clean other people's shoes. Marx snapped, *"You* should." But he was more gentle with Gertrud Kugelmann when she said to him, "I cannot think of you in a leveling society, as you have altogether aristocratic tastes and habits." Marx replied, "I cannot either. That time will come, but we will be gone by then."

Marx impressed everyone with his *Kultur*. He could talk with assurance about all the major topics—art and music, science and philosophy, classic history and great literature. Unlike many pretentious intellectuals, Marx had read practically everything and easily quoted from the sources. Cervantes, Shakespeare, Heine, Goethe, and Schiller were at his fingertips. And, still more impressive to his German audience, he was profoundly versed in all the great philosophers from Plato to Schopenhauer, about whom his opinions were authoritative and unchallengeable. He also discoursed on his favorite European writers, among them the Russian Michael Yurevic Lermontov and the Spaniard Pedro Calderón (de la Barca), both of whom he had read in the original. His comments in the fields of culture and philosophy were often merry and witty. Except for private sessions with radicals, who came from outlying towns and who met in Marx's room, he eschewed political discussion. After a decade and a half of the bitter and pinched life of a London exile, Marx, enjoying carefree days in a cultured home, was at his best—a superbly educated and entertaining *Herr Doktor* in the great German tradition of erudition.

Hanover itself, a provincial capital with fine gardens and parks, was a good setting for a relaxed existence. Life was easygoing and slow-paced. In the public gardens, which were, Marx noted, "more artistically arranged than any in London," there was good music every evening. People, young and old, could amuse themselves there freely and at almost no expense. The Hanover ambience was obviously appealing, but it had one major disadvantage: it was small-town dull and uninspiring. Marx wrote to his daughter Laura on May 13, ". . . the atmosphere is pregnant with dullness. The standard of existence is too small. It is a lot of pigmees amongst whom you want no very high frame to feel like Gulliver amidst the Lilliputians."

Marx was also sought out by Hanover nonradicals. Merkel, chief of the local Statistical Bureau, called on him and told him that he finally understood financial problems only after Marx had explained them. The Society of Europeans, a group of Prussian-hating National Unionists—"Jackasses!" Marx called them—extended him an invitation. The head of the local railroad system invited him to his home. Marx went there, met him and his "enthusiastic wife," had a good May wine, and upon his departure, was thanked "for the great honor" of his visit. And, finally, *mirabile dictu*, Otto von Bismarck, the Premier of Prussia, soon to become Chancellor of a united Germany (in 1871), made an attempt to win Marx over to his side by offering him a job. Bismarck sent "one of his satraps," the Hanover lawyer Ernest Warnebold, with an offer "to utilize me and my great talents in the interests of the German people," as Marx reported to Engels on April 24. Warnebold's visit was followed by another emissary, Rudolf von Bennigsen, a founder of the German National Union. But Marx was not for sale to Bismarck, whom he occasionally called "Pissmarck."

And then there was a romantic interlude. Gertrud Kugelmann's best friend was a Madame Tenge, *née* Bolongaro-Crevenna, married to a wealthy Westphalian landowner, Tenge-Rietberg, who lived in a *Schloss* at Rietberg, near Rheda. She was a frequent house guest at the Kugelmanns, where she occupied what she came to call "my room." Now Marx was its tenant. Frau Kugelmann invited her friend to meet the famous guest. Frau Tenge came.

She was then thirty-four years old, attractive rather than beautiful, a gentlewoman of culture, grace and distinction. She spoke perfect English, French and Italian. In religion she was an atheist, in politics she tended toward socialism, about which she did not know much, as Marx observed. But she knew poetry and literature, was a connoisseur of music and was a skilled pianist. Marx was attracted not only by her culture but by her gentle manners and utter unpretentiousness. Frau Tenge, in turn, was impressed by Marx, who embarked on a culture-oriented courtship of the lovely noblewoman. She played the *Klavier* for Marx; he recited poetry to her. They sang together, and talked endlessly. It was romance on a level of *Kultur* and romanticism.

Marx was so enthusiastic about Frau Tenge that, somewhat rashly, he sent her "Photogramm" with a description of her to London. On May 5, in a letter to his oldest daughter, twenty-three-year-old Jennychen, one of whose nicknames was "Jo" (from Louisa May Alcott's *Little Women*), Marx praised Frau Tenge as a "truly noble nature," a woman of "unassuming character" and "spontaneous friendliness." He was convinced, he concluded, that if Jennychen and Frau Tenge met, they would become friends in no time. Jennychen, knowing that a picture of an attractive younger woman would hurt her mother, apparently hid or destroyed

Frau Tenge's "Photogramm." Marx, somewhat obtusely, later wondered how the picture could have been "lost."

The daughters were clearly jealous. Laura, then engaged to be married to Paul Lafargue and busy learning to ride and cook, took time out to write her father, inquiring if Frau Tenge was beautiful, intellectual, and whether he was flirting with her. Marx's reply, written in English, was somewhat coy. Addressing Laura by her customary nickname, Marx wrote on May 13:

> My pretty little Cacadou:
>
> My best thanks for your letter, and that of the worthy Quoquo [daughter Eleanor]. You complain that I had given no signs of life, but on reviewing the question you will find that, on the whole, I have given weekly signals. Moreover, you know that I am not of a "demonstrative" character, of rather retiring habitudes, a slow writer, a clumsy sort of man, or as Quoquo has it, an anxious man. . . . As to Mrs. Tenge, I wonder that you ask me how she looks, whether she is pretty? I have sent Jenny her photogramm, hidden behind my own. How could it have been lost? Now, to answer your questions, she is 33 years of age, mother of 5 children, rather interesting than pretty, and certainly no professional wit. But she is a superior woman. As to "flirting," he would be rather a bold man who were to try it. As to "admiration," I owe it, and there may, perhaps, have been on her side, some over-estimation of your most humble and "modest" master. You know, if no one is a prophet on his own dunghill (speaking symbolically), people are easily over-valued by strangers who, *legen sie nicht aus, so legen sie doch unter* [if they don't interpret you correctly, they interpret you anyhow] and find what they were resolved upon to find in a fellah. . . .
>
> Your master,
OLD NICK.

Frau Tenge carried with her a visitors' book and, before she departed from Hanover, asked Marx to write something in it. He did, expressing his admiration for her in the following lines:

> *La vida es sueño, un frenesie, una ilusión,*
> So lehrt uns Meister Calderón.

Doch zähl ich's zu den schönsten Illusionen,
Das Fremdenbuch Tenge-Crevenna zu bewohnen.

[Life is a dream, a frenzy, an illusion,
So teaches us Master Calderón.
Still I count it among the most beautiful illusions,
To inhabit the visitors' book of Tenge-Crevenna].

After Marx had left Hanover, Frau Kugelmann found in
his room a sheet of paper on which he had written a different, somewhat more personal version:

La vida es sueño, un frenesie, una ilusión.
So lehrt uns Meister Calderón.
Doch wenn Tonmeere Deiner Hand entschäumen,
Möcht ich für alle Ewigkeiten träumen.
Es zähmt des Lebens wilde Phrenesie
Der Zauber weiblich edler Harmonie,
Doch zähl ich's zu den schönsten Illusionen,
Das Fremdenbuch Tenge-Crevenna zu bewohnen.

[Life is a dream, a frenzy, an illusion,
So teaches us Master Calderón.
But when seas of sound pour forth from thy hand,
I could dream for all eternity.
This spell of feminine noble harmony
Tames life's wild frenzy.
Still I count it among the most beautiful illusions,
To inhabit the visitors' book of Tenge-Crevenna.]

Altogether, for Marx this first visit to Hanover—there was
to be another one, with daughter Eleanor, in 1869—was a
joyful interlude. He referred to it to his host on June 10 as
"among the most beautiful and delightful oases in the desert
of life." Nor did he forget Frau Tenge. Some two years later,
he concluded a letter to Kugelmann written on March 3,
1869, with the question *"Was macht Madame Tenge?"*

The Hanover visit was further enhanced by a memorable
event. On May 8, his forty-ninth birthday, Marx received
from Hamburg the first proofs of *Capital*. After so many
years of labor, the printed sheets came as a most happy birthday present.

Marx dreaded the thought of returning to his home with its
piled-up miseries, complaints, and relentless pressures. His

family was *"in profundis"* [in distress], as he said, without money and mired in debt. After the peace and comfort of Hanover, London would be more unendurable than ever.

Marx left Hanover on May 16, spent a day with Meissner in Hamburg, and sailed for London on May 17. Before reaching home, he had a little adventure with another aristocratic lady. A few hours before the boat's arrival in London, at 2 o'clock in the afternoon of May 19, he heard a German girl, "whose military bearing had already struck me," declare that she had to be in Weston supra Mare that evening and did not know how she would manage it all with her many pieces of luggage. It was Sunday, a Sabbath day in Victorian England when "helping hands are in short supply," as Marx put it. Gallantly he came to the rescue of what he called *"la donna errante* [the errant lady]." Since she had to go to the North-Western Station, which he thought he had to pass, he offered to drop her off there. But his sense of direction was, as usual, less than adequate. Upon inquiry, he discovered that her railroad station was at the opposite end of London from his own direction. But, "as a good knight," he was stuck with his promise and had to make, as he put it, a *bonne mine à mauvais jeu* [the best of a bad situation]. When they got to the station, they learned that the train would not leave until 8 o'clock that evening. So, in Marx's words, "I was in for it." They had nearly six hours to kill. Marx did not abandon the young lady at the station. Clearly in no pressing hurry to go home, he took her walking in Hyde Park and eating in "ice shops," until train time.

The young woman was Elisabeth von Puttkammer, a niece of Bismarck, with whom she had just spent several weeks in Berlin. A proud scion of Prussia's military nobility, she attracted her opposite. Marx wrote of her:

> She was a gay, educated girl, but aristocratic and black-and-white [the colors of the royal flag] to the tip of her nose. She was not a little surprised to discover that she had fallen into "red" hands. I consoled her, however, that our rendezvous would end "without bloodshed," and I saw her depart for her destination *saine et sauve* [safe and sound].[6]

[6]Marx to Kugelmann, June 10, 1867.

Marx got home late that evening. It is doubtful whether he told his wife that he had spent most of the day and evening with young Elisabeth von Puttkammer. He did not remain home long. Two days after his arrival, on May 21, he went to Manchester. There he stayed with Engels for nearly two weeks.[7] Then he returned home, to his cares and carbuncles.

The Publication

On July 25, 1867, Marx wrote a brief Preface to *Das Kapital*. He explained that the work was a continuation of *Zur Kritik der Politischen Oekonomie* and the "long pause" that had intervened since 1859 when the latter had been published was "due to an illness of many years' duration that again and again interrupted my work." He warned that the reader might find the first chapter, containing a scientific analysis of commodities, difficult, particularly since economics was such a complex subject. "Why? Because the fully developed body is more easy of study than are the cells of that body. In the analysis of economics forms, moreover, neither microscopes nor chemical reagents are of use. The force of abstraction must replace both."

Marx succinctly summarized his economic philosophy, which he claimed to be scientific and of universal validity. He was dealing with forces and categories, and not personalities. He treated the individual, whether capitalist or landlord, as merely the personification of economic categories, the embodiment of class relations and class interests. Since economic formations were a process of natural history, as he claimed, individuals, even if they rise above it, were nevertheless the creatures of that process.

Expecting criticism, Marx reminded the reader that in political economy scientific inquiry has to meet not only the usual hostility to science, but also a group of virulent special enemies: "The peculiar nature of the material [political economy] deals with, summons as foes into the field of battle the most violent, mean and malignant passions of the human breast, the Furies of private interest." Referring to the Church of England, which was a rich land and property owner, he added with typical irony, "The English Established

Church, for example, will more readily pardon an attack on 38 of its 39 articles than on the $\frac{1}{39}$th of its income."

The world, however, was changing, despite "purple mantles or black hassocks." Marx stated that he expected no immediate miracle, but the signs of the times indicated the beginning of a break in the old order: "They show that, within the ruling classes themselves, a foreboding is dawning that the present society is no solid crystal, but an organism capable of change, and is constantly changing."

Three weeks after he wrote the Preface, Marx finished correcting the final proofs of the whole book. At two o'clock in the morning of August 16, having put the last touches on the galleys, Marx penned a brief note to Engels. In it, he expressed his infinite gratitude and obligation to the friend whose continuous financial assistance and unfailing moral support had enabled him to produce his book:

Dear Fred: Have just finished correcting the *last sheet* (59) of the book . . . Preface ditto corrected and returned yesterday. So *this volume is finished*. Only YOU alone I have to thank for making this possible! Without your self-sacrifice on my behalf I could never possibly have done the enormous work for the three volumes. I embrace you, full of thanks. [The last sentence was written in English.]

Das Kapital, Volume I, came out on September 14, 1867, in an edition of 1,000 copies. The price was 3 Taler and 10 groschen per copy. The culmination of nearly a quarter of a century of intermittent research and writing, it was to be the last book Marx published in his lifetime. Stresses, distresses, numerous illnesses and carbuncles conspired to prevent the completion of the other volumes of *Das Kapital*, although he lived on for another sixteen years after the publication of Volume I.

Das Kapital is, of course, the masterpiece on which Marx's worldwide reputation rests. Into its preparation went an immense amount of learning and literary sources, both historic and contemporary, amounting to about 1,500 titles. Volume I, described on the title page as "The Process of Capitalist Production," dealt with such technical questions as Commodities and Money, the Transformation of Money into Capital, the Production of Absolute and Relative Surplus-Value, Wages, and the Accumulation of Capital. But it was much more than just another book on political economy. It was a literary *chef d'oeuvre*, imbued with moral passion and great personal style. Marx himself, referring to the book's construction, rightly called it a "work of art."

Das Kapital is both a work of immense scholarship and an original literary creation. Underlying the factory reports, the labor statistics, the financial data, the economic theories and other components are deep convictions and intellectual brilliance, illuminated by sardonic flashes. Here, for example, is a passage on the accumulation of capital:

> This primitive accumulation plays in political economy approximately the same role as original sin in theology. Adam bit into the apple, and thereupon sin came upon the human race. Its origin is supposed to be explained as an anecdote of the past. In times long past, there was, on the one side, an industrious, intelligent, and above all, a frugal elite; and, on the other, lazy ones, spending their substance, and more, in dissipation. The legend of the theological original sin tells us, to be sure, how man came to be condemned to eat his bread by the sweat of his brow; but the history of economic original sin reveals to us why there are people to whom this is by no means necessary. Never mind! So it came to pass that the former sort accumulated wealth, and the latter sort in the end had nothing to sell except their own skin. And from this original sin dates the poverty of the great mass that, despite all its labor, still has nothing to sell but itself, and the wealth of the few that increases constantly, although they have long ceased to work.[8]

The qualities of style, irony, moral judgment, vision and social relevance[9] have made *Das Kapital* a world classic. They also help to explain why the book, whose economic theories are nowadays considered outdated, is a work that has "changed the course of history," in the words of the American economist, Paul A. Samuelson, not an admirer of Marx.

---

[8]Translated by Saul K. Padover from the 4th German edition of *Das Kapital* (Hamburg, 1890), Vol. I, Ch. 23, Sec. 1. In the English translation of 1887, this passage is found in Chapter 26.

[9]Professor Robert Heilbroner: "Why then bother with Marxian economics when, as virtually every economist will tell you, it is 'wrong'? The reason is that unlike neoclassical analysis, which is 'right,' the

The Battle for Recognition

With the fiasco of *Zur Kritik der Politischen Oekonomie* always a rankling memory, Marx was determined this time not to permit the world, most especially the German world, to ignore his work. Now he would fight for recognition with all the means in his power. On November 30, 1867, a few weeks after the publication of *Das Kapital,* Marx wrote to Victor Schily, a German friend in Paris, "My publisher [Meissner] is satisfied with the sales. The gang of liberal and vulgar economists will, of course, try, as much as possible, to do harm through their well-tested means, the *conspiration de silence.* This time, however, they will not succeed."

Marx's preparations for publicity began even before the publication of the book. On September 13, 1867, the day before *Das Kapital* came out in Hamburg, Marx, accompanied by Paul Lafargue, his prospective son-in-law, went to Manchester to plan with Engels a campaign to publicize the book. The three of them set up a fairly elaborate publicity machinery. The basic plan was to mobilize friends and acquaintances in Germany and elsewhere on the Continent to promote the book.

The campaign called for at least four kinds of activity: distribution of copies to key people and publications likely to be interested; urging translations in foreign languages; goading fellow radicals to publicize the work, and wherever possible, to print extracts from it in the socialist and communist press; and, finally, reviews, written by Engels, with Marx's occasional help, for free distribution among journals, preferably the "bourgeois" press, which radicals professed to despise. Engels, operating out of Manchester, and Kugelmann, working out of Hanover, were to be the prime movers in the publicity campaign.

A few efforts were made to publicize *Das Kapital* in England. Copies were sent to the historian Edward Spencer Beesly, and the journalist Peter Fox (Andre), both of them prominent members of the First International.

When the second German edition of *Das Kapital* came out

Marxian model has in surfeit the quality of social relevance that is so egregiously lacking in the other." Quoted in Saul K. Padover, "Marx Redivivus," in *New School Bulletin,* March 31, 1969.

in 1872, Marx sent a copy to Darwin, whose work he had always admired as a scientific corroboration of his own materialist philosophy. Darwin acknowledged receipt of the book in a courteous note, written on October 1, 1873, modestly hinting that the work was beyond his competence:

> Dear Sir: I thank you for the honour which you have done me by sending me your great work on Capital; and I heartily wish that I was more worthy to receive it, by understanding more of the deep and important subject of political economy. Though our studies have been so different, I believe that we both earnestly desire the extension of knowledge, and that this in the long run is sure to add to the happiness of Mankind.
>
> I remain, dear Sir, Yours faithfully,
> Charles Darwin.

A few years later, in 1880, when Marx was still working on Volume II of *Das Kapital,* he asked Darwin for the honor of dedicating it to him. The famous scientist, then in his seventy-first year, politely refused, mainly on the ground that he did not wish to hurt his family's religious sensibilities. Darwin was obviously referring to Marx's materialism and atheism.

There was no serious review of *Das Kapital* in the English press, nor an English translation of it during Marx's lifetime. A critique which Engels wrote for *The Fortnightly Review* in mid-1868 was rejected with the comment that it was "too scientific for the English magazine-reading public." One of the rare notices of the book appeared in the *Saturday Review of Politics, Literature, Science and Art* on January 25, 1868. The *Review* was a conservative London weekly, which, in a discussion of several other books, made the following comment on Marx, "The author's views may be as pernicious as we conceive them to be, but there can be no question as to the plausibility of his logic, the vigour of his rhetoric, and the charm with which he invests the driest problems of Political Economy."

To which Marx's comment was: "Ouff!"

Copies of *Das Kapital* were sent to a number of influential Europeans, among them Marx's estranged friend Ferdinand Freiligrath in London, the anarchist theoretician Jean-Jacques Elisée Reclus in Paris, and the academic economist Karl Wilhelm Contzen in Leipzig. A copy to Michael Bakunin, Marx's anarchist enemy-friend, went unacknowledged. But in 1868

Bakunin began to translate *Das Kapital* into Russian, a task he never completed.

Although the pressure brought by Engels and Kugelmann on their German friends and acquaintances to publicize *Das Kapital* was not altogether wasted, it was not conspicuously successful. For a long time, there was only one professional review, written by Eugen Dühring, a *Privatdozent* [lecturer] at the University of Berlin. The review appeared in *Ergänzungsblätter zur Kenntniss der Gegenwart* [Supplementary Pages to a Knowledge of the Present], a semi-popular monthly published in Hildburghausen in 1867 (Vol. III, pp. 182-86). It was not precisely a prestigious journal. Marx, grateful for any attention in Germany, thought that, despite Dühring's misunderstanding of much in *Das Kapital*, the review was, nevertheless, "very decent." Engels, on the other hand, was not pleased.

By the end of 1867, only a handful of German publications had bothered to notice *Das Kapital* or print any extracts from its Preface.[10] Marx, deeply disturbed, came down with severe attacks of carbuncles, bronchitis, liver ailments, and other afflictions that persisted until his death in 1883. He felt that he could not continue work on his second volume unless there was some positive response in Germany to the first one. He was particularly troubled by the fact that the working class paid so little attention to *Das Kapital*. He had somehow expected that poorly educated workers would rush out to buy an expensive work that was too deep even for intellectuals. After so many years of labor, anxiety and effort, it was a "torment," in Jenny's words, to get no real response from the proletariat. She wrote to Kugelmann on December 24, 1867, "If the working people had any conception of the sacrifices that were necessary to complete this work, which was written for them and in their interest, they would perhaps show somewhat greater interest."

Marx was convinced that the fate of his book depended upon "party friends" in Germany. He wanted to have them beat the timbrels for *Das Kapital* everywhere. It did not mat-

[10]In the year 1867, notices or publications of portions of the Preface appeared in *Der Beobachter* (Stuttgart daily), September 7; *Der Vorbote* (Geneva monthly), September, October, November; *Courrier Français* (Paris weekly), October 1; *La Liberté* (Brussels daily), October 13; *Libertà e Giustizia* (Naples weekly), October 27. An English notice appeared in *The Bee-Hive Newspaper* (London weekly organ of the First International), September 7.

ter what was written about the book, so long as it was mentioned at all, and as soon as possible. The one thing he could
not bear was to be ignored again. Wrenched by his anxieties,
he wrote to Kugelmann on October 11, 1867 in near despair:

A massive critique—whether from friend or foe—can be
expected only bye and bye, as so voluminous and in part
difficult work requires time to read and digest. But its
success is not going to be determined by massive criticism but, to speak plainly, by sounding the alarm and
striking the drum, which would also force the enemies to
speak out. Chiefly, *what* is being said is not as important
as that it is *said. Above all, no time is to be lost.*

Engels struck the same tone. He, too, urged Marx's gynecologist friend in Hanover to do something—anything!—to
get notices in the German press.

The main thing [he wrote to Kugelmann on November
8 and 20, 1867] is that the book be discussed again and
again. And since Marx cannot act freely in this matter,
and also feels embarrassed, like a virgin, we others must
do it. Be so kind as to let me know what success you
have had in this thing up to now and which papers you
believe can still be used. In this, to use the words of our
old friend Jesus Christ, we must act as innocent as doves
and be as cunning as serpents.

The worst thing, Engels continued, was to be ignored. He
told Kugelmann that even unfriendly reviews, including attacks on *Das Kapital*, would be welcome. If the book were
mentioned in fifteen or twenty newspapers, Engels wrote, notice would be taken of the work "simply as an important phenomenon that deserves consideration." Then the "whole
gang" of nonradical economists would begin to "howl" and
be *compelled* to pay attention to the book.

Although he wanted the book to be bruited about all over
Germany, Marx despised publicity in certain publications that
had a mass appeal, as "vulgar." This was, of course, in line
with his contempt for public opinion which he expressed in
the last paragraph of the Preface to *Das Kapital*: "Every
judgment of scientific criticism I welcome. Vis-à-vis the prejudices of so-called public opinion, to which I have never made

concessions, I apply, as ever before, the slogan of the great Florentine: *Segui il tuo corso, e lascia dir le genti!*"[11]

When Kugelmann suggested that an advertisement of *Das Kapital* be placed in *Gartenlaube,* an illustrated "family paper," Marx was offended. He urged his friend "definitely to give up this joke." He said that being mentioned in publications designed for the common masses was "*beneath* the character of a scholarly man." By way of example, he told Kugelmann that when Meyers' *Konversationslexikon* had asked him for a biographic note about himself, he ignored it as beneath his dignity: "I did not even answer the letter. Everybody must attain salvation in his own way."

Kugelmann, whom Marx called "my most intimate friend in Germany," exerted every effort in favor of *Das Kaptial.* "You," Marx told him, "have done more for my book than all of Germany together." But it was not enough. The campaign strategy for the book met with only a limited success. The reviews that Engels himself wrote were sent out to the German press and were published in seven papers, none of them of great consequence.[12] In London, Marx anxiously scanned the German press for signs of recognition or mentions. These were scant, indeed, amounting altogether to about a dozen.[13] To his chagrin, the important segment of the middle-class German press, which Marx pretended to despise but read avidly, paid no attention whatever to *Das Kapital.* To him, of course, the silence was a conspiracy. "The great bourgeois and reactionary papers," he wrote to Sigfrid Meyer on July 4, 1868, "such as the *Kölnische,*[14] *Augsburger,*[15] *Neue*

---

[11]Follow thine own course, and let people say what they will: Dante, *Divine Comedy,* "Purgatory."

[12]In 1867: *Die Zukunft* (Berlin daily), October 30; *Elberfelder Zeitung* (daily), November 2; *Düsseldorfer Zeitung* (daily), November 17; *Barmer Zeitung* (daily), December 19; *Der Beobachter* (Stuttgart daily), December 27.

In 1868: *Neue Badische Landeszeitung* (Mannheim daily), January 21; *Demokratisches Wochenblatt* (Leipzig weekly), March 21 and 28.

[13]Among the reviews were a series of twelve articles, entitled "Das Werk von Carl [*sic*] Marx," in *Der Social-Demokrat* (a Social Democratic publication appearing three times weekly in Berlin), January 22 to May 6, 1868; *Börsenhalle für Deutschland* (Hamburg daily), February 14, 1868; *Literarisches Centralblatt für Deutschland* (Leipzig weekly), July 4, 1868.

[14]*Kölnische Zeitung* (Cologne daily).

[15]*Allgemeine Zeitung* (Augsburg daily).

Preussische,[16] *Vossische,*[17] etc., have carefully kept their mouths shut."

The German academics and professional economists were also mostly silent. In addition to Dühring, there seem to have been only two reviews in the first several years after the publication of *Das Kapital.* Marx thought both of them ridiculous. One, published anonymously in the quarterly *Vierteljahrschrift für Volkswirthschaft und Kulturgeschichte,*[18] claimed that Marx was a pupil of the French economist Frédéric Bastiat, an advocate of class "harmonies,"[18] instead of class struggles. Marx considered the review a "farce," thought the editor of the journal, the economist Julius Faucher, a "buffoon," and called him *"Mannequin Piss* Faucher," a reference to the famous statue of the urinating boy in a public fountain in Brussels.

The other professional review appeared two years later, in *Jahrbücher für Nationalökonomie und Statistik,*[20] written by Karl Friedrich Rösler, an economist who indulged in what Marx called bourgeois "drivel," in lieu of hard economic categories or realities. In a letter to Engels written on July 20, 1870, Marx described Rösler's review as "philosophic twaddle worthy of Moses Mendelssohn, smart-assing, peevish, know-it-all, nit-picking." The whole thing, said Marx, then suffering from rheumatism and coughing, made him laugh. "My physical condition hardly predisposes me to merriment, but I have cried with laughter over this essay, bona fide tears of mirth."

In the Postscript to the second German edition of *Das Kapital,* which Meissner brought out in 1873, Marx made an effort to explain why the "learned and unlearned spokesmen of the German bourgeoisie tried at first to kill *Das Kapital* by silence, as they had managed to do with my earlier writings." His theory was that the German economic system was behind that of England and France, where sharp class struggles had already surfaced as expressions of ripe historic development. This was not the case in Germany, where the bourgeoisie had not yet developed any original work in political economy. German economists followed foreign thinkers. They either

[16]*Neue Preussische Zeitung* (Berlin daily).
[17]*Vossische Zeitung* (Berlin daily).
[18]Vol. XX, Berlin, 1868.
[19]Bastiat, *Harmonies Économiques* (Paris, 1851).
[20]Published by the economist and statistician Bruno Hildebrand, Jena, 1870.

"flocked to the banner" of Bastiat, the most "superficial" apologist of "vulgar economy," or followed John Stuart Mill, who attempted "to reconcile the irreconcilables." Marx wrote, "Just as in the classical time of bourgeois economy, so also in the time of its decline, the Germans remained mere schoolboys, imitators and followers, petty retailers and hawkers in the service of the great foreign wholesale concern."

Das Kapital's Slow Triumph

After Marx's death, Engels prepared a third edition of Volume I, which came out in 1883, and a fourth in 1890. Engels also brought out Volume II in 1885 and III in 1894 from the hardly legible manuscripts, notes and tables which Marx had left behind. The statistical charts had to be recalculated, as Marx had no competence with figures. Engels was then suffering from cancer of the esophagus, of which he was to die on August 5, 1895, but he continued his selfless job of preparing Volume III of Das Kapital for publication. It was no easy task. On April 11, 1894, he wrote to Marx's daughter, Laura Lafargue, then living in Le Perreux, France, "I am awfully busy; deep in the Rent of Land (Vol. III) which causes me a deal of trouble by Mohr's tables being almost without exception miscalculated—you know what a genius he was for figures!—and having to be recast."

The sale of Das Kapital in Germany was small but fairly constant. Several hundred copies were sold annually. The royalties were £130 (2,600 Marks) in 1886; £43 in 1889; £45 in 1890; £38 in 1892. The money went to Marx's two surviving daughters, Laura and Eleanor. They needed it. Laura and her husband, Paul Lafargue, often appealed to Engels for financial help, as Marx had done. Engels, who always complied, left half of his own estate to the two Marx daughters.

Marx's ideas, or at least the concepts known as Marxism, also made their way slowly but steadily in Germany. They began to take effect with the rise and growth of the Social-Democratic Party, in which Marx took a critical interest. In May 1875, Germany's two main labor parties, the Social-Democratic Worker's Party and the Lassalle-founded General Association of German Workers, met in Gotha and united into a Socialist Labor Party, which later became the German Social-Democratic Party. One of the main leaders in bringing about the union and in the new grouping was Wilhelm

Liebknecht, a loyal friend and adherent of Marx, whom the latter treated with a measure of affectionate disdain, sneering at him in private as bumbling and dim. To the Gotha congress Marx sent a trenchant critique, known as the "Gotha Programme," which formed a basic document for the rapidly growing Social-Democratic Party.[21] Within some two decades after Marx's death, it had grown into Germany's largest single political party. By the outbreak of World War I, the Social-Democratic Party was the most powerful socialist group in Europe, and probably in the world. But by then its Marxist socialism was seriously diluted, as Lenin and other harsh critics were soon to charge in the name of Marx.

Elsewhere, *Das Kapital* made quicker headway than it did in Germany. The first foreign translation of the work was not into English or French, the languages of the foremost capitalist countries, but Russian, that of Europe's most economically backward major power. The Russian censors cleared *Das Kapital* on the ground that, being scientific, it would have no meaning to the ignorant common people, and hence, presumably, would be no threat to Czarism!

The Russian translation of *Das Kaptial*, by the economist Nicolai Frantzevich Danielson and the liberal landowner German Alexandrovich Lopatin, came out in 1872, published by Nicolai Petrovich Polyakov, in St. Petersburg, and was an immediate success. On an edition of 3,000 copies, about 900 were sold within the first month, something of a record in a country with a relatively small circle of educated people. The book was widely discussed by intellectuals and professional economists. "Most journals and newspapers," Danielson informed Marx, "have carried reviews. All of them—with one exception—have been very laudatory." Marx was so delighted with the Russian notices that he mentioned them in his Postscript to the second German edition, quoting from the review by Professor Nicolai Ivanovich Sieber in the *Sankt-Petersburgskye Vedomosti* [St. Petersburg Journal] (April 20, 1872):

The presentation of the subject, with the exception of one or two exceptionally special parts, is distinguished by its comprehensibility to the general reader, its clarity, and, in spite of the scientific intricacy of the subject, by

[21] For text, see Saul K. Padover, ed., *Karl Marx on Revolution* (New York, 1971), pp. 488-506.

an unusual liveliness. In this respect the author in no way resembles . . . the majority of German scholars who . . . write their books in a language so dry and obscure that the heads of ordinary mortals are cracked by it.

Marx was pleased also with another professional review, by a St. Petersburg University professor, Illarion Ignatzyevich Kaufmann, in the prestigious *Vestnik Evropy* [European Messenger] (May 1872), from which he also quoted in his Postscript to the second German edition:

At first sight . . . Marx is the most ideal of ideal philosophers, always in the German, *i.e.,* the bad sense of the word. But in point of fact he is infinitely more realistic than all his forerunners in the work of economic criticism. He can in no sense be called an idealist.

Marx's book was having a growing effect in Russia in circles that mattered most, among students and intellectuals. In 1873 and 1874, rioting radical students in big Russian cities quoted from *Das Kapital* in their propaganda. The work was still being debated in important Russian journals as late as 1879, the year when both Joseph Stalin and Leon Trotsky were born, and Lenin was a nine-year-old schoolboy. Marx continued to be pleasantly surprised at his success in the land of the Czars. In 1880, he wrote to a friend that in Russia, a country he usually despised and feared as barbaric, he was "more read and appreciated than anywhere else." His influence on Russian radicalism, if not necessarily on the science of economics,[22] particularly on Lenin, who was to become his most powerful disciple, was to be continuous posthumously, through the Russian Revolution of 1917, and into our own time.

But satisfactory as the Russian success was to Marx, his greatest desire was for a French translation. For to him, France continued to be the historic land of revolutions and the intellectual pace-setter of Europe. From the very first, he considered a French translation of "the highest importance."[23]

---

[22] A Russian economist, Ludwig Slonimski, in his book, *Attempt at a Critique of Karl Marx's Economic Theories* (German translation, Berlin, 1899), concluded: "In the history of the . . . labor movement Marx's work plays a significant role; but he did not advance economic science by a single step!"

[23] Marx to Ludwig Büchner, May 1, 1867.

He was convinced that such a translation would not only emancipate the French from the "false views" to which Proudhonism, with its idealized petty bourgeoisie, had enslaved them, but would also serve as a platform for all of Europe, then under the influence of France. As Marx's daughter Eleanor, echoing "Papa's" thoughts, wrote to Danielson on January 23, 1872, "I hope very much that as soon as a French edition has come out, an English one will follow—the English are aping everything the French do; only when something comes from *Paris* does it have success here."

There were years of effort and negotiation involving French translators. Joseph Roy, translator of Feuerbach's work, began the translation of *Das Kapital,* but did not finish it. The work was continued by Charles Keller, a French socialist and member of the First International. But Marx was not satisfied with their work; in the end he himself thoroughly corrected and revised the French translation.

A publisher was found in Maurice Lachâtre (La Châtre), a French journalist and Communard who offered a 2,000-franc advance.[24] After some years of stormy relationship— Marx once called Lachâtre a "disgusting charlatan"[25]—the French translation of *Das Kapital* was published in November 1875. An edition of 10,000 copies quickly sold out. This all but assured the success of the book on the Continent.

An English translation was long in coming. It did not appear until 1887, two decades after the German edition and four years after Marx's death. One problem involved in the delay was linguistic expertise. A translation of seven chapters by the English socialist Henry Mayers Hyndman[26] was exposed by Engels as completely inaccurate. "Marx," Engels wrote, "is one of the most forceful, most terse and most exact writers of our time. To convey his meaning properly, one has to be a master not only of the German but also of the English language."[27] There were apparently few such masters to be found in England. The English translation was finally made by two friends of Marx and Engels, the jurist Samuel

[24]Paul Lafargue to Frederick Engels, December 12, 1871.
[25]Marx to Paul Lafargue, March 21, 1872.
[26]Hyndman, writing under the pseudonym "John Broadhouse," published the first chapter of *Capital* in the October 1885 issue of *To-Day,* a London socialist monthly of which he was editor.
[27]Engels, "How Marx Should Not Be Translated," in *The Commonwealth,* November 1885.

Moore and the journalist Edward Aveling. Both Engels and Eleanor Marx, who lived with Aveling, supervised and helped with the translation, for which Engels wrote a Preface in 1886. It is a translation that is not always strictly accurate.

This English translation, issued by the London publisher Swan Sonnenschein & Co., was more a labor of love and prestige than a response to demand. Selling at 30 shillings in 1887 and at 10 shillings 6 pence in 1889, *Capital* found few buyers. There was one anonymous review in *The Athenaeum* of March 5, 1887. The royalties amounted to £12.3.9 for 1887–1888, and to a mere £1.3.1 in 1893–1894. The English were obviously not interested in Marxism. In 1906, Charles H. Kerr Co., a Chicago publishing firm, brought out a "revised and amplified" translation by Ernest Untermann; it was no great improvement on the Moore-Aveling translation.

Capital did better in the United States than in England, but for a ludicrous reason. In 1890, a Barnum-type publisher in New York, noting that Volume I contained a section entitled "The Accumulation of Capital" (Part VII, Chapters xxiii-xxv), cunningly printed a circular stating that in *Capital*, a deep tome by a learned German scholar, one can learn "how to accumulate capital," and sent it to all the bank officials in the United States. The greedy men in the money business, eager to make a killing, responded predictably. An edition of 5,000 copies of *Capital* was sold out. Marx would have been sardonically amused to find himself a best seller among capitalists in a country which he called "the most modern form of bourgeois society."[28]

Das Kapital, as well as Marx's other social-economic writings, made their way gradually around the world. In the 19th century, the censorship prevailing in countries like Italy, Poland, Portugal and Spain, among others, slowed up translations of Marx's work but did not ultimately prevent them. Italian and Spanish translations came out in 1886 and a Polish one, in Leipzig, in 1890. There was also a Danish translation in 1885 and a complete Dutch one in 1894.

What is known as Marxism has had, and still has, a universal appeal, and not merely in countries where substantial numbers of the population have economic and social grievances. Marx speaks both to the heart and the mind, in-

[28]For Marx's opinions of America and American capitalism, see Saul K. Padover, ed., *Marx on America and the Civil War* (New York, 1972).

voking hopes alleged to be based on "science." That Marx's communism and his economics are not, as he fondly believed, "scientific" in any meaningful sense of the word, has little relevance in terms of communicating ideas. Marx's economic writings, in particular the massive *Das Kapital*, are the Scriptures for those who aspire to transform the world. Marx himself looms as a latter-day prophet—often an angry prophet—who used the tools and data of political economy to propound his vision.

Today, Marx's views are reverently taught, if not necessarily applied in practice, in countries that, in their total, make up about one-third of the human race.

XXI
The First International

The Start

In September 1864, when the International Working Men's Association—known as the First International—was founded in St. Martin's Hall, London, Marx was still a relatively obscure refugee journalist in the British capital. After the traumatic defeat of the 1848–49 revolutions in Europe, he had become politically inactive in England.

In London, his main contacts were with other European radicals and refugees, particularly German and French, with many of whom he maintained a hostile relationship. While showing a deep interest in British politics, institutions and movements, which he followed assiduously, he frequently reported to the *New-York Daily Tribune*, he generally kept himself aloof from English activists, including trade unionists. With rare exceptions, one of them being the Chartist leader and editor Ernest Charles Jones, Marx had few close connections with English radicals or laborites. He led the politically isolated life of an unassimilated Continental refugee. The First International was to bring about a change in Marx's political inaction and isolation.

It is still not clear why Marx was invited to what turned out to be a historic meeting at St. Martin's Hall. Until about a week before the meeting, on September 28, he apparently knew nothing about any preparations for it. He was told about it by a thirty-year-old French radical republican living in London, Victor Le Lubez, who invited him to come as a representative of German workers. Marx accepted and proposed that he be joined by Johann Georg Eccarius, a tailor living in London, as another German representative. Unlike Marx, Eccarius was, of course, a bona fide worker. As it turned out, Marx and Eccarius were to become the two mainstays of the International from its inception to its demise eight years later.

The St. Martin's Hall meeting was jammed with a large number of assorted international radicals. There were English Owenites and Chartists, French Proudhonists and Blanquists, Irish nationalists, Polish patriots, Italian Mazzinians and German socialists. It was a salmagundi momentarily united not by a commonly shared ideology or even by genuine internationalism, but by an accumulated burden of variegated grievances, crying for an outlet. The English were against special privilege, the French against Bonapartism, the Irish against Britain, the Poles against Russia, the Italians against Austria and the Germans against capitalism. There was no real interconnection among them, except what Marx later tried to provide in the organization that followed the meeting. Under the chairmanship of Edward Spencer Beesly, an English Positivist historian and professor at London University, radical oratory was given free rein. Marx himself did not speak. He was present as a "silent figure on the platform."

The meeting voted unanimously to appoint a provisional committee to work out a program and statutes for the proposed international organization. Marx was appointed a member of the committee, which met a week later and, being large and unwieldy, agreed on a small subcommittee to do the actual work. Marx became a member of this subcommittee. The only other German on it was "my old friend, the tailor Eccarius," as Marx wrote to a communist friend in Solingen. The subcommittee met in Marx's home and, so powerful was his intellectual ascendancy and certainty of purpose, that it authorized him to draw up the program, in the form of an Inaugural Address, and the Rules and Provisional Statutes of the organization. Henceforth, Marx was to remain the predominant spirit and the indomitable personality that held the International Association together for eight stormy years, until it was shattered by bitter internal dissensions.

Marx, then suffering from a "virulent carbuncle on the penis" and chest, spent a week drafting the Inaugural Address and the Statutes of the International. On November 1, these were adopted and, three weeks later, published by the Provisional Committee. The latter then transformed itself into the Central Council—soon to become the General Council—as the governing body of the International. For the next eight years, Marx tried to use the General Council, whose weekly sessions he rarely failed to attend, except when tortured by illness or absent from London, as an instrument to further his long-range revolutionary vision.

Thanks to Marx, the First International became a major event in the history of revolution.

The Organization of the General Council

The really active and constant members of the General Council consisted of a small group of Europeans resident in London and a larger body of Englishmen. The importance of the Continental Europeans was greater than their numbers. They not only stayed the course but also held a balance of power in the Council. The most important among them, in addition to Eccarius, were Hermann Jung, a Swiss-German watchmaker; Friedrich Lessner, a tailor; and Karl Pfaender, an artist. There was also a Frenchman, Eugène Dupont, a musical-instrument maker. Another member, at least for one year, was Heinrich Bolleter, keeper of a tavern at 2 Nassau Street, where foreign workers sometimes held their meetings.

The non-English members of the General Council came to be known as Marx's coterie, providing him with a strong and continuing base of support. Some of them occupied key positions throughout most of the life of the International. Thus Jung was the long-time Corresponding Secretary for Switzerland, then a center of radicalism; Dupont served an equally long term as Corresponding Secretary for France, the most important country on the Continent; and Eccarius, the Council's General Secretary for four years, was also, for two years, Corresponding Secretary for America. In addition, Eccarius was the International's occasional newspaper correspondent.

Marx eventually had trouble with Eccarius, whom he gave loyal support, often despite his better judgment. The tailor was a morose communist, pushy and ambitious, clearly suffering from an inferiority complex. Eccarius' tactlessness created resentment among xenophobic English members. Marx nearly always defended him and as a result made enemies among some of the British. In 1871, Eccarius finally broke with his patron, which led Marx to label him a "scoundrel" and Engels to call him a "traitor to our cause." It is interesting to note that after the Vienna Archives were opened in 1918, they were found to contain materials which led critics to accuse Eccarius of having been a spy who sold information about the International to the Austrian government. Although Eccarius was often in desperate need of money, and was likely to take it where he found it, the case against him has not been conclusively proven.

Spies were then a constant source of concern to Continental radicals, whether at home or in exile. Marx himself, frequently their target, had a touch of paranoia on the subject, and not without justification. Radical and revolutionary groups were systematically infiltrated by police spies and secret agents in the pay of Europe's autocratic governments, notably those of Austria, France, Prussia and Russia. Spies and informers, suspected or real, were frequently exposed and expelled from radical organizations.

The English majority on the General Council represented the skilled trades—bakers, plasterers, printers and shoemakers. They were neither proletarians in the Marxist sense, nor *déclassés* in the tradition of the European uprooted, but solid, perhaps even stolid, products of England's stable and orderly society. Although they had the usual class-consciousness of workers in a traditionally stratified system, these men were neither at war with queen and country nor alienated from their basic culture.

The Political Program

The Inaugural Address which Marx wrote, a brochure of approximately ten printed pages, was the basic general charter of the International. A far cry from the flamingly revolutionary *Communist Manifesto,* it reflected a subtle shift in Marx's political expectations and a strategic awareness of the essentially nonrevolutionary character of the General Council.

In the Inaugural Address, as well as in his subsequent activities and official writings on behalf of the International, Marx showed more moderation and political realism than he had evinced in his revolutionary days on the Continent a generation earlier. In part, of course, this was due to greater personal maturity and the ripening of his thought. He was forty-six when the International was founded and had had time to read widely and deeply in nondoctrinaire literature: economics, trade reports, labor statistics, political history, and discussions of social problems in general.

In part, Marx's comparative moderation was the result of

his experiences in England. For a generation he had been exposed to British life, where the Parliamentary system, with all its shortcomings, did work in practice. Despite social injustices, economic inequalities and deep class feelings on both sides of the social scale, the British government was not oppressive. Like Voltaire, who had also lived in London as a political refugee a century or so earlier, Marx found a surprising amount of freedom and public decency in England. Unlike the Continent, Britain suffered neither from police brutality nor from intellectual persecution. There was no official censorship of the press, for example; and elections, though occasionally corrupt, were generally free and open. Basic British stability, involving a widespread respect for law, suggested to Marx, as it did also to English Chartists and trade unionists, the possibility of achieving social and economic change without a violent revolution, at least in countries, such as Britian, Holland and the United States, where political democracy prevailed.

The Inaugural Address consisted of two main parts. The first was devoted to British economic and social conditions, which were obviously of special interest to the English members of the International. But they were also important from the point of view of general political-economic theory, for Britain was then the center of world capitalism. The example of Britain in matters such as investments, business enterprise, technological advances, colonialism, wages, standards of living and, above all, the role of labor in an increasingly industrialized society was bound to have an impact on other countries, including France and Germany, then in various stages of capitalist development. "England," Marx wrote, "heads the Europe of commerce and industry."

The Address stated that England had undergone an unrivaled expansion of its industry since the defeat of the 1848–1849 European revolutions, but that there had been no comparable benefit for the workers. Marx quoted statistics and government reports to show the immensity of the wealth accumulated by the few—some of them with yearly incomes of £50,000 and upwards—and the shocking misery, pauperism, "broken health, tainted morals and mental ruin" suffered by working people. "And yet," he pointed out, "the period passed since the revolutions of 1848 has not been without its compensating features."

Two victories had been achieved by English labor in the

period between 1848 and 1864. One was the ten-hour day, and the other the cooperative movement.

For a long time, Marx wrote, English economists, such as Andrew Ure,[1] Nassau William Senior,[2] and "other sages of that stamp," had predicted that any restriction of the hours of labor "must sound the death knell of British industry, which, vampire-like, could but live by sucking blood, and children's blood, too." The workers agitating for a shorter working day had been obliged to fight fiercely not only against avarice but also against the political economy of the middle class, with its "blind rules of the supply and demand laws." Despite all this, the Ten Hours' Bill was passed by Parliament. This, Marx wrote, was a victory of principle.

A still greater victory of "the political economy of labor over the political economy of property" was the cooperative movement. The value of cooperative experiments, the seeds of which were laid by Robert Owen in Britain, lay in showing the possibility of modern economic production on a large scale without "the existence of a class of masters employing a class of hands." Cooperative production "cannot be over-rated," because, properly organized, it could free workers from domination and exploitation and cause them to work not as reluctant slaves, but "with a willing hand, a ready mind and a joyous heart."

But, Marx warned, the cooperative movement would be futile if it remained confined to casual efforts of small groups. A few "private workmen" could never be strong enough to stop the growth of big monopolies or free the masses from their misery. To be effective, it was necessary to develop cooperatives on a national scale, supported by national means. Since the "lords of the land and the lords of capital" could be expected to use their political privileges to perpetuate their economic power, labor must use its political power to achieve economic emancipation.

In the second part of the Inaugural Address Marx briefly developed a foreign policy for the working class, pointing out that international politics was its vital concern, as a result of

[1]Ure, *The Philosophy of Manufactures: or an Exposition of the Scientific, Moral and Commercial Economy of the Factory System of Great Britain* (2d ed., London, 1835).

[2]Senior, *Three Lectures on the Rate of Wages* (London, 1830); *An Outline of the Science of Political Economy* (London, 1836); *Letters on the Factory Act, as it affects the Cotton Manufacture* (London, 1837).

the integral connection between the oppressive and unjust
policies pursued by governments at home and abroad. Labor
could not emancipate itself so long as it did not stop governments from following "criminal designs," playing upon "national prejudices" and squandering "in piratical wars the
people's blood and treasure" abroad. The imperialist policies
of Europe's ruling classes had permitted the assassination of
Poland and the foreign encroachments and aggressions of
Russia, "that barbarous power, whose head is at St. Petersburg, and whose hands are in every Cabinet of Europe."

Oppressive foreign policies must be countered by labor on
an international scale. Workers should use "all means in their
power," including public denunciations and protests, such as
the one that prevented the British government from supporting the slave states in the American Civil War, to vindicate
the "laws of morals and justice" that ought to govern nations
in their relations with each other. "The fight for such a foreign policy," Marx wrote, "forms part of the general struggle
for the emancipation of the working classes."

He concluded with a familiar slogan: "Workers of all
countries, unite!"

The International's official statements, which Marx drafted,
did not advocate communism, violent revolution or the overthrow of the existing order of society for the attainment of
proletarian ends. They opposed injustice, war, exploitation
and oppression; they defended the rights of workers and supported strikes not only in England but also in Belgium,
France, Germany, Spain and Switzerland. In his role as actual, though never titular, head of the International, Marx
carefully avoided extreme formulations, so that his
documents would be, as Engels summed it up in 1890, "ac-
ceptable to the English trade unions, to the followers of
Proudhon in France, Belgium, Italy and Spain, and to the
Lassalleans in Germany." Indeed, Marx often acted as a
moderating influence in the sometimes heated weekly sessions
of the General Council.

Printer's Ink

Marx was always acutely aware of the value of propaganda, and he strove to have the work of the International
publicized as widely as possible.

The first journal to print the International's official

documents and reports was a London weekly, which in the course of its existence, between 1861 and 1876, was known successively as the *Bee-Hive*, the *Bee-Hive Newspaper* and the *Penny Bee-Hive*. Each of them had the drawing of a bee-hive, symbol of busyness, on its masthead. The *Bee-Hive* was not a house organ of the International but an indepen- dent trade union journal, with a tendency, which infuriated Marx, to garble its reports. In April 1870, at his suggestion, the General Council broke with the *Bee-Hive* altogether, and, in effect, excommunicated it as an enemy of labor.

But by that time the International had long ceased to rely exclusively on the *Bee-Hive*. By January 1865, it had at least five publications which it could claim as its own, four of them on the Continent. In London, the International took over the *Miner and Workman's Advocate*, renamed it the *Workman's Advocate*, and appointed a multinational editorial board, of which Marx was a member, to run it. The paper championed the usual radical causes, which were also favored by the International: direct taxation, manhood suffrage, a shorter work week, cooperatives and nationalization of land.

Altogether, in the course of its eight-year existence, the In- ternational had about eighteen organs in various European cities, including Amsterdam, Antwerp, Barcelona, Brussels, Geneva, Madrid, Naples and Paris. It even had a weekly in Palma de Majorca. Some of these publications had small cir- culations limited to the labor unions affiliated with the Inter- national and were short-lived; others, among them Bakuninist organs in Switzerland and Proudhonist ones in France, did not follow the line laid down by the General Council in Lon- don; but each of them claimed affiliation with the Interna- tional, and in its own way, reflected some of its programs.

Marx also used friendly labor, leftist or socialist publica- tions to propagate the ideas of the International or to correct misconceptions about its policies. Among journals more or less sympathetic to the International were the *Eastern Post* in London, *Le Réveil* in Paris, the *Social-Demokrat* in Berlin and the *Volkswille* in Vienna.

Urged by Marx, the International made determined efforts to have its actions and programs reported also in the bour- geois press. Theoretically, of course, he was hostile to the bourgeois press as a paid servant of capitalism and an enemy of the proletariat, but in practice he was addicted to newspa- pers and his work-room in London was piled helter-skelter with them. The bigger the paper's circulation and the greater its influence, the more it impressed Marx—and often enraged him. It was a proud day when the London *Times,* the powerful voice of the British financial and political establishment, published a document of the International.

Organization and Policies

The International was organized as a democratic body, with free elections of members and open discussion. Occasionally it worked behind "front" organizations which it helped to set up. One of them was the Reform League, organized in 1865, of whose twelve-man steering committee six were also members of the International's General Council. The Reform League, which Marx called "our work," organized street demonstrations and public meetings in favor of universal suffrage. Marx delighted in these activities.

In general, the policies and activities of the International were aboveboard and nonconspiratorial. This, indeed, was one of the reasons for the bitter quarrel, which was to rend the organization in the last years of its existence, between the publicity-conscious Marx and the inveterate conspirator Michael Bakunin.

The International was organized like a federal republic, with elected legislative and executive bodies, and a constituent base consisting of local Sections organized in many cities in England and Western Europe (except Germany, where foreign affiliations were illegal). The Sections were given charters and membership cards (a penny apiece) by the General Council. In each country, the Sections were connected with a Federal Council, which, in turn, was in contact with London.

The legislative branch of the International was the annual Congress, which met in the month of September for a period of from three to five days. Delegates were chosen by the various Sections according to the number of their members. The Congress checked the mandates of the delegates to assure against fraudulent representation. The number of delegates varied with each Congress. There were sixty at the Geneva Congress in 1866, sixty-four at Lausanne in 1867, one hundred at Brussels in 1868, seventy-eight at Basel in 1869, twenty-three at London in 1871,[3] and sixty-five at the final one in The Hague in 1872. Marx never attended a Congress on the Continent, except the one at The Hague, where he went to prevent Bakunin and the anarchists from taking over the International.

Congresses followed prepared agendas and, when necessary, worked through *ad hoc* committees. They heard reports, amended the rules, debated issues, voted on policies and passed resolutions. They also had the power to expel members and to recognize affiliated bodies. The decisions and resolutions of the Congress were supposed to be binding on the constituent Sections and national Councils, but in practice they were impossible to enforce. Neither the Congress nor the General Council had the power to make recalcitrant or discontented Sections obey decisions, even if they were passed by a majority of the delegates.

The General Council

The Executive of the International was the General Council, the guiding and policy-making body, as well as its communications center. The Council held weekly meetings, which were rarely attended by the full membership. Attendance, except for extraordinary sessions, varied anywhere from around ten to fifteen members, the average being probably about a dozen. During the first three years of its existence, the Council had a president, George Odger, a shoemaker, elected annually. In September 1866, the English members proposed Marx as president, but he declined in favor of Odger's reelection. Marx felt that it was preferable for the nominal head of the International to be an Englishman, rather than a European refugee speaking with a heavy Teutonic accent. Soon afterwards, however, Marx quarreled with Odger and moved that the presidency be abolished and meetings of the Council be chaired by a presiding officer chosen weekly. Odger, an ambitious trade unionist, never forgave Marx. In 1871, he was one of the few prominent members of the Council to refuse to sign *The Civil War in France*, a

[3]Because of the Franco-Prussian War, there was no Congress in 1870; the sparsely attended Congress of 1871 was held in London, owing to the still-unsettled conditions on the Continent.

pamphlet which Marx wrote for the International in defense of the Paris Commune.

The work of the Council was carried out by a General Secretary, who was paid 10 shillings weekly, and permanent Corresponding Secretaries for countries in which the International had either direct affiliation or a special interest. Among the affiliates were Austria-Hungary, Belgium, Denmark, France, Italy, Spain, Switzerland and the United States. Germany, Ireland and Poland were nonaffiliates but nevertheless a concern of the Council. The Secretaries were responsible for maintaining contact with the affiliates and national groups, forwarding instructions, writing letters, receiving correspondence and requesting information. The Secretaries, in turn, reported at the Council sessions, which they attended regularly, like Marx.

The Council also served as a final court of appeals. This was particularly true in the last four years of its existence, when it was often called upon to adjudicate among competing jurisdictions, conflicting interpretations and clashing personalities of the squabbling Sections in Belgium, France, Italy, Switzerland and the United States. Many radicals, particularly the verbalizers and pseudo-intellectuals who often spoke in the name of labor, were addicted to furious altercations and doctrinal disputes. They provided drama and zest in lives that were otherwise indigent, impotent and frustrated. As a court of appeals, the Council of the International was bound to find itself in a losing position. Satisfying one group of *enragés* usually meant infuriating another. As acrimony grew, the Council's decisions tended to be ignored, which in turn led to expulsion of the offending person or Section. In the end, the technique of expulsion only contributed to the disintegration of the International.

Marx's Role

From the very first, other members of the General Council, less literate and less sure in their purpose than Marx, were glad to have him to take over responsibility. This was particularly true when it came to the all-important function of formulating positions. "I am," Marx told Engels in 1865, "in fact the head of the thing."

For Marx, the International came as a once-in-a-lifetime chance for action and expression through an organized channel that had the possibility of reaching the world proletariat. Not even in his younger years in Germany, when he was the editor of the *Neue Rheinische Zeitung* in 1848–1849, did he have a similar opportunity to affect the course of history, as he visualized it.

Marx knew that he could never again be active on the Continent, where no country would accept him.

The International was also of personal importance to Marx. It afforded him the opportunity to break out of his relatively isolated existence and widen his contacts and his social life.

As a member of the General Council, he came to know British trade unionists and could not help being interested in their pragmatism and nondoctrinaire attitudes toward labor and social problems. Occasionally he invited some of the trade unionists to his house, where his charming wife provided food, cooked by Lenchen (sometimes a "very frugal dinner," as Marx put it on some of his invitations), and he supplied rich conversation. The English trade unionists had never been exposed to anyone like Dr. Marx, with his vast erudition, philosophic sweep and positive opinions expressed in fluent English with a heavy *tschoirrman* accent. According to all testimony, Marx was an impressive, if not an overwhelming, conversationalist.

As the guiding spirit of the International, he was also a magnet for European visitors to England. Radicals from the Continent would drop in to visit him when in London. Among them were journalists, agitators, politicians, conspirators—even bona fide labor leaders: Austrians, Belgians, Dutchmen, Frenchmen, Germans, Hungarians, Italians, Poles, Russians, Spaniards and Swiss. Some of them later turned out to be spies or double agents, but all of them were welcomed by Marx as fresh sources of gossip about outstanding Continental political figures and radical personalities. The information Marx received was often of dubious veracity, but he loved to believe the worst about political leaders, particularly his own enemies.

His pet aversion was Napoleon III, a subject of the juiciest Paris gossip, which Marx loved to hear and spread. The Empress Eugénie, Marx wrote to Adolf Cluss on March 25, 1853, suffered from the affliction of farting in public, a "tympoptano mania" which the poor woman could not control. Marx commented, in French, *"Ce n' est qu'un petit bruit, un murmure, un rien; mais enfin, vous savez que les Français ont le nez au plus petit vent*—['Tis but a small noise, a murmur, a nothing, but, after all, you know the French have a nose for the smallest wind.]"

For Marx, the International involved burdens and worries, which he shouldered willingly, even though he was often *"gebothered"* by them. By the end of 1865, the work absorbed so much of his time that, he complained to Engels, "it weighs on me like an incubus." Marx alleged that he would throw it off if there were anybody to take his place, but this seems unlikely.

Theory of Revolution

Marx willingly sacrificed his time and energies to the International, for he was convinced that in it he at last possessed a great instrument for world revolution, more effective than anything to be found in Europe.

However, as early as April 1856, in a speech delivered at a banquet celebrating the anniversary of the *People's Paper,* a Chartist weekly founded by Ernest Jones in 1852, Marx had struck a different note. Speaking in English, and proud of the fact that he was the only foreigner invited for the occasion, Marx stated that the real revolution that would ultimately emancipate the proletariat lay not in the sort of "noisy" and "confused" actions that had characterized the Continental uprisings of 1848–1849, but in the development of science and technology. Steam, electricity, powered machinery, Marx said, were bringing about basic transformations, first in the economic sphere and then unavoidably in the social superstructure.[4] The obvious implication of his remarks was that mere rhetoric about "revolution," of the kind spouted by Bakuninists, Blanquists, Proudhonists and other agitators whose oral and written utterances showed a deplorable ignorance of economics, were mere phase-mongering and wishfulfillment.

After years of research in economics, Marx had concluded that science was the true revolutionary force that was transforming society. The new world of industrialization produced by science was bound to require larger numbers of workers to serve the growing industries. At some point in history, the

---

[4]For text, see Saul K. Padover, ed., *Karl Marx on Revolution* (New York, 1971), pp. 59–60.

working class would become numerous and strong enough to make a successful bid for power.

Revolution, in the sense of actual transformation of the basic forms and institutions of society, thus depended on concrete economic development, and not on the will of a charismatic revolutionary or utopian dreamer. Not all countries were in the same stage of development or moved at the same tempo. Most of the world, including "barbaric" Russia, was still in a pre-industrial stage, agricultural or nomadic, and therefore not ripe for revolution. This was something that the wilder radicals of Marx's time, against whom he struggled bitterly in the International, failed to grasp.

Thus, though the working class was historically predestined to rule, there was no way of foretelling the precise moment at which it would seize power. In the interim, the proletariat must bide its time and prepare itself for its role. It must avoid hasty and premature action, such as that of the Paris Commune of 1871, for example, which could be ruinous.

While awaiting the final seizure of power, the workers must take advantage of every opportunity to acquire experience and hasten the revolutionary process. They must learn effective methods of organization, without which nothing could be achieved in the modern world. They should engage in incessant struggles, even for limited objectives.

Organized action would give the workers invaluable training for their ultimate role. They would acquire political experience through the organization of their own parties and mass demonstrations, economic experience through cooperatives and well-led strikes, intellectual experience through the acquisition of skills and technical, as well as cultural, education, fraternal experience through support given to the strivings for independence of oppressed peoples like the Irish and the Poles, experience in international affairs through consistent opposition to imperialistic and nationalistic wars.

These organized activities would not only supply workers with experience, but also strengthen their class consciousness and provide them with steady purpose and inspiration. In addition, they would help to ripen the conditions for a real revolution. The final form of the revolution would be forged by such class-oriented struggles. Any other approach, Marx wrote, is nothing but "chewed-over general banalities."

Such, in essence, was Marx's post-*Communist Manifesto* view of revolution, as he developed it in the period when he dominated the International. His basic ideas were not always clear to his contemporaries, for he often lacked precision and spoke in generalities when embattled and antagonistic. This, together with his tone of dogmatism and anger, was likely to intensify both the uncertainty and the opposition.

To the end of his life, however, Marx held steadfast to the idea that the proletarian revolution could not simply be invented by the imagination, but would be determined in its method and outcome by actual conditions.

Marx Assigns a Revolutionary Role to England

As the internal splits of the International gradually came to the fore, Continental members criticized the choice of London as the headquarters of the General Council, on the grounds that it was too removed from revolutionary ferment. A revolutionary center, they argued, should be where the revolutionists were: on the Continent, and, more particularly, in France.

Marx used his great dialectical skill to defend the choice of London as the proper locus, and in the process he developed a theory assigning England to a special role in the revolution to come. He believed that Victorian England was then undergoing its final stages of industrial-economic transformation. In England, the basic economic revolution had gone farther than anywhere else, and its example was bound to affect the rest of the world, and ultimately to be followed by it. Consequently, for those who were charged with the responsibility of charting and guiding the course of future revolution—that is to say, the General Council of the International—the place to be was where the action was, namely capitalist London, and not small-town Geneva or petty-bourgeois Paris. Only in London, the world's center of international finance, commerce, colonialism, science and technology, could the final development of the capitalist system be properly observed; only there could the social-political-economic lessons emerging from its maturation be learnt. Marx vigorously elucidated his theory that Britain was ripening for revolution when he defended the policies of the General Council against increasingly disruptive assaults by impatient Continental radicals, who accused him of having ceased to be a real revolutionary.

The English, of course, never undertook the starring role Marx had assigned to them, nor did his General Council ever succeed in transforming British trade unionists into Continental Jacobins.

Battle with Bakunin

By the end of 1868, in the fourth year of its existence, the International began to run into serious trouble. Its disruptive difficulties, unexpected by Marx and contrary to his theories, ultimately grew to be beyond control.

One of the major conflicts within the International centered around Michael Bukunin. Marx's clash with Bakunin was symbolic of the conflicting forces within European radicalism itself. The two men represented deeply divergent views of the meaning of revolution and the role of the working class. Theirs was a struggle between the ideas of order and of anarchy, of collectivism and individualism. Marx's primary concern was with power, to be achieved through political organization. Bakunin ultimately rejected all authority, proletarian, republican or monarchical, in favor of individual freedom, total and uncontrolled. "The liberty of man," Bakunin wrote, "consists solely in this, that he obeys the laws of nature, because he has himself recognized them as such, and not because they have been imposed upon him externally by a foreign will whatsoever, human or divine, collective or individual." For Marx, on the other hand, freedom and individualism did not exist outside the scope of organized systems.

The two men, who had first met in Paris in 1844, when Marx was twenty-six years old and Bakunin thirty, admired each other's revolutionary passion, but they never understood, liked or trusted one another. Their characters and experiences were worlds apart. Marx, as the son of a middle-class Rhineland lawyer imbued with the tradition of Rousseau and Voltaire, had grown up in an atmosphere of bourgeois orderliness, legality and comparative intellectual freedom. Bakunin, the son of a wealthy Russian landowner, was shaped in an environment of Czarist despotism and feudal cruelty.

An an officer of the Imperial Guards, which he entered at the age of seventeen, he had witnessed harsh repression of the Poles, which revolted him. He soon rebelled against Czarism in Russia, then against tyranny everywhere, and finally against all political institutions. Rejecting national loyalties, he became a professional international revolutionist. At a time when Marx was pursuing a sedentary career as a journalist, Bakunin fought in revolutionary skirmishes, gun in hand.

Bakunin, physically a giant and a man of awesome courage, paid a harsh price for his revolutionary activities. After fighting in various uprisings in 1848, he was captured in Saxony and condemned to death, but was turned over to the Austrians, who condemned him to death once again. Execution was postponed, and Bakunin spent several months in jail, in chains. The Austrians delivered him to the Russians, who imprisoned him in the fearful fortresses of Petropavlovsk and Schluesselberg. He was savagely maltreated, contracted scurvy, lost his teeth. After five years of solitary confinement, he petitioned Czar Nicholas I for a pardon, which was granted after a fashion: in 1857 he was exiled to Siberia for life. Four years later, he succeeded in escaping and making his way, via Japan and California, back to Europe. Early in November 1864, shortly after the International was organized, Marx saw him in London for the first time in sixteen years. He was impressed with Bakunin and thought that he had matured and changed for the better.

But the sympathy and appreciation did not last.

Bakunin first settled in Italy, where he established a journal to preach his own brand of radicalism. He also founded a secret revolutionary society, consisting of small groups of conspirators, with branches in France, Poland and Spain. Then he moved to Switzerland. In 1867, the restless Bakunin tried to take over the League of Peace and Freedom, a pacifist group, and, having failed to do so, he joined the International. He became editor of *L'Égalité*, a weekly in Geneva, which served as the platform for his ideas.

Jumping from scheme to scheme, Bakunin continued to agitate, plot and orate. He rarely completed anything. His fellow exile, the Russian writer Alexander Herzen, said of him that he always "took the second month of pregnancy for the ninth." But Bakunin, the heavy-footed giant, clad in a Russian peasant blouse, and enveloped in perpetual cigarette smoke, had a dramatic impact on audiences consisting precisely of the kind of people Marx's International was hoping to reach, organize and influence. A genuine tribune of the people and a blazing orator, Bakunin stirred his hearers, radical workers and half-baked intellectuals, to frenzy with his impassioned tirades against tyranny and hatred of all systems, governments and organized political activities. Undisciplined and reckless, by turns artless and devious, the demonic Bakunin was, as Marx belatedly discovered, a very dangerous man.

Bakunin's fragmentary writings show that his basic ideas were not only in conflict with the methods and objectives of the International, but also a direct challenge to Marx and the whole German socialist school. Bakunin distrusted Germans as born lackeys, devoid of any sense of freedom, and believed that anything organized by them, or in line with their theories, whether Marxist or Lassallean, would end in despotism in the name of socialism. In the light of the Russian Revolution of 1917, led by the Marx-inspired Lenin, who can doubt Bakunin's remarkable prescience?

In October 1868, in Geneva, Bakunin secretly organized an *Alliance Internationale de la Démocratie Socialiste*. This International Alliance of Socialist Democracy was meant to function alongside Marx's International. Bakunin claimed that his "Alliance" aimed to restore the "idealism" lacking in the International. The "Alliance" declared itself in favor of the equality of all classes, the abolition of the state and the rejection of open political struggle on the part of the workers—a program sharply at variance with Marx's philosophy and the aims of the International. When the news of the "Alliance" first reached Marx in London, his initial reaction was to ignore it as *"fadaise* [twaddle]," *"Scheisse* [shit]" and "Russian idealism." But he soon sensed the potential danger and took steps against it.

Accordingly, on December 22, the General Council issued a formal statement, written by Marx, outlawing the "Alliance" as a branch of the International and declaring its statutes "null and void."

"I do not trust any Russian," Marx told Engels. He was right to be distrustful. While Bakunin formally agreed to dissolve the "Alliance" and remain faithful to the International, he continued secretly to work against it. His aim was to undermine its leadership with a view to taking over the organization. Bakunin did this with "Russian cunning," as Engels called it, and deliberate deception.

For about four years, Marx, whose suspicions of Bakunin grew almost paranoid in intensity, continued to battle him inside the International. It was ultimately a vain effort, first because Bakunin was sly and slippery, and secondly because he developed a loyal following among the anarchist branches of the International, particularly in the important French-speaking and Latin countries. Under the influence of Bakunin, they challenged Marx's leadership of the International and attacked its policies in publications such as *L'Égalité*.

Its final disintegration was hastened by the crises engendered by the Franco-Prussian War and the Paris Commune.

The Franco-Prussian War

The war between France and Prussia, which began on July 19, 1870, had an immediate impact on both the International and the balance of power in Europe. Among other things, it resulted in Germany becoming a united empire and France a divided republic.

Marx came to see that the war, being both nationalist and imperialist, was likely to arouse confusing emotions among working people in the belligerent countries. The International, he felt, owed it to the workers to provide them with orientation and guidance. On July 23, he completed the "First Address of the International on the Franco-Prussian War." With a donation of £20 from the London Peace Society, 30,-000 copies of the "Address" were printed in German and French, and distributed in Europe by the General Council.[5]

The "Address," which Marx was pleased to hear was praised by no less a thinker than John Stuart Mill,[6] appealed to the working class on both sides to refrain from supporting the war. It also alerted the German workers to a menace Marx particularly dreaded, namely, that if the war were prolonged, the Prussians might appeal for help to the Russian Czar, who would then enter Germany and make that country a permanent base for his long-cherished plan to dominate Europe.

Marx was always haunted by the fear that the Russian feudal hordes would someday pour across Europe's frontiers, destroying Western civilization, and wiping out the hard-won gains of Europe's relatively free working class—especially after 1848–1849, when the Czar's "Cossacks" had helped the Austrian Emperor to smash the revolutions in the Habsburg Empire.

Events moved rapidly, and a few days after the French

[5] Marx to Engels, August 17, 1870.
[6] Marx to Engels, August 8, 1870.

proclaimed the Third Republic on September 4, 1870, with a Provisional Government under the leadership of General Louis Jules Trochu and Léon Gambetta, a republican politician, Marx issued the "Second Address of the International on the Franco-Prussian War." In it, he appealed to German labor to protest against Bismarck's policy of wresting Alsace-Lorraine from France and annexing it to the new German Empire, and to work for peace and the recognition of the new French Republic. He also urged the French workers, particularly members of the International, not to be tricked by nationalist memories but to support the Republic and use it for their own ends.

Marx's appeals had no effect. In Germany there were some workers' demonstrations against the war, and a few socialist leaders, among them August Bebel and Wilhelm Liebknecht, went to jail for opposing it. But the war was extremely popular, even outside Prussia itself, where the common people, in what Marx called "south German beer patriotism,"[7] found a new pride in the prowess of Teutonic arms and superiority in general.

In France, where chauvinism was always endemic, the swift and humiliating defeat at the hands of the helmeted, goose-stepping Prussians, whom even Marx considered an inferior race because of their presumed Russian origins (*Prussia* comes from the word *Bo-Russia*), brought out strong nationalistic and anti-German feelings. The International in London was centered in the General Council, which in turn was dominated by Germans, and so it was not difficult for Marx's enemies in France to foment the suspicion, spread by Bakunin,[8] that it was a tool of Prussia and that Marx himself was a secret agent of Bismarck.

Increasing Troubles

The General Council was gradually disintegrating. Even Eccarius, Marx's local ally from the very beginning of the International, rebelled against his authority. The immediate occasion had to do with the United States, where the International's branches were splitting apart into independent groups of dubious ideological purity. At the Council's session

[7]Marx to Engels, August 17, 1870.
[8]Marx to Engels, August 3, 1870.

of March 12, 1872, it was resolved that in future "no new American Sections would be recognized unless they consisted of at least two-thirds wage workers." Eccarius, then Secretary for the United States, told Marx that he would not forward the various resolutions to America and that he was resigning from his position.

The defection of Eccarius, crazy or not,[9] at a time of political crisis, was a particularly hard blow to Marx, but he doggedly continued the operations of the General Council. Despite ill health, he persisted in attending its sessions. After February 1872, the Council met in Rathbone Place, and occasionally also in Marx's or Engels' house. Some of the meetings lasted from four o'clock in the afternoon to one in the morning. In addition, there were manifestos and "mountains of letters"[10] to answer. Battling to preserve the International, Marx neglected his own work, delayed the revision of the second German edition of *Das Kapital* and postponed editing its French translation, which needed his skilled linguistic help.

Reluctantly, Marx came to accept the idea that he could not continue to carry the whole burden of the International and do his own work at the same time. In the spring of 1872, he decided to terminate his leadership of the squabbling International after its next Congress, which was to take place in The Hague in September.

The Hague Congress

In ending his own role in the International and thus hastening its eventual dissolution, Marx's motivation was essentially political. In Europe, the organization was not only in disarray, particularly in Switzerland and among the Latins, but in danger of being taken over by Bakunin and his anarchist followers. The thought of Russians and other raw, undisciplined Europeans seizing the International scared and angered Marx. He was determined to purge the organization of Bakuninists, whom Engels called an "ignorant and unclean element." The situation, he wrote, "cannot go on."[11]

On September 1, Marx, his wife and his daughter Eleanor, accompanied by Engels, arrived at The Hague to participate

[9]Engels to Liebknecht, May 27–28, 1872: Eccarius "is crazy."
[10]Jennychen to Ludwig and Gertrud Kugelmann, June 27, 1872.
[11]Engels to Paul Lafargue, March 11, 1872.

in the seventh and last Congress of the International. Lodgings were hard to obtain. Paul Lafargue said that he and his wife chased "like maniacs" to find quarters. Marx had suggested that the delegates wear blue ribbons for identification, in case they got lost in the city.

The Hague swarmed with journalists and secret police agents from a number of European countries which kept dossiers on Marx. The conclave of radicals in the Dutch capital, taking place one year after the Paris Commune, was naturally a matter of anxiety to Europe's governments. A leading French politician, Jules Simon (later Prime Minister), vainly urged the Dutch not to allow the Congress to take place. The unintimidated Hollanders assured European ambassadors in The Hague that they had made preparations to prevent disorder. They mobilized troops, which patrolled the main streets. Sentries were doubled. The Hague looked like a city under martial law.

The French were particularly concerned with the Congress. They sent to The Hague a special squad commanded by a police commissioner from Paris. The squad reported to the Paris Prefecture that the notorious Marx, who lived in great luxury, was plotting to soften up France to prepare it for German conquest, to assassinate Thiers and the King of Spain, and to stir up trouble in Holland so as to give the Germans an excuse for annexing it.[12]

Gossip and rumor were rife. The city burghers looked upon Marx and the other delegates of the International as a species of brigands. The Hague *Dagblaad* warned its uneasy readers to be careful with their possessions. Now that the "scroundrels of the Paris Commune" were coming, the newspaper urged its readers not to let women and children walk alone in the streets, to leave their earrings at home, and to close the jewelry shops. But the Dutch police provided the radicals and their convention hall on Lombardstraat with conscientious protection.

The Congress opened on Monday, September 2, but the first three days were devoted to the crucial matter of examining credentials. There were bitter disputes, in which Marx was an active participant. He himself had three mandates, from the General Council, from Section One in New York, and from Leipzig. His son-in-law Lafargue had two, from

---

[12]Copies of the police dossiers are to be found in the Amsterdam International Institute of Social History, E 79 and E 82.

Portugal and Spain. Engels also had two, from Section Six in New York and from Breslau. Altogether there were ninety-five mandates, distributed among sixty-five accredited delegates.

The Congress, which sat in the Concordia, a dance hall on Lombardstraat, was one of the largest and most representative in the history of the International. The sixty-five delegates represented fifteen countries, the biggest contingent being French, with eighteen members, many of them Blanquists, who were partly romantic revolutionists. The second largest group was German, consisting of fifteen delegates, among them such leading radicals as Bernhard Becker, a writer and editor; Joseph Dietzgen, a labor philosopher; Adolph Hepner, a founder of the Social-Democratic party; and Marx's friend Ludwig Kugelmann. There were also seven Belgians, five Englishmen and five Spaniards, four Dutchmen and four Swiss, two Austrians, and one Dane, one Hungarian, one Irishman and one Pole. The majority of them, including the Germans, were pro-Marx, but there was a strong anti-Marx minority, consisting mainly of assorted anarchists and Bakuninists. Roughly, the pro-Marxists could garner about forty out of the sixty-five votes.

The most conspicuous absentee, the essential cause of The Hague Congress, was Bakunin himself.

Marx was, of course, the dominant figure. His fame, or notoriety, was such that, in the words of the London *Standard* correspondent, he was "pestered by requests for interviews from people in all countries and politics."[13] His appearance, too, the big, hirsute head, the swarthy complexion and the gray beard, was impressive. In addition, Marx wore a black broadcloth suit and a monocle, which he pressed to his right eye when he wanted to look at anybody.

The real work of the Congress began on Thursday, September 5. The meeting hall was located in a workers' district, standing near a prison, laundries, small shops, seedy cabarets and beer halls. It swarmed with people. Sessions were also held in the evening to attract workers, who came boisterously, in larger numbers than the Concordia could accommodate, adding to the decibels and compounding the confusion.

The real work of the Congress took place in committees, which were the scenes of intense and bitter conflict between

[13]Bernstein, *The First International in America*, p. 149.

the Marxists and the Bakuninists. Apart from personal antipathies, it was a struggle for the soul of the radical movement in Europe: the Marxists believed in guided central authority and in organized political action; the Bakuninists and anarchists rejected both in favor of individual and local autonomy, including activities through secret societies. Specifically, the anti-Marxists challenged the right of the General Council in London to enforce its decisions and suspend recalcitrant Sections and federations. James Guillaume, the Swiss editor of the Bakuninist journals *Le Progrès* and *La Solidarité*, defended autonomous action of the International branches and denied the General Council's authority to dictate to or suspend anybody.

The Bakuninists suffered defeat when a committee, investigating a batch of documents on the Alliance of Socialist Democracy, determined that the evident purpose of this anarchist organization was to disrupt and destroy the International. In a vote of 3 to 2, the committee recommended that Bakunin be expelled from the International. When the recommendation was reported, a furious Spanish anarchist, who was in the habit of wearing a red flag around his waist, pulled a gun and shouted at the *rapporteur, "Un homme comme ça devrait être traité à coups de revolver!* [A man like that ought to be treated with revolver shots!]" He was disarmed, and the Congress voted overwhelmingly to expel Bakunin and Guillaume.

But expulsion did not solve the problem of the anarchists. The Bakuninist spirit prevailed among Swiss and Latin workers, as Marx well knew. They believed in immediate and direct violence, without benefit of open political parties or revolutionary theory. Marx feared that if the International remained in Europe, its archives and organization would be seized by anarchists who would commit great infamies and *Dummheiten* [idiocies], as Engels put it, in the name of the International.

On the last day of the Congress, Marx scribbled a note in French, which was signed by ten of his friends and adherents.[14] It read, "We are proposing that for the year

[14]Maltman Barry, English journalist; Eugène Dupont, French musical-instrument maker living in London; Frederick Engels; Benjamin Le Moussu, French engraver; Friedrich Lessner, German tailor living in London; Charles Longuet, French journalist, who married Marx's daughter Jenny in October 1872; J. Patrick McDonnel (or MacDonnell), Irish socialist; Auguste Serraillier, French shoemaker living in London;

1872–1873 the seat of the General Council be transferred to New York. . . ."

The proposal, made by Engels, shocked the Congress and led to an outburst of oratory, pro and con. Edouard Vaillant, a French socialist physician, cried out that New York would be about the same as the moon. Blanquists argued that the seat of the General Council should remain in London, where the French immigrants were. The delegates were almost evenly divided on the issue, but it carried by a narrow vote of 26 to 23, with nine abstentions. Among those who voted for New York were Marx's enemies, rightly believing that in America the General Council would cease to be under his influence and would lose its prestige among European workers.

The Congress came to a close on Saturday, September 7, with a singing of the *Marseillaise* and a general handshaking by everybody.

When the Congress was over, Marx, who had never slept at all while it was in progress, went with his family to nearby Scheveningen, where he invited friends for dinner and a concert on the terrace of the Grand Hotel. They were all under the surveillance of the Dutch police. The spy reported on the doings of the Marx group and went out of his way to remark that Laura Lafargue was "very charming."[15] As for Lafargue himself, Marx, when he introduced Cuno to him, remarked in an attempt at humor, "Cuno, I am told that you are going to America, so you may do there what one of my daughters has done towards solving the color question, by marrying a nigger, for Lafargue is of colored descent."

On Sunday, September 8, Hendrik Gerhard, a pro-Bakunin Dutch tailor, invited Marx and other delegates to a meeting organized by the local Section of the International in Amsterdam. Marx went there with Engels and Lafargue, as well as a few friends, such as Sorge and Becker, to find that most of the delegates there were antagonistic. What had been a friendly majority in The Hague was now a minority in Amsterdam. There was the usual radical oratory, which allayed no animosities. When James Guillaume, the expelled Bakuninist, heard that Marx was going to make a speech, he took a walk in the park, followed by three like-minded Span-

George Sexton, English socialist physician; Walery Wroblewsky, Polish revolutionary, General in the Paris Commune.

[15]Quoted in H. Gemkow, *Karl Marx. Eine Biographie* (Berlin, 1967), p. 361.

ish delegates. They missed a speech that is of special importance in the history of Marxism.

The text of Marx's address, which he delivered in German and French,[16] is known from the notes of the German, Belgian, French and Dutch correspondents who were there. Their reports coincide in fundamentals, with a few variations. In the German version, published in *Der Volksstaat* (October 2, 1872), the idea of violence is minimized and in the Belgian one it is stressed. In a highly abbreviated Dutch version that appeared in the Amsterdam *Allgemeen Handelsblaad*, the subject of violence is not mentioned.[17]

Marx started out by saying that the reason for the choice of The Hague for the Congress of the International was that in the 18th century kings and potentates were in the habit of meeting there "to discuss the interests of their dynasties." So this was precisely the place "to reinforce the existence, propagation and hope for the future of our great Association."

The Hague Congress, he went on to say, reaffirmed the principle of the necessity for the working class to fight the old, disintegrating society on political and social grounds. Marx stated that he considered the anarchists' doctrine of abstention from organized political action "dangerous and fatal to our cause." For someday the worker must seize political power and build up a new organization of labor, if he is not to lose heaven on earth, like "the old Christians who neglected and despised politics."

But the methods of achieving the workers' goals would not be everywhere the same. They would vary with the nature and institutions of each land. In democracies, power could be attained without a resort to violence; in autocracies force would be necessary.

[16]For an English translation of the text, based on the one published in the Brussels weekly, *La Liberté* (September 15, 1872), see Saul K. Padover, ed., *Karl Marx on Revolution* (New York, 1971), pp. 63–65.

[17]According to the correspondent of the *Allgemeen Handelsblaad*, Marx said: ". . . A strong centralization of power in the hands of the General Council is urgently indicated, in view of the pending [Great Power] Congress of Berlin, which, in the view of the speaker, can be expected to make a general attack on the proletariat and the persecution and oppression of the working class. So long as the International does not appear as a firmly united body, so long as its movement is not centralized . . . its efforts will be in vain. The speaker gave the Paris Commune as an example. Why was it defeated? Because it was and remained isolated. If revolutions had broken out simultaneously with Paris in Berlin, Vienna and other capitals, the Commune would have had better expectations for success."

You know that the institutions, mores, and traditions of
various countries must be taken into consideration, and
we do not deny that there are countries—such as America, England, and if I were more familiar with your institutions, I would perhaps also add Holland—where the
workers can attain their goal by peaceful means. This
being the case, we must also recognize the fact that in
most countries on the Continent the lever of our revolution must be force; it is force to which we must someday
appeal in order to erect the rule of labor.

In *Der Volksstaat* version this last sentence was replaced
by the words: "But not in all countries is this the case."

Marx's admission of the possibility of revolution without
violence in democratic countries was to be a crucial point in
the conflict between communist and socialists in the 20th century, particularly after the Russian Revolution of 1917.

In his Amsterdam speech Marx also defended the transfer
of the General Council headquarters to New York on the
ground that the United States was becoming increasingly a
country dominated by labor. Referring to those who wondered about the transfer to New York, he asked, "Do they
then forget that America will be the workers' continent par
excellence, that half a million—workers—emigrate there
yearly, and that on such soil, where the worker dominates,
the International is bound to strike strong roots?"

Nine days after the Amsterdam speech, on September 17,
Marx and his family were back in London.

The End of the International

Marx thoroughly misjudged the future of both America
and the International. The Hague Congress with its divisive
principle of exclusion, as well as the removal of the General
Council to New York, in effect put an end to the International and terminated Marx's power over it.

It was in America that the International was finally interred. It fell prey to the usual bickerings, squabblings and
countermovements, as well as attempted takeovers by indigenous radical groups like those headed by the suffragette
Tennessee Claflin. Marx tried to direct the Council in New
York by remote control, but refused to give up the archives
in London on the ground that they were "absolutely indispens-

able" in the struggle against opponents in Europe. This created more resentment. A number of the members of the Council soon resigned or were expelled. No money was coming in from Europe, and the Council found itself, in Sorge's words, "absolutely without funds." In 1874, Sorge resigned. Engels wrote him on September 12–17, "With your resignation, the old International is completely finished. And that is good. It belonged to the Second Empire."

On July 15, 1876, the General Council held a meeting in Philadelphia, attended by fourteen delegates, and dissolved the International. Some two years later, in a *Chicago Tribune* interview held on December 18, 1878, Marx rationalized its demise: "The International Society has outlived its usefulness and exists no longer. . . . The growth of socialism of late years has been so great that its existence has become unnecessary."[18]

The First International left lasting memories in the European socialist and labor movements. It served as a precedent for the Second International, founded in Paris in 1889, six years after Marx's death. The Second International, representing Marxist Social Democratic parties, which were making rapid progress on the Continent, particularly in Germany,[19] was torn by sharply opposing interpretations of Marx's thought. Did Marx believe in the possibility of achieving socialism, at least in advanced countries, through democratic means, as he suggested in Amsterdam in September 1872, or did he exclusively advocate violence and dictatorship?

A quarter of a century after the Second International was founed, it came to an end with the outbreak of World War I in 1914. But the crucial debate over what Marx had actually said and meant in regard to revolution did not stop. After World War I, a Third International, known as the Comintern, was established, in March 1919, by Russian communists, built around Lenin's interpretation of Marxism.[20] Lenin's espousal of violence, in the name of Marx, led to a split in the ranks

---

[18]*Chicago Tribune*, January 5, 1879.

[19]In the German Parliamentary elections of January 1912, the Social Democratic party polled 4,250,000 votes or 31% of the total, winning 110 deputies, and thus becoming the largest of Germany's six political parties.

[20]For the debates between Marxist communists and socialists, see Saul K. Padover, "Kautsky and the Materialist Interpretation of History," in J. L. Cate and E. N. Anderson, eds., *Medieval and Historiographical Essays in Honor of James Westfall Thompson* (University of Chicago Press, 1938), pp. 439–64.

of socialist parties everywhere, supporters of dictatorship calling themselves communists, and advocates of democracy keeping the name of socialists or social-democrats. The Russian-led Comintern became the center of the worldwide communist movement, at least up to the period of World War II. Today, communists all over the world, in the Soviet Union as well as in China, in Europe and Africa and the Americas, invoke the name of Karl Marx.

XXII
The Paris Commune

Organization

A major cause of the destruction of the International was the Paris Commune. It was also a shattering experience for Marx, who had nourished himself on an optimistic vision of revolution.

After the surrender of Napoleon III and the French armies at Sedan on September 2, 1870, the Germans moved on Paris and besieged it. The French capital, whose Emperor was a prisoner of war, was leaderless and threatened with starvation in an especially cold winter. A French Government of National Defense was set up in Bordeaux, where the National Assembly elected Adolphe Thiers chief executive. Thiers, a conservative politician-historian who had a loathing for what he called the "vile multitude," made a peace treaty with Germany, which had in the meantime become a united empire under the victorious Prussians, led by Otto von Bismarck.[1] The treaty provided for the French cession of Alsace-Lorraine to Germany and an indemnity of five billion francs. A German army of occupation was to remain in France until the money was paid. Despite fierce opposition, voiced in particular by men like Georges Clemenceau and Léon Gambetta, both future Premiers of France, the Assembly ratified the treaty on March 1, 1871.

The peace treaty brought no peace to Paris, which did not recognize the Thiers government sitting at Versailles, the hated symbol of the *ancien régime*. Paris had set up its own National Guard and was in a state of near-insurrection. On March 18, Thiers sent regular French troops to disarm the

---

[1]On January 18, 1871, in the Hall of Mirrors at Versailles, Wilhelm III, King of Prussia, was proclaimed Kaiser [Emperor], becoming Kaiser Wilhelm I.

Paris National Guard, but the soldiers fraternized with the people. In the prevailing revolutionary atmosphere, two generals, Claude-Martin Lecomte and Clément Thomas, the latter, as Marx pointed out in his *Civil War in France,* being a political bully-boy rather than a professional officer, were shot to death. The Versailles army withdrew. Paris, then in the hands of radicals, was openly at war with the national government at Versailles.

On March 26, about a week after the two generals were killed, Paris elected a municipal council, the Commune, under the auspices of the National Guard. *Commune* in French means *township,* but in the muddle and bloodshed that soon ensued, the word became confused with *communism.* Marx's reputation and writings contributed not a little to this confusion.

In reality, the Commune was neither communistic nor particularly revolutionary. The majority of its members were not even socialists, but more or less moderate republicans.

Insofar as the Communards had a political philosophy, it was neither Marxist nor anarchist, but autonomist. The Communards wanted Paris to be an independent republic, united in a loose federation with other autonomous French communes. Each commune was to enjoy full democratic rights—of conscience, of education, of voting, of work—and absolute freedom of action within its own borders.

This made little economic or political sense, and it was certainly not in line with Marx's own basic philosophy. In fact, most of the rest of France, accustomed to centuries of highly centralized government and administration, refused to follow the example of Paris, although half a dozen cities did set up temporary communes.[2] But the passions—or fears—stirred up by Paris drowned out moderation on all sides.

Marx heard about the turmoil in Paris on March 19, one day after the Versailles troops were compelled to withdraw from the capital. He immediately set to work to help the beleaguered city. At his behest, the General Council of the International voted to ask English workers "to express sympathy with the Paris movement."[3]

At first, Marx viewed events in Paris with elation. He was enthusiastic about the revolutionary aspects of the Commune, which he considered the "incubation of a new society." On

---

[2] Le Creusot, Limoges, Lyon, Marseilles, Narbonne, Toulouse.
[3] Minutes of the General Council, March 21, 1871.

behalf of the Commune, he wrote "many hundreds of letters" to all parts of the world where the International had Sections.

On April 17, in a letter to Kugelmann, Marx explained that the Commune had to be viewed as an event of world significance. The revolutionary Parisians had no choice but to take up the fight against the Versailles *canaille* in Paris, because to succumb without a struggle would have been a "far greater misfortune than the destruction of any number of 'leaders.' " In long-range terms, the Commune represented a new stage in the class struggle between workers and capitalists. "Whatever the outcome," Marx wrote, "a new point of departure of world significance has been won." But, despite the fact that he was soon to become notorious throughout Europe as the leader and chief villain of the Commune, there was little he could actually do for the Paris radicals.

The Destruction of the Commune

Early in April, the Thiers government in Versailles sent the regular French army against Paris. Following an agreement with Bismarck, this army was soon reinforced by Marshal MacMahon and his troops, who had surrendered to the Germans at Sedan in 1870, and who were now released from captivity. While the victorious Prussians watched with *Schadenfreude* from their encampments on the eastern heights, extending in a semicircle from near St. Denis to Charenton, overlooking Paris, the French army began to batter its way from the western side of the capital.

The Paris National Guard, with its political "generals" and fancy uniforms, was obviously no match for a professional army, although the revolutionary workers fighting in the ranks often displayed unexampled and reckless bravery.

The unequal war between the Communards and the French regulars continued for six weeks, as the Communards were bloodily beaten from one barricade to another. The last holdouts were on the heights of the Buttes Chaumont and Le Père Lachaise, in the extreme eastern part of the city, and there, on Sunday, May 28, the remnants of the Communards, some 6,000 men, were simply slaughtered.

The atrocities deliberately committed by the French army against its own people vastly exceeded anything the Communards ever did. In the week of May 21–28, the so-called "Bloody May Week," the French army, its leaders fueled by fierce class hatred, indulged in carnage on a scale never before seen in modern Europe, and not to be seen again until the days of Franco and Hitler. No exact figures are available, but the estimate of slain civilians—working-class people, or men and women who resembled them—ranges from a minimum of 20,000 to a maximum of 36,000. The 20th Arondissement, a working-class district, was laid waste. In a continuing reign of terror, 20,000 working-class people were court-martialed and a large number of them condemned to penal colonies.

Marx and his family were horrified and angry at the slaughter of working people in a city they loved and one which they, as well as the rest of Europe, had long considered the center of Western civilization.

Conservatives, in search of a scapegoat for the events in Paris, found one in Marx. The International was held responsible for the Commune, and the General Council, led by Marx, was viewed as the center of a revolutionary conspiracy. On March 14, 1871, *Paris-Journal*, which Marx described as "one of the most successful organs of the Paris police press," set the tone with an article entitled *"Le Grand Chef de l'Internationale."* The *Grand Chef*, it stated, "is, as is known, a German and, what is even worse, a Prussian. His name is Karl Marx, he lives in Berlin."

Marx reacted to the attacks on him and on the Commune with unrestrained anger. He defended the Commune in the General Council of the International, saying that it was being destroyed with the aid of the Prussians, "acting as gendarmes for Thiers."[4] He attacked the English press as "bloodhounds of Thiers." Its "slanders against the Commune and against the International were invented to service his bloody policy."[5] In April and May 1871, while the Commune was being crushed, Marx wrote a bitter and eloquent brochure in its defense. Entitled *The Civil War in France*, it was issued in English, in the name of the General Council, June 1871.[6] More significantly, a Russian edition, edited by Lenin, came out in Odessa in 1905, the year of the first revolution against Czarism, when the first Soviet was set up in St. Petersburg. Communists consider *The Civil War in France* "a most im-

---

[4]Minutes of the General Council, May 23, 1871.

[5]*Ibid.*, June 6, 1871.

[6]The title page stated: "Printed and Published for the Council by Edward Truelove, 256 High Holborn, 1871. Price Twopence."

portant work of scientific communism."[7] The brochure concluded with these impassioned words:

> Workingmen's Paris, with its Commune, will be forever
> celebrated as the glorious harbinger of a new society. Its
> martyrs are enshrined in the great heart of the working
> class. Its exterminators' history has already nailed to that
> eternal pillory from which all the prayers of their priests
> will not avail to redeem them.

The immediate effect of *The Civil War in France* was to
strengthen Marx's identification with the Commune and to
weaken further the already undermined International. The
Commune was then in such disrepute that a number of the
English members of the General Council refused to sign the
brochure. The vilification of Marx continued. He was, as he
expressed it in English to Kugelmann on June 18, 1871, "at
this moment the best calumniated and the most menaced man
of London."

Interviews with American Newspapermen

Marx's notoriety spread across the Atlantic. Two American
newspapers, the *New York World* and the *New York Herald,*
published interviews with him. They gave him what he hoped
would be a chance to refute the lies about himself, the Commune and the International.

The *New York World*'s correspondent, R. Landor, visited
Marx's home in the evening of July 3, 1871, and published
his interview about two weeks later, on July 18. It was
reprinted in *Woodhull & Claflin's Weekly* on August 12.

Landor went to see Marx with some trepidation. He did
not know what to expect in this den of "revolution incar-
nate," home of the "real founder and guiding spirit of the International Society." While waiting for Marx to come into the
drawing room, Landor reported, he "peered cautiously into
the vase on the side-table for a bomb." He also "sniffed for
petroleum, but the smell was the smell of roses." Instead of
bombs, Landor found on the table an album with views of
the Rhine.

---

[7]For text, see Saul K. Padover, ed., *Karl Marx on Revolution* (New
York, 1971), pp. 332–72.

Marx's home, Landor reported, was that of a "well-to-do man of the middle class." The drawing room, in which the interview took place, could have been the "very comfortable quarters of a thriving stockbroker" on the verge of making his fortune. It was "comfort personified," the apartment of a man of taste and easy means.

Landor asked Marx whether the International, many of whose members were active in the Commune, was part of the plot. Marx denied that there was such a conspiracy. "The insurrection in Paris," he said, "was made by the workmen of Paris. The ablest of the workmen must necessarily have been its leaders and administrators; but the ablest of the workmen happen also to be members of the International Association. Yet the Association, as such, may be in no way responsible for their action."

Marx went on to explain that the International could not have directed the Commune because it was not a governmental body with the power of control or of giving orders. The International was, rather, a "bond of union" of working people.

Landor asked, "Union to what end?"

Marx replied:

The economical emancipation of the working class by the conquest of political power. The use of that political power to the attainment of social ends. . . . The Association does not dictate the form of political movements; it only requires a pledge as to their end. It is a network of affiliated societies spreading all over the world of labor.

Marx elaborated on the idea that the International was based on diversity, and not homogeneity. It recognized that nations and their problems differed widely, and hence that solutions must also vary according to the state and nature of the country. In free countries, problems could be solved through a peaceful process; in oppressed lands, violence was the answer:

In England, for instance, the way to show political power lies open to the working class. Insurrection would be madness where peaceful agitation would more swiftly and surely do the work. In France a hundred laws of repression and a moral antagonism between classes seem to necessitate the violent solution of social war. The choice of that solution is the affair of the working classes of that country. The International does not presume to dictate in the matter and hardly to advise.

But even where free agitation and voting were open to the working class, as in England, Marx was dubious whether it would be permitted to seize power. The bourgeoisie would not allow such seizure beyond a certain point. "The English middle class," he said, "has always shown itself willing enough to accept the verdict of the majority, so long as it enjoyed the monopoly of voting power. But mark me, as soon as it finds itself outvoted on what it considers vital questions we shall see here a new slaveowners' war."

What about the United States? Marx replied that hitherto a number of special circumstances had prevented the labor problem in America from assuming the same importance as it had in Europe.[8] But conditions there, he said, were rapidly changing, and soon a growing laboring class would emerge in America too, "distinct from the rest of the community and divorced from capital."

Marx's interview with the *New York Herald* correspondent was more extensive but less accurately reported than the one in the *New York World*.

The conversation between Marx and the *Herald* correspondent ranged from personalities to policies, with emphasis on the Paris Commune, the International and capitalism. According to the *Herald* reporter, Marx expressed harsh and contemptuous judgments of many French activists, including Communards.

The conversation shifted to the capitalist system, and Marx expounded his theory of revolution. He explained that capitalism was a necessary stage in human progress, naturally developing into a higher form of perfection, "just as the flower must fall to give way to the fruit, or the blade of green must spring before the corn can ripen." The present stage of capitalism had led to many beneficial developments: railroads, commerce, steamships, canals, helping to bring the remotest parts of the world together. "All this is progress, but at what a cost of human toil and suffering has it been brought about?"

[8] See Saul K. Padover, ed., *Karl Marx on America and the Civil War* (New York, 1972).

Now the unjust and cruel capitalist system was no longer needed, and it would be cast aside for something better and nobler.

The changeover would begin in England, where capital and labor were already organized. Would it be violent? asked the interviewer. Marx replied, "We do not intend to make war. We hope to be able to gain our rights in a legal and lawful way by act of Parliament, and it is the aristocracy and the moneyed men who will rebel. It is they who will attempt a revolution. But we have the force of numbers. We shall have the strength of intelligence and discipline."

Marx was then asked about the revolutionary role in the International, which he claimed had a membership of at least two million, in other countries. What about Russia? Here Marx's answer was prophetic. He said that the Czarist government did not permit organizations like the International, but "there is a revolution coming in Russia . . . slowly but surely."

The Russian revolution would be made by two discontented classes, the workers, and the smaller nobility which had been ruined by the abolition of serfdom. Once these two elements combined, they "will overthrow that tyrannical form of government easily when the first weak czar succeeds to the throne."

How about the United States? Marx expected no violence in the United States, unless "some of your great iron or other monopolies should take it into their hands to employ force to put down strikes, as they had done in one or two instances, in which case they will be swept away like chaff before the wind."

What was the International's program in the United States?

To emancipate the workingman from the rule of politicians, and to combat monopoly in all the many forms it is assuming there, especially that of the public lands. We want no more monstrous land grabs, no more grants to swindling railroad concerns, no more schemes for robbing the people of their birthright for the benefit of a few purse-proud monopolists.

He added:

Let these men be warned in time; their ill-gotten goods

shall be taken from them, and their wealth shall vanish like the baseless fabric of a vision.

The *Herald*'s correspondent concluded that the International was greatly misrepresented and overrated. It would never accomplish its objectives, he wrote, because they ran counter to human nature. As for Marx's theory of the abolition of property, the American correspondent remarked that "even the poorest mechanic [i.e., worker] in the United States will scout at it, hoping, as they all do, to one day have property of their own."

XXIII
Paterfamilias

Marx, the harsh critic and angry radical in his public life and writings, was a different man in private. In his personal life, he was extraordinarily kind and generous and, when not tormented by illnesses, jolly.

When he could afford it, Marx dressed elegantly and expensively, and in his middle years he wore a monocle with all the aplomb of a bourgeois gentleman. The monocle, suspended from the neck, went well with his finely tailored frock coats.

He loved music and the theater. When health and finances permitted, he and Jenny entertained guests with charm, gaiety and amusing conversation. The girls played musical instruments and knew how to sing *Lieder*, and so did their Papa. At New Year's Eve parties, Marx, elegant and nimble, led his ladies in stately dances.

To Marx, wine was a pleasure and a panacea and he was capable of imbibing quantities of alcoholic liquids. He was proud of the fact that his father had owned a little vineyard on the Moselle. Once in 1866 when François Lafargue, Paul's father, sent him some wine from Bordeaux, Marx thanked him for the gift and wrote on November 12, "As I come from a wine-growing region and am an ex-vineyard owner, I know well how to appreciate the value of wine. I even agree a little with old Luther, who said that a man who does not like wine will never amount to anything much."

Whenever he or members of his family, including Lenchen, were sick, as they frequently were, they drank wine, if they had it. The doctors prescribed it as a medicine for practically everything; it was supposed to obliterate pain and mitigate fever. In the decades that Marx lived in desperate poverty in

London, he often asked Engels to send him not only money but wine. Engels, who had his own wine cellar, would send hampers of wine, which the Marx family would line up admiringly in rows like "soldiers," and whose arrival was always a cause for celebration. When Engels visited London he and Marx would sometimes go reveling in pubs at night to the annoyance of Jenny, who never fully approved of Engels' bohemian habits. But, being a Rhinelander herself, she, too, enjoyed wine and so, later on, did her daughters.

Marx's humor, which his wife shared, was biting and unsparing, but spiced with a keen sense of the ridiculous. In his first critical political essay, "Remarks on the Latest Prussian Censorship Instruction,"[1] he remarked, "I treat the ridiculous seriously when I treat it with ridicule." He loved humor, not merely for its own sake, but also as ammunition against enemies. He liked to quote a stanza written by his friend, the revolutionary poet Georg Weerth:

> *Es gibt nichts Schönfes auf der Welt*
> *Als seine Feinde zu beissen,*
> *Als über alle die plumpen Gesellen*
> *Seine schlechten Witze zu reissen!*

Freely translated:

> There is nothing finer in the world
> Than to bite one's foes,
> To inflict one's bad jokes
> On all those loutish blokes.

Marx's favorite poet was Heinrich Heine, probably Germany's foremost lyricist and certainly its greatest wit. As a man of wide-ranging culture, at home in the Western world's great literature, much of which he read in the original languages, including Russian and Rumanian, Marx frequently cited such authors as Balzac, Cervantes, Dante, Goethe and Schiller. The dramatist he most admired was Shakespeare. But it was Heine, whose sardonic humor he shared, whom he loved to quote when he wanted to make an amusing or barbed point. Thus, when he wished to show his disapproval of sentimentality, he referred to a satiric verse from Heine:

---

[1]Text in Saul K. Padover, ed., *Karl Marx on Freedom of the Press and Censorship* (New York, 1974), pp. 89–108.

Ein Fräulein stand am Meere,
Ihr war so weh und bang,
Es gramte sie so sehre,
Der Sonnenuntergang.

In free translation:

A girl stood by the ocean shore
With pain and fear beset.
Why is she so with worry sore?
Because the sun has set.

In reporting a dispute between two egoistic German socialists, Wilhelm Liebknecht and Johann Baptist von Schweitzer, Marx quoted the satiric lines from Heine's "Disputation on a Theological Altercation Between Father Joseph and Rabbi Judah":

Doch es will mich schier bedünken,
das der Rabbi und der Mönch,
dass sie beide stunken.

Which may be rendered in English:

Still, I truly think
That the rabbi and the monk
Both equally stink.

Marx's comments on men and events were often as sardonic as those of Heine. When Liebknecht, whom he liked but occasionally criticized for political bumbling, became a father, Marx remarked, "Liebknecht has finally achieved something, namely a young Liebknecht." A certain mediocre German journalist, Eugen Oswald, inspired Marx to remark drily that he was "quite a decent fellow, even though he has not yet invented gunpowder." Referring to the two leading French politicians of the Louis Philippe era, Marx commented, "M. Guizot depicts M. Thiers and M. Thiers depicts M. Guizot as a traitor, and unfortunately they are both right." Of a famous German mystic, Marx said, "The shoemaker Jakob Boehme was a great philosopher. Many a professional philosopher is only a great shoemaker." At the news, in 1861, that an attempt had been made on the life of the Prussian

King, Wilhelm I, Marx wondered about the intelligence of the would-be assassin: "How can any human being with ordinary sense risk his own life to kill a brainless jackass?" His comment on the crowned autocrat of Russia, a country he despised and dreaded, was worthy of Heine: "The Czar is great, God is greater, but the Czar is still young."

Marx also had a taste for the bawdy. In informing Engels that Wilhelm Pieper, a young communist refugee in London, had syphilis, Marx commented, "His experiences have taught the worthy lad to look at female beings from the medical standpoint."[2] Observing that his brother-in-law, Edgar von Westphalen, was more interested in food than in women, he remarked, "The sexual drive has gone to his stomach."[3] Marx once was elected "constable of the vestry of St. Pancras," and when he ignored it, he received a summons to appear before the vestry "to show cause why my goods and chattels should not be distrained." The astonished and bemused Marx reported to Engels that a friend gave him this advice: "I should tell them that I was a foreigner and that they should kiss me in the arse."[4]

In one letter to Engels, written in his forty-ninth year, on October 19, 1867, Marx told him about a couple of new carbuncles in the vicinity of his penis and quoted Mathurin Régnier's[5] satiric verses on *chaude pisse* [hot piss], which he thought had never been "described more poetically anywhere else":

> *Mon cas, qui se léve et se hausse*
> *Bave d'une estrange façon;*
> *Belle, vous fournistes la sausse,*
> *Lors que je fournis le poisson.*
>
> *Las! si ce membre eut l'arrogance*
> *De fouiller trop les lieux sacrez,*
> *Qu'on luy pardonne son offence,*
> *Car il pleure assez ses péchez.*

[2] Marx to Engels, April 4, 1854.
[3] Marx to Engels, August 9, 1865.
[4] Marx to Engels, June 27, 1868.
[5] Mathurin Régnier (1573–1613) was a famous French satirist and author of licentious epigrams.

Freely translated:

> My dingus, which rises and gets higher,
> Foams in a strange fashion;
> Beauty, you furnish the sauce,
> While I furnish the fish.
>
> Alack! if this member had the arrogance
> To rummage too much in sacred places,
> His offense should be pardoned
> Because he weeps enough over his sins.

Then Marx went on to quote Régnier on the function of the male *membrum* in a stanza entitled "Fluxion of Love":

> *L'amour est une affection*
> *Qui, par les yeux, dans le coeur entre,*
> *Et, par la forme de fluxion,*
> *S'execoule par le bas du ventre.*

In English:

> Love is an emotion
> That enters the heart through the eyes,
> And, in the form of a fluxion,
> Flows through the bottom of the belly.

Finally, a verse called "Lisette Killed by Régnier":

> *Lisette, à qui l'on faisait tort,*
> *Vint à Régnier tout éplorée,*
> *Je te pry, donne moi la mort*
> *Que j'ay tant de fois desirée!*
> *Luy, ne la refusant en rien,*
> *Tire son . . . vous m'entendez bien,*
> *Et dedans le ventre la frappe.*
> *Elle, voulant finir ses jours*
> *Luy dit: Mon coeur pousse toujours,*
> *De crainte que je n'en rechappe.*
> *Régnier, las de la secourir,*
> *Craignant une second plainte,*
> *Luy dit: Hastez-vous de mourir,*
> *Car mon poignard n' a plus de pointe.*

In free translation:

> Lisette, who has been wronged,
> Comes to Régnier all in tears,
> I beg you, give me the death
> That I have wished for so many times!
> He, refusing her nothing,
> Pulls out his . . . . , you know what I mean,
> And strikes inside her belly.
> She, desiring to finish her days,
> Says to him: My heart always beats
> With the fear that I will recover.
> Régnier, tired of succoring her,
> Fearing a second plea,
> Says to her: Hasten to die,
> Because my dagger no longer has a point.

Marx also told a story about a healthy father confessor who, after spending twenty-four hours in a Russian convent, came out dead. "The nuns rode him to death," he wrote, and added that of course father confessors "do *not enter* every day." Disgusted by the Catholicism of David Urquhart, a British Tory diplomat, Marx stated that it reminded him of an Italian nun who prayed to the Madonna: "I beseech you, Holy Virgin, give me somebody with whom I can sin."[6]

In the *New-York Daily Tribune* (September 20, 1854), Marx ventured a comment on the Spanish Queen Christina and her lover, the toreador José Muñoz Benavente (a) Pucheta:

The relation of Christina and this same Muñoz can only be understood from the answer given by Don Quixote to Sancho Panza's question why he was in love with such a low country wench as his Dulcinea, when he could have princesses at his feet: "A lady," answered the worthy knight, "surrounded by a host of high-bred, rich and witty followers, was asked why she took for her lover a simple peasant. 'You must know,' said the lady, 'that for the office for which I use him he possesses more philosophy than Aristotle himself.' "

[6]Marx to Engels, November 7, 1867.

A self-assured male, Marx had a genuine affection and esteem for women. He treated his own wife and daughters not only with tenderness, but also with respect for their minds. His confidence in Jenny's judgment and wisdom was such that he consulted her about everything, including politics. This trust he also extended to Lenchen. As for his own daughters, he raised them to be women of cultural and intellectual independence, and in turn, appreciating the respect he showed them, they admired and adored him.

Marx believed that women had always played a crucial role in social transformation. He also thought that the position of the "beautiful sex" was an index of social progress: "Anybody who knows anything of history also knows that great social changes are impossible without the female ferment. Social progress can be measured accurately by the social status of the beautiful sex (the ugly ones included)."[7]

He was outraged at the maltreatment and exploitation of women in the capitalist system, as can be seen in the shocking data he marshaled on the subject in his *Das Kapital*.[8] In this, as in his intimate relationships, he was a man of immense compassion—his daughter Eleanor referred to his kindliness and patience as "really sublime"—easily moved to pity for the weak and oppressed, foremost among them being women and children. Wife-beating, then common in England, particularly among the working classes, filled him with such rage that, according to a friend, he would have gladly flogged such an offender "to the point of death."

His instinctive compassion for women once got him in trouble in his early years in London. He was riding in an omnibus with Wilhelm Liebknecht when he heard a shrill female voice screaming "Murder! Murder!" At this sound of the strumpet, Marx leaped from the carriage and, followed by a reluctant Liebknecht, rushed to the rescue of the lady, who, it happened, was a drunken wife whom her husband was trying to get home. As Marx, obviously an alien and speaking broken English, barged in, the wrangling couple, instantly reconciled by the onset of a stranger, turned furiously on him, the intoxicated female going after his provocatively magnificent beard. A crowd soon joined in the attack on the "damned foreigners," who were finally rescued by two burly constables.

[7]Marx to Kugelmann, December 12, 1868.
[8]See Saul K. Padover, ed., *Karl Marx on Education, Women and Children* (New York, 1975), pp. 47–107.

Husband

Marx's marriage lasted thirty-eight years. His married life was one of cruel economic hardship and deeply personal companionship. Jenny's self-sacrifice for the husband she adored all her life, and of whom she was always jealous where other women were concerned, was total. So was her devotion to his cause and his revolutionary ideas. She shared his enthusiasms, his prejudices, his convictions, his tastes and his humor. Her insights and wit matched his. With the indispensable aid of Lenchen, she held the family together in the most desperate circumstances and sustained Marx with her courage, her belief in him, her aristocratic pride and her keen intelligence.

Thirteen years after their marriage, Marx was still capable of writing to his forty-two-year-old wife a love letter imbued with extraordinary youthful passion. The letter was written from Mancheser, where Marx was on a week's visit to Engels, on June 21, 1856:

My heart's beloved:

I am writing you again, because I am alone and because it troubles me always to have a dialogue with you in my head, without you knowing anything about it or hearing it or being able to answer. Poor as your photograph is, it does perform a service for me, and I now understand how even the "black Madonna," the most disgraceful portrait of the Mother of God, could find indestructible admirers. . . . Those black Madonna pictures have never been more kissed, looked at, and adored than your photograph, which . . . absolutely does not reflect your darling, sweet, kissable, *"dolce,"* face. . . . I have you vividly before me, and I carry you on my hands, and I kiss you from head to foot, and I fall on my knees before you, and I groan: "Madame, I love you. . . ."

He went on to say that his momentary separation from her only revealed how great his love for her was and how it energized and regenerated his whole existence as a man. He concluded:

There are actually many females in the world, and some among them are beautiful. But where could I find a face whose every feature, every wrinkle, is a reminder of the greatest and sweetest memories of my life? Even my endless pains, my irreplaceable losses, I read in your sweet countenance, and I kiss away the pain when I kiss your sweet face. "Buried in her arms, awakened by her kisses"—namely, in your arms and by your kisses, and I grant the Brahmins and Pythagoras their doctrine of regeneration and Christianity its doctrine of Resurrection.

Marx expressed somewhat similar sentiments in a letter to his wife seven years later. His mother had died at four o'clock on the afternoon of November 20, 1863, "to the day and hour of her wedding," as she had predicted she would. Marx went to Trier a week later to collect what part of the estate he was entitled to.[9] He stayed, not with his sister Emilie Conradi or any other relatives, but at an inn, the Gasthof von Venedig. His mother's death did not affect him, but Trier, his and Jenny's childhood home, moved him very deeply. The city brought a flood of sweet memories of his youth and the earliest days of his love, and he made daily pilgrimages to the old von Westphalen house on the Römerstrasse which had harbored his "best treasure." For more than a week he did not write home, but when he finally did, on December 15, 1863, after twenty-one years of marriage he could still write to his "Dear, Heart's beloved Jenny" as though they were young lovers. When Jenny was away from home, he would write to his "sweet, dear, peerless Heart," as he did on August 8, 1856, that his longing for her (and the children) was "quite indescribable."

Jenny, of course, reciprocated his feelings. She was as proud of him as he was of her and as deeply in love. She considered herself, as she told Joseph Weydemeyer, "one of the chosen, happy, favored ones," because she could be by the side of her "dear husband" whom she called the "prop of my life." In their early years in London she acted as his

---

[9]Marx found that the estate was sealed, subject finally to administration by Lion Philips, his mother's Dutch brother-in-law, who was her executor. With her "mania for over-management," as Marx called it, his mother left everything for Philips to decide. A notarized copy of her first will provided that her daughter Emilie get all furniture and linens (but not the silver), her daughter Sophie the portrait of Marx's father, and "her son Carl a release from his debt of 1,100 Taler."

secretary, and she considered those days when she was privileged to copy his scratchy handwriting as "the happiest of my life."

In later years, when Marx was away from home, he flirted with other women, as he did with Madame Tenge in Hanover in 1867. Letters he wrote to his Dutch cousin, Antoinette Philips, who was nineteen years his junior, come close to being outright *billets doux*. Nevertheless, Jenny was the only woman in his life. When she died, of cancer, in December 1881, something in Marx died with her. He survived her by only fifteen months.

Father

Marx's extraordinary love for children, his own and others, is the most luminous feature of his character. A friend who knew him intimately said of him that he was himself "a child among children." When out walking on Hampstead Heath he would stop and play with them. Though he disapproved of adult mendicants, Marx could not resist child beggars, particularly ragged little girls, whose hair he would stroke and for whom he would empty his pockets of small change. Marx used to say that what he liked most about Christ was His love for children. On Sundays, in good weather, when his children were young, he and the whole family would go marching to Hampstead Heath, where they would picnic and romp. Marx would play the "maddest and merriest" games with his offspring, sometimes walking on all fours, pretending he was a horse, which the children gleefully rode. After a hearty meal—roast veal, bread, cheese, fruit, savories, tea or ginger beer, carried to the Heath by Lenchen in a hamper—they would straggle home tired but happy, the children singing folksongs, the others, including Papa Marx, belting out *Volkslieder* such as "*O Strassburg, O Strassburg, du wunderschöne Stadt!*"

Marx was also a superb storyteller with a fertile imagination. As a boy in Trier he had invented amusing stories to mollify his siblings after he had bullied them. Now as a father in London walking with his children, he would often entertain them with fairy tales by the mile. When they wanted more, they would beg him, "Tell us another mile." His youngest daughter, Eleanor, recalled how much she had loved the adventures of Hans Roeckle, which Marx invented and spun out for months and months and which never came to an end. Roeckle was a magician who had all kinds of toys in his shop: wooden men and women, giants and dwarfs, kings and queens, masters and apprentices, birds and animals, as numerous as in Noah's Ark. Always in need of money, Roeckle had to sell his most beautiful pieces, piece by piece, to the devil. But after many adventures, the toys would always come back to Roeckle's shop—and a new cycle of tales would begin. "Some of these stories," Eleanor wrote, "were gruesome and hair-raising . . . others were funny, but all were told with an inexhaustible reservoir of inventiveness, fantasy and humor."

The three Marx daughters, who inherited their father's intelligence and their mother's beauty, were given an excellent education. They were exposed to literature and political ideas early in life. Marx read to his children such classics as Homer, the *Niebelungenlied, Don Quixote, A Thousand and One Nights*. "Shakespeare," the youngest daughter recalled, "was our house bible; at the age of six I knew whole scenes from Shakespeare by memory." On her sixth birthday, Eleanor was given her first novel, Frederick Marryat's *Peter Simple* (1834), and subsequently books by James Fenimore Cooper and Sir Walter Scott, which Marx, an avid novel reader in several languages, read and discussed with his daughters. They went to private schools, and their education included singing, dancing and music lessons, even though Marx had no money for a piano. He wrote to Engels on April 23, 1857:

> The girls are growing very much, and their education becomes expensive also. In the ladies seminary which they attend, they receive private lessons from an Italian, a Frenchman and a drawing master. Now I have to get a music fellow. They are learning with extraordinary rapidity. The smallest—the baby[10]—is a remarkable wag and maintains that she has two brains.

The household often had to deprive itself of necessities to pay for the girls' tuition, which was frequently in arrears. In 1866 Marx owed £25 tuition for three school quarters, and

[10]Eleanor, born in 1855, was then two years old.

had to pay it at the expense of rent, for fear they would be expelled. At the age of twenty-one, Laura was still taking private music lessons,[11] for Marx and his wife were determined that their children should have a respectable bourgeois upbringing. After all, they were the granddaughters of a baron and the daughters of a baroness. Jenny actually had printed visiting cards identifying her as "Baroness von Westphalen."[12]

The Marx girls grew up to be radical and multilingual, like their parents." Such a relationship would enrich education sixteen and Eleanor six, their mother wrote to Louise Weydemeyer:

> They are completely at home in English, and they know French well. In Italian they understand Dante, they also read some Spanish; only in German is there a hitch, and although I make every effort to give them a German lesson now and then, still they manage to parry it, and my authority here does not carry very far.

In Marx's view, education was a shared experience between parents and their offspring, and not a forcible imposition of discipline. "Children," he used to say, "should educate their parents. "Such a relationship would enrich education and assure mutual respect and love. His daughters, one of whom described him as an "ideal friend," rewarded him with lifelong devotion.

The Daughters:
Jenny Longuet ("Jennychen")

Jenny, or Jennychen [little Jenny], was the oldest of the Marx children, the first to survive childhood and the first to die in adulthood. A beautiful and fragile girl, she was the only one of his daughters to provide Marx with surviving grandchildren, on whom he doted. When at the age of twenty-four she accepted a position as a language teacher to

[11]Marx to Engels, May 10, 1866.
[12]Marx wrote on September 2, 1864, to Jenny, who was then in Brighton, warning her to be careful "with your Baroness cards," lest his enemy, Arnold Ruge, use it against him.

help her father financially, Marx was very upset, fearing that a full day's work would be hard on her health.

Jennychen met her future husband, Charles Longuet, in London when she was about twenty-seven years old. Longuet was a French journalist of Norman descent, and had been a member of the Paris Commune, as editor of its organ, *Journal Officiel de la Commune*. After the fall of the Commune, Longuet, then thirty-two years old, settled as a refugee in London, where he became a member of the General Council of the International and often visited Marx. No Frenchman could possibly be unaware that Marx was the father of beautiful unmarried daughters. Longuet quietly courted the frail and lovely Jenny. At the Marx home, he would occasionally try to impress the family with his culinary art, preparing *Sole à la Normande*, his national dish, and *Boeuf à la mode*. Engels, who knew about such things, pronounced Longuet's cooking as "no great success." But the young Frenchman was more successful in the arts of love. In March 1872, Jennychen and Longuet became engaged and there was "jubilation" in the Marx household.

But if Jenny was happy, her mother had grave doubts about her daughter's future as Mme. Longuet. She liked the young Frenchman, whom she described as "a very gifted, brave, decent man," but his economic prospects were dim. She did not see how he would support a wife and family. Looking back on the years of their own financial misery, she was afraid that her daughter might repeat the pattern of her parents. In addition, she feared that Longuet, who was supporting himself precariously by giving French lessons, would turn out to have the instability which she considered characteristic of Frenchmen.

Jenny's forebodings turned out to be correct. Longuet married his *"chère petite Jenny,"* as he called her, on October 10, 1872. Like Marx himself, he could hardly make a living. The young couple moved to Oxford, where Longuet vainly hoped to establish himself as a teacher. They then returned to London, where, Jennychen wrote, she was happier than in the "right-thinking, arrogant Oxford," and where she could at least always visit her "dear Mohr." For a long time, she and her husband desperately tried to find paying jobs.

In 1874, both Longuets found teaching jobs. Jennychen got a position at Clement Dane School, where she taught German; her salary was £15 per quarter, a sum which she supplemented, despite her precarious health, by giving private lessons. Charles Longuet became a teacher of French at King's College. Between them they earned enough to eke out a living in their small London house in Leighton Grove.

Like her mother, Jennychen was pregnant nearly every year of her married life, which was a relatively short one. In September 1873, less than a year after her marriage, she gave birth to a boy, named Charles, who died of diarrhea in July 1874, before his first birthday. She was suffering from asthma, and his death came as a specially harsh blow.

The second Longuet child was born in May 1876. He was named Jean Laurent Frederick. As Marx explained to Engels on May 25, "He is called Jean (after Longuet's father), Laurent (nickname of Laura), Frederick (in your honor)."

Jean Laurent Frederick, nicknamed "Johnny," was one of four Longuet children to survive well into the 20th century. Marx came to adore the boy, his first surviving grandson. He could never have enough of him. "The little man," he wrote to Jennychen, on September 16, 1878, when Johnny was two years old, "is the apple of my eye."

Johnny grew up to follow in his father's and grandfather's footsteps. He became one of the leaders of the French Socialist Party. He died in 1938, leaving two sons, Robert (born in 1899), who became a lawyer, and Karl (born in 1904), a sculptor. Strangely enough, this Karl was the only one of the Longuet offspring to bear the famous grandfather's first name.

Jenny Longuet's third child, Henry ("Harry"), was born in 1878. Delicate in health, he was backward and seemed retarded, requiring special care. He died in the same year as his mother, at the age of five, and is buried in Highgate Cemetery.

A fourth son was born on August 18, 1879, when the sick Jennychen was at Ramsgate with her mother and other members of the family. The boy was given the name Edgar, after Edgar von Westphalen and her mother's own little son, who died in 1855. Marx heard the news of the birth of Edgar when he was in St. Hélier, Jersey Island, where, accompanied by his daughter Eleanor, he had gone in search of health, but found only a steady rainfall. Concerned about Jennychen's health, he rushed back to be near her.

Edgar Longuet, nicknamed "Wolf," also his grandfather's favorite, became a physician and, like his brother Jean

Laurent Frederick, a member of the French Socialist Party. In 1938, he joined the Communists. He died in 1950, at the age of seventy-one, leaving three sons and a daughter. Their names were in the family tradition: Charles (born in 1901), a salesman; Frédéric (born in 1904), a painter; Jenny (1906–1939); and Paul (born in 1909), a Madagascar planter.

In the summer of 1880, after the July 11 amnesty, Charles Longuet returned to France, where he became an influential editor of *La Justice*, a radical daily founded by Georges Clemenceau, "chief of the extreme Left," as Marx called him.[13] Longuet was subsequently also a member of the Paris Municipal Council. The ailing Jennychen remained for a time in London, where she badly missed her husband. Every time the postman knocked, her heart beat with the expectation of a letter from him. "Only since you have been away, my dear Charles," she wrote him, in English, "do I feel how dear you are to me and how lonely my life would be without you!" She informed him that the children were "blooming like roses" and that little Edgar was particularly enchanting, so sunny in disposition and quick-witted in spirit that she feared something untoward might happen to him. She also worried about her husband's neuralgia.[14]

The French amnesty of 1880 was a mixed blessing for Karl and Jenny Marx. Since Longuet could now return legally to France, it was unavoidable that his family would join him there. Suddenly Marx and his wife, in their old age, found themselves facing the grim possibility of being separated from their beloved daughter and grandchildren.

> What has recently perhaps worsened my condition is the great worry that presses on us "old" ones. For us the French amnesty is, according to all expectations, the equivalent of losing all our children and children's children. And in my present condition, my own moving to Paris would create too much anxiety. Formerly, I would have quickly tied up my little bundle and would have

---

[13]Marx to Sorge, November 5, 1880; original letter in New York Public Library MS Division.
[14]Jenny Longuet to Charles Longuet, October 1, 1880. Other letters by her, to "My dear Charles" or "My dearest Charles," are to be found in International Institute for Social History, Amsterdam, MS G 213–51.

galloped after the dear grandchildren. Now the machine cannot be put into operation so easily any more.[15]

In February 1881, Jennychen, pregnant again, moved to France with her three little boys, to join her husband. This was, as Eleanor Marx wrote a friend, a "sad blow for Papa and Mama as they are so devoted to the children." She did not know what her parents would do without their grandchildren. They would have been happy if Jennychen had left with them at least one of her babies, even frail and retarded little Harry. But she took all her children with her, although it was doubtful whether she was strong enough to care for them effectively. Eleanor Marx has left us a description of the Longuet boys, her little nephews:

He [Johnny] will be five next May and is a dear little fellow. He is a very beautiful boy—with a face like a picture of Murillo. The second boy—*my* boy—Harry is not pretty, and is backward—but I love him best of all, because I think his nature is by far the sweetest of the three, and he is one of those children who seem destined to suffer. Tho' so backward now I am sure he will develop wonderfully—and I should not be surprised if this apparently stupid child turned out the deepest of them all. The youngest child—Jenny's special favorite [Edgar] is not so handsome as Johnny but is strong and healthy, bright—and terribly spoilt.

Eleanor concluded:

You can imagine how fond their grandparents are of them and with what sorrow they look forward to losing them.[16]

The Longuets settled in Argenteuil, ten kilometers from Paris' Porte de Clichy, a town known in the 20th century for its asparagus and in Marx's day for its restored Romanesque cathedral, which possessed Christ's seamless tunic, allegedly a gift from the medieval Emperor Charlemagne. The cathedral

[15]In Luise Dornemann, *Jenny Marx, Der Lebensweg einer Sozialistin* (Berlin, 1968), p. 320.
[16]Eleanor Marx to Natalie Liebknecht, February 12, 1881.

in Trier also had such a tunic—a miraculous phenomenon
that must have delighted the ironic Marx when he visited Argenteuil, which he did at least three times before his daughter's death. Such visits were an emotional necessity, since
being with his family gave him a special peace of mind, as he
explained to his daughter Laura: "Under peace I understand
'family life,' the voices of children, this whole microscopic
little world, which is much more interesting than the macro-
scopic."

The children, especially Johnny, could do anything with
their grandpapa. When Johnny was sent to London a few
times to stay with his grandparents, the ailing Marx was stimulated into new life, playing games with the boy as if he were
himself a child. In the gravel and grass garden of 41 Maitland Park Road, where Marx moved in March 1874, and
lived for nine years until his death, Johnny would make his
grand-père go down on all fours, climb on his back, and
shout in two languages, "Go on! *Plus vite!* Hurrah!" The
white-haired Marx, in his sixties, would meekly trot along,
while Johnny yelled, "You naughty horse! *En avant!*"
Grandpa Marx, sweat pouring down his face, was entranced.

Jennychen, constantly ill, was sustained by the love and devotion of her father, who kept in constant touch with her. On
August 18, 1881, after returning to London from one of his
visits to Argenteuil, Marx wrote his daughter, "The pleasure
of having been with you and the dear children has given me
more joy than I could find anywhere." On December 17, in
describing the Christmas presents he was sending "our little
ones,"[17] he told Jennychen that the best service she could ren-
der him was to be well, that he hoped to continue to spend
many a beautiful day by her side, and "worthily to fulfill my
function as grandpa."

Her concern for him was as profound as his was for her.
Once, after Marx wrote her a long, gossipy letter from Algiers, where he had gone in a vain search for relief from his
chronic cough and carbuncles—"I must tell you that in this
Villa-Hotel, the two ladies, its managers, did everything in

[17]Eleanor, helped by Engels, took the Christmas box by cab to the
parcel company; among the contents were gifts from Lenchen: a little
coat for Harry, and one for Edgar; a woolen cap for Marcel; also a
little blue suit for Marcel from Laura; and a sailor's suit "for my dear
Johnny" from Marx.

my service, no care nor attention neglecting"[18]—Jennychen replied, "My dearest Papa, I have just received your dear letter and cannot go to bed without thanking you for the trouble you have taken to write me so much. You could not have sent me a better 'nightcap.' I shall sleep as I have not slept for some nights."[19]

Despite fragile health, Jennychen continued to produce children. In April 1881, she gave birth to another son, Marcel. Women like her and her mother seem to have accepted their child-bearing roles without protest, perhaps because their husbands and the male-dominated society expected them to do so. Marx obviously did. Instead of being dismayed, he was pleased and hailed his new grandson as a desirable addition to the ranks of the coming revolution. On April 29, he wrote to his daughter in English:

I congratulate you on your happy delivery. . . . My "women" expected that the "new world citizen" will increase the "better half" of the population; for my part, I prefer the "male" sex in children born at this turning point in history. They have before them the most revolutionary period that men ever had to endure. It is bad now to be so "old" that one can only foresee, instead of seeing.

Marx's grandson Marcel Longuet did in fact live through a period of profound and violent events—World War I, the Russian Revolution, the rise of European fascism, the defeat of France in World War II and the occupation of his homeland by the Nazis—but he did not become a revolutionist. He died in 1949, at the age of sixty-eight.

The Argenteuil household was boisterous, undisciplined and impecunious. With a sick wife and a houseful of growing children, Charles Longuet did not or could not cope. Marx was developing an antipathy for his son-in-law, who was a lingering Proudhonist. At one of his visits, he found to his dismay that Jennychen had no money for the rent. Marx appealed to Engels for a "monetary subsidy" to pay the landlord, explaining that in France they did not joke about such things.

[18]Marx to Jenny Longuet, March 16, 1882.
[19]Jenny Longuet to Marx, March 31, 1882; MS, D 3331, in International Institute for Social History, Amsterdam.

On September 16, 1882, Jennychen gave birth to her sixth
child, a girl. This was her last pregnancy. She had been gravely ill since her confinement, suffering from an abdominal
disease, probably cancer, of which she died on January 11,
1883, at the age of thirty-eight, when her infant was four
months old. To Marx, the news of her death, so soon after
his wife's, was a blow from which he did not recover. He followed his beloved daughter to the grave within seven weeks.

Jennychen's only daughter, also named Jenny, died, without issue, in 1952, at the age of seventy. She was the last of
Marx's grandchildren. Jean's son, Charles Jean Longuet, a
sculptor, lives in Paris with his wife Simone and their two
daughters, Frédérique and Anne. Little Anne in particular
seems to have inherited the beauty of her great-great-grand-
mother, Jenny Marx.

Laura Lafargue

Laura was Marx's second daughter, born in Brussels on
September 6, 1845, a little more than a year after Jennychen.
She was the only one of his children to survive into the 20th
century.

Laura was the most elegant and versatile of Marx's daughters. Her mother said of her that she was "at home in everything, be it in the wide sea or the stove or the reading room
of the British Museum or in the ballroom." A curly-haired
blonde, Laura was a striking beauty, as her mother noted:
"Laura is in some degrees lighter, blonder and more clear
complexioned, actually more attractive than her older sister,
because she has regular features and iridescent green eyes under dark brows and long eyelashes shine with the fire of
joy."[20]

She was naturally much courted. On May 1, 1865, her sister Jennychen's twenty-first birthday, Marx reported to Engels, in his customary Germanlish, that Laura had had "the
question popped" by a certain Charles Manning, born in
South America of an English father and Spanish mother. Although Manning was a rich and decent fellow, Marx wrote,
Laura "does not care a pin for him." Manning was a persis-

[20]Olga Worobjowa and Irma Sinelnikowa, *Die Töchter Von Marx*
(Berlin, 1965), p. 51.

tent suitor, but Laura "has already known how to damp" his Southern passion. However, since Laura was a friend of Manning's sister, and he was "frightfully in love," the whole thing was, as Marx put it, "a disagreeable case."

Paul Lafargue was more lucky than Manning. Paul, a twenty-four-year-old medical student, came to London in February 1866, carrying a letter of introduction to Marx from Henri Louis Tolain, a French communist. Lafargue, a Proudhonist, had been suspended from the University of Paris medical school for making revolutionary speeches at a student congress at Liège in October 1865. He was in London to learn English and to continue his medical studies, which he did at St. Bartholomew's Hospital, and was a frequent visitor in the Marx home.

Both Marx and his wife were thunderstruck when the young man revealed that his real interest in the Marx household was not politics or philosophy, but Laura. As Marx put it ironically, "The young man at first attached himself to me but soon transferred his attraction from the Old Man to the daughter."

Laura's parents, essentially bourgeois in their habits, may have been disconcerted by Lafargue's exuberant behavior. Lafargue was an olive-skinned, wavy-haired Creole, born in Santiago de Cuba of a partly French father. His paternal grandmother had been a mulatto from Santo Domingo, a refugee in Cuba during the French Revolution. His paternal grandfather was French. On his mother's side, his grandfather, Abraham Armagnac, was a Jew of French origin. His maternal grandmother had been a Caribbean Indian. Marx came to refer affectionately to Lafargue as a "nigger," a "Negrillo" or "our Creole."

On August 6, 1866, Laura yielded to the persuasions of her wooer and became, as Marx put it, "half engaged to Monsieur Lafargue, my medical Creole." He explained the situation on August 7 in a letter to Engels: "She had treated him like the others, but the emotional excesses of such Creoles, some fears that the *jeune homme* . . . would do away with himself, etc., some affection for him, cool as is always the case with Laura . . . have led to more or less a half compromise."

What the Marx family, including Laura, believed to be a semi-engagement, was apparently understood by Lafargue to be a full one. He now wished to commence intimate relations with his semi-fiancée. Probably prodded by his wife, Marx reacted like a middle-class Victorian Papa. On August 13, within a week of the "half engagement," he wrote to Lafargue, in French, a letter that deserves a special place in father-in-law literature.

He began with an ultimatum:

If you want to continue contact with my daughter, you must give up your manner of "paying court" to her. You know well that there is as yet no promise of marriage, that is still up in the air.

He went on to say that even if there were a full betrothal, it would be inappropriate to have an intimate relationship and that, despite temptations, the two young people would necessarily have "to live in chastity" for a prolonged period.

In the course of a geologic era of a single week, I have observed with shock the changes in your conduct. In my opinion, true love is expressed in reserve, modesty, and even shyness of the lover toward his idol, and never in temperamental excesses or too premature intimacy. When you invoke your Creole temperament, then I consider it my duty to step in between your temperament and my daughter with my healthy common sense. If you are unable to show your love for her in the form consonant with the London latitude, then it is advisable that you love her from a distance.

Marx then raised the question of finances:

Before your relations with Laura are definitely settled, I must be completely clear about your economic circumstances.

He acknowledged that he had a deep personal reason for asking this, for he himself had practically wrecked his own wife's life.

You know that I have sacrificed my whole fortune to the revolutionary struggle. I do not regret it. Quite the contrary. If I had to start my life over again, I would do the same. But I would not marry.

How did Lafargue propose to support a wife? Lafargue's career, Marx wrote him, was half-wrecked in France and his future in England, where he hardly knew the language, was problematical. In addition, Marx reminded him, "you are not diligent by nature, despite occasional feverish activity and good intentions." Under these circumstances, Lafargue was "destined to depend on others." Who would help him? His family in Bordeaux, France? Marx wrote:

> I know nothing about your family. Even if they live in prosperous circumstances, it does not prove that they are willing to bear sacrifices for you. I do not even know how they feel about your proposed marriage. It is necessary for me, I repeat, to have a positive clarification of all these questions.

Marx added that a "professed realist" like Lafargue could not expect him to behave like an idealist "where the future of my daughter is concerned." A man like Lafargue, who talked about the abolition of poverty, "would not want to make poverty at the expense of my child."

Marx concluded his letter with a stern warning:

> In order to anticipate every false interpretation of this letter, I call your attention to the fact that—should you feel tempted to enter into the marriage today—you will not succeed. My daughter would refuse. I would protest. You ought to have achieved something in life before you can think of marriage, and this will require a long testing period for you and Laura.

On the same day, Marx wrote to Paul's father, François Lafargue, in Bordeaux, a long letter in French, telling him that he must have "*renseignements positifs* [positive information]" about his economic condition before the matter between his son and Laura could go any further.

He was soon reassured. It turned out that the Lafargues, who had moved to France in 1851, when Paul was nine years old, were well-to-do people; they had plantations in Cuba and properties in New Orleans as well as in Bordeaux. Lafargue *père* was a wholesale wine merchant prosperous enough to promise that Paul, his only son and heir, who had received a fine education in the *lycées* of Bordeaux and Toulouse, would get a wedding gift of 100,000 francs. This was certainly a considerable fortune, but there is no indication that Paul ever received it. For the time being Marx was happy to learn that young Lafargue's economic prospects were, as he said, so "very favorable." Paul had completed his courses at the University of Paris medical school, but Marx was pleased with the senior Lafargue's stipulation that before Paul married Laura he would have to take his medical examination, first in London and then in Paris. "So far," Marx informed Engels, "the thing is settled."[21]

But it was not so easy to deal with Lafargue's passionate behavior toward Laura. Papa Marx realized that the young Creole was what he called a "verliebter Kauz [literally: a screech-owl in love]," but he often had to repeat to him that nothing would come of the whole thing unless he "calmed down to the level of English manners."

Lafargue both amused and exasperated Marx. When Laura was away as an apprentice teacher in a boarding school outside of London, the lovelorn Lafargue reminded Marx of Don Quixote. He wrote to Laura on August 28, "Il hidalgo della figura trista [The knight of the rueful countenance] left me at the corner of his house. After his heart was heavily shaken, he seems to part from me with heroic coolness."

Marx's exasperation proceeded from the fact that Lafargue was around the house too much at a time when there was little money and the family wanted badly to conceal its desperate poverty from Laura's well-to-do suitor. On December 7, after an angry outburst, Marx wrote him a brief apology, "If I hurt you with my excited monologue, I beg you to forgive me. It is wrong to become excited, even if one is right."

It was not possible to remain angry with Lafargue for long. Both Marx and his wife could not help being fond of him. Jenny was impressed by his "fine character, his deep goodness, his generosity, and his devotion to Laura." Marx wrote to Engels in his letter of August 23, "He is a thoroughly good-natured lad, but an enfant gaté [spoiled child], and much too much a child of nature."

On Laura's twenty-first birthday, September 26, 1866, Lafargue presented her with an "engaged ring," as her mother called it. Jenny Marx was both happy and pessimistic about her daughter's official engagement. Thinking back a

[21]Marx to Engels, August 23, 1866.

quarter of a century to the bitter religious undertones of her own engagement, she was pleased that this was at least one area where Laura would not have to suffer. Laura and Lafargue shared a common atheism and their parents had no church bias.

In February 1868, M. Lafargue in Bordeaux arranged the necessary papers for his son, in preparation for the wedding in April. Marx was both relieved and desperate. On the one hand, he wanted to have "this *affaire* settled" once and for all, particularly since Lafargue "practically lives in our house" and thereby the "expenses are appreciably increased."[22] On the other hand, he had no money either for the wedding or for such necessities as water and gas, for which he had just received a final summons to pay £5. The situation was so *"brûlante"* [burning] that Marx developed severe headaches and carbuncles. Twice he appealed to his Philips relatives in Holland for financial help. They did not even answer. "In regard to the Dutch," he wrote to Engels on March 14, "it seems to me that I will not extort anything from them unless I assail them in person—without previous notice. But this is out of the question just now."

Marx's appeal to Kugelmann met with some success. Kugelmann sent him £15, and, in his acknowledgment of March 17, Marx wrote that the whole matter was both unpleasant and agreeable for him. It was unpleasant because it would be "miserable" on his part to accept such a present, and so he wanted it to be considered a loan, to be repaid someday. Laura's letter to Engels, written on March 20, was much more brief:

Paul has written to you and urged all due reasons why you should do so and why you should *not* do otherwise; I have, therefore, nothing more to add than that I should be delighted to see you on the day of my marriage and very disappointed if you did not come.

When Lafargue heard that Engels was coming for the wedding, he thanked him warmly in a letter addressed to "My ever-laughing Engels":

If you find my English good, I find your French astonishing and you have not near you such a pretty master

[22]Marx to Engels, March 6, 1868.

to correct your mistakes as I have. The French *"grisettes"* who have taught you have so well earnt their money that you would need them no longer for that purpose.[23]

On April 1, Engels came to London for Laura's wedding. There was to be no religious ceremony, for as Marx found out, in England "a church wedding is not legally necessary."[24] On April 2, Marx, his carbuncles bandaged in poultices, went with Engels to the Register Office of Pancras County, Middlesex, to witness the marriage.[25]

At the end of April, the "lovesick" Lafargues returned from their honeymoon to London and settled in an apartment at Primrose Hill.[26] Lafargue, who took his doctor's degree at St. Bartholomew's, where he practiced as a surgical assistant, was admitted to the Royal College of Surgeons on July 22 and began to practice medicine. Marx commented sardonically that his son-in-law was now "licensed to kill men and beasts."[27] But at least Marx was now in a position to "borrow" money from his daughter Laura.[28]

Lafargue, more interested in politics than in medicine, for which, Marx noted, he had a real flair, decided to return to Paris. He and Laura moved there on October 16, 1868, and settled in an upper-floor apartment on the rue de Cherche-Midi. Lafargue soon discovered that there were obstacles in his way to medical practice in Paris, since the French did not recognize his English doctorate. As Marx wrote to Engels on November 7, "Our Negro, Paul Lafargue, has the ill luck of not having his English diploma honored at all, but [they] insist upon his running the gauntlet of five new examinations, instead of one or two, as he had expected."

In Paris, Lafargue became a member of the Vaugirard branch of the International. He and Laura moved in a circle of radicals, both foreign and French. Among Lafargue's foreign friends were the German 48'er Victor Schily, an old

[23]Lafargue to Engels, *ca.* March 25, 1868.

[24]Marx to Kugelmann, April 6, 1868.

[25]The certificate registered the marriage of "Paul Lafargue, 26, medical student, son of Francis Lafargue, Gentleman, [and] Jenny Laura Marx, 22, Spinster, daughter of Charles Marx, Gentleman"; MS G 349, in the International Institute for Social History, Amsterdam.

[26]Marx to Engels, April 30, 1868.

[27]Marx to Engels, July 23, 1868.

[28]Marx to Engels, September 12 and October 4, 1868.

friend of Marx; the Russian populist German Alexandrovich Lopatin (Lopatine), co-translator of the first volume of *Das Kapital* into Russian; and the Hungarian communist Leo Frankel. Marx worried about Lafargue, who, instead of pursuing his medical career, became "much too absorbed in politics."

Laura soon began to have babies. The first child, a boy, was born on January 1, 1869, nine months to the day after her wedding. He was named Charles Étienne and nicknamed "Schnaps" or "Schnappy." Eleanor Marx's nickname for her nephew, whom she loved "fanatically," was "Fouchtra."[29] Marx, thrilled by his first grandchild and worried about Laura's health, wrote to Lafargue that he wanted to visit Paris to see them. However, his letter was intercepted by the French police, who began to inquire when he was arriving, so he did not go. He was thinking of becoming naturalized as an Englishman "to be able to travel to Paris in safety,"[30] but he did not get around to doing so until a few years later.

Laura was constantly ailing, and on July 7, Marx, in his anxiety about her, risked arrest by going to Paris without a passport of his own, traveling incognito under the name "A. Williams." At Dieppe, to his surprise, the *douaniers* and the police did not bother him, "whereas, curiously enough, some innocent people (among others, a Yankee with very black hair, who was taken for an Italian) were asked for their passports, and the French passengers, according to the latest regulations, had to give their names."[31]

"A. Williams" stayed in a *"maison meublée"* on the rue St. Placide, one block from the Lafargues. Marx was "deeply shaken" to find Laura seriously ill. The house doctor, whom he consulted, urged the absolute necessity of her going to the seashore, suggesting Dieppe, where Paul agreed to take her. Lafargue also promised Marx that he would not further neglect his medical career but take his examinations upon returning from the seashore. The one bright spot in Marx's Paris visit was little "Schnappy." "Our grandson," he wrote to Paul's father on July 10, "is an enchanting boy. I have never seen so beautifully formed a child's head."

In the middle of July the Lafargues visited London, where

[29] Mark to Engels, August 10, 1869.
[30] Marx to Engels, March 20, 1869.
[31] Marx to Engels, July 14, 1869.

they stayed in the Marx home for about a month. Laura was still ailing, and so was the "most darling little man." Jenny Marx wrote to Kugelmann on September 15, "The dear little boy suffers from teething with all its usual symptoms. The little amiable face has become so thin and small, and the beaming little eyes shine so big and powerful out of the pale little face. He is a gay and tender little chap, and we will miss the little monkey so much."

Marx in the meantime, on his way to see his Hamburg publisher, stopped in Hanover, where he was a guest of the Kugelmanns for the second time.

Exactly one year after Schnappy's birth, on January 1, 1870, Laura was delivered of another child, a girl. In London, the news of Laura's latest "New Year's present" did not make her mother happy. She wished her daughter's "rapid tempo" in child-bearing would come to an end. Otherwise, she wrote sardonically, they would soon sing, "1, 2, 3, 4, 5, 6—10 little nigger-boys!"[32]

The baby, "stinted from the beginning,"[33] died two months later, at the end of February, during a severe cold spell in France. Marx was sure that the extraordinary cold contributed to the little girl's death. He sympathized profoundly with its parents at their loss, although, as he wrote them on March 5, "Still, from the same personal experience I know that all wise commonplaces and consolatory trash uttered on such occasion inflate real grief—instead of soothing it."

He was also greatly concerned about the effect the harsh cold might have on little Schnappy, his "greatest favorite." The child was, after all, partly Negro and he believed that the "dark-skinned nature" did not endure severe cold weather. In this connection, Marx expressed a satirical opinion of the leading contemporary French race-theorist, Joseph Arthur, comte de Gobineau, who was to have a disastrous influence on 20th century racists, particularly the German Nazis:

Apropos, *un certain M. de Gobineau* had published *il y a à peu pres dix ans* [about ten years ago], a work in 4 volumes, *Sur l'Inégalité des Races Humaines*,[34] written

[32]Jenny Marx to Engels, January 17, 1870.
[33]Marx to Engels, March 5, 1870.
[34]Gobineau, *Essai sur l'Inégalité des Races Humaines* [Essay on the Inequality of the Human Race] (4 vols., Paris, 1853–55).

for the purpose to prove above all that *"la race blanche* [the white race]" is a sort of God among the other human races and, of course, the noble families within the *"race blanche"* are again *la crême de la crême* [elite]. I rather suspect that M. de Gobineau, *dans ce temps là "premier secrétaire de la légation de France on Suisse"* [at that time, "first secretary of the French legation in Switzerland"], to have sprung himself not from an ancient Frankish warrior but from a modern French *huissier* [doorman]. However that may be, and despite his spite against the *"race noire* [black race]" (for such people it is always a source of satisfaction to have somebody they think themselves entitled to *mépriser* [despise]), he declares *"le nègre* [the Negro]" or *"le sang noir* [black blood]" to be the material source of art and that all the artistic creativity of the white nations depends on their mixture with *"le sang noir"* . . .

Later in 1870, Laura gave birth to a third child. It lived only seven months. Schnappy did not survive the other children very long. He died in Madrid in 1872, at the age of three and a half, after months of suffering from dysentery. Lafargue, desperate at his inability to save his children, gave up medicine altogether. The Lafargues were to have no more children.

After the 1872 Congress of the International in The Hague, the Lafargues settled in London, where they lived for ten years. As the Longuets were also there until 1881, it was a period of special satisfaction for the ailing *"Père Marx,"* as Engels called him, for now he had all his adoring and adored family together in London.

Lafargue went into the photo-engraving business, using his kitchen as a laboratory. Beguiled by impractical schemes, he was always on the verge of some big job, but never really landed one. His mother-in-law wrote that he worked like a "true Nigger" but that his nature was of such buoyancy that for him "the sky was always full of violins." She wished that he had stuck to medicine: "It is a pity that he became unfaithful to old Father Aesculapius."[35]

Engels always came to the rescue of the needy Lafargues in France. In thanking him, Laura wrote on December 15,

[35]Jenny Marx to Friedrich Adolph Sorge, January 20 or 21, 1877.

1886, that everything pleasant in her life, from a good dinner or an extra glass of beer to a good book, was connected with him in her thought. She expressed her longing for the country where Engels lived and where she was raised in a two-line stanza, asking the shade of Robert Burns to forgive her:

> My heart is in England (my heart is not here)
> With her brown kippered herrings and blond
> Pilsner beer!

In May 1887, Lafargue was a candidate for the Paris Municipal Council from the V. Arrondissement, which included the Jardin des Plantes and the Zoo. On April 26 Engels congratulated him for being the candidate of the plants and the animals: "Being, in his quality as a nigger, a degree nearer to the rest of the animal kingdom than the rest of us, he is undoubtedly the most appropriate representative of that district. Let us hope the animals will have the best of it in this struggle against the beasts."

Lafargue lost to the *"bêtes,"* receiving only 568 votes, coming in third.

Late in 1887, the Lafargues rented a house in Le Perreux, near Nogent-sur-Marne, twenty minutes by train from Paris. In November, when Laura thanked Engels for his latest check and invited him to visit the house into which they moved in December, she wrote, "We shall have a bit of a bedroom to offer you and plenty of fresh country air, pretty river scenery and a kitchen and a flower garden into the bargain."

The Lafargues remained in Le Perreux until Engels' death in 1895.

It was a cheerless life in a land which Laura described to Engels on December 21 as a *"pays enchanté mais non enchanteur* [enchanted but not enchanting country]." She added that whenever she visited her sister in Argenteuil, "Jenny and I do nothing but rail against la belle France."

In August and September 1882, Laura accompanied Marx, who was then taking sulphur baths at Enghien, on trips to Lausanne and Vevey, Switzerland. She was still a strikingly beautiful blonde and an appreciative listener for her widowed father, who was in an unrestrainedly talkative mood. When Marx died half a year later in London, Laura, who had inherited her mother's Victorian prudishness as well as her good looks, committed a crime against history by destroying her parents' intimate correspondence, including their love letters.

On November 14, 1894, Engels, suffering from cancer of the larynx, informed Laura and Eleanor, *"Mein lieben Mädels* [My dear girls]," that he was leaving each of them one-eighth of his estate.[36] He was gallant and bibulous to the end. One of his last letters, written in English from Eastbourne on July 23, 1895, was to Laura:

> My dear Löhr,
>
> To-morrow we return to London. There seems to be at last a crisis approaching in my potato field on my neck, so that the swellings may be opened and relief secured. At last! So there is hope of this long lane coming to a turning. And high time it is. . . . I am not in strength to write long letters, so goody-bye. Here's your good health in a bumper of *lait de poule* [mulled egg] fortified by a dose of *cognac vieux* [old brandy].

Less than two weeks after he wrote that letter, at 11 o'clock in the evening of August 5, Engels died, at the age of seventy-five. He had wanted no burial or funeral ceremonies. The urn with his ashes, in the presence of some eighty friends, including Eleanor Marx and Edward Aveling, was dropped into the English Channel at Eastbourne, the fashionable resort where he had spent many happy vacations.

Engels' extraordinary beneficence to the Marx family continued even after his death. Thanks to the inheritance from Engels, the Lafargues were able to buy a two-story, thirty-room house in Draveil (Juvisy-sur-Orge), twenty-five kilometers from Paris, near the Seine. It was an opulent estate, with outhouses and a *maison* for a gardener. The garden was a veritable park with numerous fruit trees and a lot of game. When sister Eleanor visited there in 1897, she was disturbed by the lavishness of the Lafargue establishment. The "orangerie" alone was so big that it might be converted into a meeting hall. She felt that socialists should not live in such a luxury and worried about the future of French Marxism. She wrote to Karl Kautsky that she would not "exchange my little Den [in London] with this palace." Here Laura and Paul

---

[36]Engels' will was drafted on July 23, 1893, and a codicil was added on November 14, 1894.

spent the rest of their lives. They continued to be devoted to each other, she soft-spoken and low-voiced, he booming and ebullient. They had many visitors.

In 1910, two shabby Russian strangers came by bicycle from Paris to see them. The Lafargues received their visitors with great cordiality. Paul talked to the man about philosophy; Laura took the woman for a walk in the park, where they chatted about the role of women in the Russian revolutionary movement. Later the Russian woman recalled emotionally the walk with Marx's last living offspring: "I was very excited—here was after all the daughter of Marx who was before me; I looked at her intensely, instinctively I sought in her features those of her father."[37]

The Russian visitors were Vladimir Ilyich Lenin and Nadeshda Konstantinovna Krupskaya, his wife.

The following year, on November 26, 1911, the gardener entered the house and found both Lafargues dead in their chairs. They had returned late from Paris and were still festively dressed. Lafargue, the ex-doctor, had injected cyanide in Laura's arm and then into his own. He left a letter saying that he had long ago decided to die at seventy, a crucial period when old age begins. Now he and Laura found themselves without means and did not want to be a burden to the socialist party. Laura accepted the decision to terminate their lives. Laura was then sixty-six years old, and Paul was sixty-nine. They had been married for more than forty-three years.

At the funeral, Lenin, speaking in the name of the Russian Social Democratic party, lauded Lafargue as "one of the most gifted and thorough of all those who propagated Marxist ideas."[38]

Helene and Henry Frederick
(Freddy) Demuth

In December 1850, the Marxes moved to the furnished three-room apartment on 28 Dean Street, Soho. Marx was

---

[37]O. Worobjowa and I. Sinelnikowa, *Die Töchter von Marx*, p. 141.
[38]Quoted in Worobjowa, p. 143. Lafargue's Marxist ideas can be found in the following writings by him: *The Evolution of Property from Savagery to Civilization* (London, 1890); "Der Klassenkampf in Frankreich," in *Die Neue Zeit*, 1893–94; "Le matérialisme économique de Karl Marx," in *L' Ère Nouvelle*, July 1893; *Origine et évolution de la Propriété* (Paris, 1895).

penniless and in debt. "I literally don't have a farthing," he wrote to Engels on March 31, 1851, Jenny Marx was sick and pregnant, and so was Helene Demuth. Marx spoke of the "very tangled family situation."

On June 23, 1851, three months after Jenny had given birth to Franziska, who died the following year, Lenchen Demuth, then twenty-seven, was delivered of a boy, Henry Frederick. His birth certificate, registered on August 1, listed the name of his mother, but left blank that of the father.

Jenny was apparently easily persuaded that Engels was the father. She never really approved of his morals. A man who lived with a mistress, as Engels did with Mary Burns in Manchester, was capable of anything. (It is noteworthy that even though Engels was to be the most important person in her and her husband's life, she did not address him as "Friedrich" or "Frederick" or "Fred," but always as "Herr Engels.")

Some two months before Lenchen gave birth to her baby, Engels was informed of the situation. As a preliminary, Marx hinted at a "mystery" which he called "tragicomic." He would reveal the mystery, "in which you also play a role," in a few words next time.[39] But by April 2 Marx had changed his mind and decided to tell Engels in person, instead of by letter: "In regard to the mystery, I will not write to you about it, since cost what it may, I will visit you at the end of April. I must leave here for eight days."

Marx went to Manchester on April 17 and remained for several days. He persuaded Engels to accept responsibility for Lenchen's child, who was named Frederick, after him.

Lenchen, with her total devotion to Jenny and the Marx family, never betrayed the secret; she let her baby be brought up by a working-class family, for whom Engels occasionally sent her money.[40] If Jenny had known the truth, it might have killed her, or at the very least destroyed her marriage. This was the reason why, although Marx loved children and was a doting father, he never permitted himself to acknowledge "Freddy" as his son.

After Marx's death, Lenchen moved into Engels' home on 122 Regent's Park Road as his housekeeper. Later Engels

---

[39]Marx to Engels, March 31, 1851.

[40]See, for example, Marx's letter to his wife, who was then visiting Trier, August 8, 1856: ". . . this morning I received a note from Frederic [sic], with 15 Thaler for Lenchen. *Tell her* that he is *very exact* in such things."

moved to a more capacious apartment a few doors away, at 128 Regent's Park Road, with a wide view of Primrose Hill, and Lenchen went with him. According to Paul Lafargue, she was as "fond of him as of the Marx family," while Engels appreciated and respected her as much as the Marxes had. To him, too, Lenchen was a "treasure."[41]

To Engels, who entertained frequently, Lenchen was indispensable. She was a great cook who, like Engels, appreciated good food, fine wine and foaming beer. At his dinners she presided at table as the *Hausfrau*. Her son Freddy visited his mother regularly once a week. As an ordinary workingman, however, he entered through the kitchen.

On November 4, 1890, Lenchen, aged sixty-seven, died of "Cancer of the Bowell, perforative Peritonitis."[42] Engels was deeply affected. He expressed his grief on November 5 in a brief note to his and Marx's friend, Friedrich Adolph Sorge, in Hoboken, New Jersey:

> Today I have sorrowful news to report. My good, dear, loyal Lenchen gently passed away after a brief and mostly painless illness. We have lived seven happy years together in this house. We have been the last two of the Old Guard from before 1848. Now I am alone again. If, for a long period of years, Marx, and in the last seven years I, found peace of mind to work, it was essentially due to her. What will happen to me now I do not know. I will also painfully miss her wonderfully tactful advice in Party affairs.

Only after Lenchen's death did the truth about Freddy's birth slowly begin to come out. On November 9, four days after Lenchen was buried in Highgate, Engels wrote to Louise Kautsky (née Strasser), a Viennese who, in 1889, had divorced the Marxist theoretician Karl Kautsky, inviting her to come and live in his house: "You are young and have a fine future before you. In three weeks I will be seventy and have only a short time to live."[43] She accepted his invitation and early in December she came to London and moved into his home as his secretary. Although Louise was thirty, attrac-

---

[41]Marx to Louise Weydemeyer, March 11, 1861: "Ask your dear husband about her; he will tell you what a treasure I have in her."

[42]Photostat of death certificate in the Karl-Marx-Haus, Trier.

[43]Engels lived on happily for another five years.

tive and gay, there could be nothing more intimate between them than that, as the seventy-year-old Engels, always susceptible to women, wrily admitted to a friend:

That Louise is a very good *Hausfrau*, I am prepared to maintain against each and every one, despite contrary assertions, and also that she is a splendid cook. But I am not entirely sure that the housewifeliness does not consist of the fact that we two are not married; and should this continue to be the case, it would be my good fortune because, given our age difference, marital and extramarital relationships are equally excluded and thus there is nothing left but the housewifeliness.[44]

Louise remained a member of Engels' household until his death, even after marrying a Viennese physician, Dr. Ludwig Freyberger, who moved in with her, treating his host free of charge. It was to her that Engels told the truth about the identity of Freddy's father, and she in turn communicated it to a few trusted friends.

Louise befriended Freddy, who continued his visits to the Engels home even after his mother's death. She saw to it that he entered through the front door and that he enjoyed, as she said, "all the privileges of visitors." In July 1894, when friends gathered in Engels' home, drinking beer and awaiting the telegraphic news of the Parliamentary election returns in Germany, Freddy Demuth was among the guests.[45]

Little is known of Freddy's last years. In the Amsterdam archives (G280) there is a rare letter written by Freddy, who was then living in Upper Clapton, London, N.E., to Laura Lafargue, on October 10, 1910. The writing is that of a poorly educated proletarian full of troubles and worries, but sheds some light on his and his family's existence:

My dear Laura. It is such a long time since I heard from you that I am again taking the liberty of writing to you which I should have done sooner, but I so much wanted to write you more hopefull news of myself and my Son and his family, and I am pleased to say that I am able

[44]Engels to August Bebel, February 2, 1892.
[45]Postal card to Natalie Liebknecht (in Berlin), July 1, 1894, signed by thirteen people, including "F. Demuth."

294KARL MARX

to do so for myself you will be glad to know that I am
well in Health.

He went on to say that he had employment and that he
was "much more pleasanter located in lodgings" than he had
been for a long time. He was living with a fellow worker and
his wife, whom he had known for many years and who were
very kind to him. His son, he wrote, was employed by a
French taxicab company, but he had to work nights, from 8
P.M. to 7 A.M., six days a week, for which he was paid 22
shillings weekly. The son's wife and "little ones" were well,
although "I am sorry to say, there has been another little girl
Born." Freddy then made a sociological comment which his
father might have approved: "To me it seems very sad,
seeing they have had so much trouble in their young lives, to
bring more children into the world appears to me very short
of a crime, but I suppose it will go on till the time comes
when the Birth of Children will be Hailed with joy instead of
sadness."

In the second half of the letter, Freddy asked Laura
whether she could do him a small favor. He had read in a
newspaper that there was an engineering firm named Demuth
Bro. of Austria. Could Laura tell him whether "perhaps they
might be connected with my mother" and if they had a
branch in London? If so, could his son get there "a better
and more remunerative Employment?" He apologized to
Laura for troubling her with "so much Personality" in his letter, but he knew, he wrote, that she would try to help, because she would realize that his son "and His children are the
only Beings I have in the world who I can call mine and although I do not see them very often it gives me great
Pleasure to Help in any way I can do so." He signed his letter: "Dear Laura affectionately yours, F. Demuth."

Soon after the letter was written, Freddy's son left for Aus-
tralia, hoping to find work on a farm. His wife and four children remained in London in Freddy's care. What happened
to all of them is unknown.

A death certificate, registered in London, names a "Frederick Lewis Demuth," an engineer by profession, who died on
January 28, 1929, aged seventy-six years, but this could have
been a different Demuth.[46]

---

[46]Displayed in the Karl-Marx-Haus, Trier.

Eleanor ("Tussy")

Eleanor was born on January 16, 1855, one month before her mother's forty-first birthday.

Eleanor was Marx's last offspring to survive childhood. (A seventh child died soon after its birth in July 1857.) Following the custom of the house, she was given many nicknames, among them "Mine Own"[47] and "Miss Lilliput."[48] But the nickname that finally stuck, and by which she is known to posterity, is "Tussy," presumably from the way she, a cat lover, pronounced "Pussy" as a child.

Although Marx regretted at Eleanor's birth that she was not a boy,"[49] he hailed his Töchterchen [little daughter] as a new "*Weltbürgerin* [world citizeness]."[50] As the youngest child in a tightly knit, affectionate household, Eleanor became everybody's pet, including that of her sisters Jenny and Laura, who were eleven and ten years older, respectively. Liebknecht, a frequent visitor to the Marx home, described her as a "little gay thing, round as a ball." Her mother wrote of her:

> The child was born at the time when my poor dear Edgar left us, and all love for the little brother, all tenderness for him was transferred to the little sister, whom the older girls cherished and tended with virtually maternal care. For that matter, there is hardly a more lovable child, pretty as a picture, naive and whimsical. The child is characterized especially by its lovable speech and story telling. This she has learned from the brothers Grimm, who are her companions day and night. All of us read ourselves deaf and dumb in the fairy tales, and woe to us if we leave out a syllable from the story of Rumpelstilzchen or King Drosselbart or Snow Maiden.

[47]Marx to Jennychen, January 11, 1865.
[48]Marx to Eleanor, July 3, 1865. In his letter to his daughter, then aged ten, he signed himself playfully, "Dr. Wunderlich [Dr. Strange, or Eccentric]."
[49]Marx to Engels, January 17, 1855.
[50]Marx to Lassalle, January 23, 1855.

Jenny concluded:

> She is Karl's true love and laughs and babbles away
> many of his worries.[51]

Tussy became Marx's particular pet. She was allowed to
scribble on his letters and loved to ride on his shoulders in
the small garden of their house on Grafton Terrace. He put
flowers in her curls and acted as her "splendid horse."

Tussy, like her sisters, came to adore her father. In fact, it
was her love and admiration for and domination by him that
was to be her undoing.

Tussy differed from her older sisters in both temperament
and appearance. Unlike them, she was not a housewifely
type, but a vigorous revolutionary activist. Where Laura, for
example, was a cool Teutonic blonde, Tussy was Semitic and
emotional. Black-haired and flashing-eyed, she bore a remarkable resemblance to her father, possessing even his thickish
nose. She once wrote to Karl Kautsky, "I, unfortunately only
inherited my father's nose . . . and not his genius."[52]

But she was in the deepest sense the image of her father.
She possessed his temperament, energy, passion and dedication to politics. Marx used to say that his wife had made a
mistake about the sex, that Eleanor should have been a boy.
After her parents' death, Tussy said that she and her mother
had loved each other passionately, but "she did not know me
as father did." She recalled her father talking about his oldest
daughter, his favorite, and saying, "Jenny is not like me, but
Tussy *is* me."[53]

Born and educated in London, Tussy was essentially
British, and English was her mother tongue, but she mastered
languages, particularly German and French, and became a
skilled translator. She had a beautiful speaking and singing
voice, and like her mother, she loved the theater, admired Sir
Henry Irving, the great Shakespearean actor, and aspired to
be an actress.

But her main interest was politics. Only six years old when
the American Civil War broke out, she followed its course
with intense concern. She studied the war maps and had her

[51]Quoted in Worobskaya, p. 31.
[52]Eleanor Marx to Karl Kautsky, December 28, 1896.
[53]Quoted in C. Tsuzuki, *The Life of Eleanor Marx*, 1855–1898 (Oxford, 1967), p. 63.

father explain the battle reports to her. As she recalled later, "At that time .. . I had the unshakable conviction that Abraham Lincoln could not succeed without my advice, and so I wrote him long letters, which Mohr had to read and take to the post office. Many years later he showed me the childish letters which had so amused him that he had preserved them."[54]

In 1876, at the age of twenty-one, she rang doorbells to solicit votes for Mrs. Westlake, a free-thinker who was running for the school board against the "Church-Party," which wanted to abolish compulsory school attendance. This resulted in some eye-opening experiences: "In one house, they asked what 'religion especially' should be taught; in another, I was told 'Education is the curse of the country— schooling will destroy us,' etc., etc. In brief, it is amusing, but withal also sad, when one comes to a worker who tells you he wants first 'to ask his factory owner.' "[55]

Tussy became a member of the Socialist League, and, with Engels, helped to found the Second International in 1889. She was a fiery orator. Henry Mayers Hyndman, a founder of the Social Democratic Federation, remarked after hearing Tussy speak at a commemoration of the Paris Commune, "Eleanor Marx made one of the finest speeches I ever heard. The woman seemed inspired with some of the eloquence of the old prophets of her race."[56]

She had her father's combativeness. Even policemen did not intimidate her. One morning she went to the Bow Street Police Station where Michael Davitt, a leader of the Irish Land League and champion of Home Rule in Parliament, had been taken upon his arrest. There was a large and angry pro-Davitt crowd in front of the Station. Tussy asked a policeman, who had a "very Hibernian countenance," whether Davitt was still inside. "No," he replied in an Irish brogue, "it's meself put him in the van." Tussy asked angrily whether there were not enough Englishmen "to do such dirty work that an Irishman must help 'put in the van' a man like Davitt who had done so much for his country." The other policeman glared at her. As she was turning away, a man walked up to

[54]See Saul K. Padover, ed., *Karl Marx on America and the Civil War* (New York, 1972), p. xxii.

[55]Eleanor Marx to Carl Hirsch, a German socialist journalist, November 25, 1876.

[56]Hyndman, *The Record of an Adventurous Life* (1911), p. 318.

her, extended his hand and said, "As an Irishman allow me to shake hands with you and thank you."[57]

She had also inherited her father's intensity and bluntness. Ludwig Kugelmann's daughter Franziska wrote that Tussy was "so boundlessly frank that she told everybody what she thought without any ceremony."[58]

In 1872, when Tussy was seventeen, she fell in love with a swaggering, thirty-four-year-old French journalist, Prosper Olivier Lissagaray. He had been a Communard, and as a refugee in London he published a short-lived weekly, *Rouge et Noire*, in which Tussy took a lively interest. Lissagaray, a French Basque count turned revolutionist, who had given up his title and been cast out by his family for his radicalism, was described by a contemporary as "insignificant in his appearance."[59] For reasons that are unclear, Marx took a strong dislike to him. Although he encouraged him in writing his authoritative book *Histoire de la Commune de 1871*, the German translation of which he supervised,[60] Marx did not want him for a son-in-law. Nevertheless, Tussy and the French ex-count became engaged.

Marx did everything to dampen Tussy's ardor and discourage the engagement. But he had to act with unwonted delicacy to spare her feelings. In a letter to Engels, on May 31, 1873, Marx reported that Tussy accused him of being unjust to Lissagaray: "The reproach is unfounded. I ask nothing of him except that he give proof, instead of phrases, that he is better than his reputation and that there is any reason whatever for anybody to rely upon him. The damn thing is that for the sake of the child I must proceed considerately and carefully."

Tussy was torn between her passion for Lissagaray and her love for her father, whom she would not disobey. While teaching school in Brighton, she pleaded with Marx for permission to see Lissagaray. It was a letter full of pathos:

I want to know, dear Mohr, when I may see L again. It is so *very* hard *never* to see him. I have been doing my

---

[57]Eleanor Marx to Liebknecht, February 12, 1881.

[58]Franziska Kugelmann, "Small Traits of Marx's Great Character," written for the Institute of Marxism-Leninism, 1928.

[59]Franziska Kugelmann, *op. cit.*

[60]Marx to Wilhem Bracke, April 21, 1877. The German title of the book was *Geschichte der Commune von 1871*, published in Brunswick in 1877.

best to be patient, but it is so difficult, and I don't feel as if I could be much longer. I do not expect you to say that he can come here—I should not even wish it, but could I not, now and then go for a little walk with him? You let me go out with Outline,[61] with Frankel,[62] why not with him? No one moreover will be astonished to see us together, as everybody knows we are engaged. . . .

When I was so very ill at Brighton (during a week I fainted 2 or 3 times a day) L came to see me, each time left me stronger and happier, and more able to bear the rather heavy load laid on my shoulders. It is *so* long since I saw him, and I am beginning to feel so very miserable notwithstanding all my efforts to be merry and cheerful. I cannot much longer.

She concluded:

Believe me, dear Mohr, if I could see him now and then it could do me more good than all Mrs. Anderson's[63] prescriptions put together.[64]

Marx, worried about Tussy's health, yielded. "I am," he wrote to Kugelmann on August 4, 1874, "in this regard less stoical than in other things, and family afflictions always hit me hard." But he remained adamant in his opposition to Lissagaray as a son-in-law. This antipathy was shared by other members of the Marx family. Lissagaray was barely welcome when he came visiting. Laura and Paul Lafargue, when they lived in London, refused to shake hands with him.

Tussy remained loyal to both her father and to Lissagaray. She was so proud of her fiancé's work that she translated it into English.[65] After the German edition came out (1877), she sent a copy to Heinrich Graetz, the renowned German-

[61]Nicolai Issaakovich Outine (Utin) (1845–1883), a Russian revolutionary editor and member of the Russian Section of the First International.

[62]Leo Frankel (1844–1896), Hungarian revolutionist, Communard, and member of the First International.

[63]Elizabeth Garrett Anderson (1836–1917), Tussy's doctor.

[64]Quoted in Tsuzuki, *op. cit.*, p. 35. The letter is undated; it was probably written in 1873 or 1874. Marx refers to Dr. Anderson's treating Tussy, in a letter to Dr. Kugelmann, August 4, 1874.

[65]*History of the Commune of 1871* was published in London by Reeves and Turner in 1876.

Jewish historian,[66] whom she and her father had met in Karlsbad when they were on a cure in 1876. In acknowledging receipt of Lissagaray's *History of the Commune of 1871,* Graetz congratulated Tussy on "such a bridegroom," saying that the book had "realism, style and conviction."[67]

Tussy's relations with Lissagaray continued for about a decade, even after he moved back to France. When he wrote her, he addressed her as *"Ma petite femme."* During the period of their engagement, she was buffeted by frequent illnesses, which were clearly psychosomatic. Her stomach was often upset and revolted against food. She suffered from depressions. Marx thought, or pretended to think, that Tussy's problem was a "woman's disease" that had a "hysterical element."[68]

In the end, Marx did win his silent battle against Lissagaray, but at a heavy cost to Tussy's health and future. She obeyed her father, but her compliance was to be devastating for her. In the summer of 1881, when Marx returned to London after visiting Jennychen in France, he found Tussy a physical and nervous wreck, as he reported to Jennychen on August 18: "Tussychen is pale and thin, for weeks she has eaten nothing (literally). Her nervous system is in a state of extreme depression; hence the constant sleeplessness, trembling hands, nervous facial tic, etc."

The Marx family's hostility to Lissagaray continued even after he moved to France. He and Paul Lafargue were also in political and journalistic conflict. Early in 1882, Tussy finally made the agonizing decision to break off her engagement to Lissagaray. On January 15 she wrote her sister Jenny about it and asked the Longuets to treat him as a friend, nevertheless: "He has been very good, and gentle, and patient with me." Jennychen was not displeased with Tussy's decision. Thinking of her own marriage to Longuet, she once wrote to Tussy, "these Frenchmen at the best of times make pitiable husbands."[69] On February 24, 1882, Jenny informed her father that Tussy had terminated her engagement. Marx replied on March 16, "I am very pleased to learn from your letter that Tussy has solved the catastrophe tactfully."

---

[66]Graetz (1817–1891) worked for twenty-two years on his monumental *Geschichte der Juden* [*History of the Jews*]. A five-volume English translation of the *History* came out in 1891–1895.

[67]Graetz to Marx, February 1, 1877.

[68]Marx to Engels, August 14, 1874.

[69]Quoted in Tsuzuki (no date), p. 66.

But Tussy soon entered into an arrangement with another man, Edward Aveling, that was to end in a real catastrophe.

Edward Aveling, the son of an Irish Protestant minister, was a doctor, a naturalist, a follower of Darwin, an atheist and a popular lecturer. He and Tussy first met in 1873, when she was eighteen and he twenty-four. The occasion of the meeting was a lecture on the theory of natural selection at the Orphan Working School, Hampstead, near Marx's home. Tussy and her parents were in the audience. At the end of the talk, the man with the "tremendous leonine head" went over to Aveling and congratulated him.

After Marx's death, Aveling, then editor of *Progress*, an atheist monthly, invited Tussy to write an obituary on her father. This renewed contact led to their intimate relationship. Even as a little girl, Tussy had considered "Edward" one of her favorite masculine names. Edward Aveling was a man of wit and charm, and already known as a secularist radical. An additional attraction was his admiration for Marx's work, which led to his conversion to socialism.

In the summer of 1884, when Tussy was twenty-nine years old, she went to live with Aveling. She knew that he had a wife from whom he was separated and that she was defying convention, as she wrote on June 30 to her friend Dollie Maitland Radford:

> I am going to live with Edward Aveling as his wife. You know he is married, and that I cannot be his wife *legally*, but it will be a *true* marriage to me—just as much as if a dozen registrars had officiated . . . if love, a perfect sympathy in tastes and work, and a striving for the same ends can make people happy, we shall be so.

She was aware, she wrote to Dollie, that people brought up with the old ideas and prejudices would think her wrong, but she was prepared to accept that. She added that Helene Demuth, who had been "as a mother to us," and Engels, "my father's oldest and dearest friend," approved what she was doing and were "perfectly satisfied." Engels took Aveling into his circle of socialist friends. On July 22, in informing Laura Lafargue that Tussy and Aveling had gone off on their "honeymoon," Engels stated, "I like Edward very much and think it will be a good thing for him to come more into contact with other people besides the literary and lecturing circle in which he moved."

Aveling further strengthened his relations with the Marxist group by joining the slow-working Samuel Moore in the translation of *Das Kapital*, although he was a "perfect novice" in political economy.[70] Engels observed that Aveling had to translate "strange matter out of *unbekannten Deutsch in ein ihm unbekannten Englisch* [unknown German into an English unknown to him]."[71]

For more than a dozen years Tussy and Aveling shared an active life intellectually and politically. He dabbled in the theater and she occasionally acted on the stage. They were also busy in the Social Democratic Federation and in trade union activities. Eleanor organized Jewish immigrant women workers in Whitechapel, and to make herself understood by them she learned Yiddish. Despite her father's antipathy for Jews, she herself felt strongly Jewish and was attracted to them and their problems—the only member of her family to have such feelings. "My happiest moments," she told the socialist historian Max Beer, "are when I am in the East End amidst Jewish work people." Tussy also organized other strikes, including that of the gas workers.

Her father remained a constant and powerful presence in her mind. A dozen years after Marx's death, on March 14, 1895, she wrote to Liebknecht, "Today it is 12 years since Mohr died—and I think I miss him and my mother and Jenny more today than when we lost them." She did everything possible to promote Marx's ideas and to keep his writings alive. To support herself, she followed in his footsteps and worked in the British Museum, doing research on articles and translations. She prepared her father's writings for publication in book form. Among the books, some of which came out after her death, were *The Eastern Question*, a collection of Marx's articles in the *New-York Daily Tribune* (1897); *Value, Price, and Profit* (1898); *Secret Diplomatic History of the Eighteenth Century* (1899). One of the books she published in 1896 under her father's name, *Germany: Revolution and Counter-Revolution*, consisting of articles in the *New-York Daily Tribune*, turned out to be an unfortunate mistake; the articles had actually been written by Engels.

She and Aveling and her two black cats, one of whom was named "Deviltry Satan," lived in slummy rooms until she

---

[70]Engels to Laura Lafargue, March 31, 1884.
[71]Engels to Laura Lafargue, May 26, 1884.

came into her £9,000 inheritance from Engels. In December 1895, she purchased a house in Jew's Walk, Sydenham, and named it "The Den." She exulted in her financial security and wrote enthusiastically to Laura on December 10:

> I am Jewishly proud of my house in Jew's Walk. Voilà. Ground floor—large room (Edward's study and general room combined); dining room (opens in back garden), kitchen, scullery, pantry, coal and wine cellars, cupboards, large entrance hall. One flight of upstairs (easy)—bedroom—spare bedroom *(yours)*, servants' room, bathroom . . . *my study!!!*—Everywhere we have electric light . . . tho' gas is laid on too.

But while her living conditions improved dramatically, her relationship with Aveling steadily deteriorated. He squandered her money on himself and other women. People came to despise him as a drunk, a libertine and a cheat. According to George Bernard Shaw, Aveling was "Homeric" in his borrowings. The "scamp," as Victor Adler, the Austrian socialist, called him, cheated Tussy, stole her things, had affairs with other women, and threatened during their last years together that he would expose Freddy Demuth's true paternity and blacken Marx's name unless she gave him money. Yet Tussy remained self-sacrificingly loyal to Aveling. Early in 1898, when he became gravely ill with a kidney abscess that required an operation, she got him into one of the best hospitals, obtained the finest surgeon, and attended him as a nurse. All this was, among other things, financially ruinous. She wrote to Liebknecht on January 3:

> Sometimes I hardly know how I shall hold on! It is not only the awful anxiety, but the actual material difficulties. Our joint income is (for London) very small and my present expenses are enormous—Doctors, chemists' bills, "chairs" for going out, and so forth, added to the home that must be kept up—all this means a great deal.

Tussy's last years were full of despair, and she came to lean heavily on Freddy Demuth, her half-brother. "Come," she wrote him on September 2, 1897, "if you possibly can, this evening. It is a shame to trouble you; but I am so alone, and I am face to face with a most horrible position; *utter* ruin—everything, *to the last penny,* or utter, open disgrace."

Tussy had become a warm friend to Freddy long before she learned the truth about his paternity. Believing Engels to be his father, she was bitter at the indifference with which he treated Freddy, who, she wrote to Laura on October 13, 1888, had had a "great injustice" done to him throughout his whole life. "We should none of us," she wrote, "like to meet our pasts, I guess, in flesh and blood." Freddy was a pitifully poor workingman, whose wife, in 1892, ran away with his few possessions. Whenever she saw Freddy, Tussy was assailed by a sense of shame and of "guilt and wrong done" to him.[72]

Tussy may have suspected the truth, but until August 4, 1895, the day before Engels died of cancer of the esophagus, she clung to her conviction that he was Freddy's father. On that day, Engels, who could no longer talk, wrote on a slate who Freddy's father really was.

Louise Freyberger records Tussy's reaction in a letter to the German socialist leader August Bebel on September 2, 1898:

Dearest August:

. . . That Freddy Demuth is Marx's son, I know from the General [Engels] himself. Tussy had pressed me so hard that I asked the Old Man directly. The General was very much surprised that Tussy continued in her stubborn belief, and then gave me permission that, should the necessity arise, I should contradict the gossip that Marx had disavowed his son. . . .

That Frederick Demuth is the son of Karl Marx and Helene Demuth, has been confirmed, moreover, by the General, a few days before his death, to Mr. [Samuel] Moore, who thereupon went to Orpington to see Tussy, whom he told about it. Tussy insisted that the General *lies* and that he had always said that he himself was the father. Moore returned from Orpington and again urgently asked the General, but the Old Man stuck to his assertion that Freddy is the son of Marx, saying to Moore: *Tussy wants to make an idol of her father.*[73]

On Sunday, the day before his death, the General himself wrote it down on the slate tablet, and Tussy left the room so shaken that she forgot her hatred of me and

[72]Tussy to Laura Lafargue, December 19, 1890.
[73]The italicized words were written in English.

threw herself around my neck, crying bitterly.

The General empowered us (Mr. Moore, Ludwig [Freyberger] and me) to make use of this information only if he himself was ever accused of having treated Freddy shabbily; he said he did not want to have his name dishonored, particularly as it served no purpose. His intercession for Marx had saved the latter from a grave domestic conflict.

Louise then explained Marx's motive in not acknowledging his son, as she had heard it from Engels:

For Marx, a possible divorce from his wife, who was frightfully jealous, was ever present. He did not love the boy; the scandal would have been too great; he did not dare do anything for him. The boy was boarded with a Mrs. Louis, I believe that is what she called herself, and he was named after his foster-mother, taking the name Demuth only after Nim's [Helene Demuth] death. . . .

Freddy looks ridiculously like Marx, and it required really blind prejudice to detect in this authentic Jewish face with its thick blue-black hair any resemblance to the General. I saw the letter that Marx had written at that time [1851] to the General in Manchester—the General did not yet live in London—but I believe that he [Engels] destroyed that correspondence with the rest. . . .

That Frau Marx once left her husband in London and went to Germany and that Marx and his wife had not slept together for years, all this has been well known to Tussy . . . but she idolized her father and invented the most beautiful legends. . . .

Your Louise.

Tussy never recovered from the trauma of this revelation. Her idealized image of her father had been irreparably soiled. She tried, she said, not to judge either her father or her lover too harshly. In a letter to Freddy, written on February 5, she made an obscure reference to those who were "physically diseased" whom one should not blame, but try to cure. "I have learnt this through long suffering in ways I would not tell even you."

By 1898, tangled up in her emotions and incapable of han-

dling reality, Tussy was contemplating death. She envied her
oldest sister Jenny, who had been dead for fifteen years. As
she wrote to Freddy on January 13:

> I sometimes feel like you, Freddy, that *nothing* ever goes
> well with us. I mean you and me. Of course, poor Jenny
> had her full share of sorrow and of trouble, and Laura
> lost her children. But Jenny was fortunate enough to die,
> and sad as that was for her children, there are times
> when I think it fortunate. I would not have wished
> Jenny to have lived through what I have done.

For Tussy the end came on March 31, 1898, some two
months after her forty-third birthday. On that morning she
received a shattering letter which, according to her friend Eduard Bernstein, the German socialist theoretician, informed
her that Aveling was bigamously married under a false name
to Eva Frye, a young actress who had been his mistress. This
was the final humiliation, an insult to the idealistic concept of
free love with which she had justified her relationship with
Aveling. Tussy obtained cyanide, went upstairs, wrote a letter
to her solicitor, Arthur Wilson Crosse, and a heartbreaking
note to Aveling:

> Dear, it will soon be all over now. My last word to you
> is the same that I have said during all these long, sad
> years—love.

Tussy's last thoughts were with her father. She wrote to her
twenty-two-year-old nephew Jean Longuet, who had been a
special favorite of Marx:

> My dear, dear Johnny!
> My final word is directed to you.
> Try to be worthy of your grandfather.
>   Your Aunt Tussy,

She bathed, dressed in white and took the poison.

She was cremated in Woking on April 5. Labor leaders
from Austria, France, Germany, Russia and Poland attended
the funeral. Will Thorne, secretary of the Gasworkers Union
and a founder of the British Labour Party, was so choked up
that he could hardly talk.

Four months later, on August 2, Aveling, suffering from a

kidney disease, shunned by labor organizations, and despised by his socialist colleagues, died peacefully.

The urn with Tussy's ashes was kept in the office of the Social Democratic Federation until 1920, when it was transferred to the headquarters of the British Communist Party. In the 1950's the ashes joined the rest of the Marx family and Helene Demuth in Highgate Cemetery. Tussy and Engels had had a hand in composing the inscription on the tombstone in 1891.[74] The inscription reads:

JENNY VON WESTPHALEN
The Beloved Wife of
Karl Marx
Born 12th February 1814
Died 2d December 1881

and KARL MARX
Born May 5th 1818. Died March 14th 1883

and HARRY LONGUET
Their Grandson
Born July 4th 1878. Died March 20th 1882

and HELENA DEMUTH
Born January 1st 1823. Died November 4th 1890.

[74]Engels to Laura Lafargue, July 12, 1891: "Tussy and I have just been talking over Nimmy's [Lenchen's] inscription. After various proposals of various epithets, to all of which objections may be made, I incline to put nothing but the name."

—————— XXIV ——————
Final Years

Breakdown

After the International came to an end in Amsterdam in 1872, Marx, according to his daughter Tussy, felt relieved of his responsibility and said over and over again, *"Jetzt kommt man wieder zur Arbeit* [Now one can begin to work again]." But this was a false hope. He did go occasionally to the British Museum and worked desultorily on Volume II of *Das Kapital,* but physically and psychologically he was no longer capable of sustained creative effort. The last decade of his life was one of almost constant illness and ultimately of a desperate pursuit of cures.

In Manchester, where Marx remained from May 22 to June 3, he was treated by Dr. Eduard Gumpert and made contact with some of Engels' other friends, among them the chemist Carl Schorlemmer and the lawyer Samuel Moore, co-translator of *Das Kapital.* Moore could not be seen during the days because he was with "his Dulcinea." The first days in Manchester were "damned cold," as Marx reported to Engels on May 25, and he got the sneezes "in optima forma."

Dr. Gumpert put Marx under a strict regime. Work was to be limited to no more than two hours in the morning and two hours in the evening. Breakfast was compulsory, and so was exercise, which meant walking. As usual, wine was also prescribed as a medicine. Port, sherry and claret were considered good for strengthening the heart. Engels had often supplied Marx with this medicine. "Your wine," Marx had written him on February 10, 1866, "does wonders for me." This time, Dr. Gumpert ordered Marx to drink wine with soda. For sleeplessness, the doctor ordered very strong doses of chloral.

"Now at any rate," Engels reported to Kugelmann on July

1, "he sleeps four to five hours a night without chloral and one to one and a half hours after meals, and this is more than he has done for nearly a year—in The Hague, for example, he *practically never slept.*"

Marx was tormented by headaches, liver pains and insomnia. Strong doses of chloral did not help the sleeplessness.[1] Sometimes he thought himself "in danger of apoplexy."[2] In November 1873, Marx. accompanied by the ailing Tussy, went to Harrogate for a cure and remained there for three weeks. He made a side trip to Manchester, again to see Dr. Eduard Gumpert, who was himself suffering from enlarged hemorrhoids and faced a dangerous operation, and in whose home, filled with six children and a governess, he dined that evening.

"Gumpert," Marx wrote to Engels on November 30, "examined me physically, and found a certain elongation of the liver, which, he believed, I could cure entirely only in Karlsbad. I am to take the same waters as Tussy . . . but no mineral baths."

It was the same advice that Dr. Kugelmann had given him a few years earlier, since Karlsbad, the fashionable spa in Austrian Bohemia, was considered the place to effect a cure for intestinal disorders. Kugelmann had diagnosed Marx's carbuncles and his internal disorders as resulting from an improper diet. "The whole thing is due to bad nourishment, the latter resulting in bad digestion, and that is connected with the liver that does not function regularly."[3]

In Harrogate, Marx played chess with his daughter, followed Dr. Gumpert's orders to take walks in the fresh air— and caught cold. "Mein cold," he wrote in Germanlish to Engels on December 7, ". . . was verdammt severe." After three weeks in Harrogate, he returned to London still suffering from headaches and insomnia, and promptly had a carbuncle break out on his right cheek. It had to be operated upon, but it generated "a number of small successors." Quicksilver salve, prescribed by Dr. Gumpert, relieved the itching.[4]

The headaches and sleeplessness persisted. In the middle of

[1] Marx to Kugelmann, July 1, 1873.
[2] Marx to Sorge, September 27, 1873.
[3] Marx to Engels, April 14, 1870.
[4] Marx to Kugelmann, January 19, 1874.

April, Marx went for three weeks to the seashore in Ramsgate. He took lodgings, at 12 shillings weekly, in a somewhat raffish house on a cliff at 16 Abbot's Hill. At the entrance gate stood a nude male statue with the intimate part of his anatomy painted out by the landlord, a coach builder who dabbled in art. In the center of the small garden a little clay figure of Napoleon the First on a stone pedestal was garbed in black, yellow and red, and looked "a very manly man." The landlady had, in addition to other children, a six-week-old baby who made himself "disagreeably audible."[5] The baby's wailing did not help Marx's insomnia. His health did not improve. "Despite baths, jogging, wonderful air, careful diet, etc.," he wrote to his wife on April 20/24, "my condition is worse than in London."

In the middle of July, Marx went to Ryde, Isle of Wight, for a two-week cure. On the island, which had a temperate climate, he noted a peculiarly English mixture of capitalism and religiosity. The island, he observed, was a "little paradise" for the rich, with their houses located on the best lands and surrounded by parks. He saw posters which read: "Vote for Stanley, *the rich man*." The City Council was dominated by members of the Ryde Pier and Railroad Companies.

In Ryde, religion flourished everywhere among the natives, Marx observed. His own landlord on 11 Nelson Street was a Scripture reader for the poor and his sitting room was "adorned" by a library consisting of about two dozen volumes on theology. Marx found a similar library in the Sandown Bath House. He could not take a step without running into announcements of pious meetings. Marx commented, "In reality, the plebs here are very poor and seem to find in the church their chief distraction. It would be very interesting to find out how the original fishing population *in no time* became crushed into this God-overwhelmed condition."

Towards the end of his stay in Ryde, Marx was shocked by the news of the death of young Charles Longuet. The death of his little grandson made his home almost unbearable, as Marx wrote to Jennychen on August 14 upon his return to London:

The house has died since the little angel no longer animates it. I miss him all the time. My heart bleeds when I

⁵Marx to Jenny, April 19, 1874.

think of him, and how can one get out of one's mind
such a sweet and clever little man! But I hope, my child,
that you remain brave for the sake of your Old Man.
Adieu, my darling, beloved little dark one.

Your devoted,
Old Nick.

Karlsbad

Continuing sleeplessness, new carbuncles on his left loin,
and the "damned liver ailment," which was chronic, made it
impossible for Marx to do any work. He had to drop the revision of the French translation of *Das Kapital,* and this
added to his worries. "To be *unable* to work," he wrote to
Sorge on August 4, "is, in fact, a death sentence for any man
who is not a beast." Dr. Gumpert urged, indeed ordered, him
to go to Karlsbad.

Marx decided to go, although he hated to be away from
England for two weeks at a time when he was worried about
his sick daughter Jennychen. He wrote to Kugelmann on August 4, ". . . I find the family distresses always hard to take.
The more a person lives practically cut off from the world, as
I do, the more his feelings are entangled in the narrowest
circle."

He was also concerned about the possibility that the Austrian government would expel him from Karlsbad when he
got there. His name as the notorious head of the International was then being bandied about on the Continent in connection with some political trials in St. Petersburg and
Vienna and "ridiculous riots"[6] by anarchists in Bologna and
Apulia early in August.

Since the trip to and stay in Karlsbad were expensive, on
August 14 Marx asked Engels to advance him the next quarter's allowance on his annuity. As he could not afford to
waste the money, he made an effort to protect himself politically through English citizenship. He had thought of becoming naturalized several years earlier, in 1869, when he was
planning to go to Paris in connection with a French edition
of *Das Kapital* and did not want to expose himself to the
vengeance of Napoleon III. As he wrote to Engels on March

[6] Marx to Jenny Longuet, August 14, 1874.

20 of that year, "I see no reason why I should not visit Paris *without the permission* of Herr Bonaparte." But he apparently took no steps then to become an Englishman.

On August 1, 1874, however, "Carl Marx," vouched for by four British subjects,[7] applied for British citizenship, although he felt that the Home Secretary, Robert (Bob) Lowe, Viscount Sherbrooke, who "disposes of naturalization like a sultan," would turn him down.[8] Marx's pessimism was justified. The Metropolitan Police Office (Scotland Yard) investigated him and found him to be notorious and politically disloyal. On August 17, a Scotland Yard sergeant submitted the following report:

> With reference to the above,[9] I beg to report that he is the notorious German agitator, the head of the International Society, and an advocate of the Communistic principles. This man has not been loyal to his own King and Country.

Even before his application for British naturalization was rejected, Marx decided to leave for Karlsbad.[10] On Saturday, August 15, he and Tussy, who was seriously ill and languishing for Lissagaray, left London. They took four days for the trip, to avoid tiring out Tussy, arriving in Karlsbad on August 19. The official *Carlsbader Curliste* [Cure Register] of August 22 contains the following entry: "Herr Charles Marx, *Privatier,* and daughter Eleanor from London—Residence: 'Germania'—Schlossberg, arrival August 19."[11]

The word *"Privatier"* in the Register, meaning a man of no profession, and by implication a gentleman of means, was the inspired suggestion of Dr. Leopold Fleckles, the physician recommended by Kugelmann. In view of his presumed wealth, "Charles Marx, *Privatier,"* had to pay a double Cure Tax to the city treasury, but Marx felt it was worth it. If he should be denounced as the notorious Karl Marx, former

[7]Seaton, Matheson, Manning and Adcock; Marx to Engels, August 4, 1874.
[8]Marx to Sorge, August 4, 1874.
[9]"Carl Marx—Naturalization," photostat in Karl-Marx-Haus, Trier.
[10]Marx to Jenny Longuet, August 14, 1874.
[11]For this and other details, see the booklet by Egon Erwin Kisch, *Karl Marx in Karlsbad* (Aufbau-Verlag, Berlin and Weimar, 1968).

head of the International, he would have the tax receipt to prove that he was really "Charles Marx" instead.[12]

A similar maneuver was involved in Marx's choice of lodgings. The Germania was not an expensive hotel. Even so, Marx could have obtained cheaper quarters, as he reported to Engels, but he felt that the Germania, on the Schlossplatz, provided him with a cover of respectability which, given his notoriety, was "useful, perhaps necessary." The Schlossplatz was not a *Platz* [Square] but a continuation of a lane called Schlossberg, a respectable area that was unlikely to attract police attention. Among the guests there at the same time as Marx was the well-to-do Russian novelist Ivan Turgenev. There is no indication, however, that the two men ever met.

Marx's precautions were justified. On August 30, *Der Sprudel* [*Bubbling Spring*], a Vienna journal specializing in spa affairs, which Marx called a *"Klatschblatt* [scandal sheet]," carried a news telegram from Karlsbad: "Marx, the long-time leader of the International, and the Polish Count Plater,[13] arrived in Karlsbad to take the cure." But the matter went no further. The succeeding issue of *Der Sprudel* carried a defense of Count Plater as a Polish patriot and not a Russian nihilist or member of the International. Marx himself referred to him as a "good Catholic, a liberal Aristocrat."

By coincidence, one of the Karlsbad guests at the time was also named Marx. This was Wilhelm Marx, Chief of Police of Vienna, who arrived with his wife Louise on August 6. Police Chief Marx apparently paid no attention to his namesake. The Austrian authorities left "Charles Marx" unmolested.

Marx and Tussy occupied two rooms on the ground floor of the Germania. The Kugelmanns, who had arrived there three days earlier, were on the same floor.

Kugelmann spoiled Marx's stay in Karlsbad. The Hanover doctor turned out to be, in Marx's words, a "whining and nagging" specimen, a boorish loudmouth, a yammering dogmatist, whose unceasing blabbering drove Marx, tense and nervous from sleeplessness, beyond the bounds of endurance.

Finally [Marx wrote to Engels on September 18], my patience came to an end when I could no longer stand

---

[12]Marx to Engels, September 1, 1874.
[13]Wladislaw Plater (1806–1889) participated in the Polish uprising against the Russians in 1830–31 and then went into exile.

his domestic scenes. For this archpedantic, shopkeeperish petty bourgeois philistine deludes himself that his wife, who is in every way his superior, does not understand his Faustian, higher *Weltanschauung* [ideological] nature, and torments the little lady in the most revolting way. We therefore had a fall-out; I moved to the first floor.

His room there had a fine view of the surrounding hills.[14]

There may have been another reason for Marx's rage at his Hanover friend. According to Franziska Kugelmann, her father irritated Marx by his tactless reiteration that the author of *Das Kapital* should stop wasting his time on petty political propaganda and devote his genius to the completion of the other volumes of his great work. This was obviously a sore point with Marx, who was certainly aware how much of his life he had frittered away on the International and communist affairs in general. The criticism was all the more bitter from a disciple ten years his junior.

In Karlsbad, Marx followed a strictly prescribed spa ritual, as he described it in a letter to Engels on September 18, towards the end of his stay. He rose at 5 or 5:30 in the morning, and went to the various springs to drink six glasses of mineral water, at fifteen-minute intervals between each two glasses, walking up and down in the interim. Then he had breakfast, eating fresh rolls prescribed for those taking the cure. This was followed by an hour's walk, terminating with coffee, "which is excellent here," in a coffeehouse. Thus refreshed, he took a stroll through the beautiful pine woods, where there were no birds. Marx noted sardonically, "Birds are healthy and do not like mineral vapors."

At noon, he would return to his room, take an hour-long bath, change his clothes and go to an inn for lunch. Taking a nap after eating was *"streng verboten* [strictly prohibited]." Instead, he went for another walk, alternating with excursions into the countryside. He took delight in the wooded mountains and the quick-flowing, gurgling Eger River in the "romantic Egertal." In Dallwitz, he visited the Oaks of Körner, named after the German poet and patriot, Karl Theodor

---

[14] The Germania building in Karlsbad (Karlovy Vary, in Czech), known today as *Kurhaus Marx*, carries a plaque, showing a bas-relief of Marx with the Czech legend: *"Zde Bydlel V Letech* [Here Lived in the Years] 1874, 1875, 1876 *KAREL MARX."*

Körner (1791–1813), who had spent time there recovering from wounds received at the battle against Napoleon at Leipzig in June 1813.

Marx also went to Aich, where he enjoyed watching the process of making porcelain there. He observed one worker turning a special potter's wheel on which delicate cups were made, and asked him, "Is this always your job, or have you some other?" "No," the worker replied, "I have not done anything else for years. It is only by practice that one learns to work the machine so as to get the difficult shape smooth and faultless." Marx made a "Marxist" comment to his walking companion, "Thus division of labor makes man an appendage to the machine. His power of thinking is changed into muscular memory."

On his walks he had occasional companions, including Kugelmann until their estrangement. Among the others were the Polish Count Plater and Otto Knille, a painter. Plater's insignificant looks caused Knille to remark that if anyone asked which of the two, Marx or the Polish nobleman, was the count, the answer would definitely be Marx. To Plater's disappointment, Marx eschewed political conversation. With Knille he frequently discussed art.

After his excursions, Marx would be back in Karlsbad between six and eight in the evening, have a light supper, and go to bed. On some evenings he attended the theater or a concert. He enjoyed listening to the fine resort orchestra under the direction of *Meister* Labitsky. Entertainments in the city always terminated at nine, so that guests could go to bed early. Before retiring, Marx would have another glass of cold mineral water. "One becomes a sort of machine," he commented, "with virtually not a free moment the whole day long." Marx and Tussy followed the Karlsbad rules strictly. "We are very exact indeed in all our 'duties,'" Tussy wrote to her sister Jenny on September 5, 1874. "Fancy Papa being ready dressed and at the '*Brunnen* [fountains]' by six o'clock, frequently still earlier!"

The Gotha Program

The only memorable work Marx did in this period was the so-called *Gotha Program*. A conference to unite Germany's two socialist parties, that of Lassalle and that of the Eisenachérs, was being prepared to take place in Gotha between May 22 and 27, 1875. Marx, concerned lest too many concessions be made to the Lassalleans, wrote a critical analysis of the proposed agenda, and, on May 5, sent it to Wilhelm Bracke, a leader of the Eisenach socialists, with a covering letter, asking him to submit it to other socialist leaders—Ignaz Auer, August Geib, August Bebel and Wilhelm Liebknecht—for examination.

Marx's critical comments on the proposed agenda for the socialist unity congress, entitled "Marginal Notes on the Program of the German Workers Party," came to be known as the *Gotha Program,* now considered to be one of the most important documents of "scientific communism."[15] The *Gotha Program* contained an attack on Lassalleanism and some sharply worded expressions that have come to be connected with Marxism. Here are some of Marx's comments:

> *Gotha program:* Labor is the source of all wealth. . . .
> *Marx:* Labor is *not the source* of all wealth. *Nature* is just as much the source of use value . . . as labor, which itself is only the manifestation of a force of nature, human labor power. . . .
> Labor becomes the source of wealth and culture only as social labor, or what is the same thing, in and through society.
> . . *Gotha program:* In present-day society, the instruments of labor are the monopoly of the ˙ capitalist class. . . .
> *Marx:* In present-day society the instruments of labor are the monopoly of the landowners (the monopoly of property in land is even the basis of the monopoly of capital) *and* the capitalists. . . .
> *Gotha program:* The working class strives for its emancipation first of all *within the framework of the present-day national state.* . . .
> *Marx:* It is altogether self-evident that, to be able to fight at all, the working class must organize itself at home *as a class.* . . . But the "framework of the present-day national state" . . . is itself in turn economically "within the framework" of the system of states. . . .

---

[15]Editorial note in *Marx-Engels Werke,* XXII, No. 127. The *Gotha Program* was first published by Engels in *Die Neue Zeit,* No. 18, 1891.

Gotha program: . . . the German workers' party strives . . . for . . . the abolition of the wage system *together with the iron* law of wages. . . .

Marx: So, in future, the German workers' party has got to believe in Lassalle's "iron law of wages"! . . . [This] nonsense is perpetrated in speaking of the "abolition of the wage system" [it should read: system of wage labor], "together with the iron law of wages." If I abolish wage labor, then naturally I abolish its laws also, whether they are of "iron" or sponge. . . .

Gotha program: The free basis of the state.

Marx: Free state—what is this?

It is by no means the aim of the workers, who have got rid of the narrow mentality of humble subjects, to set the state free. In the German Empire the "state" is almost as "free" as in Russia. Freedom consists in converting the state from an organ superimposed upon society into one completely subordinate to it. . . .

The question then arises: What transformation will the state undergo in communist society? . . . .

Between capitalist and communist society lies the period of the revolutionary transformation of the one into the other. Corresponding to this is also a political transition period in which the state can be nothing but *the revolutionary dictatorship of the proletariat.* . . . [16]

Return to Karlsbad

In March 1875, Marx moved to the house at 41 Maitland Park Road (or Crescent), where he lived until his death in 1883. Some five months later, on about August 12, he left London for a second trip to Karlsbad. This time he was not accompanied by Tussy. He went via Frankfurt, where he stopped over for two days.

On the train between Cologne and Frankfurt there was a worldly-looking Catholic priest, named Mutzelberger. He was returning from Dublin, where he had attended the hundredth anniversary of Daniel O'Connell, the Irish nationalist leader, on August 6. The priest was now going back to Frankfurt,

[16]This English text is from Marx and Engels, *Selected Works* (Progress Publishers, Moscow, 1968), pp. 319–335.

his home town, via Holland. Marx tried to engage him in
conversation about the *Kulturkampf,* Bismarck's conflict with
the Catholics in Germany. Mutzelberger was wary at first,
but in the end, as Marx put it, "the Holy Ghost came to the
rescue." The priest pulled out a bottle, found it empty, and
confessed that ever since he had left Holland he had been
thirsty. Marx brought out his own bottle of cognac, and
Mutzelberger went at it with a will. When other passengers
came in, he made bad jokes in German, but with Marx he
used English, a language he knew very well. "Our freedom in
the German Empire is so great," the priest said ironically,
"that when it comes to the *Kulturkampf* one must use English jargon." Before they got off the train in Frankfurt,
Marx gave Mutzelberger his own name and told him not to
be surprised if tomorrow's newspapers reported a conspiracy
between the Black and the Red Internationals.

The publisher of the Frankfurt daily *Frankfurter Zeitung
und Handelsblatt,* a liberal member of the Reichstag named
Leopold Sonnemann, identified Mutzelberger as virtually the
only Catholic bishop in the city, and on August 17, his newspaper carried a notice about Marx: "At the end of last week,
Herr *Karl Marx* arrived here from London. His friends were
pleasantly surprised by his vigorous appearance and cheerful
mood. He is on the way to Karlsbad, where he expects to
remain for four weeks."

Marx arrived in Karlsbad on August 15 and again put up
in the Germania. Now he was not a *"Privatier."* The city's
Kurlist registered him as "Charles Marx, Phil. Dr. *aus* London." As a mere Ph.D., he saved tax money; he now paid
only 6 Gulden for the waters and 3 for the public music.

This time, however, he did attract the attention of the police, although not from his namesake, Police Chief Marx
from Vienna, who had again arrived in Karlsbad at about the
same time that Marx came from London. On September 1,
Josef Vieth, the Karlsbad *Bezirkshauptmann* [District Cap-
tain], reported to his chief in Prague:

Charles Marx, Dr. of Philosophy from London, an outstanding leader of the democratic-social party, is now in
Karlsbad for the cure. Since the same was in Karlsbad
also last year, and gave no cause for taking measures of
suspicion, I permit myself in this report to confine myself obediently to the observation that Marx has hitherto

behaved quietly, has no great contact with other guests
and often takes long walks by himself.

Marx dutifully followed the prescribed routine of drinking
mineral water at the various springs: Felsenquelle, one glass
daily; Bernardsbrunn, two glasses; Sprudel, two glasses—a total of five hot mineral waters every morning, in addition to
one cold Schlossbrunn water in the morning and another at
bedtime.[17]

This liquid regimen, plus his vigorous walks, agreed splen-
didly with Marx. With a few exceptions, he was able to sleep
nights. The doctors, he said, considered him a "model guest."

Marx associated with three Karlsbad doctors, Eduard
Gans, and the two Fleckles, Leopold and his son Ferdinand.
Leopold, descendant of an eminent Jewish family from
Prague and a Karlsbad *Badearzt* [spa doctor] from 1839 until his death in 1879, was Marx's personal physician, as he
had been also in the previous year. His son Ferdinand was
not only a doctor but also the publisher of *Der Sprudel*, the
spa's gossip sheet.

As a friend of Marx, Ferdinand Fleckles published an article about him.[18] It contained a number of factual errors—
for example, that "Carl Marx" was born in 1810 (instead of
1818) in Saarbrücken (instead of Trier), and that his father
was "a rich Jewish merchant"—but this may have been done
deliberately, to throw the police off the track. The author of

[17]Marx to Engels, September 8, 1875. According to a Viennese
chemist, Professor Ferdinand Ragsky, the chemical content of the
mineral waters that Marx imbibed, in grams, was as follows:

Sulphate of potash	1.2564
Bicarbonate of soda	18.2160
Sodium chlorite	7.9156
Sodium carbonate	10.4593
Calcium carbonate	2.2870
Magnesium carbonate	0.9523
Strontium carbonate	0.0061
Iron oxide carbonate	0.0215
Manganese oxide	0.0046
Aluminum phosphorus oxide	0.0030
Phosphoric oxide	0.0015
Fluorine	0.0276
Silica	0.5590

This made a total of 41.7099 grams of mineral components, plus an
additional 5,8670 grams of free carbonic acid.

[18]Julius Walter, "Carl Marx," in *Der Sprudel*, September 19, 1875;
see Kisch, *op. cit.*, pp. 63–74.

the article found Marx a striking figure. He described him as a slender man, medium-sized, giving the impression of "strong, youthful elasticity," despite his "sixty-three" years. He had a large brow framed by curly white locks that reached to his powerful shoulders, a snow-white beard that "flows deep down," and brown eyes sparkling from underneath "black-bushy" eyebrows.

The author found Marx to be an enchanting conversationalist, who held his hearers' attention by the richness and artistry of his talk. "He spoke lightly, with pleasing yet artistic elegance, with striking phrases, illustrative images, and lightning-like wit at his fingertips." He was at home in Germany's high culture, his memory enriched by legendary literary figures of the romantic period, some of whom he had known personally. There was August von Schlegel, the great translator of Shakespeare, who had been one of his professors in Bonn. In Berlin, as a student, he had visited the famous salon of Bettina von Arnim, the friend of Beethoven and Goethe. And Heinrich Heine, then dead for about two decades, had been a special friend during his early days in Paris. When Marx permitted himself to discuss his own radical ideas, the author of the article stressed that he did not sound like an academic pedant or visionary agitator, but like a cultured thinker: "He is indubitably more philosopher than man of action and has more of the stuff of a historian of a movement in him, perhaps as a strategist, than a swordsman."

In addition to the two doctors Fleckles, with one of whom, Ferdinand Fleckles, Marx continued to maintain friendly contact later on,[19] he also saw a great deal of a young Russian scholar, with whom he took daily walks. This was a Maxim Maximovich Kovalevksy, a twenty-four-year-old sociologist and historian, who also visited Marx in London. For the rest of his life, until his death in 1916, Kovalevsky continued to hold Marx gratefully in memory as "a dear teacher" who had determined the course of his scientific work. Eight years before the Russian Revolution, Kovalevsky, then a liberal political figure, paid tribute to Marx as "one of the intellectual and moral leaders of mankind who are enti-

---

[19]See, for example, Marx's letter to Dr. Ferdinand Fleckles, January 21, 1877, thanking him for medicines he had sent him. Marx also advised Fleckles to continue his English studies, "for in case of necessity, England always remains the best place to set up medical quarters."

tled to be called great because they are the truest spokesmen of the progressive tendencies of their time."[20]

On Saturday, September 11, Marx left Karlsbad after almost four weeks there. He returned to London via Prague, the "old Hussite city,"[21] where he proposed to stay with the manufacturer Max Oppenheim for a couple of days.[22] After visiting several other cities, Marx arrived in London on September 20. His health seemed to be fully restored. He returned from Karlsbad, in the words of Engels, "completely changed, vigorous, fresh, cheerful and healthy, and can now seriously get back to work."[23] But that did not last.

Karlsbad for the Last Time

Marx worked only intermittently, and then not creatively. Among other things, he corrected the French edition of *Das Kapital*, which appeared in Paris at the end of November 1875. He also put in some time on the second volume. His health remained precarious. When Pyotr Lavrovich Lavrov, a Russian sociologist who had participated in the Paris Commune and now published, in London, a Russian magazine, *Vperiod*, invited him to join in a meeting for Poland, Marx, despite his deep sympathies for that country, declined on the ground of ill health. He had a recurrence of carbuncles.[24]

He also turned down an invitation, extended by Friedrich Adolph Sorge to him and Engels,[25] to attend the celebration of the Centennial of the American Revolution in Philadelphia: "I, in particular, can ill afford to waste the time, since my state of health is such that it still compels me to lose about two months in the Karlsbad cure."[26]

On August 13, accompanied by Tussy, Marx, who suffered from ceaseless headaches, left London again for Karlsbad.

The spa was reverberating with what Marx called the "*Getrommel* [drum beats] of the music-of-the-future in Bayreuth" where Wagner's *Ring of the Nibelungen* cycle was

[20]Kovalevsky, in *Vestnik Yevropy*, July 1909.
[21]Marx to Oppenheim, September 20, 1874.
[22]Marx to Oppenheim, September 9, 1875.
[23]Engels to Wilhelm Bracke, October 11, 1875.
[24]Marx to Lavrov, December 3, 1875.
[25]Sorge to Marx, March 17, 1876.
[26]Marx to Sorge, April 4, 1876.

being performed between August 13 and 17. People kept asking: What do you think of Wagner? Marx, a lover of classical music, did not think much of him or of his *"Narrenfest* [festival of fools]" in Bayreuth. In a letter to Jennychen late in August, Marx conveyed the current gossip about Wagner's menage:

> Highly characteristic of this neo-German-Prussian State-musician: He and wife (divorced from von Bülow), with Hahnrei Bülow and their mutual father-in-law Liszt, live cosily together, loving, kissing and adoring each other. If one recalls, moreover, that Liszt is a Roman monk and Madame Wagner (Cosima by name) is his "natural" daughter by Madame d'Agoult (Daniel Stern)—one can hardly imagine a better *opera text* by Offenbach than this family group with its patriarchal relationships. The happenings in this circle would also make another tetralogy—like the Nibelungen.

Marx, as usual, enjoyed life in Karlsbad. His headaches disappeared. He dutifully drank the prescribed mineral waters, which had a soporific effect. He referred to his relaxed way as pleasantly *"gedankenlos* [mindless]."

A heat wave was succeeded by rain. On clear days, Marx and Tussy took long walks. In later years, she told Liebknecht that her father was an enchanting companion: "Always in good humor, he was ever ready to enjoy everything, whether a beautiful landscape or a glass of beer. And with his comprehensive knowledge of history, he made every place we passed more alive and actual in the past than even in the present."

Marx and Tussy made many friends in Karlsbad, including two medical men and a distinguished historian. The doctors were Hermann Friedberg, professor of medicine in Breslau University, and Wilhelm Alexander Freund, a Breslau gynecologist. The historian was Heinrich Graetz. Tussy, an aspiring actress, talked about Shakespeare with Dr. Freund, whom Marx later addressed on January 21 as *"Lieber Freund Freund* [Dear Friend Friend]." With Graetz, the German-language historian of the Jewish people, Marx discussed history and world politics. Among other things, he predicted a fundamental revolution in Russia. The exact words he used are not

known, but his thinking on the subject is recorded in a
letter he wrote at about this time to a friend in America:

> Russia—and I have studied conditions there in the origi-
> nal *Russian* sources, unofficial and official (the latter ac-
> cessible to but few persons, but obtained for me through
> friends in Petersburg)—has long been on the threshold
> of an upheaval; all the elements for it are ready. . . .
> The upheaval will begin *secundum artem* [according to
> the rules of the game] with some playing at constitution-
> alism, *et puis il y aura un beau tapage* [and then there
> will be a fine ruckus]. If Mother Nature is not particu-
> larly unfavorable to us, we shall yet live to see the fun![27]

Marx and Graetz seem to have greatly appreciated each
other's company. As a token of his esteem, Marx, upon his
return to London, sent Graetz photographs of himself and
Tussy, as well as some of his writings, including *Das Kapital*.
The historian, in acknowledging the gifts on February 1,
1877, expressed the fear that he might not understand much
of *Das Kapital* but that he had read the *Civil War in France*
with great pleasure, summarizing the latter as, "Paris all
truth, Versailles all lie, and when you state it thus, it is as if
the youngest court of world history had passed its judgment
of condemnation."

Graetz then expressed his embarrassment at Marx's gifts
and wondered how he could repay them:

> I don't know what I could offer you from my own *opera
> omnia* [collected works]. The content of my 12-volume
> history [of the Jews] lies far beyond your horizon. Pos-
> sibly my work on the *Psalms* would be to some extent à
> *votre porté* [up your alley]. For the author was, in my
> view, a rough realist, who, in a fantastic, heaven-bent
> world, had the courage to express the idea that the cer-
> tainty of this world was preferable to the dubiousness of
> the other one. . . . If only there was not so much He-
> brew in my commentary!

---

[27] Marx to Friedrich Adolph Sorge in Hoboken, N.J., September 27,
1877. In an interview published in the *New York Herald*, August 3,
1871, Marx said: "There is a revolution coming in Russia, slowly, but
surely."

Marx's last days in Karlsbad were marred by Tussy's sudden illness. As a result of heavy rains, she came down with a high fever and heavy cold, verging on pneumonia, from which she was saved by the rapid treatment of Dr. Ferdinand Fleckles.[28] On September 15, after she recovered, father and daughter left Karlsbad for home.

. . Marx and Tussy traveled leisurely. From Prague they made their way to London via Germany, where they made a sentimental side trip to Kreuznach. Marx wanted to show his daughter where he and her mother had spent their honeymoon thirty-three years before. Kreuznach was also near Jenny von Westphalen's birthplace. Then they traveled, via Bingen to Liège, where they stopped overnight at the Hôtel de Suède and visited the ailing Russian Populist revolutionary Nicolai Isacovich Utin [Outine], whom Marx called "one of my most beloved friends." Utin suffered from fatty degeneration of the heart tissues and, in fact, died seven years later at the age of thirty-five.

One week after leaving Karlsbad, on September 22, father and daughter arrived in London. According to her mother, Tussy returned home "pale and emaciated."[29]

Neuenahr

No sooner had Marx returned from Karlsbad than he caught a severe cold, which became chronic. He sneezed and coughed and could not sleep. In an attempt to relieve the constant secretion of mucus, he had an operation to remove an elongated uvula, but it did not help.[30] Marx, in a letter to Dr. Freund, compared his condition to that of Martin Luther's peasant, "who mounted his horse on one side, and fell off on the other."[31] The removal of the uvula only caused continuous throat pains.[32]

Unable to do much creative work, Marx confined himself

[28] Marx to Max Oppenheim, September 9 and 12, 1876; Marx to Ida Pauli, September 10, 1876.

[29] Jenny Marx to Friedrich Adolph Sorge, January 20 or 21, 1877.

[30] Ibid.

[31] Marx to Alexander Freund, January 21, 1877. The reference is to Luther's Table Talk, where the world is compared to a drunken peasant who cannot stay in the saddle.

[32] Marx to Pyotr Lavrov, February 24, 1877.

largely to reading. He began to read and make voluminous excerpts from Friedrich Christoph Schlosser's monumental *Weltgeschichte für das deutsche Volk* [*World History for the German People*] (19 vols., 1844–1857). He also has studied a number of works on the Russian economy, in the original Russian.[33] There seems to have been something fateful in Marx's interest in Russia—and Russia's continuing interest in him.

On March 3, 1877, Marx described his miserable state of health to Engels as *"Verkältung, Verschnupfung und Verhustung* [cold, catarrh, and cough]." This was in addition to his other ailments: pleurisy, carbuncles, lung abscesses, liver troubles and sciatica. The insomnia and headaches persisted. He worried about his wife, who was, if anything, more sick than he. She suffered, among other things, from "indigestion," which later turned out to be a killing cancer. Tussy, too, was sick from tensions. As the summer came, the question in the Marx household was: Which spa to visit? Marx himself favored a fourth trip to Karlsbad but he was privately informed that the Austrian government would expel him. This time, moreover, he would have to take along his wife, who seems to have resented being left behind in the previous years; and a trip to Karlsbad for the three of them was much too expensive, particularly if they had to risk expulsion.[34]

In addition, Marx was psychologically somewhat troubled by the thought of going to Karlsbad again. While he loved the place, it had provided no lasting cure. If a fourth visit there turned out to be equally futile, then it was like "playing the last card."[35]

The doctors informed him that Bad Neuenahr, in the Ahr

[33]Among the Russian-language economic books Marx obtained and read in that period of his illness were: A. Golovatshov, *Desyat Let Reform*, (1861–1871); I.I. Kaufman, *Teoriya Kolebaniya Zen, Kutscheniyu o Dengach i Kredite*; W. Nerutschev, *Russkoye Semlevladeniye i Semledeliye*; A. Skrebizki, *Krestyanskoye Delo v Zarstvovanyye Imperatora Alexandra II*; Janson, *Opyt Statitscheskavo Issledovanya o Krestiyanskich Nadelach i Plateshach*; and Skaldin, *V Sacholustiyl i v Stolitze*. In 1881—1882, when Marx drafted an outline, entitled "Notices on the Reform of 1861 and the Russian Development connected with it," he cited a number of Russian-language statistical and other data.
[34]Marx to Engels, July 23, 1877.
[35]Marx to Engels, July 25, 1877.

Valley, was just as good as Karlsbad. Neuenahr was in country familiar to Marx, lying roughly midway between Bonn and Coblenz, and close to the Rhine; the cost would be considerably less than the trip to Karlsbad. Marx calculated that the fare for the four of them—Marx and his wife, Tussy and Lenchen (who grumbled at the thought of not being taken along on a trip to her homeland)—would amount to £70, which would include the cost of transporting the luggage.

In addition to saving transportation cost, Marx thought that Bad Neuenahr was "even hygienically better" than Karlsbad. Its mineral baths, good for digestive disorders and cardiac diseases, were weaker than those of the Bohemian resort, and in the present state of his nerves he felt that *"variatio delectat corpus* [change is good for the body]." The body has to be coddled, as he wrote in a note to Engels: "one has to diplomatize with the corpus as with all other things."

Engels, who was then spending most of July and nearly all of August with the ailing Lizzy Burns in Ramsgate,[36] approved of Neuenahr:

> Your plan has at any rate the advantage of hitting many flies with one stroke; I can only hope that the main fly, your liver, does not suffer from it. Still so many doctors are in favor that from this point of view nothing definite can be said against it. Who knows, perhaps this time Neuenahr will do you more good than Karlsbad. It is in any case a lottery, *espérons le mieux* [let's hope for the best.][37]

To expedite matters, as he put it, he sent Marx a check for £101 and invited him to come to Ramsgate for a few days.

Shortly before departing for Neuenahr, Marx visited Engels in Ramsgate. The Lafargues were also there. The visit to Engels invigorated him, and on the way back to London, he indulged in "a veritable orgy of exuberance" and could not stop talking, according to his son-in-law. He was as "merry as a grig and chattered nineteen to the dozen." Arriving at Euston Station at ten in the evening, Marx promptly lost his

[36]She died on September 12, 1878, at the age of fifty-one.
[37]Engels to Marx, July 24, 1877.

way and did not get home till after midnight. His son-in-law commented, "His knowledge of geography is scarcely more brilliant than that of French generals."[38]

The Marxes arrived in Bad Neuenahr on August 8 and put up at the Hotel Flora, a comfortable three-story, half-block-long building on the Hauptstrasse [Main Street]. Marx described the spa as a village, hardly of the rank of a market town, cut off from the outside world, since there was no railroad within the Ahr Valley.[39]

Neuenahr had a pleasant appearance, with balmy air and mostly white buildings. The *Badehaus* [bath house], which Marx and some 1,700 or 1,800 other guests (in normal years there were 3,000) used, was built in 1857, "In memory of Franz Egon Graf [Count] von Fürstenberg." It still had an aristocratic air, in the national spa style of architecture. The *Kurhaus*, where the guests took the waters, which Marx found extremely relaxing, faced Beethovenstrasse. As a youth the composer, who, like Marx, was a native of the region, had spent summers in Neuenahr between 1786 and 1792.

In Neuenahr, Marx's physician was Dr. Richard Schmitz, whom he called a "very good doctor." Schmitz found no trace of liver elongation in Marx but diagnosed the digestive apparatus as "somewhat disordered." The main trouble was of "a nervous nature." The doctor suggested that after three weeks in Neuenahr, it would be a good idea for the Marxes to complete their cure in the Schwarzwald, where they would roam the slopes and hills and breathe the pure mountain air. They went there on September 4 and remained for more than two weeks. On September 27, after an absence of nearly two months, they returned to London. Neither Marx nor Jenny was cured.

Malvern and Jersey

After Neuenahr, Marx dropped virtually all his creative writing, including the continuation of *Das Kapital*, but his curiosity about intellectual, scientific and political matters remained unabated. Between 1878 and 1882, he made sys-

[38]Paul Lafargue to Engels, August 7, 1877.
[39]Marx to Maltman Barry, August 15, 1877.

tematic studies of algebra, making extracts from the writings of pioneer mathematicians such as Leonhard Euler and Colin Maclaurin, and prepared an outline for a history of differential calculus. In the spring of 1878, he read and excerpted from the writings of agricultural chemists and geologists, and later in that year he did the same with Descartes and Leibniz.

His interest in national and international affairs never slackened, nor did his acuteness. As early as 1878, he foresaw the dissolution of the Austrian and Turkish empires (he admired the Turkish peasants as "the most efficient and moral peasantry in Europe") and a revolution in Russia.[40] He continued to consume newspapers voraciously. He would hurry to the French quarter to buy any number of editions of French papers, as if important events were still happening in Paris. This newspaper hunger was so excessive that it alarmed his family.[41] His mordant and dogmatic comments on men and measures were not affected by his ailments. An example of his bite is the opinion of British labor which he conveyed to Liebknecht in Leipzig on February 11, 1878:

> The English working class, after the period of corruption since 1848, became by and by more deeply demoralized until it finally reached a point where it became the tail of the great Liberal Party, that is, the serfs of the capitalists. Its leadership fell entirely into the hands of the venal trade-union leaders and professional agitators. These lads screamed and howled *in majorem gloriam* about the people-liberating Czar . . . but did not lift a finger for their own people in southern Wales, their brothers condemned to death by the mine owners. The wretches!

Continuing illnesses and worries took their toll of Marx's appearance. On December 18, 1878, a *Chicago Tribune* correspondent came to interview him in his London home and found him to be an old man, despite a physique that was "well knit, massive, and erect." The newspaperman, who was impressed by the "venerable exile's vast range of knowledge of men and things throughout the world," thought that he

[40]Marx to Liebknecht, February 4, 1878.
[41]Paul Lafargue to Engels, July 27, 1877.

"must be over seventy years of age."[42] Actually, Marx was ten years younger.

In 1879 and for two years thereafter, Marx sought relief in English watering-places by the sea. Fresh breezes were fine, but for a man with Marx's throat and chest condition moisture-laden air was hardly conducive to good health, especially when it rained, which it often did.

Illness, however, did not deter him from acting as political adviser to Continental radicals and socialists who came to seek his counsel in London. In March 1880, one of his frequent visitors was Lev (Leo) Hartmann, the Russian Populist who, in 1879, had been one of the participants in an abortive attempt by the Narodnaya Volya revolutionary group to assassinate Czar Alexander II and who, two years later, emigrated to the United States, where he died in 1908. Later, in the spring, Jules Guesde, a thirty-five-year-old French radical Marxist, came to London to consult Marx and Engels, together with Paul Lafargue, about founding a socialist labor party in France. The four of them, meeting in Engels' home, drafted a detailed program, together with a preamble written by Marx, for the new French socialist party. The "minimal program," as worked out by Guesde and Lafargue, with the approval of Marx and Engels, consisted of thirteen points, four political and nine economic.

A. Political

1. Abolition of all laws against the press, assemblies and associations.
2. Abolition of all budgets for religious purposes.
3. General arming of the people.
4. The administration and the police to be subject to the commune.

B. Economic

1. No work on Monday. Eight-hour work day for adults. Prohibition of work by children under fourteen. Six-hour work day for youths between sixteen and eighteen.
2. Minimum wage, to be determined annually according to the cost of living.

[42]The interview was published in the *Chicago Tribune*, January 5, 1879, signed "H." For full text, see Saul K. Padover, ed., *Karl Marx on the First International* (New York, 1973), pp. 351–61.

3. Equal pay for men and women.
4. Scientific and technical education for all children at public expense.
5. Exclusion of entrepreneurs (capitalists) from the administration of workers' mutual aid societies, insurance companies, etc.
6. Responsibility of entrepreneurs for industrial accidents.
7. Participation of labor in the working arrangements in shops, including the imposition of fines and wage deductions.
8. Revision of all contracts connected with public ownership (banks, railroads, mines, etc.) and control of State workshops by the workers.
9. Abolition of all indirect taxes and the transformation of all direct taxes into one progressive tax for incomes above 3,000 francs and for inheritances of over 20,000 francs.[43]

Marx had other radical visitors that year, including the English socialist Henry Mayers Hyndman, who in 1881 founded the Democratic Federation, which became the Social Democratic Federation three years later. Until the summer of 1881 when Marx claimed that Hyndman had plagiarized his ideas and broke off the relationship,[44] Hyndman visited him[45] and wrote him at least eighteen letters.[46] He was introduced to Marx by the German radical journalist Carl Hirsch, who courted Tussy when he lived in London after 1879. Hyndman, then thirty-eight years old, was awed:

The first impression of Marx as I saw him was that of a powerful, shaggy, untamed old man, ready, not to say eager, to enter into conflict and rather suspicious himself of immediate attack.

[43]This socialist program was published in *L' Égalité*, June 30, 1880; in *Prolétaire*, July 10, 1880; in *Revue Socialiste*, July 20, 1880.
[44]In a booklet entitled *England for All* (1881), Hyndman quoted verbatim from *Das Kapital* without mentioning either the book or its author. Marx upbraided him in a letter written on July 2, 1881, but which may not have been mailed.
[45]For a description of one visit by Hyndman and his "brusk, unconventional and blunt" wife, see Marx to Jenny Longuet, April 11, 1881.
[46]Photocopies of the letters are to be found in the International Institute for Social History, Amsterdam. (D2381/99).

After two hours of conversation, Hyndman concluded that Marx's talk was on as high a level as his writing.

"Among Marx's visitors was the German socialist leader, August Bebel. Before Bebel left London, he called on the Marx family to say goodbye. Jenny Marx, whom Bebel had found handsome and charming, was confined to her bed. Marx had told him he could go into the bedroom and talk to her but not for more than fifteen minutes. Bebel and Jenny got into such a lively conversation that he forgot the time: "Marx became impatient and came in and severely asked whether I wanted to be the death of his wife. I bade farewell in sorrow."[47]

At the end of July, Marx and his wife traveled to Manchester to consult Dr. Gumpert about their respective ailments. Then they went to Ramsgate, where they remained until September 13. Although the resort did not help them, it was, nevertheless, a happy occasion, since for the last time the whole Marx family, including the daughters, the sons-in-law and the grandchildren were there together. So was Engels.[48] Jenny's "dangerous liver sickness"[49] was so grave that Marx thought she was close to death. He wrote from Ramsgate:

. . . At present I am incapable of doing theoretical work. I have been sent here by the doctors in order "to do nothing" and to cure my nerves through *far niente* (do nothing). My wife's sickness, from which she has suffered for a long time, suddenly got worse, so that she is threatened with a *fatal* end.[50]

Increasingly, Marx was preoccupied with Jenny's illness. An acquaintance, the biologist Sir Edwin Ray Lankester, recommended his colleague, Dr. Donkin. Marx thought him to be a bright and intelligent person, but in fact, as he wrote to Jennychen, using English words, "one man [is] as good, and perhaps better, than another man." A change of medical advisers, he noted, cheers his wife at first and she is full of

---

[47]August Bebel, *Aus Meinem Leben* (Stuttgart, 1911; new edition, Berlin, 1958).

[48]Engels to Johann Philipp Becker, August 17, 1880: "We are all here, Marx, his wife, his daughters and their husbands and children, and the stay here does Marx good."

[49]Marx to Sorge, August 30, 1880.

[50]Marx to Danielson, September 12, 1880.

praise for the "new Aesculapius," but the novelty of a new doctor soon wears off.[51]

Jenny's pains did not prevent her from going to the theater, which she loved, a few times weekly. But Marx had no illusions about her disease. "In regard to *Möhmchen* [little mother]," he wrote on June 6 to Jennychen, whom he addressed as "My dearest Don Quixote," "you must be clear in your mind that for the ailment from which she suffers there is no cure, and in fact she grows weaker." He wrote in the same vein to Sorge on June 20, "Confidentially, my wife's illness is unfortunately incurable."

Marx himself was suffering from uninterrupted coughing, insomnia, pain in the throat and rheumatism. At the end of June, he and Jenny went to Eastbourne. They returned to London, essentially unchanged, after about three weeks at the seashore.

Without the grandchildren, they continued to find their home unbearably empty. Every time he heard children's voices outside his study, he would run to the window, in the vain hope of seeing little Edgar, or Henry or Jean, though he knew that they were on the other side of the Channel. "Not a day passes," he wrote to Jennychen on June 6, "without my thoughts dwelling with you and your darling children."

So anxious was Marx to see his children that he decided to take the chance of visiting France, a country in which he had not lived for thirty-two years, since his expulsion in 1849. A double risk was involved: the effect of the trip on Jenny and possible arrest by the French government.

Engels supplied Marx with £120 for the trip. Marx, knowing that the Longuets were hard up, in turn sent his daughter money to buy beds for him and his wife, as well as Lenchen, an action that embarrassed Jennychen. She was then ill and pregnant, and trembling with excitement at the expectation of her parents' arrival.

On July 26, Marx, Lenchen and Jenny, who was in great pain when they left their home in Maitland Park, took the train to Dover. When they embarked on the boat, she immediately went to the ladies' cabin, where she lay down on a sofa. The passage across the Channel was calm, the weather beautiful. Reaching Calais, they decided to continue the journey to Paris, despite Jenny's uncontrollable diarrhea. At 7:30 in the evening they reached Paris, where Longuet was waiting

[51]Marx to Jenny Longuet, April 11, 1881.

for them at the railroad station, and took a cab to the Gare St. Lazare for the twenty-minute train ride to Argenteuil. They arrived at the Longuet home, 11 Boulevard Thiers, at about 10 o'clock that night. It was a grueling journey for a woman with terminal stomach cancer.

At the Paris railroad station, Longuet told Marx that an influential political friend had assured him that Marx had "absolutely nothing to fear from the French police."[52] The friend was Georges Clemenceau, then a radical member of the French Parliament.

The stay in the Longuet home was enlivened by a domestic drama. The scenario, as Marx pointed out, was like a play by Kotzebue.[53]

Jennychen had a cook, "a very lively girl from the country." The girl's last employer, the wife of a local physician named Reynaud, had given her a "negative" recommendation, to the effect that she had left her employment *voluntarily*. But Longuet's mother, a meddling old woman who was always trying to bully Jennychen, wrote to Madame Reynaud, inquiring about the character of the girl.

Madame Reynaud was a handsome coquette and her husband a "wild jackass." The doings of this pair were the talk of Argenteuil. The Reynauds had not known that their former maid had found a new job in town, let alone one in the household of Longuet, an intimate friend of Dr. Dourlen, whose wife was an intimate enemy of Madame Reynaud. This, indeed, needed looking into.

So one afternoon Madame Reynaud, whom Jennychen had not met before, came visiting. She told Jennychen that the girl had had dirty affairs with men and, worse still, she had stolen a gold ring from her. The lady assured Jennychen that she wanted to keep the matter "*en famille*," without recourse to the "authorities." Jennychen summoned the girl. Madame Reynaud chatted with her and threatened her at the same time. The girl confessed and returned the ring. Whereupon Dr. Reynaud denounced her to the *juge de paix*.

Jennychen appealed to the *juge de paix*, who said the matter was out of his hands the moment the girl was officially accused. Surprised at Madame Longuet's defense of her employee, he asked her: "But you don't want to defend theft"?

[52]Marx to Engels, July 27, 1881.
[53]August Friedrich Ferdinand von Kotzebue (1761–1819) was a German novelist and popular playwright.

Karl Marx's daughter answered: "No, Monsieur, but begin by arresting all the big thieves of Argenteuil, and those of Paris to boot." The judge took her written desposition in defense of the girl and said it might help her. But in the meantime, the Longuet home, now housing six adults and four children, was without a maid and cook.

Jenny Marx was treated by Dr. Dourlen, who lived close by. He prescribed opium pills to relieve her pains, which Dr. Donkin had hesitated to do in London. When she felt better, Marx took her on a visit to Paris. It was a beautiful day, and they drove through the streets in an open carriage. She loved it, but on Marx the great city made the impression of a *"foire perpétuelle* [perpetual fair]."[54] Jenny had attacks of sudden pain, and they had to sit down at terrace cafes. She barely managed to get back to Argenteuil.

In Argenteuil, as in London, Marx rarely had a night's sleep. The headaches persisted. His head was so congested that he felt as if he had a "millstone grinding inside" it.

His visit in Argenteuil was cut short by the news that Tussy was seriously ill and that Dr. Donkin was on the point of going to the Hebrides for his holiday. He telegraphed the doctor to postpone his departure and hurried back to London. A few hours after his arrival Dr. Donkin came, gave Tussy a thorough examination, and found nothing organically wrong with her except a derangement of the stomach. She had not eaten for a long time and was in a state of "utter nervous dejection." The doctor warned her that she was in deadly danger if she persisted in her course. She promised to obey his prescriptions.

Two days later, Jenny and Lenchen departed from Argenteuil. Marx had found it painful to leave his wife, but since, as he wrote to Engels, the "real support for her is Helen," his own presence was not absolutely necessary. In addition, his departure would hasten her decision to leave Argenteuil, which she was reluctant to do, knowing she would never again see her daughter and grandchildren. However, Marx felt that with her growing debility she would be better off at home. He planned that Jenny and Lenchen should travel, first class, by slow stages, staying overnight at Amiens, resting for a day or more at Boulogne, and embarking for Folkestone.[55]

[54] Marx to Engels, August 9, 1881.
[55] Marx to Engels, who was then on a cure at Bridlington Quay, August 18, 1881.

After her return from France, Jenny hardly left her bed. She was lying in the large front room, and Marx, suffering from bronchitis complicated by pleurisy, lay in an adjoining smaller room in the rear. Tussy and Lenchen attended them day and night, taking turns at resting for an hour. Once Marx managed to get up and make his way into his wife's room. For a short while, as Tussy recalled it, they were together again, like young lovers, rather than "an old man devastated by illness and a dying old woman who were taking leave from one another for life." He expected Jenny to die any moment.[56] For the last three weeks before her death he did not see her. He felt suicidal, wanting, as he wrote to a Russian friend, "to turn my back on this evil world."[57]

Up to the end, she managed to smile and even make jokes. She laughed as she told Laura, then still in London, that a suit she and Marx had bought for five-year-old Johnny in Paris made him look like a "little *bourgeoisgentilhomme* [bourgeois gentleman]."[58]

Jenny's last words were addressed to "Karl," showing that the only man in her life was uppermost in her mind to the end. She said, curiously enough, in English, "Karl, my strength is broken."[59] There was no death struggle, just a gentle passing away. "Her eyes," as Marx reported to his daughter, "were brighter, larger, more radiant than ever."[60]

When Engels came in, he infuriated Tussy by saying, "Moor is now also dead."

She was soon to realize that he was prophetic.

Jenny was buried in unconsecrated ground in Highgate Cemetery on December 5. Dr. Donkin absolutely forbade the sick Marx to attend the funeral, particularly as the weather was bad. Engels delivered a short speech at her grave.

[56]Marx to Karl Kautsky, October 1, 1881, mentioning the "imminent catastrophe" awaiting his wife; on the same day he also wrote to Minna Kautsky, a novelist and mother of Karl Kautsky, referring to Jenny's *fatal* illness."
[57]Marx to Nicolai Frantzevich Danielson, December 13, 1881.
[58]Marx to Jenny Longuet, December 17, 1881.
[59]Lafargue, *Reminiscences*; also Liebknecht, *Karl Marx zum Gedächtnis* (Nuremberg, 1896).
[60]Marx to Jenny Longuet, December 7, 1881. Tussy, in her letter to Jennychen of December 3, in which she enclosed some of their mother's hair ("soft and beautiful as a girl's"), made the same comment: "The look in her eyes was simply indescribable. Not only that they were so clear—clear as one only sees *children's* eyes—but the sweet expression as she saw & recognized us—which she did to the end."

The outpouring of letters of condolence confirmed, if confirmation was necessary, Engels' evaluation of Jenny's life and character. The tributes came from far and wide.

Samuel Moore, co-translator of *Das Kapital*, wrote to Laura from Manchester:

I am very much grieved at the sad news of your mama's death contained in your letter & feel that your loss must be terrible. . . . I only hope that your Father in his present weak state of health will be able to hold up under the terrible blow which this loss will inflict upon him. . . .[61]

From Paris, Sibylle Hess, the widow of Moses Hess, both of whom Marx had often denigrated, wrote him a touching letter on December 11:

Just now I received the *Sozialdemokrat* from Zurich. Ach, what a terrible surprise when I read the death notice of your dear wife, written by our gallant Engels. In her, nature has truly destroyed its own masterpiece; for in my whole life I have never encountered another such a spirited and amiable woman. I first learned to love and to appreciate her when we all lived together in Brussels, and from that time on she has remained in my memory full of love and reverence. . . . I find it impossible to describe to you how deeply the news has shaken me. . . .

On December 12, Wilhelm Liebknecht, who for years had been a visitor in the Marx home during his time of exile in London, wrote a poignant note from Leipzig:

The news of the death of your wife shook me deeply. What more can I say? You know what the gallant lady was to me—above all, it is her I have to thank that I did not become wrecked in the days of misery as a refugee in London.

From Hungary, Leo Frankel, the Hungarian communist and former Paris Communard, wrote Marx a letter on December 18 that was full of romantic, fanatical revolutionary rhodomontade:

[61]Moore to Laura Lafargue, December 3, 1881; MS in the International Institute for Social History, Amsterdam (G 330).

. . . like a battlefield commander, who, when his adjutant . . . is torn from his side by a bullet, may not yield to his grief, but must continue to storm forward to destroy the enemy and his army and to lead to victory—you too, who have undertaken this battle of the disinherited and the oppressed against the ruling vileness, must not permit yourself to be overwhelmed by your grief over the loss of your noble wife and fellow-fighter. Men like you belong neither to a family nor to a fatherland, but to *mankind*. In the first instance, the proletariat has a claim on you. You have led it to battle. You have forged for it the intellectual weapons with which it fights, and to it you must dedicate your life.

Ventnor

After Jenny's death, Marx spent the remaining fifteen months of his life in pursuit of health, traveling from resort to resort, seeking dry weather, sunshine and cure. Much of the time he found only rain. He was in a bad state: "From the last sickness I have emerged doubly crippled, morally through the loss of my wife, physically on account of a thickening of the pleura and an increased irritation of the trachea."[62]

For the pleura, the medical remedy was tattooing the chest and back with iodine. The only effect this had was to cause a painful burning of the skin. For Marx's mental state, medicine had no remedy. The only effective antidote to depression, he told his daughter ironically, was physical pain: "Put the prospect of the end of the world on one side, and a man with an acute toothache on the other!"[63]

On December 30, 1881, Marx went with Tussy to Ventnor on the Isle of Wight. Before he left, Engels gave him £40, of which Marx spent about half for necessities and some £17 for the fare. His lodging in Ventnor, No. 1 St. Boniface Gardens, was expensive. The rooms cost 2 guineas weekly, plus another 4 guineas for coal, gas and food. On January 12 Marx asked Engels for more money. Engels sent him £20.

So far as his health was concerned, it was all a waste of good sterling. It rained practically every day. At night the

[62]Marx to Sorge, December 15, 1881.
[63]Marx to Jenny Longuet, December 7, 1881.

howling gales and storms made any attempt at sleep impossible. Mornings the sky was leaden, overcast, "Londonlike," and the temperature much colder than London's. Marx's cough was unrelieved, his breathing difficult. When he took a walk, mostly in the rain, he had to carry a "lock-jaw, alias respirator."[64] Sometimes he managed to get a bit of sleep without opium. As if he did not have enough trouble, his bad teeth made his cheeks swell.[65]

His physical troubles were aggravated by Tussy's behavior. Pining for Lissagaray, she was in poor mental and physical condition. Nervous, tense and sleepless, she read or wrote the whole day, hardly speaking to her father. "My companion," he wrote confidentially to Laura on January 4, "is practically not at all. . . . Indeed, she does give the impression that she is staying with me out of a sense of duty, bearing it all as a self-sacrificing martyr."

On January 16, Marx left Ventnor, which was "enveloped in fog."[66] When he was on the Isle of Wight, where it was cold and rainy, the weather in London was dry and summery. This balminess "disappeared," as he wrote to a friend, "upon my return there."[67] His bronchitis was worse than ever.

Marx's coughing got to be so bad that both Dr. Donkin and Engels concluded that he would have to go to a warmer, drier climate. Italy was out of the question, because it required a passport. Engels decided Marx should go to Algiers, which he assumed without further investigation had a salubrious climate. Later, when Algiers, too, proved unsatisfactory, Marx blamed his "good old Fred," who, as he wrote confidentially to Jennychen on March 16, "may easily kill someone out of love."

Algiers

Marx went to Algiers via Argenteuil, to see Jennychen and the four grandchildren. He then took a train from Paris to Marseilles, via Lyons. The locomotive had what he called a "distemper" at Cassis and Valence, and arrived at Marseilles at 2 A.M., two hours late. There was a biting wind and it was

[64]Marx to Engels, January 5, 1882.
[65]Marx to Engels, January 15, 1882.
[66]Eleanor Marx to Jenny Longuet, January 23, 1882; MS in the International Institute for Social History, Amsterdam, (G 269).
[67]Marx to Lavrov, January 3, 1882.

bitterly cold. At the station in Marseilles, while waiting for the luggage to be moved to his hotel, *Au Petit Louvre*, on the Rue de Cannebière, Marx had to resort to alcohol again and again.

The office of *Paquebots à Vapeur des Postes Françaises* [Steam Packets of the French Postal Services] was in the same hotel, so that Marx immediately bought a first-class ticket on the steamer *Said* and had his luggage checked in at the same time. No passport was required; the name of the passenger written on the ticket was sufficient.

Marx embarked on the *Said*, an "excellent steamer" in the late afternoon of February 18, and arrived in Algiers two days later. The cabin was comfortable, but he could not sleep. His ordinary insomnia was aggravated by howling winds and "the diabolical din of the machinery."[68]

Bad weather continued to hound him. The passage across the Mediterranean was through rain and fog. Algiers, normally sunny, was having an abominable season of rain and cold. Upon his arrival, Marx encountered the wettest weather in months. His breathing was agonizing, and he felt helpless and lost: "Sleepless, without appetite, heavy coughing, somewhat baffled, not without fits of *profunda melancholia* [profound melancholy], à la the great Don Quixote."[69]

He communicated his misery not only to Engels but also to his children. They could only extend their sympathy. Jennychen, herself ailing, wrote:

My dearest Papa, . . .
I wrote at once to . . . tell you how unspeakably annoyed & disappointed I feel to think that you are still pursued by the damp cold weather. Is it not frightful to travel in such a crazy year. The world seems positively to be standing on its head.[70]

Marx stayed in a hotel-pension, the Victoria, which was on high ground on the Mustapha Supérieur Boulevard.[71] From

[68]Marx to Engels, February 21, 1882.
[69]Marx to Engels, March 1, 1882.
[70]Jennychen to Marx, February 24, 1881; MS in the International Institute for Social History, Amsterdam (D3330).
[71]In a letter to Lafargue on March 20, 1881, Marx described the location of his hotel:
Finally, my brave Gascon, "what does Mustapha Supérieur mean:" Mustapha is a name like John. When you leave Algiers by way of the rue d'Isly, you see before you a long street; on one side, at the foot of the hills are Moorish villas, surrounded by gardens (one of these is the

his villa, he had a magnificent view of the harbor, the bay, and, when it was clear, of snow-capped mountains in the distance. The splendid scenery brought no relief to his insomnia. Marx at first felt worse than he had in London, for in his sleepless nights he was haunted by the memory of his dead wife. As he confided to Engels on March 1 in English, "By the by, you know that few people are more averse to demonstrative Pathos; still, it would be a lie [not] to confess that my thought [is] to a great part absorbed by reminiscence of my wife, such a part of my best part of life!"

Marx's guide in Algiers was Fermé, a French republican lawyer who had been banished under Napoleon III, and was now a judge. A friend of Charles Longuet, Fermé provided Marx with information about Algiers, the Moslem population, and the condition of the French colony. Fermé, who was married to an *indigène* [native], was not happy in Algiers; he did not like the climate, his family often suffered from fevers and he was underpaid. He was considering a better offer, either in Tunis or in New Caledonia, where, as a judge, he would be paid 10,000 francs annually.

Medically, Marx was treated by a Dr. Stephann, a native of Germany, who was considered to be the best physician in Algiers. Marx described him as a "very resolute, sharp fellow." The doctor prescribed a spoonful of arsenate of soda, mixed with water, to be taken before every meal, and a spoonful of codeine mixed with *julep gommeux* to relieve the cough. Dr. Stephann suggested he take moderate morning walks, weather permitting.

For the pleurisy, which had caused a serious weakening of Marx's left side, Dr. Stephann prescribed regular *vésicatoires* (blisterings). This process consisted of tattooing with collodion cantharidal on the left side of the back and chest, and opening the resulting blisters to let out the water.

Hotel Victoria); on the other side, terraced houses line the street. Mustapha Inférieur begins at the declivity of Mustapha Supérieur and goes down to the sea. Both Mustaphas form one community, whose mayor (this man bears neither an Arabic nor a French name, but a German one) communicates with the inhabitants from time to time by merely posting various official bulletins. You see, a very mild regime obtains here. In Mustapha Supérieur new buildings are constantly being erected, old ones torn down, etc., and even though the workers, natives here, are healthy men, within the first three days they fall sick with fever. Hence a part of their wages consists of a daily dose of quinine, provided for them by the entrepeneurs. One can observe the same system in various areas of South America.

Marx was fortunate in the choice of the Hotel Victoria, where both management and guests were friendly and helpful. The two ladies who managed the hotel, Marx wrote in English, "did everything in my service, no care nor attention neglecting." One of the guests of the hotel was a young pharmacist named Maurice Castelhaz, who performed the blistering service on Marx gratis: "Mr. Castelhaz . . . is so kind as to tattoo me, then open the water-filled blisters, then put linen on the somewhat rough skin, etc. He does all such things in the most genteel way, and offers these voluntary services in the most delicate manner."[72]

The blistering was painful and could be messy. It caused itching, but scratching was forbidden. One night the blisters burst open simultaneously and caused a "veritable inundation" in his bed. In the morning, Castelhaz found Marx amid wet sheets, soggy flannels and shirt, and bandaged him gently. The medical treatments affected Marx's mind, as he wrote apologetically to Engels on March 31:

> Mon cher, You, like other family members, will be struck by the mistakes of my orthography, construction, false grammar; it always strikes me—in my state of great distraction—only *post festum* [later]. Shows you, there is something to be said for *sana mens in sano corpore* [a healthy mind in a healthy body].

But the treatments and medication, together with the clear air, also led to some improvement in his condition. By the end of March, he could sleep better and his coughing was milder. In the middle of April, Dr. Stephann pronounced the pleurisy cleared but expressed himself dissatisfied with Marx's bronchitis, which was not likely to improve in Algiers' wet weather.

Dr. Stephann did not encourage strenuous walking, but Marx did make a few excursions. One of them was to the *Jardin Hamma* or *Jardin d'Essai*, a botanical garden in Mustapha Inférieur, in the company of Maurice Castelhaz and his mother and another hotel guest, Madame Claude of Neufchâtel. Marx was enchanted by the beauty and variety of the tropical garden. He and his companions had coffee in a Moorish cafe and observed half a dozen Moors, sitting in an inclined position, their legs crossed, sipping coffee and

[72]Marx to Jenny Longuet, March 16, 1882.

playing cards. Marx commented on them in a letter to Laura
on April 13/14, in English:

> Most striking this spectacle: Some of these Maures were
> dressed pretentiously, even richly, others in, for once I
> dare call it *blouses*, sometime of white woollen appear-
> ance, now in rags and tatters—but in the eyes of a true
> Mussulman such accidents, good or bad luck, do not dis-
> tinguish Mahomet's children.
>
> *Absolute equality in their social intercourse*, not af-
> fected; on the contrary, only when demoralized, they be-
> ..come aware of it; as to the hatred against Christians and
> the hope of an ultimate victory over these infidels, their
> politicians justly consider this same feeling and practice
> of absolute equality (not of wealth or position but of
> personality) a guarantee of keeping up the one, of not
> giving up the latter.
>
> Nevertheless, they will go to the devil without a revo-
> lutionary movement.

Perhaps because of his lifelong nickname, Marx was particularly fascinated by the Moors, about whom he also read
numerous books.[73]

> In Algeria, [he wrote to Jennychen on April 6/7] the
> Moors are called Arabs; a small minority of them, hav-
> ing moved from the desert and from their communities,
> live in the cities alongside the Europeans. On the aver-
> age they are taller than the French, have oval faces,
> eagle noses, large and brilliant black hair and beards,
> and their complexion runs the scale from nearly white to
> dark-bronze colors.
>
> Their dress—even when ragged—is elegant and grace-
> ful, the *culotte* [knee pants] (or a cloak, rather a toga,
> of fine white wool) or a capot *à capuchon* [Capuchin
> hood]; the headdress . . . is a turban or a piece of white
> muslin; . . . in general they leave the legs bare, also the
> feet, but sometimes they wear pantuffles of yellow or red
> Morocco leather. Even the poorest Moor excels the
> greatest European actor in the *"art de se draper* [art of

---

[73]Paul Lafargue to Engels, June 16, 1882. "Marx has come back with
his head full of Africa and the Arabs; he took advantage of his stay in
Algiers to devour its library. . . . (In parenthesis I must tell you that
Marx is as dark as a chestnut; he is a real Moor now.)"

draping himself]" in his cloak and in keeping a natural, graceful and dignified bearing.

The character of the Moslems, Marx noted, contributed to Algiers being one of the most unrestrained cities imaginable. Police forces were reduced to an absolute minimum. The atmosphere of the place was one of complete *laissez-faire*. "Moslems," he wrote to Laura on April 13, "in fact recognize no subordination; they are neither subjects nor administrative objects, recognizing no authority."

The nomadic Arabs of the country, according to Marx, had degenerated, but they retained some qualities enabling them to survive in the struggle for existence. They also were aware that they had once produced great philosophers, scholars, etc., and that the Europeans now despised them for their present ignorance.

The weather in Algiers continued to be violently changeable and generally unfavorable to a man suffering from bronchitis. Rain and thunder would be succeeded by hours of sun and heat or by "wind concerts." Overall, it was "abominable."[74] Marx never had a fully restful night.[75]

By the end of April, Marx received his last tattooing. His cough continued, and he could no longer endure the African city. [76]

Monte Carlo

On May 2, Marx sailed back to France on the *Said*, the same ship that had taken him to Algiers. He went to Monte Carlo, via Nice, at the recommendation of Dr. Stephann, in the hope of finding dry weather and sunshine.

In the last days of his stay in Algiers, there was a hot and humid sirocco, laden with sand from the desert. Marx could hardly breathe. The passage across the Mediterranean brought him no relief, as the storm was also raging at sea. Marx arrived in Marseilles, on the morning of May 5, in a heavy rain. It also rained in Nice, where Marx stayed for two days, and in Monte Carlo, where it had not rained for months.[77] "Of course," Marx wrote to Jennychen, "I had the

[74] Marx to Jenny Longuet, April 6.
[75] Marx to Engels, April 18, 1882.
[76] Marx to Engels, April 28, 1882.
[77] Marx to Engels, May 8, 1882.

comical consequence of importing here with me the *first two rainy days* (since January); it seems to have waited only for my arrival from Algiers."[78]

In Monte Carlo, where Marx stayed for about a month in the Hotel de Russie, he went to see Dr. Kunemann, an Alsatian physician recommended by Dr. Stephann. Marx found him a scientifically well-trained man, but a conservative—a "republican philistine"; hence he did not discuss politics or identify himself as a revolutionist.

Dr. Kunemann so scared Marx with his diagnosis that he decided not to let his daughters know about it. As he informed Engels on May 20, "Notabene. What I write the children is the truth, but *not the whole truth*. Why worry them?"

After examining Marx, the physician found that the pleurisy had returned and the bronchitis was chronic. He recommended a renewal of the *vésicatoires*. Kunemann's treatments, as well as an improvement in the weather, brought Marx some relief. But Kunemann was not optimistic about his patient's future. He told him that his affected lungs needed new "gymnastics," and would benefit from thin mountain air.

Marx was amused by Monte Carlo, which he called Gerolstein, an operetta setting in a splendid location, lacking only music by Offenbach. The gambling casino attracted colorful characters, including the wife of a Russian diplomat who won 100 francs and lost 6,000, as well as mondaines and demimondaines. Marx thought the whole thing silly: "What childishness this gambling table is compared to the Stock Exchange!"[79]

On June 3, after almost a month in Monte Carlo, Marx took a train to Cannes, on the way to Argenteuil to visit his daughter. Dr. Kunemann told Marx to rest in Cannes for a couple of days, rather than stop over in a number of places, because he might catch cold in railroad stations. The physician advised him to carry two bottles of good Bordeaux wine, to drink and eat well, not to walk too much and "to think as little as possible."[80]

Again, the weather did not cooperate. In Cannes, Marx encountered a hot wind, with swirling dust. Nature, he remarked grimly, had its own kind of "philistine humor," as was to be found in the Old Testament, where it tells that the

---

[78]Marx to Jenny Longuet, May 8, 1882; he made a similar observation in a letter to Tussy on May 21, 1882.
[79]Marx to Tussy, May 28, 1882.
[80]Marx to Engels, June 5, 1882.

snake was condemned to be nourished by earthly muck, and in Darwin's book *The Formation of Vegetable Mould, Through the Action of Worms, with Observation on Their Habits* (London, 1881). The Riviera had recently experienced a violent storm; a lightning bolt struck the Mentone railroad station, and another one smote the sole of a shoe of a "wandering philistine" nearby, but left the philistine himself intact.[81]

From Cannes, Marx sent a card to Jennychen in Argenteuil, announcing his arrival, which he wanted to be unheralded:

> Dearest Child:
>
> I'll come at *some of the first days* of the week beginning on the 6th June. I cannot specify. . . . I have always found that nothing has done me more harm than people at the station waiting for me. . . .[82]

He explained that he needed absolute rest and wanted to be alone with his family:

> Under "rest" I understand "family life," the "noise of children," this "microscopic world" that is much more interesting than the "macroscopic" one.

When Marx arrived in Paris on June 6, Lafargue, who met him there, found him excited, animated, his head full of Africa and Arabs, and uncontrollably talkative. After a time, he exclaimed to Lafargue, "But you haven't told me anything [about the family]!" Lafargue replied, "Good heavens, you didn't give me a chance to get a word in!"[83]

Argenteuil and Enghien

In Argenteuil Dr. Dourlen recommended that he try the "sulphurous waters" at Enghien, which was fifteen minutes away. As Marx reported to Engels on June 9, in English, "Dr. D. found the tone and strength of my body much other

[81]*Ibid.*
[82]Marx to Jenny Longuet, June 4, 1882; MS in the International Institute for Social History, Amsterdam (C580).
[83]Lafargue to Engels, June 16, 1882.

than when I left; he was even astonished that I was in so good a condition after two relapses and after 14 *vésicatoires*."

Marx began his cure at Enghien on June 17. He followed a strict daily routine, spending most of the day with Jennychen and the children and taking walks when the weather was favorable, which often it was not. He would rise at seven-thirty in the morning and take a 9 o'clock train to Enghien, returning to Argenteuil at noon for *déjeuner en famille*. He did this for three weeks.

The Enghien sulphur bath routine was as follows: After the *Spritzbad*, "alias douche," he would get onto a raised board, and the attendants would then spray him with a hose. They handled it the way a virtuoso did his instrument, bombarding the whole "corpus," as Marx said, except the head, with a spray for three minutes, progressively increasing the power of the spray "crescendo." Then he would go to the inhalation hall, where the atmosphere was dark with sulphur fumes, and stay there for about half an hour. Every five minutes the patient would go to a table to inhale sulphuric steam from a special tin tube with valves. The inhalers in the steam-filled room were garbed from head to foot, like mummies, in rubber outfits. They marched behind each other to the table with the pipe. "An innocent scene from Dante's inferno," was Marx's comment.[84] Lafargue, hearing about it, called it "a highly picturesque and grotesque sight."[85] These sulphur baths were exhausting, which was probably their purpose, and Marx thought they were leading him to imbecility. They made him look pink, but did not alleviate his cough or the pain in his throat. Nor did they help his insomnia. To add to his woes, he was afflicted with an extremely painful sciatica, which Dr. Dourlen treated with laudanum massages.[86]

As usual, the weather was not favorable. Warm days alternated with cold ones and rain. "It is my fault," Marx remarked. "I bring bad weather with me." In the Middle Ages, he said, he would have been burned as a sorcerer.

Switzerland

While taking the sulphur treatment in Enghien, Marx was planning to go to Switzerland at the recommendation of his

[84]Marx to Engels, July 4, 1882.
[85]Lafargue to Engels, June 19, 1882.
[86]Marx to Engels, June 24, 1882.

doctors, Dourlen and a colleague named Feugier. They believed that Swiss mountain air would do his pulmonary condition some good. He asked Laura, who was then still in London, to accompany him. Addressing her as "Best Child," Marx wrote her a postal card on June 17, in French: "I can in fact hardly again undertake a trip alone. You see, it is more or less your duty to accompany the Old Man of the Mountain."

Marx was not altogether happy in Argenteuil. He was worried about his ill and pregnant daughter,[87] who found it difficult to cope with four small children, particularly the oldest one, Johnny, who was running a little wild and was losing his good manners. Tussy had come over to help out and to take Johnny in hand. Marx wanted Tussy, "an excellent disciplinarian," to take Johnny to London and have him go to school there. Longuet, whom Marx considered an indifferent husband, was not cooperative.

"Herr Longuet," he confided to Engels on August 10, "does 'nothing' for the child, but his 'love' consists in not having him removed from himself during the few moments of time when he is visible, since in Argenteuil he is mostly in bed until noon, and leaves for Paris at 5 in the afternoon."

In the same letter, Marx asked Engels for money, since, after paying the doctors and other necessary expenses, he had little left for the trip to Switzerland. On August 20 Engels sent him 1,200 francs.

On August 22, after six weeks in Argenteuil, Marx, accompanied by Laura, set out for Switzerland. The weather, as Marx grimly noted, was naturally abominable: muggy, gusty and rainy.[88] They spent the night in Dijon, and then went to Lausanne, where they stayed for three days in the Hotel du Nord. Of course, it rained when they arrived at nine in the evening. Marx's first question was to the waiter in the hotel: "Since when has it been raining here?" Answer: "For the last two days." Marx's comment: *C'est drôle* [It's funny]!"[89]

From rainy Lausanne, Marx and Laura went to nearby Vevey, also on the Lake of Geneva, where they stayed in the Hotel du Léman. Here the weather was better, and Marx,

[87]On September 16, 1882, Jenny Longuet gave birth to a daughter, who was also named Jenny.
[88]Marx to Engels, August 21, 1882.
[89]Marx to Engels, August 24, 1882.

despite occasional rainstorms, felt well enough to take trips on the lake and to climb vineyard slopes at Montreux.[90]

While in Switzerland, Marx received some advice on drinking. His Argenteuil doctor, Feugier, sent him a prescription for the waters he was to imbibe. In the winter he was to take one glass of *"eau sulfurique,"* every morning, either that of Enghien or of Challes in Savoy. Otherwise, he was to alternate his mineral water input monthly: *"un mois l'eau d'Enghien, l'autre mois l'eau de Challes."*[91]

Engels also sent advice; he was less silly and certainly more pleasurable. He recommended Ivorne, a local wine, a red Neuchâteler; Cortaillod, "which bubbles a little"; and finally Veltliner (Valtellina), "the best wine in Switzerland." He recalled that when he had been in Switzerland as a refugee in 1849, also staying in the Hotel du Léman, the ordinary Burgundy, Maçon and Beaujolais were good and not expensive. Engels concluded, "Drink away gallantly at all these kinds, and if in the long run you get bored with all the wandering about remember that it is the only way for you to regain your old form."[92]

Marx happily took Engels' advice, which was backed up with continued financial generosity. "Your self-sacrificing concern for me," Marx wrote to him on Septemebr 16, "is unbelievable, and deep inside of me I am often ashamed."

The air in Vevey was salubrious, and Marx's breathing improved "crescendo," as he said. In the company of a loving daughter, he was as happy as his condition permitted and he talked at great length about his future plans, the third German edition of *Das Kapital*, his work on mathematics and the world in general. He wanted attention all the time, so that she could hardly get a chance to maintain even necessary correspondence. "Papa," Laura wrote to Engels, "has the incorrigible habit of wanting to talk and be talked to as soon as ever I take pen in hand and consequently I write these lines under a running fire of wit and wisdom which is quite stultifying."

On September 25, after a month in Vevey, Marx and Laura left the town to return home. They went by way of

[90] Marx to Engels, September 4, 1882.
[91] Dr. Feugier to Marx, August 26, 1882; MS, in the International Institute for Social History, Amsterdam (E 89).
[92] Engels to Marx, August 26, 1882.

Geneva, to visit Johann Philipp Becker, an old revolutionary friend, admired by both Marx and Jenny. Marx expected to spend a few days in Geneva, but ran into awful weather.

On his way back to London, Marx stopped off in Argenteuil, to spend a few days with Jennychen, then dying of cancer. This was the last time he was to see his most beloved daughter. He was examined by Dr. Dourlen, who warned him not to cross the English Channel at night and not to stay in London, with its wet weather, more than three weeks. Naturally enough, when he left Argenteuil it was raining, or as he put it: "Here it pours from the so-called sky."[93]

Ventnor Again

In London, where Marx arrived early in October, he was examined by Dr. Donkin, who found him somewhat improved, but recommended that he spend the rest of the fall and the winter months in the south of England. On October 30, Marx took a train for Ventnor, Isle of Wight, where again he was a lodger at No. 1 St. Boniface Gardens. On the eve before he left London, Engels came over for supper. They stayed up until one in the morning drinking rum.[94]

The weather in Ventnor alternated between rain and sunshine. On clear days, Marx strolled the hilly promenade along the ocean, enjoying the combined mountain and sea air. But his spasmodic coughing and expectoration continued unabated.[95]

Early in November he developed muscular rheumatism on the left side of his chest, the region of his pleurisy. The pain was such that he required the services of a doctor, who prescribed rubbing the chest with liniment so long as the pain lasted.[96]

There was no improvement in Marx's condition, "rather the reverse," as he put it. He could not do much but read, books and newspapers. Among the works he read were J. Lubbock's *The Origin of Civilisation and the Primitive Condition*

[93]Marx to Engels, September 28, 1882.
[94]Engels to Lafargue, October 30, 1882.
[95]Marx to Tussy, November 10, 1882.
[96]Marx to Engels, November 8, 1882.

of Man, which he had begun to excerpt in London. He occupied himself with mathematics, particularly algebra and differential calculus.[97] At this time, Marx may also have read a Russian book by V.P. Vorontzov, *Sudby Kapitalismu v Rossiyi* [*The Fate of Capitalism in Russia*], which discussed the "influence of the socialists of the Marxist school." Such recognition pleased Marx, as he wrote to Laura in English on December 14:

> Some recent Russian publications, printed in Holy Russia, not abroad, show the great run of my theories in that country. Nowhere my success is to be more delightful; it gives me the satisfaction that I damage a power, which, besides England, is the true bulwark of the old society.[98]

Marx's condition deteriorated steadily. By early January, 1883, his cough was continuous, his throat was strangling with mucus and he vomited daily. Sometimes swallowing became almost impossible. He could not breathe for several seconds.[99] On top of it all, he was constantly worried about Jennychen in Argenteuil, wishing his condition would permit him to cross the Channel to be by her side.

On January 11, Jennychen died of cancer of the bladder, leaving five children, including a four-month-old baby girl. Marx hurried back to London and asked Tussy to go to Argenteuil to stay with the Longuet children.

Jennychen's burial in Argenteuil was attended by leading French and foreign socialists, including a number of Communards, now amnestied, as well as correspondents of radical newspapers.

Engels wrote her obituary in *Der Sozialdemokrat.*

---

[97] Discussion of Marx's mathematics in Engels to Marx, November 21; and Marx to Engels, November 22, 1882.

[98] On March 18, 1883, on the day after Marx was buried, the students of the Petrovsky Agricultural Academy in Moscow sent a telegram to London, asking Engels to lay a wreath on the coffin of the "unforgettable author of *Capital*" with the following inscription: "To the defender of the rights of the workers in theory and their realization in practice." The students offered to pay for the wreath as soon as Engels let them know the cost: Engels, "Zum Tode von Karl Marx" [On the Death of Karl Marx], in *Der Sozialdemokrat,* May 3, 1883.

[99] Marx to Tussy, January 9, 1883.

The End

For Marx, the death of his firstborn, most beloved child
was a shattering final blow. He survived Jennychen by only
two months. Towards the end, in addition to bronchitis and
laryngitis, he developed a lung tumor, which began to bleed
and which was probably the immediate cause of his death.

Death came quietly and suddenly while he was sitting in
his easy chair at about three o'clock on the afternoon of
March 14, 1883. In two more months he would have reached
his sixty-fifth birthday.

Engels, the guardian and architect of Marx's reputation as
the foremost philosopher of socialism, immediately set about
to announce the news. He sent telegrams—"Marx passed
away suddenly this afternoon at 3 o'clock"—and letters to
Longuet, to Sorge, to Frau Bebel.[100]

On March 15 Engels described Marx's last moments to
Sorge, in Hoboken:

Yesterday afternoon—which is the best time for visiting
him—I arrived to find the house was in tears; it seemed
to be the end. I inquired about it. . . . A small hemor-
rhage, but a sudden collapse. Our good old Lenchen,
who tended Marx as no mother tends her child, went
upstairs, came down. He was half asleep, she said, and I
could go up. When we entered, we found him there
asleep, but not to wake again.

Medical art, Engels went on to say, might have prolonged
Marx's life for a few more years, but it would have been a
vegetable existence, which he would never have tolerated.
"Death," Marx used to say, quoting Epicurus, "is no misfortune for him who dies but for him who outlives." Engels
concluded: "Mankind is shorter by a head, and the greatest
head of our time to boot."

To Liebknecht, Engels wrote on March 14:

Despite the fact that I saw him tonight stretched out on
his bed, the fixed stare of the corpse in his face, I still

[100]August Bebel was supposed to have been freed from a Leipzig jail
on March 9.

cannot think that this brilliant mind has ceased to fructify the proletarian movement of both worlds with his mighty thoughts. What we all are, we owe to him . . . without him, we would still sit in garbage and confusion.

To Johann Philipp Becker in Geneva, Engels wrote on March 15:

. . . The mightiest brain of our party has ceased to think, the strongest heart I ever knew has stopped beating. . . . We two are thus now altogether the last of the Old Guard of before 1848. The bullets whistle, friends fall, but this is not the first time we two see this.

The burial in Highgate Cemetery, in the grave next to his wife, took place on Saturday noon, March 17. Not many people were present—probably no more than twenty. Among them were Tussy, and Marx's two sons-in-law, Lafargue and Longuet, but not Laura, who was too ill to come. There were at least three Englishmen: Edward Aveling, Sir Edwin Ray Lankester, and Ernest Radford, a lawyer Marx had known through Tussy's friend, the actress Dolly Maitland. The others were German: Carl Schorlemmer, Friedrich Lessner and Georg Lochner, Marx's communist colleagues who had played roles in the First International, and Gottlieb Lemke, a member of the German Workers *Bildungsverein* in London. Lemke laid two wreaths on the coffin, one from the *Bildungsverein* and the other from the editorial staff of *Der Sozialdemokrat*.

Longuet read in French a message from Pyotr Lavrov in the name of the Russian socialists, hailing Marx as the "outstanding master among all socialists." Liebknecht spoke in German as the representative of the German Social Democrats, concluding, "Dead, living Friend. We will follow the path thou hast shown us until the aim has been attained. This we vow on your grave."

Engels delivered the main obituary in English:

Karl Marx was one of those outstanding men few of whom are produced in any century. Charles Darwin discovered the laws of evolution of organic nature on our planet. Marx is the discoverer of the fundamental law that determines the course and development of human history. . . .

Above all, he saw in science a great lever of history, a revolutionary force in the best sense of the term. And in this sense, he applied his immense knowledge, especially of history, to all the fields he mastered.

For he was truly a revolutionary, as he called himself. The struggle for the emancipation of the wage-earning class from the fetters of the modern capitalist system of exploitation was his true mission. . . .

Nobody can fight for a cause without making enemies. And he had many of them. Throughout the greatest part of his political life he was the most hated and most calumniated man in Europe. But he hardly paid attention to the calumnies. . . . At the end of his life, he could proudly glimpse millions of followers in the mines of Siberia as well as in the workshops of Europe and America. He saw his economic theories becoming the indisputable basis of socialism throughout the whole world.

The published version of Engel's obituary concluded with the words:

His name will live on through the centuries, and so will his work.[101]

[101]Engels, "The Burial of Karl Marx," in *Der Sozialdemokrat*, March 22, 1883.

Appendix I

Chronology:
The Life of Karl Marx

1814
FEBRUARY 12   *Birth of Jenny von Westphalen, Marx's future wife, in Salzwedel, Prussia.*

1818
MAY 5   *Birth of Karl Marx, son of lawyer Heinrich Marx and Dutch-born Henriette Marx (nee Presborg or Presburg or Presborck), in Trier, No. 664 Brückengasse (now No. 10 Brückenstrasse).*

1823
JANUARY 1   *Birth of Helene Demuth.*

1824
AUGUST 26   *Baptized, together with seven siblings (Sophie, Hermann, Henriette, Luise, Emilie, Karoline, and Eduard), in Lutheran church. The Marx family had been Jewish.*

1830
OCTOBER   *Enters Friedrich Wilhelm Gymnasium in Trier, where he remains until September 1835.*

1835
SEPTEMBER 24   *Graduates from Gymnasium.*
OCTOBER 15   *Matriculates at Bonn University as "Studiosus juris et cameralium," attending lectures in law, Roman history, and Greek mythology. Address: 1 Stocken Strasse, then 764 Joseph Strasse.*

1836

AUGUST

Fights a student duel, is wounded in right eye.

AUGUST 22

Leaves Bonn for Trier, where he becomes secretly engaged to Jenny von Westphalen.

MID OCTOBER

By post coach to Berlin, taking up quarters first at 61 Mittelstrasse, then 50 Alte Jacobstrasse.

OCTOBER 22

Matriculates at Berlin University, Faculty of Law, attending lectures in philosophy, law, art history. He remains in Berlin four and a half years, until March 30, 1841.

1837

Reads Hegel, other philosophers and jurists; writes plays, fifty-six poems ("Book of Love" and "Book of Poems," dedicated to Jenny von Westphalen; and "Wild Songs," dedicated to his father); meets Young Hegelians, the so-called Freien; has a nervous breakdown.

NOVEMBER 10

Writes 4,000-word letter to father, explaining his readings, writings, search for truth, and his undisciplined behavior.

1838

MAY 10

Death of his father, Heinrich Marx, in Trier.

1839–40

Studies Greek philosophers and works on his doctoral dissertation, Differenz der demokritischen und epikureischen Naturphilosophie [Difference Between the Democritean and Epicurean Philosophy of Nature].

1841

JANUARY 23

Publication of two poems, "Der Spielmann" and "Nachtliebe," in Athenaeum; the only poems Marx ever published.

MARCH 30

Completes studies at Berlin University.

APRIL 15

Receives Ph.D. degree from Jena University, in absentia.

MID APRIL

Leaves Berlin for Trier, where he remains until early July.

MAY 4

Declared unfit for military service because of affected lungs.

EARLY JULY–
MID-OCTOBER

Moves to Bonn in vain expectation of a university professorship.

1842

JANUARY 15– FEBRUARY 10	*Writes on Prussian censorship for Ruge's* Deutsche Jahrbücher; *because of censorship difficulties the article is not published until February 1843, in Swiss-based* Anekdota zur neuesten deutschen Philosophie und Publicistik, *Vol.* I.
LATE JANUARY	*Writes article, "Luther As Arbiter Between Strauss and Feuerbach," published in* Anekdota, *Vol.* II, 1843.
MARCH 3	*Death of Ludwig von Westphalen, Jenny's father.*
MAY 5	*Begins a series of six articles on debates over freedom of the press in the Rhenish Landtag, in* Rheinische Zeitung *(May 5, 8, 10, 12, 15, 19).*
AUGUST 9	*Publishes "The Philosophical Manifesto of the Historical School of Law," in* Rheinische Zeitung *(the censor cut out the section on marriage).*
MID-OCTOBER	*Becomes editor in chief of* Rheinische Zeitung *and moves to Cologne from Bonn.*
OCTOBER 16	*Publishes article on communism in* Rheinische Zeitung.
OCTOBER– EARLY 1843	*Begins study of French utopians: Fourier, Cabet, Proudhon, etc.*
NOVEMBER	*Marx and Engels meet for the first time, in office of* Rheinische Zeitung.
NOVEMBER 15	*Publishes critical article on religious aspects of divorce law in* Rheinische Zeitung.
LATE NOVEMBER	*Breaks with Young Hegelians over* Rheinische Zeitung *policy.*
DECEMBER 19	*Publishes critical article on divorce law in* Rheinische Zeitung.

1843

JANUARY 1–16	*Publishes a series of seven articles on the suppression of the* Leipziger Allgemeine Zeitung *in* Rheinische Zeitung *(January 1, 4, 6, 8, 10, 13, 16).*
MARCH 17	*Resigns from* Rheinische Zeitung *(closed by censorship on April 1).*
LATE MARCH	*Travels in Holland.*
JUNE 19	*Marries Jenny von Westphalen at Kreuznach.*
SUMMER	*Writes "Critique of Hegel's Philosophy of Law" and "On the Jewish Question."*

LATE OCTOBER   *Moves to Paris: 41 Rue Vanneau, Fbg. St.*
                Germain; and becomes coeditor (with Ruge)
                of Deutsch-Französische Jahrbücher.

1844

LATE FEBRUARY   *Publishes first double issue of* Deutsch-
                Französische Jahrbücher, *containing his two*
                articles "Critique of Hegel's Philosophy of
                Law" and "On the Jewish Question."

MARCH 23   *Meets Michael Bakunin in Paris.*

MARCH 26   *Break with Arnold Ruge and suspension of*
                Deutsch-Französische Jahrbücher.

APRIL–AUGUST   *Works on the* Economic and Philosophic
                Manuscripts *of 1844 (first published in*
                Berlin, 1932).

APRIL 16   *Prussian Government issues order for Marx's*
                arrest for "high treason and lèse majesté" if
                he enters Prussia.

MAY 1   *Birth of daughter Jenny in Paris.*

JULY   *Meets Pierre Joseph Proudhon.*

AUGUST 7, 10   *Publishes anti-Ruge articles, "The King of*
                Prussia," etc., in Vorwärts!, *a twice-weekly*
                German-language publication in Paris.

AUGUST 28   *Meets Engels for the second time, and*
                strikes up a permanent friendship.

SEPTEMBER   *Begins to meet with French workingmen's*
                groups and to study economic and socialist
                theorists.

AUTUMN   *Meets Proudhon and other revolutionists.*

WINTER   *Begins writing* Economic and Philosophic
                Manuscripts.

1845

MID JANUARY   *Receives order of expulsion from Paris.*

FEBRUARY 1   *Signs contract with Darmstadt publisher,*
                Karl Leske, for a two-volume work, Critique
                of Political and National Economy.

FEBRUARY 2   *Meets utopian communist Étienne Cabet.*

FEBRUARY 3   *Moves to Brussels: 4 Rue d'Alliance, outside*
                Porte de Louvain.

FEBRUARY 24   *Publication of* Die Heilige Familie [The
                Holy Family], *a polemic against Bruno*
                Bauer and colleagues, written in collabora-
                tion with Engels.

SPRING   *Writes "Thesis on Feuerbach" (first pub-*

	lished by Engels in his Ludwig Feuerbach, *in 1888).*
JULY 12	*In company of Engels, visits London and Manchester for first time.*
AUGUST 20	*Participates in Chartist conference in London.*
AUGUST 24	*Returns to Brussels.*
SEPTEMBER	*Begins work on the* Deutsche Ideologie [The German Ideology].
SEPTEMBER 6	*Birth of daughter Laura.*
NOVEMBER 10	*Requests release from Prussian citizenship.*
DECEMBER 1	*Gives up Prussian citizenship.*

1846

EARLY IN YEAR	*Founds, with Engels, a Communist Correspondence Committee in Brussels.*
MARCH 30	*Vehement confrontation with German radical Wilhelm Weitling.*
LATE APRIL	*Meets German radical Wilhelm Wolff, who becomes a life-long friend.*
MAY	*Moves to hotel Au Bois Sauvage: 19/21 Plaine Ste. Gudule.*
SUMMER	*Completes, with Engels,* The Germany Ideology, *but can find no publisher in Germany.*

1847

JANUARY 3– FEBRUARY, 1848	*Writes for* Deutsche-Brüsseler-Zeitung, *a radical paper in Brussels.*
MID JANUARY	*Moves to new address: 42 Rue d'Orléans, Fbg. de Namour, Brussels.*
JANUARY–APRIL	Works on Misère de la Philosophie [Poverty of Philosophy].
EARLY JUNE	*Organizes, with Engels, German Communist League, in Brussels.*
EARLY JULY	*Publication, in French, of* Misère de la Philosophie, Réponse à la Philosophie de la Misère de M. Proudhon, *in Paris and Brussels (a German edition came out in 1885).*
LATE AUGUST	*Founds, with Engels, German Workers' Association, for propagation of communist ideas.*
NOVEMBER 15	*Elected vice-president of the Brussels Association Démocratique.*

NOVEMBER 29	*Participates, with Engels, in international meeting of Fraternal Democrats in London.*
NOVEMBER 29– DECEMBER 8	*Particiates, with Engels, London congress of Communist League, which commissions Marx to draw up the* Manifesto.
DECEMBER 13	*Returns to Brussels from London.*
DECEMBER 17	*Birth of son Edgar.*
LATE DECEMBER	*Lectures before German Workers' Association on* Wage Labor and Capital, *published later as a pamphlet in 1884, 1891, and 1925.*

1848

LATE JANUARY	*Completes, with Engels,* Manifesto of the Communist Party *and sends it to London to be printed.*
FEBRUARY 24	*Publication, in German, of* Manifesto.
FEBRUARY 25	*Resigns as vice-president of the Brussels Association Démocratique.*
MARCH 1	*Receives invitation from French Provisional Government to return to Paris.*
MARCH 3	*Receives order of expulsion from Brussels.*
MARCH 4	*Arrested in Brussels.*
MARCH 5	*Arrives in Paris; address: 10 Rue Neuve Ménilmontant (Bld. Beaumarchais).*
MARCH 8–9	*Helps found Club of German Workers in Paris.*
MARCH 12	*Elected president of Communist League.*
MARCH 21, 29	*Writes, with Engels, "Demands of the Communist Party in Germany."*
APRIL 6	*Leaves Paris, with Engels, to participate in German revolution.*
APRIL 11	*Arrives in Cologne; address: No. 7 Apostelstrasse.*
MID APRIL	*Works on plans to establish the daily,* Neue Rheinische Zeitung.
JUNE 1	*Publishes first issue of* Neue Rheinische Zeitung, *subtitled* Organ der Demokratie [Organ of Democracy]. *It started with 6,000 subscribers, and appeared until May 19, 1849.*
EARLY JULY	Neue Rheinische Zeitung *investigated by police.*
JULY 20	*Attacks Prussian censorship in an article in* Neue Rheinische Zeitung.

JULY 21	Elected member of Cologne Democratic Society.
AUGUST 3	Denied citizenship by Prussian Government.
AUGUST 23– SEPTEMBER 11	Trip to Berlin and Vienna to raise money for Neue Rheinische Zeitung.
SEPTEMBER 11	Returns to Cologne.
SEPTEMBER 25	Outbreak of revolution in Cologne.
SEPTEMBER 26	Neue Rheinische Zeitung suspended under martial law.
OCTOBER 5	Reappearance of Neue Rheinische Zeitung.
NOVEMBER	Meets Charles A. Dana, who is later (1852) to appoint him London correspondent of New-York Daily Tribune.
NOVEMBER 14, 20, 23, 26	Appears in court on charges of lèse majesté and incitement to rebellion.
DECEMBER 2	Summoned to court again.
DECEMBER 6	Indicted.
DECEMBER 20–21	Court trial. Decision postponed.

1849

FEBRUARY 7–8	Tried in Cologne court and acquitted by jury.
MAY 16	Receives order of expulsion from Prussia.
MAY 19	Publication of last issue of Neue Rheinische Zeitung.
JUNE 3	Arrives in Paris.
JULY	Joined by wife and children; address: 45 Rue de Lille.
JULY 19	Receives order of expulsion from Paris.
AUGUST 24	Leaves Paris for London.
LATE AUGUST	Helps to reconstitute Communist League in London.
EARLY SEPTEMBER	Joins German Workers' Educational Society.
SEPTEMBER 17	Joined by pregnant wife and their children; lives in rooming house on Leicester Square.
NOVEMBER 5	Birth of son, Heinrich Guido, called "Föx-chen," because he was born on Guy Fawkes Day.
NOVEMBER 10	Engels arrives in London.
DECEMBER	Works with Engels on publication of Neue Rheinische Zeitung. Politisch-Ökonomische Revue.

1850

JANUARY	*Illness.*
MARCH 6	*First issue of* Neue Rheinische Zeitung. Politisch-Ökonomische Revue, *printed in Hamburg in an edition of 2,500 copies, and dated January, 1850.*
LATE MARCH	*Second issue of the Revue, dated February, 1850, 2,000 copies.*
APRIL 17	*Third issue of the Revue, dated March, 1850.*
MAY 19	*Fourth issue of the Revue, dated March–April, 1850.*
NOVEMBER 29	*Fifth-sixth, and last, double issue of the Revue, dated May–October, 1850.*
MARCH– NOVEMBER	*Publication of* The Class Struggles in France, 1848 to 1850, *as a series in the Revue. In 1895 Engels published the whole in book form under this title.*
SPRING	*Evicted from German hotel in Leicester Square and moves to squalid quarters: 64 Dean Street, Soho.*
MID APRIL	*Meets Wilhelm Liebknecht on excursion of German Workers' Educational Society.*
JULY	*Begins study of political economy in British Museum.*
SEPTEMBER 17	*Quits Workers' Educational Society over doctrinal dispute.*
LATE NOVEMBER	*Engels moves to Manchester, to enter business and help support Marx financially, which he will do for the rest of the latter's life.*
NOVEMBER 19	*Death of one-year-old son Heinrich Guido.*
NOVEMBER 30	*First publication of* Manifesto of the Communist Party *in English (translation by Helen McFarlane), in George Julian Harney's* Red Republican, *a Chartist weekly.*
DECEMBER	*Moves to small three-room furnished apartment: 28 Dean Street, Soho, where the Marx family lives until September 1856.*

1851

MARCH 28	*Birth of daughter Franziska.*
APRIL 17	*Visits Engels in Manchester.*
LATE APRIL	*Publication of first part of* Gesammelte Aufsätze von Karl Marx [Collected Essays by Karl Marx], *by Hermann Becker in Cologne.*

MAY–DECEMBER	*Works in British Museum daily "from 10 A.M. to 7 P.M."*
JUNE 23	*Birth of Frederick Demuth, Marx's illegitimate son by his housekeeper, Helene Demuth.*
AUGUST 7	*Receives invitation from Dana to write for New-York Daily Tribune.*
NOVEMBER 5–15	*Visits Engels in Manchester.*
DECEMBER 19– MARCH 25, 1852	*Works on* Der achtzehnte Brumaire des Louis Bonaparte [*The Eighteenth Brumaire of Louis Bonaparte*].

1852

JANUARY	*Ill with hemorrhoids and barely able to work.*
JANUARY–MAY	*Publication of* Der achtzehnte Brumaire des Louis Bonaparte, *in two installments, in Joseph Weydemeyer's New York German-language weekly,* Die Revolution. *A revised edition came out in book form in Hamburg, 1869.*
APRIL 14	*Death of daughter Franziska.*
LATE MAY– MID JUNE	*Visits Engels in Manchester, where they work on booklet,* Die grossen Männer des Exils [*The Great Men of the Exile*].
JULY–AUGUST	*Resumes research in British Museum.*
AUGUST 21	*Publication of Marx's own article (translated by Engels), "The Elections in England: Tories and Whigs," in* New-York Daily Tribune. (*His last* Tribune *article was published March 10, 1862.*)
OCTOBER 2–23	*Reprint of the* Tribune *article in the Chartist weekly, the* People's Paper (*October 2, 9, 16, 23*).
NOVEMBER 17	*Dissolution, at Marx's suggestion, of Communist League.*
DECEMBER 14	*Ill with hemorrhoids.*

1853

LATE JANUARY	*Publication of* Enthüllungen über den Kölner Kommunisten Prozess [*Revelations About the Cologne Communist Trial*], *in Basel.*
MARCH	*Grave liver inflammation ("I came near to croaking this week," Marx to Engels, March 10).*

APRIL 24 · *Publication of* Enthüllungen *as a pamphlet in Boston.*

APRIL 30–
MAY 19 · *Visit to Engels in Manchester.*

OCTOBER 19–
JANUARY 11,
1854 · *Publishes six articles, "Lord Palmerston," in* New-York Daily Tribune; *the series also appeared, in eight articles, in the Chartist weekly, the* People's Paper *(October 22, 29, November 5, 12, 19, December 10, 17, 24, 1853).*

NOVEMBER 21–28 · *Writes* Der Ritter vom edelmütigen Bewusstsein [The Knight of Magnanimous Consciousness], *a satire against August Willich.*

1854

MID JANUARY · *Publication of* Der Ritter *as a brochure in New York.*

MARCH 6 · *Publishes article, "The Oriental War," in the Capetown* Zuid Afrikaan.

MAY · *Illness—tumors, toothaches, etc.—and inability to work.*

SEPTEMBER 9–
DECEMBER 2 · *Publishes a series of eight articles, "Revolutionary Spain," in* New-York Daily Tribune *(September 9, 25, October 20, 27, 30, November 24, December 1, 2).*

1855

JANUARY 2–
OCTOBER 8 · *Publication of first article, "Rückblicke [Retrospects]," in the Breslau daily,* Neue Oder-Zeitung. *Altogether, Marx contributed 112 articles (a few of them in collaboration with Engels), many of which also appeared in the* New-York Daily Tribune, *to the* Neue Oder-Zeitung. *The last article, "The French Bank —Reinforcements for the Crimea—The New Field Marshals," came out October 8, 1855.*

JANUARY 16 · *Birth of daughter Eleanor (Tussy).*

FEBRUARY 9–
MARCH · *Illness and eye inflammation.*

APRIL 6 · *Death of eight-year-old son Edgar (Musch).*

APRIL 18–
MAY 6 · *Marx and wife visit Engels in Manchester.*

MAY 16 · *Publication of Palmerston articles as a pamphlet in Tucker's* Political Fly-Sheets.

JUNE · *Illness and "atrocious toothache."*

JULY 28– AUGUST 15	Publication of a series of six articles, "Lord John Russell," in Neue Oder-Zeitung (July 28, August 4, 7, 8, 10, 15).
JULY– SEPTEMBER 12	Lives with family in Peter Imandt's cottage: 3 York Place, Denmark Street, Camberwell.
SEPTEMBER 12– EARLY DECEMBER	Marx family lives with Engels in Manchester: 34 Butler Street, Green Keys.
DECEMBER 29– FEBRUARY 16, 1856	Republication of Palmerston articles from the People's Paper in Urquhart's Free Press; they were also published as a separate brochure, No. 5 of "Free Press Serials."

1856

JANUARY– FEBRUARY	Ill with hemorrhoids.
FEBRUARY– APRIL	Research in British Museum (though "plagued by hemorrhoids") on Russo-British diplomatic relations in seventeenth and eighteenth centuries.
APRIL 5–26	Publishes a series of four articles, "The Fall of Kars," in the People's Paper (April 5, 12, 19, 26).
APRIL 14	Speech at anniversary banquet of the People's Paper on revolution and the proletariat.
MAY 18–JUNE 5	Illness and inability to work.
JUNE 7– MID JUNE	Visits Engels in Manchester.
JUNE 21–JULY 11	Publication of a series of three articles, "The French Crédit Mobilier," in New-York Daily Tribune (June 21, 24, July 11).
JUNE 21	Begins writing Diplomatic History of the Seventeenth Century. (This work was not completed.)
JULY 23	Death of Marx's mother-in-law, Caroline von Westphalen.
EARLY OCTOBER	Moves from Soho to new house in undeveloped suburb: 9 Grafton Terrace, Maitland Park, Haverstock Hill. The Marx family lived here until 1864.

1857

JANUARY–JULY	Illness and inability to work (Mrs. Marx to Engels, April 12: "Der Chaley has a headache, terrible toothaches, pains in the ears,

head, eyes, throat, and God knows what else. Neither opium pills nor creosote helps").

MAY — *Studies Danish and Swedish.*

LATE AUGUST–MID SEPTEMBER — *Works on introduction to a book on political economy. The introduction was first published in Die Neue Zeit in 1903.*

SEPTEMBER–APRIL, 1858 — *Writes sixteen articles—eight in collaboration with Engels—for the New American Cyclopaedia, published in New York.*

1858

FEBRUARY–LATE MAY — *Illness—liver, toothaches, etc.—and inability to work.*

MAY 6–24 — *Visits Engels in Manchester.*

AUGUST — *Begins writing Zur Kritik der Politischen Ökonomie [Critique of Political Economy].*

EARLY NOVEMBER — *Toothaches and inability to work.*

1859

JANUARY 26 — *Manuscript of Critique of Political Economy sent to publisher Franz Duncker in Berlin.*

JUNE 4 — *Introduction to Zur Kritik published in Das Volk, a radical German-language London weekly.*

JUNE 11 — *Publication of Zur Kritik, First Part, in an edition of 1,000 copies. (An English translation did not appear until 1909.)*

JUNE 12–JULY 2 — *Visits Engels in Manchester.*

JULY 3 — *Becomes editor of Das Volk.*

JULY 30 — *Publishes article, "Invasion!" in Das Volk.*

JULY 30–AUGUST 20 — *Series of four articles, "Quid pro Quo," published in Das Volk (July 30, August 6, 13, 20).*

AUGUST 20 — *Das Volk ceases publication.*

1860

JANUARY–EARLY FEBRUARY — *Works on Second Part of Zur Kritik der Politischen Ökonomie (never completed).*

MAY–NOVEMBER 17 — *Works on Herr Vogt, a bitter, violent, and financially ruinous pamphlet against Karl Vogt, whom Marx accused of being a Bonapartist agent.*

LATE NOVEMBER — *Illness and toothaches.*

DECEMBER 1	*Publication of* Herr Vogt, *by A. Petsch & Co., "German Bookseller," 78 Fenchurch Street, London, E.C.*
DECEMBER	*Illness; reading Darwin's* Natural Selection *(Marx to Engels, December 19: ". . . it is the book that contains the natural-history basis of our philosophy").*

1861

JANUARY	*Suffers from inflammation of the liver.*
JANUARY– OCTOBER 11	New-York Daily Tribune *suspends Marx's correspondenceship, printing none of his articles.*
FEBRUARY 28– MARCH 16	*Visits uncle, Lion Philips, in Zalt-Bommel, Holland.*
MARCH 17– APRIL 12	*Visit with Ferdinand Lassalle in Berlin.*
APRIL 10	*Applies for restoration of Prussian citizenship.*
APRIL 12–29	*Travels from Berlin to the Rhineland, visiting his mother in Trier and returning to London via Holland.*
EARLY JUNE	*Begins work on* Das Kapital.
JUNE	*Research on U.S. Civil War.*
EARLY JULY	*Eye inflammation (Marx to Engels, July 5: "For three days now I have had a disgusting eye inflammation, which prevents all writing and reading").*
LATE AUGUST– MID SEPTEMBER	*Visits Engels in Manchester.*
SEPTEMBER 18	*Writes "The American Question in England," the first article of his to be published in* New-York Daily Tribune *in the year 1861 (October 11). For the rest of the year the* Tribune *publishes only seven more of his articles.*
OCTOBER 25	*First publication ("The North American Civil War") in* Die Presse, *a Vienna daily.*
NOVEMBER	*Prussian Government denies Marx's application for restoration of citizenship.*

1862

JANUARY– FEBRUARY	*Works on "Theories of Surplus Value."*
MARCH 10	*Publishes last article, "The Mexican Imbroglio," in* New-York Daily Tribune.

MARCH 30–
    APRIL 25   *Visits Engels in Manchester.*

AUGUST 28–
    SEPTEMBER 27   *Visits mother in Trier and uncle Lion Philips in Zalt-Bommel in connection with money matters.*

DECEMBER 5–13   *Visits Engels in Manchester.*

1863

FEBRUARY–
    LATE MAY   *Illness—inflammation of eyes and liver, coughing—and inability to work.*

MAY–AUGUST   *Intermittent research in British Museum.*

SEPTEMBER–
    DECEMBER   *Ill with carbuncles and furuncles; carbuncle operation in November.*

DECEMBER 2   *Death of mother, Henriette Marx, in Trier.*

DECEMBER 7   *Leaves London for Germany and Holland; in Trier, stays in inn, Gasthof von Venedig.*

DECEMBER 21–
    FEBRUARY 19,
    1864   *Stays with Philips family in Zalt-Bommel, where he is ill.*

1864

FEBRUARY 19   *Returns to London.*

MARCH   *Moves to new house: 1 Modena Villas, Maitland Park, Haverstock Hill, N.W. The Marx family lived here until 1873.*

MARCH 12   *Visits Engels in Manchester, to report on his trip to Germany and Holland.*

MAY 3–13   *In Manchester during final illness and death (May 9) of friend, Wilhelm Wolff, who left the Marx family the bulk of his estate, valued at £320.*

LATE MAY   *Ill with carbuncles.*

JULY 1–
    AUGUST 31   *Ill with influenza and carbuncles.*

AUGUST 31   *Death of Ferdinand Lassalle.*

JULY 20–
    AUGUST 10   *On cure in Ramsgate, 46 Hardres Street.*

SEPTEMBER 28   *Attends meeting which founds International Working Men's Association (First International), at St. Martin's Hall, London; chosen member of Provisional Committee.*

OCTOBER 6–17   *Illness and inability to work.*

OCTOBER 21–27   *Drafts Provisional Rules and Inaugural Address of the International, adopted by the Provisional Committee, November 1.*

NOVEMBER 3   *Meets Michael Bakunin for first time in sixteen years.*

EARLY NOVEMBER–
MID DECEMBER   *Ill with new carbuncles.*

NOVEMBER 29   *Completes "Address of the International Working Men's Association to Abraham Lincoln," congratulating him on his reelection to Presidency.*

DECEMBER 21, 30   *Publication of "Address and Provisional Rules of the Working Men's Association," in Der Sozialdemokrat; also published as pamphlet by Bee-Hive Newspaper Office, 10 Bolt Court, Fleet Street.*

1865

JANUARY 7–14   *Visits Engels in Manchester.*

FEBRUARY–
MID MARCH   *Ill with carbuncles.*

MARCH 19–
APRIL 8   *Visits relatives in Zalt-Bommel.*

APRIL 11   *Becomes the International's corresponding secretary for Belgium (Marx held this office until January 1866).*

MAY 2–9   *Drafts International's Address to President Andrew Johnson.*

LATE MAY–
JUNE 17   *Writes "Wages, Price and Profit."*

JUNE 20   *Delivers "Wages, Price and Profit" as a lecture before the General Council of the International.*

MAY–AUGUST   *Ill with influenza, carbuncles, etc., but working intermittently on Das Kapital.*

LATE AUGUST   *Chosen for editorial board of Workmen's Advocate, organ of the International.*

SEPTEMBER 25–29   *Attends sessions of London conference of the International.*

SEPTEMBER 29–
MID OCTOBER   *Illness and inability to work.*

OCTOBER 20–
NOVEMBER 2   *Visits Engels in Manchester.*

LATE DECEMBER   *Completes first draft of Das Kapital.*

1866

JANUARY   *Begins preparing manuscript of Das Kapital for publisher.*

MID JANUARY– MID MARCH	*Desperately ill with carbuncles and boils, interrupting work on* Das Kapital.
MARCH 15– APRIL 10	*On cure in Margate, 5 Lansell's Place.*
MID APRIL– LATE DECEMBER	*Continuing illnesses–toothaches, carbuncles, rheumatism, liver inflammation, etc; work- ing intermittently.*
SEPTEMBER 2	*Elected International's corresponding secre- tary for Germany.*
MID NOVEMBER	*Sends first part of* Das Kapital *to Meissner, Hamburg publisher.*

1867

LATE MARCH	*Completes* Das Kapital.
APRIL 10	*Leaves for Hamburg to see Meissner, his publisher.*
APRIL 12–16	*Discusses publication of* Das Kapital *with Meissner.*
APRIL 17– MAY 15	*Visits Dr. Ludwig Kugelmann, a friend and admirer, in Hanover.*
MAY 16–17	*On way back to London, again visits Meis- sner in Hamburg.*
MAY 19	*Arrives in London.*
MAY 21– JUNE 2	*Visits Engels in Manchester.*
AUGUST 15–16	*Finishes correcting proofs of* Das Kapital.
SEPTEMBER 14	*Publication of* Das Kapital *(Vol. I).*
LATE NOVEMBER	*New outbreak of carbuncles.*

1868

JANUARY– MID MAY	*Festering carbuncles all over his body; tak- ing prescribed arsenic treatment.*
APRIL 2	*Marriage of Laura Marx to Paul Lafargue.*
APRIL 22	*Begins intermittent work, for brief periods, on Vol. II of* Das Kapital.
MAY 29–JUNE 15	*Visits Engels in Manchester with daughter Eleanor.*
AUGUST 21–24	*On cure in Ramsgate.*
SEPTEMBER 24	*Reelected International's corresponding sec- retary for Germany.*
EARLY OCTOBER	*Bakunin begins translation of* Das Kapital *into Russian.*
MID NOVEMBER	*Reappearance of carbuncles.*

NOVEMBER 29	*Engels offers Marx annuity of £350 to relieve him permanently of financial distress.*
DECEMBER 1	*Appointed archivist of the International.*

1869

LATE JANUARY	*Ill with cold and fever; prepares second edition of* The Eighteenth Brumaire of Louis Bonaparte *and sends it to Meissner in Hamburg.*
MID FERBUARY– LATE MAY	*Liver illness and carbuncles.*
MAY 25–JUNE 14	*Visits Engels in Manchester, with daughter Eleanor.*
JULY 1	*Engels gives up his business in Manchester (Engels to Marx, July 1: "Hurrah! Today . . . I am a free man").*
JULY 6–12	*Incognito visit to daughter Laura Lafargue in Paris, under pseudonym of "J. Williams."*
LATE JULY	*Ill with carbuncles. Publication of second edition of* Eighteenth Brumaire *in Hamburg.*
LATE AUGUST– EARLY SEPTEMBER	*Writes "Report . . . of the International . . . to the Fourth Congress in Basel."*
SEPTEMBER 7–11	*At Basel Congress, the absent Marx is unanimously reelected member of International's General Council.*
SEPTEMBER 10	*Leaves, with daughter Eleanor, for Germany, travelling through Belgium.*
SEPTEMBER 18– OCTOBER 7	*Visits Dr. Kugelmann in Hanover.*
OCTOBER 8–9	*Visits publisher, Meissner, in Hamburg.*
OCTOBER 11	*Returns to London.*
LATE OCTOBER	*Begins to study Russian.*
NOVEMBER 30	*Becomes member of Land and Labour League, a radical organization founded October 1869.*

1870

MID JANUARY– APRIL	*Ill with liver inflammation, carbuncles and abscesses; undergoes two operations.*
APRIL 29	*Receives Russian translation of the Manifesto, to be published in Geneva.*
MAY 23– JUNE 23	*Visits Engels in Manchester with daughter Eleanor. Review of* Das Kapital *by Hermann Karl Friedrich Rösler, in* Jahrbücher

	für Nationalökonomie und Statistik, *which Marx considered so ridiculous that he laughed until he had tears in his eyes.*
JULY 19–23	*Writes* First Address of the International *on the Franco-Prussian War, published, in German and French, in an edition of 30,000 copies.*
AUGUST 9–31	*On cure for sciatica at Ramsgate,* 36 *Hardres Street.*
SEPTEMBER 6–9	*Writes* Second Address of the International *on the Franco-Prussian War, protesting annexation of Alsace-Lorraine.*
SEPTEMBER 16	*Writes last letter to Engels in Manchester.*
SEPTEMBER 22	*Engels moves to London, 122 Regents Park Road, N.W., to be near Marx.*

1871

JANUARY ON	*Continued illness—bronchitis, coughing, sleeplessness.*
MARCH 18	Paris Commune established.
APRIL 18– MAY 29	*Writes* The Civil War in France, *a pamphlet defending the Paris Commune, published in English in London, in German in Leipzig (July), and in a later edition by Engels in 1891.*
MAY 2–22	*Inability to work, due to continued illness.*
JUNE–DECEMBER	*Organizes financial assistance for Paris Commune refugees in London.*
JULY 3	*Gives interview to R. Landor, correspondent of New York* World *(published in the* World, *July 18, and in* Woodhull & Claflin's Weekly, *August 12).*
AUGUST 16–29	*On cure in Brighton, Globe Hotel, Manchester Street.*
SEPTEMBER 17–23	*Participates in London conference of the International.*
SEPTEMBER 28– OCTOBER 3	*On cure in Ramsgate with Mrs. Marx and Engels.*
OCTOBER 3	*Elected International's corresponding secretary for Russia.*
OCTOBER– LATE NOVEMBER	*Inability to work, due to illness.*

1872

| | |
| JANUARY–
EARLY MARCH | *Prepares, with Engels, the anti-Bakunin circular, "Fictitious Splits in the International."* |

JANUARY 15– FEBRUARY 15	*Negotiates with Joseph Roy for the transla- tion, and with Paris publisher Maurice Lachatre for the publication, of a French edition of* Das Kapital.
MARCH 27	*Publication of first foreign translation—in Russian—of* Das Kapital *(translation begun by Bakunin, completed by Nicolai F. Dan- ielson). Of an edition of 3,000 copies, 900 were sold in the first six weeks.*
APRIL–MAY	*Edits French translation of* The Civil War in France, *published in June in Brussels in an edition of 2,000 copies.*
JULY 9–15	*On cure in Ramsgate with Engels.*
JULY	*Publication in Leipzig of new German edi- tion of the* Manifesto, *with introduction by Marx and Engels.*
MID JULY	*Publication of first part of second German edition of* Das Kapital.
LATE AUGUST	*Chosen delegate to Hague Congress of the International.*
SEPTEMBER 1	*Arrives, with wife and daughter Eleanor, in The Hague.*
SEPTEMBER 2–7	*Participates actively in the Congress and in the struggle with the Bakuninists which led to dissolution of the International.*
SEPTEMBER 17	*Returns to London. Publication of first in- stallments of French edition of* Das Kapital.
OCTOBER 10	*Marriage of Jenny Marx to French socialist Charles Longuet.*

1873

JANUARY 24	*Writes Epilogue for second German edition of* Das Kapital.
MAY–JUNE	*Corrects and retranslates French edition of* Das Kapital.
MAY 22–JUNE 3	*Visits Dr. Eduard Gumpert (for medical consultation) and friends, including Carl Schorlemmer and Samuel Moore, the En- glish translator of* Das Kapital, *in Man- chester.*
EARLY JUNE	*Publication of second German edition of* Das Kapital.
JULY–OCTOBER	*Works in British Museum, despite ill health.*
NOVEMBER 24– DECEMBER 15	*On cure in Harrogate with daughter Elea- nor.*

1874

FEBRUARY—
MID APRIL   *Continued illness.*

MID APRIL—
MAY 5   *On cure in Ramsgate, 16 Abbott's Hill.*

MID JULY—
LATE JULY   *On cure in Ryde, Isle of Wight, 11 Nelson Street.*

AUGUST 1   *Applies for British citizenship, to obtain passport for European travel.*

AUGUST 4–9   *In Ramsgate with sick daughter, Jenny Longuet.*

AUGUST 24   *Application for British citizenship rejected.*

AUGUST 19—
SEPTEMBER 21   *On cure in Karlsbad, Hotel Germania, am Schlossberg.*

OCTOBER 3   *Returns to London.*

OCTOBER 28—
DECEMBER 18   *First publication in Germany—in* Der Volksstaat, *a Social-Democratic journal appearing twice weekly in Leipzig—of* Revelations About the Cologne Communist Trial; *it was published as a brochure in 1875.*

1875

MARCH   *Moves to 41 Maitland Park Road (or Crescent), N.W., where he is to live until his death in 1883.*

MAY 5   *Sends* Critique of the Gotha Program *to Wilhelm Bracke for the Social-Democratic congress in Gotha, Germany.*

AUGUST 15—
SEPTEMBER 11   *On cure in Karlsbad, Hotel Germania.*

SEPTEMBER 20   *Returns to London after visiting several European cities.*

LATE NOVEMBER   *Publication of French edition of* Das Kapital *(translation begun by Joseph Roy, corrected by Marx, completed by Charles Keller and others).*

1876

JULY 1   *Death of Michael Bakunin.*

JULY 15   *The General Council of the International, which Marx had moved to America in 1872 to keep it out of the hands of the Bakuninists, dissolves itself at a conference in Philadelphia.*

AUGUST 16– SEPTEMBER 15	*On cure for third time in Karlsbad, Hotel Germania, with daughter Eleanor.*

1877

MARCH 5	*Completes first part of Chapter 10 for Engels' Anti-Dühring.*
LATE MARCH	*Resumes intermittent work on second volume of Das Kapital.*
AUGUST 8	*Completes second part of Chapter 10 for Anti-Dühring.*
AUGUST 8– SEPTEMBER 27	*On cure, with sick wife, in Bad Neuenahr, Germany, Hotel Flora.*
NOVEMBER– JULY, 1878	*Works on first chapter of second volume of Das Kapital.*

1878

SEPTEMBER 4–14	*On cure, with wife and daughter Jenny Longuet, in Malvern.*

1879

AUGUST 8–20	*On cure in St. Aubin's, Isle of Jersey; Trafalgar Hotel.*
AUGUST 21– SEPTEMBER 17	*On cure with wife in Ramsgate, 62 Plains of Waterloo.*

1880

JANUARY– DECEMBER	*While ill, works intermittently on second and third volumes of Das Kapital.*
EARLY AUGUST– SEPTEMBER 13	*On cure, with wife and children, in Ramsgate.*
OCTOBER	*Meets H. M. Hyndman.*

1881

LATE JUNE– JULY 20	*On cure with wife in Eastbourne, 43 Terminus Road.*
JULY 26– AUGUST 16	*With sick wife, visits daughter Jenny Longuet in Argenteuil, 11 Boulevard Thiers.*
OCTOBER 13– MID DECEMBER	*Gravely ill.*
DECEMBER 1	*Publication of "Karl Marx," by Ernest Belfort Bax, in Modern Thought, a London monthly—the first serious pro-Marx article in the English language.*

DECEMBER 2 — *Death of wife, Jenny Marx, of cancer; Marx too ill to attend funeral.*

DECEMBER 29– JANUARY 16, 1882 — *On cure in Ventnor, Isle of Wight, 1 St. Boniface Gardens.*

1882

JANUARY 16 — *Returns to London from Ventnor.*

JANUARY 21 — *Writes (with Engels) preface to Russian translation (by G. Plekhanov) of the Manifesto; preface published in Russian weekly, Narodnaya Volya, February 5.*

FEBRUARY 9–16 — *Visits daughter Jenny Longuet in Argenteuil, on way to cure for pleurisy and bronchitis in Algiers.*

FEBRUARY 20– MAY 2 — *On cure in Algiers, Hotel Victoria.*

EARLY MAY– JUNE 3 — *In Nice and Monte Carlo, Hotel de Russie.*

JUNE 3–5 — *In Cannes.*

JUNE 6– AUGUST 22 — *Visits daughter Jenny Longuet in Argenteuil, taking sulphur baths at Enghien-les-Bains.*

AUGUST 23–27 — *Visits Lausanne with daughter Laura Lafargue.*

AUGUST 27– SEPTEMBER 25 — *Visits Vevey, Switzerland, with Laura.*

OCTOBER 30– JANUARY 12, 1883 — *On cure in Ventnor, 1 St. Boniface Gardens.*

1883

JANUARY 11 — *Death of Jenny Longuet, in Argenteuil, of cancer, causing Marx to return to London.*

JANUARY– MARCH 14 — *Gravely ill with laryngitis, bronchitis, lung tumor, etc.*

MARCH 14, 2:45 P.M. — *Dies at home in London, sitting in easy chair.*

MARCH 17 — *Buried in Highgate Cemetery, London.*

1890

NOVEMBER 4 — *Death of Helene Demuth.*

1895

AUGUST 5 — *Death of Engels.*

1898
MARCH 31   *Suicide of Eleanor Marx.*

1911
NOVEMBER 26   *Suicide of Laura and Paul Lafargue.*

1929
JANUARY 28   *Death of Frederick Demuth.*

Appendix II

Marx's Paternal Ancestors

JEHUDA BEN ELIEZER HALEVI MINZ (ca. 1408–ca. 1508)
|
ABRAHAM MINZ (ca. 1440–ca. 1525)
|
MEIER BEN ISAAC KATZENELLENBOGEN (1482–1565), renowned rabbi and head
    of Talmudic school in Padua, Italy
|
JOSEPH BEN GERSON COHEN or HACOHEN (ca. 1511–1591)
|
MOSES LVOV (d. 1788)
|
AARON LVOV (d. 1712)
|
JOSHUA HESCHEL LVOV (ca. 1693–1771)
|
MOSES LVOV (d. 1788)
|
CHAYA (EVA) LVOV (1737–1823) m MORDECHAI (MARX LEVY) (ca. 1740–1804)

| HESCHEL (Heinrich Marx's father) b. 1777 | SAMUEL b. 1781 | ESTHER b. 1786 | MOSES | BABBETTE b. 1791 | JACOB | HIRSCH | YOLEM LEVY |

Appendix III

Marx's Maternal Relatives

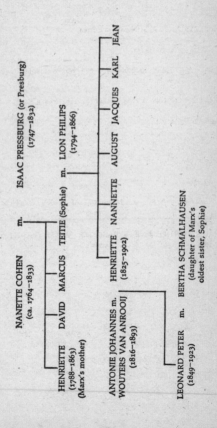

NANETTE COHEN (ca. 1764–1833)   m.   ISAAC PRESSBURG (or Presburg) (1747–1832)

HENRIETTE (1788–1863) (Marx's mother)

DAVID

MARCUS

TEITJE (Sophie)   m.   LION PHILIPS (1794–1866)

HENRIETTE (1825–1902)

NANNETTE

AUGUST   JACQUES   KARL   JEAN

ANTONIE JOHANNES WOUTERS VAN ANROOIJ (1816–1893)   m.

LEONARD PETER (1849–1923)   m.   BERTHA SCHMALHAUSEN (daughter of Marx's oldest sister, Sophie)

378

Appendix IV

Marx's Siblings

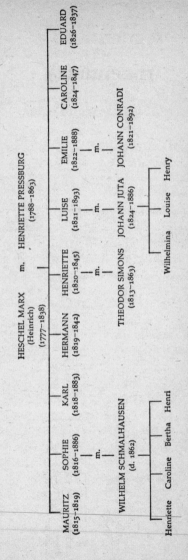

HESCHEL MARX   m.   HENRIETTE PRESSBURG
(Heinrich)   (1788–1863)
(1777–1838)

MAURITZ   SOPHIE   KARL   HERMANN   HENRIETTE   LUISE   EMILIE   CAROLINE   EDUARD
(1815–1819)   (1816–1886)   (1818–1883)   (1819–1842)   (1820–1845)   (1821–1893)   (1822–1888)   (1824–1847)   (1826–1837)

m.   m.   m.   m.

WILHELM SCHMALHAUSEN   THEODOR SIMONS   JOHANN JUTA   JOHANN CONRADI
(d. 1862)   (1813–1865)   (1824–1886)   (1821–1892)

Henriette   Caroline   Bertha   Henri   Wilhelmina   Louise   Henry

Appendix V

Marx's Descendants

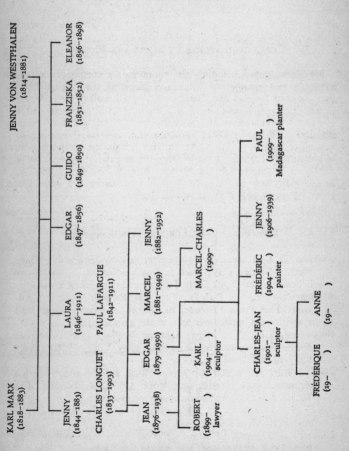

381

Bibliography

Collected Works by Marx and Engels

Marx's writings, including his voluminous correspondence, are available in a number of languages, including the original German, also in English and German. The great collection is *Marx-Engels Werke* (39 volumes, plus 2 volumes of Supplement and 1 of Index), prepared by the Moscow Institute of Marxism-Leninism and published by Dietz Verlag, Berlin, 1964-68. There is also a Russian-language edition. An English translation of the *Werke*, to run into 50 volumes, is under way; the first twelve volumes were published by International Publishers, New York, in 1975–79. The Moscow Institute of Marxism-Leninism is planning a *Marx-Engels Gesamtausgabe* in about 100 volumes.

One-Volume Collections in English

Avineri, S.: *Karl Marx on Colonialism and Modernization* (Doubleday, Garden City, 1969). Largely selections from Marx's articles in *New-York Daily Tribune* and the Vienna *Presse*.

Blackstock, P.W., and B.F. Hoselitz: *The Russian Menace to Europe* (Free Press, Glencoe, Ill., 1952). A thoroughly garbled and distorted version of some of Marx's writings.

Bottomore, T.B.: *Karl Marx: Selected Writings in Sociology & Social Philosophy* (McGraw-Hill, New York, 1956). Short but well-translated selections.

———: *Karl Marx: Early Writings*. With a Foreword by Erich Fromm (McGraw-Hill, New York, 1963). Writings on "The Jewish Question" and some economic essays.

Burns, E.: *A Handbook of Marxism; Being a Collection of Extracts* (Random House, New York, 1935).

Caute, D.: *Essential Writings of Karl Marx* (Macmillan Co., New York, 1967). Brief and eclectic selections.

Christman, H.M.: *The American Journalism of Marx and Engels* (New American Library, New York, 1966). Selections from the *New-York Daily Tribune*.

Doerig, J.A.: *Marx vs. Russia* (Ungar, New York, 1962). Selections from the *New-York Daily Tribune*, 1853–1856.

Draper, H.: *Writings on the Paris Commune by Karl Marx and Friedrich Engels* (Monthly Review, New York, 1971).

Easton, L.D. and K.H. Guddat: *Writings of the Young Marx on Philosophy and Society* (Doubleday, Garden City, 1967). Some well-translated selections of Marx's writings before 1847.

Feuer, L.S.: *Basic Writings on Politics and Philosophy. Karl Marx and Friedrich Engels* (Doubleday, Garden City, 1959). Many inferior translations by others.

Fischer, E.: *The Essential Marx* (Herder and Herder, New York, 1971). The title is misleading. These brief selections are heavily interspersed with admiring editorial comment.

Freedman, R.: *Marx on Economics* (Harcourt, Brace, New York, 1961).

————: *Marxist Social Thought* (Harcourt, Brace, New York, 1968).

Krader, L.: *The Ethnological Notebooks of Karl Marx* (Assen, Van Gorcum, 1972). Studies of Morgan, Phear, Maine, Lubbock.

McLellan, D.: *Karl Marx: Early Texts* (Barnes & Noble, New York, 1971). McLellan is a Marx scholar and biographer.

————: *The Thought of Karl Marx* (Harper & Row, New York, 1972).

Meek, R.L.: *Marx and Engels on Malthus* (International Publishers, New York, 1954).

Padover, S.K.: *The Karl Marx Library* (McGraw-Hill, New York). Seven volumes, mostly original translations:

  I *Karl Marx on Revolution* (1971)
  II *Karl Marx on America and the Civil War* (1972)
  III *Karl Marx on the First International* (1973)
  IV *Karl Marx on Freedom of the Press and Censorship* (1974)
  V *Karl Marx on Religion* (1974)
  VI *Karl Marx on Education, Women and Children* (1975)
  VII *Karl Marx on History and People* (1977)

————: *The Essential Marx. The Non-Economic Writings* (New American Library, New York, 1978).

————: *The Letters of Karl Marx* (Prentice-Hall, Englewood Cliffs, N.J., 1979).

Stenning, H.J.: *Karl Marx: Selected Essays* (Books for Libraries Press, Freeport, N.Y., 1968).

Stockhammer, M.: *Karl Marx Dictionary* (Philosophical Library, New York, 1965).

Trotsky, L.: *The Living Thoughts of Karl Marx* with an Intro-
    duction by Sidney Hook (Longmans Green & Co., London,
    England, 1939; also Fawcett Publications, New York 1963).
    "This book," writes Trotsky, "compactly sets forth the funda-
    mentals of Marx's economic teaching in Marx's own words."

SELECTED BIOGRAPHIC WRITINGS

Marx's towering stature has had an unfortunate effect on the
objectivity of writers, who have tended either to worship or to
hate him. Hence biographical writings about him should be read
with caution. This is particularly true of the full biographies. To
communist writers, for example, Marx is not a mere human figure, but a sacred one. Non-communists are likely to be inimical.
A recent, but not isolated, example of relentless antipathy is
Robert Payne's otherwise well-researched *Marx* (1968). Other bi-
ographers, ranging from Franz Mehring, whose work is now outdated, to David McLellan, are excessively pro-Marx. A few books,
notably Arnold Künzli's *Karl Marx. Eine Psychobiographie*,
(1966), are solidly and meticulously documented accounts with a
special slant. Some, such as the biographies by Carr and Schwartzschild, have bias even in their titles.

Marx

Annenkov. P.: "A Wonderful Ten Years," in *Vestnik Yevropy*,
    April, 1880; excerpts in *Reminiscences of Marx and Engels*
    (Foreign Languages Publishing House, Moscow), pp. 269-
    72.
Barker, F.: "The Life and Strange Death of Eleanor Marx," in
    The Cornhill Magazine, Autumn, 1955.
Beer, M.: *The Life and Teaching of Karl Marx* (Parsons Co.,
    London, 1921).
Berlin, I.: "Benjamin Disraeli and Karl Marx: The Search for
    Identity," in *Midstream*, August-September, 1970, pp. 29-49.
————: *Karl Marx: His Life and Environment* (Oxford University
    Press, 1939; also paperback editions).
Carr, E.H.: *Karl Marx: A Study in Fanaticism* (Dent, London,
    1934).
Lancaster, L.W.: "Karl Marx," in *Master of Political Thought*,
    Vol. III, Ch. 5 (Houghton Mifflin, Boston, n.d.), pp. 160-202.
    This is of interest as one of the first articles on Marx in
    English.
Lenin, V.I.: "Karl Marx," in *Granat Encyclopedia*, XXVIII
    (1915); also published in Lenin, *Works*, 4th Russian ed.,
    XXI, pp. 30-62, and in *Reminiscences of Marx and Engels*,
    pp. 28-57.

Liebknecht, W.: *Karl Marx: Biographical Memoirs* (Charles H. Kerr Co., Chicago, 1901).

Longuet, E.: "Some Aspects of Karl Marx's Family Life," in *Cahiers du Communisme*, March, 1949; reprinted in *Reminiscences of Marx and Engels*, pp. 258-65. By a grandson.

Marx, E.: "Karl Marx (A Few Stray Notes)," in *Reminiscences of Marx and Engels*, pp. 249–55.

Marx, J.: "Short Sketch of an Eventful Life," written before 1865; in *Reminiscences of Marx and Engels*, pp. 221-35.

McLellan, D.: *Karl Marx: His Life and Thought* (Harper & Row, New York, 1974).

McLellan, D.: *Marx Before Marxism* (Harper & Row, New York, 1970)

Mehring, F.: *Karl Marx* (University of Michigan Press, 1962)

Padover, S.K.: *Karl Marx: An Intimate Biography* (McGraw-Hill Book Co., New York, 1978).

Schwartzschild, L.: *The Red Prussian: The Life and Legend of Karl Marx* (Charles Scribner's Sons, New York, 1947).

Index